European Studies in English Literature

The symbolist tradition in English literature

This major and acclaimed study of the symbolist tradition in England focuses on the years 1850 to 1900 and discusses the poetry of such as William Morris, O'Shaughnessy, the Rossettis, Swinburne, Wilde and Yeats, paintings by Holman Hunt, Millais, Rossetti, Burne-Jones and others, and critical works by Keble, Ruskin, Carlyle, Arnold, Pater and Arthur Symons. It begins by considering the changes from romantic symbol through Victorian 'type' and 'emblem' to late romantic image, proceeding from this theoretical groundwork to discuss questions of symbolist form and style as well as dominant themes and motifs like the imaginary landscape, the ideal beloved, and manifestations of the symbolist spirituality. This study of both literature and the visual arts is comparative in nature, attempting to establish an English symbolist tradition as part of an international development linking the nineteenth and twentieth centuries.

Available now for the first time in English translation, Lothar Hönnighausen's book includes illustrations and a survey of critical works since 1971, defining major research issues and offering suggestions for future work.

European Studies in English Literature

SERIES EDITORS
Ulrich Broich, Professor of English, University of Munich
Herbert Grabes, Professor of English, University of Giessen
Dieter Mehl, Professor of English, University of Bonn

Roger Asselineau, Professor Emeritus of American Literature, University of
Paris-Sorbonne
Paul-Gabriel Boucé, Professor of English, University of Sorbonne-Nouvelle
Robert Ellrodt, Professor of English, University of Sorbonne-Nouvelle
Sylvère Monod, Professor Emeritus of English, University of
Sorbonne-Nouvelle

This series is devoted to publishing translations into English of the best
works written in European languages on English and American literature.
These may be first-rate books recently published in their original versions, or
they may be classic studies which have influenced the course of scholarship in
their field while never having been available in English before.

To begin with, the series has concentrated on works translated from the
German; but its range will expand to cover French and other languages.

TRANSLATIONS PUBLISHED
Walter Pater: The aesthetic moment by Wolfgang Iser
*The Symbolist Tradition in English Literature: A study of Pre-Raphaelitism and
'Fin de Siècle'* by Lothar Hönnighausen
The Theory and Analysis of Drama by Manfred Pfister
Oscar Wilde: The works of a conformist rebel by Norbert Kohl
The Rise of the English Street Ballad 1550–1650 by Natascha Würzbach

TITLES UNDER CONTRACT FOR TRANSLATION
Studien zum komischen Epos by Ulrich Broich
Redeformen des englischen Misterienspiels by Hans-Jürgen Diller
Die romantische Verserzählung in England by Hermann Fischer
*Studien zur Dramenform vor Shakespeare: Moralität, Interlude, Romaneskes
Drama* by Werner Habicht
*Die Frauenklage: Studien zur elegischen Verserzählung in der englischen
Literatur des Spätmittelalters und der Renaissance* by Götz Schmitz

Shakespeare et la Fête by François Laroque

The Symbolist Tradition in English Literature

A Study of Pre-Raphaelitism and *Fin de Siècle*

Lothar Hönnighausen
Professor of English and American Literature
University of Bonn

condensed and translated from the German
by Gisela Hönnighausen

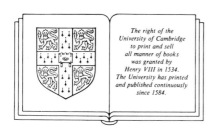

The right of the
University of Cambridge
to print and sell
all manner of books
was granted by
Henry VIII in 1534.
The University has printed
and published continuously
since 1584.

Cambridge University Press

Cambridge
New York   Port Chester
Melbourne   Sydney

Published by the Press Syndicate of the University of Cambridge
The Pitt Building, Trumpington Street, Cambridge CB2 1RP
40 West 20th Street, New York, NY 10011, USA
10 Stamford Road, Oakleigh, Melbourne 3166, Australia

Originally published in German as *Präraphaeliten und Fin de Siècle:
Symbolistische Tendenzen in der Englischen Spätromantik* by
Lothar Hönnighausen 1971
and © Wilhelm Fink Verlag, Munich, West Germany
First published in English by Cambridge University Press 1988
as *The Symbolist Tradition in English Literature: A study of
Pre-Raphaelitism and 'Fin de Siècle'*

Reprinted 1990

Printed in Great Britain at the University Press, Cambridge

British Library cataloguing in publication data
Hönnighausen, Lothar
The symbolist tradition in English literature:
a study of Pre-Raphaelitism and fin de
siècle. – (European studies in English
literature).
1. Symbolism (Art movement) – England –
History 2. Arts, English
I. Title II. Präraphaeliten und Fin de
siecle. *English* III. Series
700 NX600.S95

Library of Congress cataloguing in publication data
Hönnighausen, Lothar
[Präraphaeliten und fin de siècle. English]
The symbolist tradition in English literature : a study of Pre-
Raphaelitism and fin de siècle / Lothar Hönnighausen: condensed
and translated from the German by Gisela Hönnighausen.
   p.   cm. – (European studies in English literature)
Translation of: Präraphaeliten und fin de siècle.
Bibliography.
Includes index.
ISBN 0 521 32063 1
1. English literature – 19th century – History and criticism.
2. Symbolism (Literary movement) – Great Britain. 3. Symbolism in
literature. 4. Preraphaelitism – Great Britain. 5. Romanticism –
Great Britain. 6. Art and literature – Great Britain – History – 19th
century. I. Title. II. Series.
PR468.S9H66 1988
820'.9'008 – dc 19   87–35497   CIP

ISBN 0 521 32063 1

GG

Contents

Illustrations

Preface

This book attempts to portray Pre-Raphaelite and *fin de siècle* poetry and art as an integral part of a continuous tradition connecting romanticism with modernism. It focuses on the symbolist tendencies within this tradition because, in contrast to what terms like 'aestheticism' or 'decadence' might suggest, 'symbolism' represents a main stream in both English and international nineteenth-century literary history. Accordingly the approach is twofold and combines an assessment of the changing conceptions of the symbol from the English romantics through the Victorians to Pater, Wilde, and Yeats with the comparison of examples from the more clearly established French symbolist movement. These reflections in chapter 1 are to prepare the ground for a critical appraisal of the particular forms in which the various conceptions of the symbol are poetically realized ('Typology and allegory' and 'Poet and poetry') and of the modes in which symbolist contents are set forth in major motifs ('The imaginary landscape'; 'The ideal beloved'; 'Late romantic spirituality').

The study of the shifting conceptions of the symbol and of the 'Pre-Raphaelite' affinities of non-Pre-Raphaelite authors such as James Thomson B.V. is intended to guard against the restrictive effect of classification and to widen our perspective of Pre-Raphaelitism. For a similar reason the works of minor authors are also included in our discussion. I hope to establish or confirm literary patterns from their work that in our studies of the major authors will keep us from relying too exclusively on biographical explanation. The additional attention paid to the relationship between poetry and painting seemed to arise naturally with the subject and not only from my own interest in the sister arts. The comparative approach will perhaps not appear surprising in a book offering a view complementary to the Anglo-American perspective on the subject.

I have acknowledged my manifold debts to previous scholarship in notes and bibliography, but should single out one author to whom I am particularly indebted: William E. Fredeman, the distinguished scholar and collector whose pioneer efforts opened the field.

I owe special thanks to my wife and fellow 'Pre-Raphaelitist', Dr Gisela Hönnighausen, for sharing her scholarly insights with me and for giving stimulating advice. At a time when I was under pressure from other scholarly obligations, she stepped in and made the English edition of the book possible. She very skilfully condensed the original book and translated it; she patiently let me do a lot of rewriting of what she had translated, but kept me from turning it into a 'deconstructionist, all-over' piece. In translating she had the expert assistance first of Ms Jo Van Vliet and later of Mr Rupert Glasgow whose intelligent and sensitive suggestions were also of great help when I revised the final draft. I should also like to thank Mr Christoph Irmscher and Ms Sabine Gülicher for competent bibliographical work and Ms Dana Loewy for producing a meticulous typescript.

When I wrote in the late sixties about the Victorian fascination with 'old-fashioned' typologies and emblems and at the same time with unnaturally clear and scientifically rendered details, about the iconography of Rossetti's symbolic portraits and the role of Pater's art criticism in the development of modernist poetics, part of the fun was discovering something, the excitement of 'a peak in Darien'. Since the publication of the original version of the book in 1971 by Wilhelm Fink Verlag, Munich, much important work has been done by others and the several aspects of the topic are now known in much greater detail. In the *Postscript* of this book I discuss studies related to a comprehensive view of the English symbolist tradition, indicating major research issues and how we might deal with them in our future work.

University of Bonn   L. H.

Introduction

The subject of this study of late romantic poetry from 1850 to 1900 is the work of the Pre-Raphaelites and the poets of the *fin de siècle*. The expression 'late romantic' seems to be a reasonable 'blanket' term[1] to cover the literature of an age characterized by the development from romanticism to modernism. Within this transitional period, a number of distinct literary trends meet and interact, and attempts to categorize and define literary terms are consequently to be found in abundance. A variety of designations ('decadence', 'aestheticism', 'symbolist movement') thus refer to the same phase,[2] while works as disparate as Millais's *Christ in the House of His Parents* and Burne-Jones's *Perseus* cycle, Morris's *Guenevere* volume and Rossetti's *House of Life* are all incorporated in the single concept of Pre-Raphaelitism.[3] Ever since Holman Hunt's claim that the designation applied exclusively to his own style, the question whether Pre-Raphaelitism was a typical manifestation of Victorian England or rather an anti-Victorian parallel to French aestheticism[4] has been a perennial bone of contention, and this remains the case today. In this situation, applying the spirit of the 'perspectivism'[5] which emerged with Nietzsche, Wilde and other late-nineteenth-century thinkers, it is perhaps most profitable to consider such terms as 'decadence' and 'symbolism' as interesting perspectives rather than as absolute designations.

The use of the expression 'symbolist tendencies' as the point of departure for this study arises from the conviction that, in the literary as well as in the visual arts of the nineteenth century,[6] an international movement was at work,[7] which, having initially come to light in the symbols of the German and English romantics, went through a series of phases, before the so-called French symbolist school of the nineties[8] achieved its most extreme and seemingly its final expression. The considerable latitude within late romantic symbolism occurs as a direct consequence of the different histories of French, English and German romanticism. In French literature the symbolist tendencies from Baudelaire to Mallarmé clearly represent a new experience and culminate in the creation of literary masterpieces, while in the England of Keble, Ruskin and the Pre-Raphaelites, comparable effects never reach the poetic heights of Blake, Wordsworth and Keats, failing to develop beyond an epigonic

1

restoration of the medieval 'language of types'. Beginning with Swinburne, however, there are new impulses in Victorian England and it is possible to trace a marked proclivity to incorporate symbolist inspiration from across the Channel within the indigenous tradition of romantic symbolism.[9] Our study consists, therefore, in an examination of the symbol in the English tradition and its transformations in the course of the nineteenth century, followed by an analysis of specific manifestations of the French symbolist movement. It is important to recognize, however, that 'what soaked through to England of the new *art poétique* was something very much less than the difficult and disturbing process by which Mallarmé and Rimbaud were transforming French verse'.[10] Swinburne and other English francophiles of the time – O'Shaughnessy, Payne, L. Johnson or Dowson – are linked to the French not only by their fascination with the symbolic and the resultant search for a new and fitting poetic medium, but primarily by their thematic and stylistic similarities and their underlying sensibility. Considering symbolism solely in terms of Mallarmé's preface to Ghil's *Traité du Verbe*, in terms of the manifesto itself or the ideals of the narrowly defined 'symbolist school', it is clear that, from Rossetti and Swinburne to Dowson and the young Yeats, England did not produce a symbolist of note. If, however, we proceed from precursors of the movement like Baudelaire, or even from Verlaine, whose position was somewhat apart from the symbolist school itself,[11] a series of poetological and stylistic parallels can be discerned, allowing us to speak of symbolist tendencies in late English romanticism.[12]

Just as Emile Blémont and Gabriel Sarrazin had brought the Pre-Raphaelites to the attention of those French writers tending toward symbolism, and thus demonstrated the parallels between the two movements,[13] Arthur Symons performed a similar service for his fellow Englishmen with his book on representative French symbolists. His essays on the English and French literature of the time, his books on the French symbolists as well as on Blake,[14] are crucial to the present study because of the emphasis they place on the inner continuity linking the various international manifestations of the movement. Of particular import are the introduction and conclusion to *The Symbolist Movement*. (The essay 'The Decadent Movement' can be considered a preliminary study.) Starting with a discussion of the terminology, Symons ascertains that 'the terms Impressionism and Symbolism define correctly enough the two main branches of that movement'.[15] In fact, however, these two elements are often found in juxtaposition, or in a fusion peculiar to symbolism, the 'spiritual vision' generating originality of perception, and the impressionistic disassembly of reality, as in Verlaine, suggesting a new spirituality.[16]

Like Yeats's early essays,[17] which have contributed so significantly to the discussion of symbolism, Arthur Symons's observations are based on the assumption that it is a European movement.[18] The dedication in *The Symbolist Movement* is addressed to Yeats not only as a friend, but also as 'the chief representative of that movement in our country', who had recognized and laid stress on its broader connections in 'Symbolism in Painting':

Wagner's dramas, Keats' odes, Blake's pictures and poems, Calvert's pictures, Rossetti's pictures, Villiers de l'Isle-Adam's plays, and the black-and-white art of Mr Beardsley and Mr Ricketts, and the lithographs of Mr Shannon, and the pictures of Mr Whistler, and the plays of M. Maeterlinck, and the poetry of Verlaine, in our day, but differ from the religious art of Giotto and his disciples in having accepted all symbolisms.[19]

The quotation is of interest for a number of reasons. In England, as in other countries, a continuous tradition extends from the romantics Blake and Keats through to the contemporary artists Ricketts and Shannon, constituting part of a transnational movement encompassing all the arts. Its symbolist foundation led Yeats and Symons alike to the conclusion that symbolism was a concept intrinsic to literature. The choice of Giotto and Orcagna as focal points reveals the Pre-Raphaelite heritage unequivocally and enables Yeats to differentiate between a timeless symbolic disposition in all art and contemporary variants of it. The self-consciousness of the movement strikes Symons as typical of the decadent spirit of the times: 'What distinguishes the Symbolism of our day from Symbolism of the past is that it has now become conscious of itself.'[20]

The quotation from Carlyle which serves as an epigraph to Symons's introduction places additional emphasis on the international nature of the movement: 'It is in and through Symbols that man, consciously or unconsciously, lives, works, and has his being: Those ages, moreover, are accounted the noblest which can the best recognise symbolical worth, and prize it highest.'[21] The choice of this epigraph is by no means arbitrary, for the introduction makes further reference to Carlyle. The well-known attempt to depict the duality of the symbol as simultaneous concealment and revelation prepares the ground for the definition in *Sartor Resartus:*[22]

In the Symbol proper, what we can call a Symbol, there is ever, more or less distinctly and directly, some embodiment and revelation of the Infinite; the Infinite is made to blend itself with the Finite, to stand visible, and as it were, attainable there.[23]

In Symons's eyes this formulation is equally applicable to the outlook of the French symbolists.

In conjunction with Carlyle's Anglo-German conception of the symbol, the relationship between symbolism and transcendentalism must also be taken into account. Yet when Symons cites the ageing Spanish writer Campoamor as an advocate of *transcendental art*, an art 'in which we should recognise much of what is most essential in the doctrine of Symbolism',[24] he is not using the concept in the Kantian sense, but rather in the somewhat vaguer sense of American transcendentalism. As is often the case with poetological problems, parody offers an amusingly distorted but nonetheless illuminating impression of the movement and its wider implications:

> If you're anxious for to shine in the high aesthetic line as
>   a man of culture rare,
> You must get up all the germs of the transcendental
>   terms, and plant them everywhere.
> You must lie upon the daisies and discourse in novel
>   phrases of your complicated state of mind,
> The meaning doesn't matter if it's only idle chatter of a
>   transcendental kind.[25]

If the symbolist movement in England seemed limited to providing material for Gilbert and Sullivan, it was the shortcomings of the symbolist poetry that were to blame, rather than any unfamiliarity with the symbolist poetics, as an appraisal of Symons's introduction clearly shows. Symbolism, he says, is:

a form of expression, at the best but approximate, essentially but arbitrary, until it has obtained the force of a convention, for an unseen reality apprehended by the consciousness. It is sometimes permitted us to hope that our convention is indeed the reflection rather than merely the sign of that unseen reality. We have done much if we have found a recognisable sign.[26]

Symons explains the rejection of rhetoric and external description as an attempt to manipulate the suggestive effects of the poetic medium in order 'to spiritualize literature'.[27] He had already announced this inclination towards 'spiritualization' in the dedication: 'I speak often in this book of Mysticism.'[28] The notion of mysticism, apparently an essential aspect of symbolism, is lent an interesting new dimension by the reference to Plotinus in the conclusion. Symbolist mysticism does not dispel 'the final uncertainty . . . but we seem to knock less helplessly at closed doors, coming so much closer to the once terrifying eternity of things about us, as we come to look upon these things as shadows, through which we have our shadowy passage'.[29] This debt to Platonic–Plotinian thought during the period from 1850 to 1900 is motivated less by a belief in the permanence of the ideas than by a fear of the 'terrifying eternity of things'. This seems to be the real reason for the strange fascination Plato continues to hold for the late romantics. Plato's theory of ideas has lost the authority it had still possessed for Shelley's generation, but the vague escapist need for a form of idealism led Pater's contemporaries to cling to the relics of Platonism: 'it is at least with a certain relief that we turn to an ancient doctrine, so much the more likely to be true because it has so much the air of a dream'.[30] The quotations from Plato with which Wilde embellished his essays, as well as Wratislaw's introduction to a translation of *The Republic*[31] document this fashionable interest in an idealism with a rather questionable metaphysical basis. Significantly, the Platonism of the nineties is satirized in the same song as the 'germs of the transcendental terms'.[32]

The philosopher who had called poets liars is zestfully misinterpreted by the master of the paradoxical shock effect: 'Lying and poetry are arts – arts as Plato saw, not unconnected with each other';[33] beyond this, Wilde sees Plato in the same light as Pater does, as an 'aesthete', 'a critic of Beauty'.[34] As Wilde makes clear with a misleading reference to Pater, it is not a question of the beauty of ideas: 'Who, as Mr Pater suggests somewhere, would exchange the curve of a single rose-leaf for that formless intangible Being which Plato rates so high?'[35] The distortion of the Platonic conception of *theoria* (or contemplation), equally important for Wilde and Symons alike though in slightly differing respects, should also be seen in this context. The *bios theoretikos*, celebrated as 'the true ideal'[36] by Wilde, no longer comes to fruition in a truly Platonic contemplation of the Ideas, but has been transformed into the aestheticist viewpoint of the world. In contrast to the self-abandonment to the state of being characterizing Plato's *theoria*, Wilde's *bios theoretikos* consists in an intensive cultivation of the sensibility in order to attain a life of becoming in Pater's sense: 'the contemplative life, the life that has for its aim not *doing*, but *being*, and not *being* merely, but *becoming* – that is what the critical spirit can give us'.[37] The true reality of the symbolists is a self-made dream world, 'that spiritual universe which we are weaving for ourselves, each out of the thread of the great fabric'.[38] The development from Shelley's Platonism to that of Pater is representative of the affinities and differences between romanticism and late romantic symbolism. What distinguishes the late romantic version of symbolism from that of other periods is a new and striking self-consciousness, colouring both intellect and sensibility, and, as a result of this, a complete reorientation of its literary theory, forms and motifs.[39] To establish the parallel relationship between French symbolism and the trend here referred to as English 'symbolist tendencies' (because of its less conspicuous features) therefore entails a comprehensive treatment of examples from all three areas: poetics, forms and motifs. Given the close connection between symbolist literature and painting, it seems advisable also to include the sister arts in our comparative study of the symbolist tendencies in late English romanticism. This approach is primarily intended to give a new perspective to English literary studies but may perhaps also help to prepare the way for a comprehensive examination of the many different national manifestations of symbolism.

Although late romantic symbolism may not be as clearly centred on the concept of the symbol, the problem remains the focus of interest in the period from 1850 to 1900 and is consequently taken as the starting-point for this study. Having looked in the first chapter at the continuity underlying the changes and development of the symbol, the second and third chapters investigate the various symbolistic modes of expression. While those Pre-Raphaelites who follow in Holman Hunt's footsteps never succeed in overcoming the discrepancy between the typological model and the demand for the realistic depiction of detail, others like Rossetti and Burne-Jones develop means of expression suited to their inner experiences through a return to the emblematic tradition and a revival of allegory. These continue to enjoy an immense popularity with the writers of the nineties, the more so because they recognize that Baudelaire had himself employed many of the same techniques. In chapters 2 and 3, we are not only concerned with specific forms of typological and allegorical expression, but also with the genre of the mood-poem and the interrelationship of the arts as well as with matters of detail such as compound formations, manneristic imagery and synaesthesia.

While it sometimes proves difficult to classify the style of Rossetti, Swinburne, Thompson or Dowson as 'symbolist' in comparison with the poetically more sophisticated French examples, this problem does not arise in the studies of motif and theme undertaken in the second half of the book. Since for both the Pre-Raphaelites and their French contemporaries the development of their dream and nightmare landscapes is directly related to their particular experience of time it is here that the discussion of these landscapes opens. Chapter 5 investigates to what extent the female figure in these landscapes becomes a symbol of yearning as well as an embodiment of secret fears. As the *femme fatale* motif is well known and has been treated so thoroughly by Praz, the fifth chapter is dedicated primarily to the complementary relationship in which she stands *vis-à-vis* the several variants of the symbolic figure of the ideal beloved. With its description of late romantic forms of mysticism the final chapter turns to a characteristic trait of symbolism emphasized by Symons, and attempts to ascertain whether the tensions between worlds of nightmare and escapist dream, between *femme fatale*

and ideal beloved correspond to a similar relationship between the contemporary guilt complexes and escapist religiosity. The discussion comes
full circle with reflections on the various aspects of late romantic
spirituality, returning to problems originally considered in conjunction
with the symbol from a different point of view.

1 Changing conceptions of the symbol in the nineteenth century

From romantic symbol to Victorian typology (Keble, Ruskin, Carlyle)

It is a principle inherent to perspectivism that any point of view can be complemented by another. Just as the term 'symbolism' designates one of many possible approaches, so the specific variation it finds with Arthur Symons constitutes but one avenue for exploring symbolist tendencies in late English romanticism. Its various transformations derive from the same source, the romantic conception of the symbol.[1] For Wordsworth the poet is a symbolist insofar as he seeks to express his deeper understanding of the inner relationship between self and world.[2] Walter Pater finds Wordsworth's 'joyful and penetrative conviction of the existence of certain latent affinities between nature and the human mind' embodied in the lines:

> How exquisitely the individual mind
>   to the external world
> Is fitted; and how exquisitely, too
> The external world is fitted to the mind.[3]

The 'spirit of life' fills man and nature equally and reveals itself in sudden epiphanies, the 'spots of time' of the *Prelude*. During these moments of ecstasy 'we see into the life of things'[4] and recognize that natural phenomena constitute 'types and symbols of eternity'.[5] What strikes Wordsworth with the immediacy of spontaneous inspiration serves Coleridge, under the influence of German idealism, as the object of elaborate and abstract reflection. Nevertheless the two authors share the same romantic conception of an analogy between mind and nature.[6]

In the work of John Keble, the theologian known for his affiliation with the Oxford Movement, the change from the romantic to the Victorian understanding of the symbol becomes strikingly manifest. Keble likewise proceeds from the romantic idea of a directly experienced harmony between man and nature, but he clearly is more interested in the rediscovery of the theological concepts than in the natural details into which they are projected:

9

If we suppose Poetry in general to mean the expression of an overflowing mind, relieving itself . . . may it not be affirmed that [God] condescends in like manner to have a Poetry of His own, a set of holy and divine associations and meanings, wherewith it is His will to invest all material things?[7]

The Victorian urge to discover a symbolic meaning behind everything is one explanation for the strong appeal which the typologies of the Middle Ages and Renaissance, rediscovered in the wake of romantic interest in medievalism, held for Keble and his contemporaries. At a time when the unity and dignity of human life were being threatened by the spread of scientific and mechanical theories,[8] the medieval mode of analogical thinking was received favourably because, unlike the pantheism of the romantics, it was firmly based on the theocentric Christian outlook. Keble's *The Christian Year* (1827) and Isaac Williams's *Baptistry* (1842) are two outstanding examples of the Anglo-Catholic transformation of romantic symbolism and, at the same time, bear witness to the Victorian revival of the emblematic tradition in the nineteenth century.[9] Keble's poem 'Septuagesima'[10] offers valuable insight into the typological outlook of the Victorians:

> There is a book, who runs may read,
> Which heavenly truth imparts,
> And all the lore its scholars need,
> Pure eyes and Christian hearts.

Alluding to the traditional image of nature as the second book of God, the Oxford don playfully addresses its readers as 'scholars', whose erudition lies, accordingly, in their Christian belief.[11] In the course of his poem Keble develops the vertical correspondence implicit in the line 'The works of God above, below' (stanza II, line 1), deriving a religious meaning from each natural detail. Particularly prominent is the tendency toward allegory, later to become so popular with the Victorians:

> Faith is their fix'd unswerving root,
> Hope their unfading flower,
> Fair deeds of charity their fruit,
> The glory of their bower. (stanza VII)

This tendency to create allegorical patterns is related to the proclivity to develop rather forced analogies like the one in the ninth stanza, where Hebrews 12.29 and John 2.8 [12] are meant to clash and to converge simultaneously:

> The raging Fire, the roaring Wind,
> Thy boundless power display;
> But in the gentler breeze we find
> The Spirit's viewless way.

Given such verses it is no longer surprising that the late romantics look to the religious lyrics of the sixteenth and seventeenth centuries for inspiration. Interest in the Metaphysicals increases concurrently with the displacement of the romantic experience of the symbol by subtle theological analogies.[13]

In the concluding stanza of *The Christian Year* Keble interprets the symbolic understanding of the world as an expedient which has become necessary due to original sin.[14] This demonstrates how far Keble has diverged from the romantic conception of the symbol based on the pantheistic and optimistic feeling of oneness with nature. However, Keble's poetry lectures juxtapose both romantic and Christian elements, for the *homo religiosus* is as overwhelmed by the magnitude of the universe as the poet of the Coleridge generation. Keble attempts to reconcile the two elements, on the one hand religion and on the other hand poetry, by which he primarily means the poetry of Wordsworth:

Moreover, a true and holy religion will turn such aids [of poetry] to the fullest account, because it, most of all, feels itself overwhelmed in the presence of the boundless vastness of the universe: . . . what aid can be imagined more grateful and more timely than the presence of Poetry, which leads men to the secret sources of Nature, and supplies a rich wealth of similes.[15]

True to the spirit of Victorian didacticism[16] Keble transforms the immediate experience of the symbolic in nature into theological evidence for the existence of God. For this new and considerably modified form, in which the romantic symbol continues to be present for the Victorians, the transformative influence of Christian piety on literature is of special significance:

For, once let that magic wand, as the phrase goes, touch any region of Nature, forthwith all that before seemed secular and profane is illumed with a new and celestial light: men come to realize that the various images and similes of things, and all other poetic charms, are not merely the play of a keen and clever mind, nor to be put down as empty fancies: but rather they guide us by gentle hints and no uncertain signs, to the very utterances of Nature, or we may more truly say, of the author of Nature.[17]

Keble shows too little interest in a realistic perception of nature and the theological intentions are too prevalent a feature for his 'Septuagesima' to be considered a convincing poem; but it nevertheless has some value for literary history because it lets us more clearly visualize the transition between Wordsworth and Matthew Arnold. Since Keble had tied Christian theology to the romantic conception of nature, the philosophical crisis became all the more acute when scientific discoveries made an optimistic, sympathetic view of nature impossible. It is not until the end of the century with Francis Thompson's clear distinction between pantheist philosophy and the Christian understanding of nature that a solution is offered in the mysticism of St Francis:

through the thin partition of his consolation Pantheism can hear the groans of its neighbour, Pessimism.

Absolute Nature lives not in our life, nor yet is lifeless, but lives in the life of God: and in so far, and so far merely, as man himself lives in that life, does he come into sympathy with Nature, and Nature with him. Not Shelley, not Wordsworth himself, ever drew so close to the heart of nature as the Seraph of Assisi.[18]

Although John Ruskin with his evangelical background provides a vivid contrast to a High Church Anglican like Keble, both hold similar views as regards the nature of symbolism. Under Ruskin's influence typology takes on a new dimension that makes it one of the most prominent features of Victorian art and thought:

I trust that some day the language of Types will be more read and understood by us than it has been for centuries; and when this language, a better one than either Greek or Latin, is again recognized amongst us, we shall find, or remember that as the other visible elements of the universe – its air, its water and its flame set forth, in their pure energies, the life-giving, purifying, and sanctifying influences of the Deity upon His creatures, so the earth, in its purity, sets forth His eternity and His Truth.[19]

The language of types gains in importance with the development of a more rational and systematic approach to the symbol.

To achieve an understanding of a phenomenon as complex as nineteenth-century symbolism, it must be borne in mind that the most diverging conceptions of the symbolic concur in some central points. Thus, when Carlyle, in the chapter on symbols in *Sartor Resartus*, concludes that 'the Universe is but one vast symbol of God',[20] it corresponds both to Keble's image of creation as the book of God and to Ruskin's idea of a language of types in the universe. The fundamental idea of a symbolic view of life ('all visible things are emblems') also links Carlyle and Keble, although Carlyle does not derive it from the scholastic theory of an *analogia entis* as Keble does, but from the philosophy of German idealism ('. . . what thou seest is not there on its own account; strictly taken, is not there at all: Matter exists only spiritually, and to represent some Idea, and body it forth').[21] Moreover, Keble, Carlyle and Ruskin all turn to symbolism for the same reasons. The intellectual background to the diverse modes of nineteenth-century symbolism is well illustrated in *Sartor Resartus*, where reflections on the essence of the symbol are accompanied by vehement attacks against the 'Genius of Mechanism' and the 'Doctrine of Motives'.[22] If to the modern reader Keble's and Ruskin's typologies appear as well meant but hardly convincing attempts to ward off the threat of mechanical determinism envisaged by Darwinism, their contemporaneity with Carlyle's symbolism calls to mind that they are also striving to maintain a spiritual order in life.[23]

It would, however, be an over-simplification to explain the predilection for analogies, types, emblems, and allegories exclusively as a protest against the predominance of scientific and causal thinking. All these forms of the symbolic are equally symptomatic of an aesthetic sentiment emerging as a reaction against the growing ugliness and desolation of an industrial age. What made the paintings of Hunt, Millais, and their friends so attractive to a new industrial class of entrepreneurs and *nouveaux riches* was not only the crude realism and garish colours indicative of their artistic taste but also the 'entertainment value' in deciphering hidden messages. The typological implications of realistically captured details made art understandable in practical terms while the prevalence of moral themes satisfied the Victorian desire for spiritual edification. Holman Hunt's interpretation of his own painting *The Light of the World* (Pl. 1) shows the middle-class mind at work solving an edifying and entertaining typological rebus:

The closed door was the obstinately shut mind, the weeds the cumber of daily neglect, the accumulated hindrance of sloth; the orchard the garden of delectable fruit for the dainty feast of the soul. The music of the still small voice was the summons to the sluggard to awaken and become a zealous labourer under the Divine Master; the bat flitting about only in darkness was a natural symbol of ignorance; the kingly and priestly dress of Christ, the sign of His reign over the body and the soul . . . In making it a night scene, lit mainly by the lantern carried by Christ, I had followed the metaphorical explanation in the Psalms, 'Thy word is a lamp unto my feet.'[24]

Since Ruskin sees nature in its entirety as a reflection of God, 'the visible objects of Nature complete as a type of the human nature',[25] it is not surprising that he should also subject art to a typological interpretation:

You need not be in the least afraid of pushing these analogies too far . . . There is no moral vice, no moral virtue, which has not its *precise* prototype in the art of painting; so that you may at your will illustrate the moral habit by the art, or the art by the moral habit.[26]

Ruskin handled typologies with so much ingenuity and enthusiasm that he failed to see what an anachronism they constituted at a time when Darwin was conceiving and publishing *On the Origin of Species by Means of Natural Selection* (1859).[27]

The crisis of the romantic approach to nature and its impact on the symbol (Arnold, J. Thomson B.V.)

Some of the contemporaries, however, began to have doubts whether the message,[28] which thus far had seemed to emanate from nature, was not in truth an echo of what Ruskin had previously read into it. Matthew

1   William Holman Hunt, *The Light of the World*

Arnold's poetry reflects this crisis of the romantic experience of nature, a crisis which led to a re-assessment of its philosophical foundations and, ultimately, to a revised conception of the symbol. As in the macrocosmos passage of Goethe's *Faust*, nature responds to the overbearing familiarity of Arnold's 'The Youth of Nature' by adopting an attitude of extreme aloofness: 'Yourselves and your fellows ye know not; and me, / The mateless, the one, will ye know?'[29] Having been so cruelly rejected, the late romantic is forced to reconsider the Wordsworthian relationship between man and nature. Although it proves to be illusory, it nonetheless gives rise to a feeling of superiority, since the mere ability of the human imagination to experience such relationships is proof of man's 'thousand gifts'.

> Man, man is the king of the world!
> Fools that these mystics are
> Who prate of Nature!
>
> . . .
>
> Nature is nothing: her charm
> Lives in our eyes which can paint,
> Lives in our hearts which can feel.[30]

Ruskin's interpretation of Hunt's painting *The Light of the World* (letter to *The Times*, 5 May 1854)

The legend beneath it is beautiful verse − "Behold I stand at the door and knock. If any man hear my voice, and open the door, I will come in to him, and will sup with him, and he with me." Rev. iii. 20. On the left-hand side of the picture is seen this door of the human soul. It is fast barred; its bars and nails are rusty; it is knitted and bound to its stanchions by creeping tendrils of ivy, showing that it has never been opened. A bat hovers about it; its threshold is overgrown with brambles, nettles, and fruitless corn − the wild grass, "whereof the mower filleth not his hand, nor he that bindeth the sheaves his bosom". Christ approaches it in the night-time − Christ, in His everlasting offices of Prophet, Priest, and King. He wears the white robe, representing the power of the Spirit upon Him; the jewelled robe and breast-plate, representing the sacerdotal investiture; the rayed crown of gold, in-woven with the crown of thorns; not dead thorns, but now bearing soft leaves of the healing of the nations.

Now, when Christ enters any human heart, He bears with Him a twofold light; first, the light of conscience, which displays past sin, and afterwards the light of peace, the hope of salvation. The lantern, carried in Christ's left hand, is this light of conscience. Its fire is red and fierce; it falls only on the closed door, on the weeds which encumber it, and on an apple shaken from one of the trees of the orchard, thus making that the entire awakening of the conscience is not merely to committed, but to hereditary guilt.

The light is suspended by a chain wrapt about the wrist of the figure, showing that the light which reveals sin appears to the sinner also to chain the hand of Christ. The light which proceeds from the head of the figure, on the contrary, is that of the hope of salvation; it springs from the crown of thorns, and, though itself sad, subdued, and full of softness, is yet so powerful that it entirely melts into the glow of it the forms of the leaves and boughs, which it crosses, showing that every earthly object must be hidden by this light, where its sphere extends.

This euphoria, however, proves to be impermanent. Nevertheless the fundamental belief in an analogical relationship between man and nature is so deep-rooted that the late romantic continues to entertain hopes of learning from it; but if the stars can still be regarded as 'typical',[31] it is only in terms of the self-sufficiency and passivity with which they endure the indifferent universe. As the title of Arnold's 'In Utrumque Paratus' indicates, the speaker wavers between resignation to this situation and the vague hope that some order uniting man and nature might be preserved. It is in James Thomson's 'The City of Dreadful Night' that this disillusionment comes to a head; a harmonious relationship to nature is now impossible: 'Fond man! they are not haughty, are not tender; / There is no heart or mind in all their splendour'.[32] The atheist minister in the cathedral scene destroys the possibility of both pantheist symbols and Christian typology alike:

> I find *no hint* throughout the Universe
> Of good or ill, of blessing or of curse;
> I find alone Necessity Supreme.[33]

The same kind of pessimism prevails in Yeats's poem 'The Sad Shepherd':

> And he called loudly to the stars to bend
> From their pale thrones and comfort him, but they
> Among themselves laugh and sing alway.[34]

One consequence of this experience is the hostility toward nature so prevalent in the nineties. Numerous late-romantic poets in England espouse Baudelaire's and Huysmans's cult of the artificial not so much out of artistic conviction but out of bitterness that the Wordsworthian belief in harmony between man and nature can no longer be maintained. Oscar Wilde flirts with the notion of *l'art pour l'art*, appearing modern and a francophile in his emphasis on the formal aspects of art, but the ironic phrasing of his new aesthetic doctrine still bears the imprint of Arnold's and Thomson's[35] disappointment with nature: 'And then Nature is so indifferent, so unappreciative'.[36] With characteristic rhetorical flair Wilde declares the nineteenth century a major turning-point in history due to the influence of Darwin[37] and Renan alone. This may seem somewhat exaggerated, but there can be little doubt that the changing conception of the symbol at the end of the century was significantly influenced by their theories – 'the one the critic of the Book of Nature, the other the critic of the books of God'.[38]

The beginnings of the new symbolism (Pater, Wilde, Yeats)

In the works of Walter Pater the transformation from the romantic to the modern symbol is strikingly manifest.[39] 'To regard all things and principles of things as inconstant modes or fashions has more and more become the tendency of modern thought'[40]: in these opening lines of his 'Conclusion' to *The Renaissance*, Pater summarizes the contemporary situation. Not only a 'correspondence' between God and creation, man and nature, but every form of symbolism has become impossible. What remains after all experience has been reduced to single, isolated impressions enclosed within the confines of the individual mind is a world of unrelated perceptions hostile to the very idea of the symbol. The only feasible solution seems to be a permanent striving for 'a life of constant and eager observations',[41] a heightening of the perceptive faculties. However, if perspectivism as a method is applied to the writings of Walter Pater, who himself introduced perspectivism in England, it becomes clear that the 'Conclusion' to his well-known essay represents only one possible intellectual standpoint. The hero in Pater's *Marius the Epicurean* observes a 'delighted mystic sense'[42] in the works of his friend Flavian; he himself is given to a 'dreamy idealism'[43] connected with the same deep yearning for 'something permanent in its character, to hold by'[44], which constitutes an essential impulse in *Plato and Platonism*[45] as well. It may seem surprising to find a marked interest for Plato in an author who advocates the 'wholesome scepticism of Hume or Mill'[46] and who attacks Coleridge's obsession with 'fixed principles' and his futile and 'disinterested struggle against the relative spirit'.[47]

Pater initially turns to Plato with epistemological questions. 'The drift of momentary acts of sight and passion and thought', which appears as the pivotal base of his thought in the 'Conclusion' to the essay *The Renaissance*,[48] dictates the need for some kind of structure. It is for this reason that the first chapter on Heraclitus in *Plato and Platonism* is followed by a chapter on Parmenides. But being an epigonic eclecticist, or, if you like, an avant-garde perspectivist, Pater divests the Platonic ideas of their substantiality and reduces them to structures of the mind. Opposed as he is to philosophical abstractness and consequently hostile to Coleridge's transcendental idealism, he describes these ideas metaphorically in the manner of the essayist: 'a recrudescence of polytheism in that abstract world; a return of the many gods of Homer, veiled now as abstract notions . . .'[49]

The animistic misinterpretation of his ideas had increased Plato's attractiveness for the romantics; their empathetic kind of symbolism presupposed an animated cosmos. That Pater retained a secret yearning for this tradition is evinced not only in *Marius the Epicurean* and in his book on Plato, but also in his 'Wordsworth' essay: 'To him every natural object seemed to possess more or less of a moral or spiritual life, to be capable of a companionship with man, full of expression, of inexplicable affinities and delicacies of intercourse.'[50]

Pater's theoretical contribution to symbolism corresponds to his traditional position in literary history. The late romantic epigone valiantly modifies traditional ideas in order to preserve them. Obviously, the 'drift of momentary acts of sight and passion and thought' from which he attempts to grasp as many moments as possible does not afford him the satisfaction that one might expect after the reflections in the 'Conclusion'. His interpretation of Platonic ideas and romantic 'animism' as well as his interest in ritual and myth imply a surprisingly uncritical inclination to transcend a world of appearances and integrate it into a vaguely typological system of correspondences.

His way of conceiving religion came then to be in effect what it ever afterwards remained – a sacred history indeed, but still more a sacred ideal, a transcendent version or representation, under intenser and more expressive light and shade, of human life and its familiar or exceptional incidents, birth, death, marriage, youth, age, tears, joy, rest, sleep, waking – a mirror towards which men might turn away their eyes from vanity and dullness, and see themselves therein as angels, with their daily meat and drink, even, become a kind of sacred transaction – a complementary strain or burden, applied to our everyday existence, whereby the stray snatches of music in it re-set themselves, and fall into the scheme of some higher and more consistent harmony.[51]

Behind the longing for 'such heavenly companionship, and sacred double of their life' which constitutes the main impulse for Deleal's 'constant substitution of the typical for the actual', one can sense the hidden hopes of the sceptic also expressed in *Marius the Epicurean*: 'Dared one hope that there is a heart, even as ours, in that divine "Assistant" of one's thoughts – a heart even as mine, behind this vain show of things.'[52]

Together with this late romantic use of a modified Victorian typology in 'The Child in the House' another tendency of the age can be detected, namely that toward a modern symbolism in the French vein, which finds its specific expression in England in numerous mood-poems from Olive Custance to Yeats. Like Proust, Pater purports to establish a system of empirical associations as a foundation for a symbolism aspiring to overcome the world of appearances:[53]

a system of visible symbolism weaves itself through all our thoughts and passions; and irresistibly, little shapes, voices, accidents . . . become parts of the great chain wherewith we are bound.[54]

From an empiricist point of view this 'visible symbolism' seems to arise from the perception of external impressions, while from an idealistic viewpoint it proves to be nothing but a projection of the mind: 'all language involves translation from inward to outward'.[55] In his essay 'Style' Pater attempts to reconcile these two diverging modes of thought:

Into the mind sensitive to 'form', a flood of random sounds, colours, incidents is ever penetrating from the world without, to become, by sympathetic selection, a part of its very structure, and in turn, the visible vesture and expression of that other world it sees so steadily within, may already with a partial conformity thereto, be refined, enlarged, corrected, at a hundred points; and it is just there, just at those doubtful points that the function of style, as tact or taste, intervenes.[56]

In its isolation the self withdraws into 'that other world it sees so steadily within'. This refined and esoteric state of mind, characterized by a fusion of sensuality and indeterminate spirituality, could not be expressed in the straightforward analogies and typologies of the mid-Victorians. It required a new and sophisticated medium, inspired by the stylistic awareness of the French symbolists.

After its metamorphosis into the Victorian 'type' the romantic symbol has developed by the turn of the century into a *chiffre* expressing the moods and subjective states of the modern mind. The fact that terms such as 'type', 'typical'[57] continue to be frequently used despite their changed connotations points to the continuity of symbolist tendencies throughout the nineteenth century. Since the symbol no longer embodies an *analogia entis* but an analogy of experience and expression, the question of style has become all-important. Characteristically, Pater defines this new expressive symbolism – which anticipates Eliot's 'objective correlative' – within the context of his essay on style.

Pater has not only developed this new conception of symbolism, which replaces the Victorian typology in his aesthetic theory, but made it the decisive category in his literary criticism. The inner coherence of the symbolist tradition becomes clear when he applies his own symbolist standpoint to an interpretation of Rossetti's works: 'his primary aim, as regards form or expression in his verse was its exact equivalence to those *data* within'.[58] In the last analysis the symbolist conception of style is another manifestation of the idealism Pater shares with his hero Marius and which is only reconcilable with his empiricism if one accepts the relative spirit as the basis of his thought. 'It was easier to conceive of the material fabric of things as but an element in a world of thought – as a thought in a mind, than of mind as an element, or accident, or passing condition in a world of matter, because mind was really nearer to himself.'[59] Pater himself may not have produced any symbolist works, but his theoretical observations establish him firmly within the symbolist tradition.

What enabled Walter Pater and Arthur Symons, for whom symbolism represented 'the turn of the soul',[60] to transcend the barrenness of James Thomson's (B.V.) negative philosophy was the rediscovery of the soul. This symbolist soul may have had, ontologically speaking, a somewhat dubious status, but it undoubtedly provided the powerful impulse which preserves Pater's conception of style from empty formalism. In keeping with the widespread mystical tendencies of the period Pater harks back to the ideas of 'that mystical German' (probably Böhme) and Swedenborg, who, in his words, had regarded the body as 'a process, an expansion of the soul'.[61] It is in this philosophical stance that the roots of Pater's 'expressive' symbolism are to be found:

For such an orderly soul, as life proceeds, all sorts of delicate affinities establish themselves, between herself and the doors and passage-ways, the lights and shadows, of her dwelling-place, until she may seem incorporate with it – until at last, in the entire expressiveness of what is outward, there is for her, to speak properly, between outward and inward, no longer any distinction at all; and the light which creeps at a particular hour on a particular picture or space upon the wall, the scent of flowers in the air at a particular window, become to her, not so much apprehended objects, as themselves powers of apprehension and doorways to things beyond – . . .[62]

In his poetic works as well as in his observations on the theory of symbolism Oscar Wilde once again demonstrates his amazing powers of assimilation. It would be mistaken to expect a systematic approach from the master of epigram and *bon mot*; Wilde clearly does not share Pater's unflagging interest in the problem as a whole. Yet his 'De Profundis' essay deserves consideration within our survey of symbolist tendencies because it incorporates the whole gamut of nineteenth-century variations on the theme in an eclectic form. The formulation, 'I was a man who stood in symbolic relations to the art and culture of my age',[63] is the telling self-depiction of a man whose main artistic achievement consists in the creation of the persona Oscar Wilde. To support this claim he turns to Carlyle's symbolic interpretation of the 'Lives of heroic god-inspired Men',[64] among whom Christ holds the highest position.[65]

Wilde uses the same argument to prove the symbolic character of art that Carlyle did in *Sartor Resartus*: 'Art is a symbol, because man is a symbol.'[66] Like Carlyle's 'Poet and inspired Maker; who, Prometheus-like, can shape new Symbols',[67] Wilde's Christ – the Christ of Renan's *La Vie de Jésus* and Strauss's *The Life of Jesus Critically Examined*[68] – becomes a symbol, 'the image of the Man of Sorrows'.[69] Upon closer consideration, however, it proves not to be a symbol conceived by man, but the fulfilment of a divine prefiguration: 'Christ found the type and fixed it, and the dream of a Virgilian poet, either at Jerusalem or at Babylon, became in the long progress of the centuries incarnate in him for whom the world was waiting.' When Wilde interprets every work of art and every human life as prophecy become reality, he is combining the Victorian predilection for typologies with the quasi-religious taste of the aestheticists:

The song of Isaiah, 'He is despised and rejected of men, a man of sorrows and acquainted with grief: and we hid as it were our faces from him', had seemed to him to prefigure himself, and in him the prophecy was fulfilled. We must not be afraid of such a phrase. Every single work of art is the fulfilment of a pro- phecy: for every work of art is the conversion of an idea into an image. Every single human being should be the fulfilment of a prophecy: for every human being should be the realisation of some ideal, either in the mind of God or in the mind of man.[70]

According to Wilde, Christ did not give the world its 'most eternal symbol'[71] in the cross alone; he sees Christ's entire life as 'the most wonderful of poems',[72] a symbolic work which the Church re-enacts again and again as a 'mystic presentation'[73] in its liturgical rites. In his self-representation[74] as Man of Sorrows Christ endowed his humanness with a symbolic dimension:[75]

But while Christ did not say to men, 'Live for others', he pointed out that there was no difference at all between the lives of others and one's own life. By this means he gave to man an extended, a Titan personality. Since his coming the history of each separate individual is, or can be made, the history of the world.[76]

Although Wilde enjoys shocking the Victorians by denying that Christ preached brotherly love, his modified form of the Christian command- ment remains clearly indebted to the tradition of Victorian analogical thinking.

Christ is an artist in the Victorian sense because he 'found the type and fixed it' while simultaneously meeting Pater's aestheticist demands for an 'artistic acceptance of all experience'[77] and 'self-perfection'.[78] Pater's Oxford student Oscar Wilde places Christ among the ranks of poets[79] because his entire life was a fulfilment of the same expressive symbolism theoretically outlined in the works of Wilde's teacher. He also interprets the relationship of 'idea' and 'image' in the light of Pater's Platonism: 'Truth in art is the unity of a thing within itself: the outward rendered expressive of the inward; the soul made incarnate; the body instinct with spirit.'[80] The fact that Wilde could see the sacramental nature of art 'typified' in the incarnation of Christ bespeaks the continuity linking the sacramental theory of the Oxford Movement with the blasphemous fusion of sensuality and spirituality in both French and English sym- bolism, from Rossetti and Swinburne to Symons and Yeats.

The blasphemous inversion of religious concepts and metaphors is but one consequence of expressive symbolism. In the absence of a timeless world order the artist is left with only the perceptions and moods of the isolated subject to symbolize, and the symbols tend to become more and more cryptic. The suggestive power of these private symbols or ciphers increases precisely because of this subjective quality. This stage in the history of English symbolism is only achieved by Yeats and Eliot, but Walter Pater and Oscar Wilde deserve credit for having laid the necessary theoretical groundwork.[81] From this perspective Yeats's early essays are no longer to be seen as preparations for the rather special case of *A Vision*,[82] but as marking the final stage of a more general movement in the nineteenth century.

In the preface to Blake's works co-edited by Yeats and Ellis, the early romantic emerges as the father of symbolism. Such an interpretation is only possible because Yeats himself shares basic idealistic convictions that, however diverse they may be, dominate all of nineteenth-century literature from romanticism to Pater. 'The sensations and observations are merely the symbols or correspondence whereby the intellectual nature realizes or grows conscious of itself in detail.'[83] Blake's concept of the sovereign imagination[84] is fused with Hegel's concept of the 'conscious movements in the secular process of the eternal mind'.[85] Yeats's idea of the symbol has to be seen within this epistemological context. Ellis's and Yeats's bold recourse to Böhme, Swedenborg and occultism may be of little interest to the Blake scholar,[86] but it does illustrate Yeats's own position within the symbolist movement. Thus, the striking affinities between Yeats's analysis of the relationship between body and soul[87] and certain passages in *Marius the Epicurean*[88] can be explained in terms of the same fascination with mysticism and the occult which links the French and English symbolists.[89]

Deeply aware of living in an epigonic age, the young Yeats is conscious that the symbol occurs in a wide variety of manifestations. He differentiates between the 'traditional symbolism' in Rossetti's painting and the 'personal symbolism' of Wagner,[90] between 'emotional symbols' that unconsciously awaken purely emotional responses and 'intellectual symbols', 'symbols that evoke ideas alone, or ideas mingled with emotions'.[91] Like Blake and Goethe, he is anxious to distinguish between symbol and allegory, thus underlining his participation in the same continuous tradition. It seems surprising that in the wake of Verlaine's 'Art Poétique' he should still speak of intellectual symbols, which are usually associated with Victorian paintings of ideas by Watts and his school, yet what Yeats understands by the concept is definitely not the obtrusive illustration of abstract or moral themes: 'for symbols, associated with ideas that are more than fragments of the shadows thrown upon the intellect by the emotions they evoke, are the playthings of the *allegorist* or the pedant, and soon pass away'.[92]

Yeats was, of course, familiar with Verlaine's poetics and poetry,[93] but a comparison of poems on a similar topic like 'Ephemera' and 'Colloque Sentimental' shows that he clearly follows his own muse. What distinguishes his early poetry from that of the French symbolists[94] is, in addition to the Irish features, the presence of Pre-Raphaelite traits.[95] Nonetheless, a poem like 'The White Birds' shows Yeats striving to invest Pre-Raphaelite flower emblems with the suggestiveness of Verlaine's symbolism.

> A weariness comes from those dreamers, dew-dabbled, the lily
> and rose;
> . . .
> Soon far from the rose and the lily and fret of the flames would
> we be,
> Were we only white birds, my beloved, buoyed out on the
> foam of the sea![96]

But although the rose and the lily have lost the precise meaning inherent to them in Rossetti's paintings, their new implications still encompass the traditional connotations. Since unfulfilled love in this life constitutes one of the basic and painful experiences of the Pre-Raphaelites, it comes as no surprise that the originally positive emblems (rose = love; lily = purity) turn into symbols of frustration for Yeats. As negative symbols they contrast with the image of the white birds which expresses the lovers' longing to escape into an erotic world of dreams.

Yeats attempted to develop a symbolic language,[97] resorting to various sources including Irish and classical mythology, Pre-Raphaelitism and the occult, yet his early theoretical writings and poetry prove that the only viable symbolism is the 'arbitrary symbolism' which he believed he had found in the literature of Blake and Villiers de l'Isle-Adam.[98] It is in Yeats's works that the expressive symbolism of Pater finds its final and definitive articulation. 'True art is expressive and symbolic, and makes every form, every sound, every colour, every gesture, a signature of some unanalysable imaginative essence.'[99] In the wake of Pater's theories Yeats asserts that a 'continuous indefinable symbolism' is the 'substance of all style'.[100] With the rise of expressive symbolism the question of style is of course in the ascendant: 'metaphors are not profound enough to be moving, when they are not symbols, and when they are symbols they are the most perfect of all, because the most subtle outside of pure sound . . .'[101] For Yeats the same inner affinity exists between symbolic imagery and 'pure sound' that led Pater, as well as Mallarmé and Verlaine, to identify poetry and music. Musical structures within poetry ('when sound, and colour, and form are in a musical relation')[102] underline Yeats's poetics of *l'art pour l'art*; the sound of 'wavering, meditative, organic rhythms'[103] engenders that particular state of trance 'in which the mind liberated from the pressure of the will is unfolded in symbols'.[104]

According to Yeats, activity, 'doing this or that',[105] is an impediment to all true experience of the symbol. This proclivity to passive contemplation is essential to all symbolism[106] and pervades nineteenth-century poetry as a continuous, though often varied, feature. Pater and Wilde find this contemplation exemplified in Plato's *theoria*, to which they apply an aestheticist interpretation. Rossetti renders this state in imagery that is well known to the psychoanalyst ('Willowwood'). For Nerval, who is cited by Yeats, symbols reveal their meaning during his bouts of madness.[107] Yeats had himself experienced these symbolist visions – either directly or conjured by occult signs – in dreams[108] and daydreams.[109] Postulating a 'great mind and great memory', which could be summoned by symbols, the pupil of Mme Blavatsky and McGregor Mathers attempts to develop in a systematic way the idea 'that the borders of the mind' and 'the borders of the memory . . . are ever shifting',[110] an experience central to Coleridge's 'Kubla Khan' and Poe's 'Ulalume', and to give this idea a foundation in occultism.[111] In his fascination with magic and occult practices Yeats goes far beyond the latent mysticism of Walter Pater, for whom the problems of observation and expression remained the central issue. Nevertheless both authors are in agreement on the basic ideas of expressive symbolism.

All sounds, all colours, all forms, either because of their preordained energies or because of long association, evoke indefinable and yet precise emotions, or as I prefer to think, call down among us certain disembodied powers, whose footsteps over our hearts we call emotions.[112]

What above all imparts an inner continuity to the numerous manifestations of symbolism in the nineteenth century is the urge to capture at least a glimpse of 'a part of the Divine Essence'.[113] A comparison of Ruskin's rational typology and Yeats's 'continuous indefinable symbolism' brings to light the radical transformations to which the notion of symbolism was subject before the initially romantic conviction that 'Revelation' demands a special language could finally establish itself.

The problem of correspondences

The complex phenomenon of symbolism cannot be reduced to the question of changes in the understanding of the symbol alone because it manifests itself in subject-matter as well as in form and style, and beyond that in the emergence of a new sensibility. Yet the concepts symbol, typology, and correspondence serve as the foundations for an international movement in both literature and the other arts in the nineteenth century. Considering the widespread eclecticism of the period and the numerous forms in which symbolism appears, it would be mistaken to speak of symbolism as a style in the same sense that we refer to gothic or baroque styles.[114] Basic symbolist traits can, however, be detected behind the stylistic imitations,[115] behind the experiments with old and new techniques and – in spite of the national and individual variations – they form a common basis for the many affinities between French and English literature of the age.

The precursor of French symbolism was, of course, Charles Baudelaire (1821–67); his works together with those of Verlaine were among those most frequently translated into English at the time. Baudelaire is a fitting subject for comparison because he does not adopt the extreme stance held by Mallarmé, whose esoteric language remained, despite their assertions to the contrary, foreign to most English poets of the nineties. Although it is difficult to imagine poems less alike in their philosophic and poetic orientation than Keble's 'Septuagesima' and Baudelaire's 'Correspondances', there is no doubt that both poems are based on the same idea of correspondence which enjoyed popularity in the nineteenth century for a number of very different reasons:

nous arrivons à cette vérité que tout est hiéroglyphique, et nous savons que les symboles ne sont obscurs que d'une manière relative, c'est-à-dire selon la pureté, la bonne volonté ou la clairvoyance native des âmes. Or qu'est-ce qu'un poète . . . si ce n'est un traducteur, un déchiffreur: Chez les excellents poètes, il n'y a pas de métaphore, de comparaison ou d'épithète qui ne soit d'une adaptation mathématiquement exacte dans la circonstance actuelle, parce que ces comparaisons, ces métaphores et ces épithètes sont puisées dans l'inépuisable fonds de l'universelle analogie.[116]

What unites Baudelaire's understanding of correspondence with that of Keble or Ruskin is his conviction that the poet does not create but interprets correspondences already in existence as part of a universal analogy.

While the Victorians did not attempt to go beyond this objective and fixed pattern so well suited to their moral and didactic purposes, Baudelaire transforms correspondence – in the sense of Pater's expressive symbolism – into the experience of a subjective and dynamic relationship:

Tout l'univers visible n'est qu'un magasin d'images et de signes auxquels l'imagination donnera une place et une valeur relative; c'est une espèce de pâture que l'imagination doit digérer et transformer.[117]

Correspondences no longer reveal an existing world order to the religious mind but, deprived of their metaphysical foundations, now reflect the unorthodox activity of the poetic imagination and provide a new and indeterminate spirituality with a structural pattern. It is therefore quite understandable that most English poets of the time felt a greater affinity for Blake's visionary imagination than for the religious enthusiasm of Wordsworth's late nature poetry. The forests of symbols through which man is passing in Baudelaire's sonnet still observe him with the customary familiarity ('avec des regards familiers'),[118] yet he himself perceives the message issuing from the pillars of the temple of nature as nothing more than 'confuses paroles'. As a result of the impenetrability of the hidden message the horizontal correspondence ('Les parfums, les couleurs et les sons se répondent')[119] replaces the vertical.

The opening poem to Gautier's *Emaux et Camées*, significantly called 'Affinités Secrètes', marks a decisive transitional stage. The idea expressed in Gautier's poem is not yet that of Baudelaire's symbolic correspondence but of a metamorphosis of 'forms of being' based on a mystical harmony within the universe. Although he adds the subtitle 'Madrigal Panthéiste', it soon becomes evident how far removed Gautier's pantheism is from Wordsworth's. The poem begins with a description of the amorous union of two pearls, two roses and two doves. Their ephemeral nature, evoked at the end of the enumeration ('La perle fond, . . . / La fleur se fane et l'oiseau fuit')[120] allows them to pass into a higher form of existence.

> En se quittant, chaque parcelle
> S'en va dans le creuset profond
> Grossir la pâte universelle
> Faite des formes que Dieu fond.
>
> Par de lentes métamorphoses,
> Les marbres blancs en blanches chairs
> Les fleurs roses en lèvres roses
> Se refont dans des corps divers.[121]

The 'affinités secrètes' arise from such continuous metamorphoses ('De là naissent ces sympathies'). After this relationship has been developed with great ingenuity for eight further stanzas, the speaker incorporates his own feelings of love into the pantheist framework. Gautier's mannered handling of the 'affinités secrètes' demonstrates that the age no longer shares the romantics' feeling of oneness with nature. At the same time, it announces the emergence of a new kind of symbolism that distinguishes itself from 'the Symbolism of the past' because 'it has now become conscious of itself'.[122]

It is this consciousness that characterizes all attempts to re-establish the time-honoured idea of correspondence in the nineteenth century. The concept of correspondence, which in the age of the Metaphysicals[123] constituted an integral part of the philosophical world order, now serves Keble as a justification for his efforts to re-establish the threatened cosmic order in accordance with his reactionary ideals. Browning regards correspondence as an interesting historical model without universal validity.[124] Like the French symbolists, Yeats turned to occult theories and practices to fulfil his spiritual needs, because, unlike those of orthodox Christian religion, they make allowance for a certain intellectual scepticism. Thus he saw the 'Emerald Tablet'[125] as a mystical alternative to religious beliefs rendered unacceptable by scientific advances in the nineteenth century. In the course of their occult studies, French as well as English poets discover a common source for the correspondence model in the figure of Swedenborg. It was above all through the influence of Blake and his followers that Swedenborg became known in England; in France Balzac was one of his best-known transmitters.[126] The impact of the idea of correspondence on the Victorian Pre-Raphaelites as well as on the poets of the nineties under the influence of Baudelaire will become evident in the analysis of poetic form in the two following chapters.

2　Typology and allegory in late romantic literature

Typologies

'He has got her to the Royal Academy. She has gone to the Prae-Raffaelites. Oh! She is walking Prae-Raffaelitism herself. Symbols and emblems! Unfortunate John! Symbolic, suggestive teaching, speaking to the eye . . .'[1] These malicious remarks made by Miss Marston concerning an acquaintance in Charlotte Yonge's novel *Heartsease* are still of some interest today because they summarize major characteristics of Pre-Raphaelitism. The belief that 'all things are types and symbols', which is also predominant in the works of writers as disparate as Bell Scott,[2] who is only distantly related to the Pre-Raphaelite Brotherhood, and De Quincey,[3] had recieved formative impulses from the Evangelical, as well as from the Oxford, Movement. This is quite understandable since the typological approach conforms to religious traditions revived in the nineteenth century for didactic and apologetic reasons. Hence when Hunt and Shields took up religious themes in their paintings, placing them in an emblematic framework, they met with the enthusiastic approval of the clergy. The Revd Richard Glover, well aware of Hunt's emblematic intentions, saw fit to instruct the members of his parish accordingly during a discussion of *The Light of the World*: 'The great truths of the picture, remember, were not produced out of the fancy of the artist, but are the truths of God's Holy Word. The picture is a divine parable in paint, and a human commentary in colour.'[4] Similarly, Chapman's sermons on Shields's painting at St Luke (Camberwell) prove that the artist and the clergyman share the same religious and typological outlook.[5]

This sort of intent to emblematize involves the artists in impassioned discussions of details, which, although difficult for the modern reader to appreciate, are of crucial importance for a thorough understanding of Pre-Raphaelite painting and poetry. Soliciting Shields's advice on the 'correct colours for the draperies of Faith', G. F. Watts received a response that reveals much about the inspirations and techniques of the time.

I am no authority! I know none on the subject but the Authority of the Word revealed. Paul declares Faith is God's gift. She is Heaven born . . . The fine linen

28

of the Saints symbolises their righteousness in the Apocalypse, and it is said that their robes were made white in the blood of the Lamb! . . . it is the best I can offer in response to your question. I bow to tradition only where it agrees with the written word.[6]

There are various reasons why an entire period would consciously embrace what in the nineteenth century was essentially an anachronistic way of thinking like the typology. As the creators of their own analogical systems the Victorians could assure themselves of their validity at any given moment; the ensuing experience of congruence and order provided this generation unsettled by countless symptoms of crisis with the illusion of security. Because of their transparency and sense of direction these types complied with the deep-rooted urge to conceal inner uncertainty behind didactic principles. In addition, the analogies and symmetries of the typological mode of thought satisfied the growing aspiration for beauty arising in reaction to industrial ugliness through the development of decorativeness.[7]

The remarkable ingenuity evident in the combination of otherwise unrelated topics and motifs is a prominent feature of typological painting and poetry in the nineteenth century. In his poem 'Ave' Rossetti adopts an image from medieval theology because of the conceit inherent in it:

> Now sitting fourth beside the Three,
> Thyself a woman-Trinity, –
> Being a daughter borne to God,
> Mother of Christ from stall to rood,
> And wife unto the Holy Ghost.[8]

Such theological speculation might seem mannered in the age of Renan yet it links the works of the agnostic Dante Gabriel Rossetti and his devout sister. In a letter to Shields, for instance, Christina Rossetti dwells upon the meaning of the word 'Azazel' in the manner of medieval etymologists.[9] Even if the individual interpretations occasionally display a particular inventiveness, the main objective of the Victorian typology remains a general validity based on rational transparence and sound orthodox dogma. An article about Frederick Shields written by Horace Scudder and published in the *Atlantic Monthly* in 1882 with the revealing title 'An English Interpreter' demonstrates this rather vividly:

It is in the interpretative function of art that Mr Shields has shown his great power; and the interpretation is not of a historical tradition nor of an individual fancy, but of a catholic and comprehensive conception of spiritual life.[10]

Prefiguration is one of the most common variants of the typology in the nineteenth century. The theological tradition of a correlation between the Old and New Testament allows the Pre-Raphaelites to discover numerous prefigurations in the childhood of Jesus:

> Ah! knew'st thou of the end, when first
> That Babe was on thy bosom nurs'd? –
> Or when he tottered round thy knee
> Did thy great sorrow dawn on thee? – [11]

To the modern eye, paintings like Millais's *Christ in the House of His Parents* or Rossetti's *The Passover in the Holy Family* seem like genre paintings; due to their epigonal character they no longer portray momentous events in the life of Christ but minor episodes. But the minute attention to detail together with the inclination for the idyllic and the sentimental are often countered by the posed arrangement of the figures, endowing the painting with an aura of meaningfulness beyond the domestic tranquillity. Rossetti's sonnet on *The Passover in the Holy Family*, which fulfils the function of the *subscriptio* of traditional emblems, proves that the painting's vague symbolic suggestiveness, important though it appears to our modern sensitivity, is rather a side-effect, the main goal of the painter–poet being typological clarity.

> Here meet together the prefiguring day
> And day prefigured. . . .
> Lo! the slain lamb confronts the Lamb to slay.[12]

While the illustrations of Alciat or Quarles are strictly functionalized in order to elucidate the abstract theme, Pre-Raphaelite paintings are often so laden with minor scenes and realistic details that the intended message is virtually obscured. Frequently there is also a tension between the aesthetic and typological arrangement of images which produces mannered and obtrusive formulations like 'the slain lamb confronts the Lamb to slay'. Finally, the co-presence of the prefiguring and prefigured event, the contraction of two time levels in the timelessness of the 'symbolic moment' created problems which the realism of the Pre-Raphaelites was unable to accommodate and which ultimately led to the distortion characteristic of Pre-Raphaelite art.

The typological mind is inventive and experimental; thus in *Mary Magdalene at the Door of Simon the Pharisee* Dante Gabriel Rossetti earnestly attempts to present the prefiguration in a sophisticated antithesis that, however, first becomes fully understandable in his sonnet. In the brief description of the painting appended to the sonnet, Rossetti explains that its intentional symmetry is meant to express the heroine's difficult decision. 'In the drawing Mary has left a festal procession, and is ascending by a sudden impulse the steps of the house where she sees Christ. Her lover has followed her and is trying to turn her back.'[13] Rossetti's endeavour to translate Leonardo Da Vinci's *Our Lady of the*

Rocks into the language of a sonnet is comparable to that of Shields, who, according to Scudder, discovers an additional allegorical dimension to biblical scenes.[14]

Among the distinctive Pre-Raphaelite examples of typological art is James Collinson's 'The Child Jesus, A Record Typical of the Five Sorrowful Mysteries'. This elaborate work opened the second issue of *The Germ* and was praised in the most enthusiastic terms by Dante Gabriel Rossetti in a letter to his mother. Rossetti's comment that the author's inclusion of two additional episodes makes it 'emblematical of the five sorrowful mysteries of the Atonement'[15] betrays the nineteenth-century predilection for systematic completeness and numerical principles of order borrowed from the devotional tradition. William Michael Rossetti is considerably more reluctant in granting approval: 'nor is there much invention in the symbolical incidents'.[16] What he apparently finds lacking is not originality in devising new prefigurations (in Collinson's work there are hardly any prefigurations known from legends or tradition) but their persuasive power as 'types'.[17]

Yet it would be a misconception to judge the episodes on the basis of their 'typical' allusiveness alone. Equally important – as the nature of Collinson's and other Pre-Raphaelite depictions reveals[18] – are the idyllic and sentimental appeal of the scenes. The Victorian public which enjoyed Arthur Hughes's *The Woodsman's Child* with the squirrel watching the woodsman's sleeping daughter and was deeply touched by the sheepdog's devotion in Landseer's *The Old Shepherd's Chief Mourner* must have been moved to tears by the idea of the child Jesus playing with a lamb. Our difficulties with the typological art of the nineteenth century mainly stem from the fact that the artists did not restrict themselves to establishing one major prefiguration but insisted on giving symbolic overtones to as many details as possible in the seemingly realistic descriptions. In Collinson's poem, to cite just one example, the maltreated donkey is a foal of the ass that carried Mary and her child into Egypt.[19] The deliberateness behind these prefigurations becomes particularly obvious at the end of the scene, in which the Crucifixion is anticipated in a number of typological details. What distinguishes the Victorian from the medieval experience of typological schemes is the sentimental awareness of the symbolic relation which the characters invite the reader to share with them. In a dream Mary sees how Jesus's baby lamb marked with a tiny red cross dies near a leafless tree mourned by its mother. Jesus himself interprets this scene as a prefigurement, a vision sent by God, and connects it with the passage from Isaiah[20] which the two of them had read together the evening before.

There is little doubt that Collinson's sense of analogy is far more developed than his sense of taste. His admittedly second-rate poem still deserves some consideration, however, because the Christian prefigurations employed by the Pre-Raphaelites constitute one of the most striking manifestations of the late romantic yearning for the continuity of a spiritual tradition in England. Towards the end of the Victorian era the romantic belief in harmony has been irretrievably lost, causing many authors to search for new points of orientation. Russell (AE) finds them in pantheist mysticism ('Star Teachers' or 'The Secret') or in elements from Platonic philosophy ('The Symbol Seduces', 'Symbolism').[21] It is this endeavour to participate in a new cosmic unity which in France leads Nerval to understand the microcosm as a cabalistic reflection of a macrocosm and explains why the analogies of a Fourier and the correspondence theory of a Swedenborg held so much fascination for Baudelaire.[22]

It is symptomatic of the fragmentation of an outgoing age when Francis Thompson on the one hand admires Shelley's 'Ode to the Setting Sun' as 'instinctive perception . . . of the underlying analogies, the secret subterranean passages, between matter and soul', but, at the same time, tries to remake it as a Victorian typology.[23] The beginning and end of the poem throw considerable light on the way Victorian typologies work. The sun and the cross are not related in a strictly typological sense, yet the conspicuousness of their combination demonstrates that the author intends more than straightforward description:

> . . . Thy straight
> Long Beam lies steady on the Cross.[24]

> . . . The Cross stands gaunt and long
> 'Twixt me and yet bright skies, a presaged dole.
> Even so, O Cross! thine is the victory.
>   . . .
> Brightness may emanate in Heaven from thee.[25]

Similarly elaborate treatment of symbolic relationships can be found in the works of most epigonal poets at the end of the nineteenth and beginning of the twentieth centuries.[26] The poem 'A Flaw',[27] published as late as 1908 by Michael Field, a pseudonym for Katherine Bradley and Edith Cooper, still bears the marks of late romantic deliberateness in its accumulation of antitheses, but, under the influence of Pater and Wilde, the character of the correspondence has changed considerably. In the face of belated assurances like the one Francis Thompson makes in 'The Heart II', 'Nature is whole in her least things exprest',[28] Oscar Wilde emphasizes his aestheticist position in 'The Critic as Artist' by declaring: 'Beauty is the symbol of symbols. Beauty reveals everything, because it expresses nothing. When it shows itself, it shows us the whole fiery-coloured world.'[29] Oscar Wilde's aestheticist rhetoric cannot disguise the fact that there is no longer any ontological base for either spiritual prefigurations or correspondence of being. Victorian typology has given way to the only remaining analogy between inner experience and the 'objective correlative'.

The realism of the Pre-Raphaelites

While Oscar Wilde develops his aestheticist understanding of the symbol in opposition to Victorian typology, his praise of lying is meant as an attack against the realistic tendencies of the time: 'and if something cannot be done to check, or at least to modify, our monstrous worship of facts, Art will become sterile and beauty will pass away from the land'.[30] Thus it seems natural that the question of the subject should be central to Pre-Raphaelite poetics as expounded in *The Germ*. Tupper, for instance, maintains that 'works of Fine Art delight us by the interest the objects they depict excite in the beholder, just as those objects in nature would excite his interest'.[31] In the second part of his essay Tupper continues his argument and discusses 'the propriety of selecting the subject from the past or the present time', an important issue for Pre-Raphaelite realism and historicism. Strong realistic impulses around 1850 led to modifications in the representation of the romantics' favourite realms: nature and the medieval world. Holman Hunt strongly objects to the idealized medievalism of the Nazarenes[32] which had been introduced into England by artists like Dyce and enthusiastically received by Rossetti and most other Pre-Raphaelites. These conflicting attitudes were destined to result in a controversy dividing the Pre-Raphaelite Brotherhood itself. Pre-Raphaelitism as originally conceived by Hunt strove to unite realism and Victorian typology, but now undergoes transformations, and in Oxford, under Rossetti's leadership, some artists attempt to create a new symbolic suggestiveness by adopting escapist themes and stylized techniques from the Middle Ages in their works.

A direct result of the conflict between the fascination for the Middle Ages and the exact representation of reality was the compromise to capture the world of Chaucer and the Chronicles with utmost realist precision in poems like Morris's 'The Haystack in the Floods' and paintings like Ford Madox Brown's *Chaucer at the Court of Edward III*.[33]

The first care of the painter, after having selected his subject, should be to make himself thoroughly acquainted with the character of the times, and habits of the people which he is about to represent; and next, to consult the proper authorities for his costume, and such objects as may fill his canvas.[34]

Ford Madox Brown's objectives are the same as those which motivated Holman Hunt to travel to the Holy Land in order to paint biblical themes with maximal accuracy. While historical subjects (e.g. *Early Britons Sheltering a Missionary from the Druids*) appealed to artists like Hunt because they lend themselves to the truthful depiction of details, reality was only attractive to the Morris of the *Guenevere* volume if it was that of a long-forgotten age. Predictably, the doubtful compromise between the two branches of the movement was to be short-lived. Whereas Burne-Jones withdrew to a world of symbolist stylization, Millais shifted his focus to contemporary subject-matter. Tupper's question thus seems programmatic:

If, as every poet, every painter, every sculptor will acknowledge, his best and most original ideas are derived from his own times . . . why transfer them to distant periods, and make them *not things of today*? . . . Why to love a *Ladie in bower*, and not a wife's fire-side?[35]

Relatively rare for Pre-Raphaelite realism are direct and convincing portrayals of the modern world at work. Bell Scott's painting *Newcastle Quayside in 1861*, although it does not attain the artistic achievement of Menzel's *Eisenwalzwerk*, stands out as a valiant but uncommon attempt in this direction. Ford Madox Brown's *Work* and Rossetti's *Found* try to convey too much and further the propagation of a message rather than the depiction of modern everyday life. The deeper reasons behind this are illustrated in the essay 'Modern Giants', one of Stephens's contributions to *The Germ*. Like Tupper, he turns from historical to contemporary themes: 'there is the poetry of the things about us; our railways, factories, mines, roaring cities, steam vessels, and the endless novelties and wonders produced every day', but, without becoming aware of his own inconsistency, he proposes interpreting modern technology according to typological categories deriving from and reflecting the totally different economic, social, and philosophical world of the Middle Ages:

You point out to others . . . the sentiment of a flowing river with the moon on it, as an emblem of the after-peace, but you see not this in the long white cloud of steam, the locomotive pours forth under the same moon, rushing on; the perfect type of the same, with the presentiment of the struggle beforehand.[36]

Tupper concludes his discussion of the merits of the reproduction 'of real life or nature in its own real garb and time' with a revealing example:

the writer remembers to have seen an incident in the streets where a black-haired, sordid, wicked-headed man, was striking the butt of his whip at the neck of a horse, to urge him round an angle of the pavement; a smocked countryman offered him the loan of his mules: a blacksmith standing by, showed him how to free the wheel, by only swerving the animal to the left: he, taking no notice whatever, went on striking and striking; whilst a woman waiting to cross, with a child in her one hand, and with the other pushing its little head close to her side, looked with wide eyes at this monster.[37]

Neither Tupper nor his contemporaries seem to have realized that not real life but an underlying moral intention distorts the apparent realism dominating the composition of this scene. Such scenic representation encourages a display of crude emotions bordering on the melodramatic on the one hand, and sentimentality on the other; nevertheless, their very overtness enabled the Victorians to reach their goal: the illustration of a moral abstract. In accordance with the tastes of an art-loving Victorian public, Tupper endows every detail with a precise function within the didactic scheme. The Pre-Raphaelite treatment of socially relevant themes also displays the same fatal tendency to see more than what is actually there. Rossetti's remark to the prostitute in 'Jenny' – 'You know not what a book you seem, / Half-read by lightning in a dream'[38] – mirrors the technique of Victorian interpretation. Melodramatic, sentimental and moralistic features are even more obtrusive in the poems of mediocre authors of the time.[39]

Not only Rossetti but minor Pre-Raphaelites as well see Giotto and Orcagna, Dante and Pugliesi as their ideals. Strangely enough, in Stephens's eyes, the stylized art of the Early Italians is marked by 'a firm attachment to truth in every point of representation'.[40] Since in his essay 'The Purpose and Tendency of Early Italian Art' he discovers that 'entire adherence to the simplicity of nature'[41] in the works of the Early Italians, it would be unjustified to expect a realistic interest in nature in comparable Pre-Raphaelite works. What Stephens and his friends understand by simplicity – a rather artificial and stylized mode of naiveté – is more typical of Pre-Raphaelite painting and poetry than a truthful rendering of nature. Hunt's new version of the return to nature is characterized by the same scientific precision which Ruskin, and later Hopkins, strive for in their drawings. Curiously, it seems to have escaped Stephens how far he has actually strayed from the ideals of the Early Italians when he attempts to model his aesthetic conception of truth on that of the sciences:

The sciences have become almost exact within the present century. . . . If this adherence to fact, to experiment and not theory . . . has added so much to the knowledge of man in science; why may it not greatly assist the moral purposes of the Arts? It cannot be well to degrade a lesson by falsehood. Truth in every particular ought to be the aim of the artist.[42]

The distinctive feature of Pre-Raphaelite realism is the conflict between the two leading ideals of 'truth to nature' and the 'exact adherence to all her details', a new scientific orientation and an emphasis on the ethical dimension.[43] This idealist aspect underlying the Pre-Raphaelite interpretation of natural details can be traced back to their interest in the Early Italians, whose truthfulness to nature is seen as the result of an inner purity and harmony achieved through monastic asceticism. Thus the idea of the artists associated with *The Germ* to call themselves a 'Brotherhood' was more than just a youthful caprice.[44] Stephens, who, like Ruskin, can feel the decadence of the age, is especially receptive to the archaic innocence of Giotto and Orcagna, urging his contemporaries to emulate it in their own works: 'let us have it unstained by this vice of sensuality of mind'.[45]

As the realism of Hunt and his school have been treated thoroughly elsewhere,[46] we shall limit our discussion to some additional reflections. The striving for truth in the sense of photographic accuracy leads to the development of a unique Pre-Raphaelite sharpness of vision which focuses on the 'smallest things – weeds and stones, and the mere winkings of nature'.[47] As a consequence, every detail seems to stand out from the paintings as if photographed with a telephoto lens. Since this method is applied to every detail, an unintentional but powerful suggestiveness without any fixed symbolic meaning is produced, accounting for the sense of unnatural intensity[48] in so many Pre-Raphaelite paintings. The actual technique of painting as described by Holman Hunt[49] is crucial to this effect. Before beginning work on each new section of the painting, the artist covers the respective section of the prepared white canvas with another fresh layer of white ground from which the superfluous oil has been removed. Painting on this wet white surface is understandably a rather delicate operation, but it imparts an unusual precision and luminous clarity to the details in turn responsible for the impression of a strange fragmentation. This type of fragmentation together with the disconcerting effect of photographic accuracy and the dramatic arrangement of elements explain why Pre-Raphaelite realism appealed to Salvador Dali. Although the Pre-Raphaelites experimented widely with modes of portrayal, later to be of unmistakable significance for modern painting, there is no doubt that the upright Holman Hunt would have been shocked at the surrealist interest in his artwork. His goal was not distortion, but factualness, truth. That his is a very selective truth – the minute depiction of a natural world devoid of all revolting, dangerous, and colossal elements – and a 'realistic' form of escapism is another matter.

Pre-Raphaelitism has to be seen within the larger context of late romanticism, a period when the most diverse realist and symbolist tendencies merge in a myriad of forms.[50] Woolner's *My Beautiful Lady* can be considered a representative example of Pre-Raphaelitism insofar as parts of it opened the first issue of *The Germ*. In its final version the poem provides evidence of the tension between conflicting currents in Pre-Raphaelitism; Woolner addresses the ideal beloved in the stylized manner of the 'Blessed Damozel' ('My Lady's Voice From Heaven') and yet, in another section of the work, he refers to his father-in-law who had served in the colonial forces in India.[51] Natural phenomena, when they do appear, are always grouped together in clusters, producing the same obtrusiveness as the 'realistic' depictions of nature in Hunt's paintings. By removing the details from their natural context and repeatedly re-introducing them in different comparisons, Woolner achieves an effect quite similar to Hunt's concentration on isolated details.

> Her soul is like the simple flower
> Trembling beneath a shower.
> . . .
> My lady walks as I have seen a swan
> Swim thro' the water just where the sun shone.
> There ends of willow branches ride,
> Quivering with the current's glide,
> By the deep river-side.
> . . .
> When'er she moves there are fresh beauties stirred
> As the sunned bosom of a humming-bird
> At each pant shows some fiery hue,
> Burns gold, intensest green or blue:
> The same, yet ever new.[52]

The images seem to take on an existence of their own and divert the reader's attention from the main theme, the virtues of the beloved. Despite the marked visual quality of the vehicles in some instances, the images do not merge in an integrated tableau. The only unifying atmosphere is one of stylization evoked by the Pre-Raphaelite accuracy of detail and the subdued and mannered portrayal of nature.[53] The attentiveness the 'beautiful lady' bestows upon simple weeds and tiny creatures, taking care not to tread upon them, is indicative of the Victorian love of nature.

> Her feet spared little things that creep: –
> 'We've no more right,' she'd say,
> 'In this earth than they'.[54]

While the romantic self instinctively feels the powerful impact of nature and effortlessly encounters the reflection of its own state of mind in the landscape, the speaker in *My Beautiful Lady* consciously projects feelings onto it.

> If trees could be broken-hearted
> I am sure that the green sap smarted,
> When my lady parted.[55]

As a result of the tendency to sentimentalize the relationship between man and nature, the description of natural phenomena loses its visual

quality, becoming increasingly abstract and stylized. This is equally
noticeable in the poem 'The Seasons' contributed to the first issue of *The
Germ* by Coventry Patmore, a writer befriended by the Pre-Raphaelite
circle, and in the works of Payne and other Pre-Raphaelite epigones.[56]
The minute yet highly mannered description of the young Jesus pensively
observing a swarm of bees in Collinson's typological poem is another
example[57] and conveys the same symbolist predilections as the
disproportionately large finger pointing to a Dürer-like clump of grass
in Bell Scott's illustration to *Studies from Nature*.[58] In this sense the
title of Tupper's poem 'A Sketch from Nature' is as misleading as Bell
Scott's, because he by no means provides a realistic sketch but rather a
sentimentalized natural scene.[59] Although the realism modelled on the
scientific conception of nature destroys the feeling of immediate harmony, the spiritual needs of the romantics remain, leading to the
development of numerous compromises. Predominant among them are
the tendency to introduce a sentimental or moral element in an otherwise
straightforward scene and the inclination for descriptions of a stylized or
mannered kind.

Seen within this context, the oft-quoted fact that Rossetti was not a
nature poet[60] proves most instructive. In his sonnet 'Silent Noon' the
seemingly realistic description is, in actuality, structured acccording to a
complicated decorative pattern:

> All round our nest, far as the eye can pass
> Are golden kingcup-fields with silver edge
> Where the cow-parsley skirts the hawthorn-edge.[61]

While the stylized effect achieved by Rossetti's combination of gold and
silver, kingcup and cow-parsley is artistically more convincing, it does
not essentially differ from Tupper's 'Two sheep . . . with backs all silver,
breasts all gold'.[62] Natural phenomena form the elaborately wrought
framework for the beloved in 'Silent Noon' and 'Youth's Spring-tribute'
and retain little of their inherent visual intensity.[63] Having become
somewhat dissociated from their original context as a result of this
stylization, the details can readily fulfil the symbolic function Rossetti
has assigned to them. Since the dragonfly appears as a 'blue thread
loosened from the sky', it embodies more successfully 'this wing'd hour
. . . dropt to us from above . . . / This close companioned inarticulate
hour / When twofold silence was the song of love'.[64]

In light of the obvious Pre-Raphaelite delight in stylization, the
ornate, aesthetic nature descriptions in Oscar Wilde's[65] works can no
longer be exclusively attributed to the influence of Gautier[66] and the
French symbolist school. The literary traditions in his native England
constitute equally important sources. Wilde, in reference to Wainewright,

writes: 'Like most artificial people, he had a great love of nature',[67] and the same can be said of many French as well as English writers after 1830. The symbolically transfigured, and often mannered, in any event, artistically deliberate description of natural phenomena is but another expression of the late romantic hostility toward nature. Wilde's 'Le Jardin' and Gautier's 'Premier Sourire du Printemps' mark an inter-mediate stage; in these poems nature no longer conveys an immediate symbolic experience as in Wordsworth nor a typological lesson in Ruskin's sense. Although it does not yet furnish poetry with a system of ideograms later central to the works of Hulme, H.D. or Pound, there is little doubt that the varied late romantic experiments with the stylized depiction of nature play a crucial role in the development of the metaphors of the Imagist school.

The conflict between realist and symbolist elements

In his memoirs Holman Hunt gives an interesting account of the negative reception of his painting *The Scapegoat*. To him the emblem-atic relationship to the Bible of the realistically painted goat as well as the photographically accurate Dead Sea and its mountainous back-ground is immediately obvious. The reviewer for the *Art Journal*, however, had difficulty in seeing the connection and minces no words in his appraisal: 'There is nothing to connect the picture with sacred history.' A colleague on the *Athenaeum* was of the same opinion; his criticism must have been an even greater shock for Hunt, since he seemed inclined to take the artist's emblematic intentions into consideration:

Still the goat is but a goat, and we have no right to consider it an allegorical animal of which it can bear no eternal marks. Of course the salt may be sin and the clouds eternal rebukings of pride, and so on, but we might spin these fancies from anything.[68]

While the Pre-Raphaelites found in literature the possibility for realistic representation and clarification of underlying emblematic meaning, in the visual arts they were compelled to abandon one of their essential principles or to provide their paintings with explanatory poems as Rossetti did in *Sonnets for Pictures*.

Only from the sonnet accompanying Rossetti's painting *Found* does it become clear what the painter actually intended to depict: the young woman melodramatically turning away had once been the betrothed of the young man who now attempts to rescue her.[69]

The fact that Pre-Raphaelite painting cannot do without the accom-panying interpretative poems demonstrates that it is in truth an allegorical art of ideas ultimately literary in nature. This intellectual quality of symbols and the minute depiction of detail – due, as Bell Scott points out, to the rise of photography and typical of the Pre-Raphaelite school[70] – produce a conflict between symbolist and realist tendencies in the works of Hunt and his followers. Burne-Jones, however, astutely avoids the problem from the beginning by combining stylized portrayals and symbolic suggestiveness in his paintings. The dilemma besetting the Pre-Raphaelitism of the Hunt school illustrates why Yeats[71] as well as Wilde and Francis Thompson,[72] in their defini-tion of the symbolism of the nineties, object to an art 'striving to render by visible form or colour, the marvel of what is invisible, the splendour of what is not seen'.[73] What they propose instead is 'to avoid too definite a presentation of the Real, which would be mere imitation, and too definite a realisation of the Ideal, which would be too purely intellectual'.[74]

In an eclecticist age as enthusiastic about experimentation as the nine-teenth century, the symbolist tendencies undergo a variety of transform-ations, derive from diverse sources and come to light in many different manifestations. During the same period we encounter Hunt's realistic paintings with their emblematic dimension, Watts's paintings of ideas and Rossetti's symbolic portraits. All of these – despite considerable differences – presuppose a public interested in symbolic representation and a willingness to uncover emblematic meanings. The same holds true for the use of flower emblems which has been discovered in the works of Christina Rossetti.[75] The Victorian language of flowers enjoyed such enormous popularity because it coincided with a wide range of Victorian interests: typological implications, botanical interests, a delight in idyllic and sentimental decoration and a realistic rendering of detail are incor-porated in a variety of ways. Burne-Jones's *Flower Book*, a collection of illustrations of flower names, Swinburne's poem 'The Sundew', a Pre-Raphaelite version of the genre reaching back as far as Wordsworth's 'The Primrose of the Rock', 'To the Small Celandine' or 'To a Snowdrop' and further developments like the rose in Keble's poem for the fourth Sunday of Lent[76] all belong to the same tradition. Poems like Blake's 'Ah, Sunflower!' and 'The Lily', inspired by symbolic intentions rather than the observation of nature, seem to mediate between the emblematic tradition of the sixteenth century and its Victorian renaissance which K. J. Höltgen has discussed. In this respect the floral imagery in Wordsworth's poetry undergoes an interesting development: from the early poems like 'To a Snowdrop' or 'The Daisy' to late verses like 'Love Lies Bleeding' there is a growing affinity to Victorian flower emblems. 'The Primrose of the Rock', dated 1831, marks a transitional stage; here the direct experience of nature is secondary to its symbolic implications. Finally, in 'Love Lies Bleeding' (probably written in 1842),

Wordsworth's play on the meaning of the flower name, using it as an allusion to Adonis and the dying gladiator,[77] reflects the same delight in etymology central to Burne-Jones's *Flower Book*:

The pictures in this book are not of flowers themselves, but of subjects suggested by their names. The first meaning of many of these has long been forgotten and new meanings are here found for them in the imagination of the artist . . .[78]

His *Flower Book* intends 'not merely to illustrate' but 'to add to the meaning of words or to wring their secrets from them'. By giving them all the same format − a circle about six inches in diameter − the artist underlines the cyclical structure of the entire volume.[79]

A preference for formal symmetries or cycles also figures prominently in a literary *pendant* to Burne-Jones's collection of miniatures, Allingham's *Flower Pieces*. But while Burne-Jones, taking up a Victorian fashion, places an emphasis on the visionary and the enigmatic and approaches a symbolism similar to that of Maeterlinck, Allingham's cycle remains within the tradition of Shields's rational art and Victorian typology. *Flower Pieces*, with its twofold system of analogies − *Flowers and Poets* and *Flowers and Months* − bears witness to the Victorian liking for symmetrical arrangements. The modern reader, inclined to dismiss the assignation of flowers and poets' names[80] as a Victorian fancy, is surprised to learn in 'Prelude': 'Nor of Fancy's birth may be / Every correspondency'.[81] Allingham has recourse to pantheist and idealist ideas in his attempts to discover a deeper analogy ('Where the Inner's like the Outer') between vehicle and tenor, poet and flower emblem. The connection of the different months with particular flowers (for example, snowdrop, February; daffodil, March; primrose, April; hawthorn, May) originates in the age-old tradition of calendars that, in Keble's days, had met with a religious revival and gained in influence beyond ecclesiastical circles due to its suggestion of a more comprehensive system of order.[82] At the same time, it seems natural that this genre should thrive in an age virtually obsessed with the idea of decoration and illustration. Ingenious combinations are as characteristic of the use of flower emblems as the systematic listings of the flowers and their meanings in flower books, floral alphabets and books of etiquette.[83]

Even the sources of Swinburne's 'The Sundew' can be traced to the tradition of the Victorian floral emblems. In a typically Pre-Raphaelite manner Swinburne combines a minute rendering of detail with a tendency toward stylization: 'A little marsh-plant, yellow green, / And pricked at lip with tender red'.[84] Swinburne does not establish a direct emblematic relationship between the flower and the beloved, but evokes it by means of association in the ornate style of the Early Italians, giving his lines a quality of symbolic suggestiveness: 'My sundew, grown of gentle days'.[85] Related to Swinburne's poem, in the way the emblematic implications are conveyed, are Rossetti's lines dedicated to the 'Woodspurge'. At the heart of the poem is an emotional and spiritual experience. Having 'walked on at the wind's will' the lyric speaker stops and suddenly notices – with the acuity of Pre-Raphaelite eyes that are 'wide open' and 'fix upon' one detail – a small area on the ground where 'ten weeds' are growing, among them the flowering woodspurge with its most prominent characteristic: 'Three cups in one'. Rossetti takes up the practice of deriving a moral from such observations to invert it and ironically proclaim:

> From perfect grief there need not be
> Wisdom or even memory:
> One thing then learnt remains to me, –
> The woodspurge has a cup of three.[86]

Still, the woodspurge remains an emblem – not, it is true, a rationally conceived embodiment of objective truths as with Ruskin or Keble, but an image suggestive of an individual state of feeling. In this poem Rossetti uses the typological mode in the sense of expressive symbolism.

A similar transformation of flower emblems is noticeable in his 'Willowwood' cycle. Here a real plant, 'bloodwort', grows in close proximity to imaginary plants such as 'tear-spurge' and 'heart-stain': their telling names – analogical forms of flower names like 'woodspurge' and 'heartease' – also have an impact on the interpretation of the initially realistic plant. Thus, they become integral elements within the atmosphere and scenery of the 'Willowwood', which can no longer be understood in the light of traditional correspondences but as symbolizing the subconscious anguishes of the inner soul.[87]

Among the poets of the nineties one still finds reminiscences of the language of flowers. Le Gallienne, for instance, in his poem 'A June Lily', relates the six petals of the lily to the six years of love for his lady in an extremely mannered way.[88] Far more important, however, for the development of symbolist tendencies than the fashionable continuation of a Victorian trend is a poem like Michael Field's 'Cyclamens'. Here, the Pre-Raphaelite and imagist endeavours to concentrate on one single symbolic detail converge, and the flower emblem, once representing a direct and objective correspondence, has become the symbol of subjective experience, an example of what I would term 'expressive symbolism':

> They are terribly white:
> There is the snow on the ground,
> And a moon on the snow at night,
> The sky is cut by the winter light,

Yet I, who have all these things in ken,
Am struck to the heart by the chiselled white
Of this handful of cyclamen.[89]

Only familiarity with the typological interest of the period and the language of flowers as one of its special manifestations allows us to grasp fully the iconographical meaning attached to so many details in nineteenth century poetry and painting.

At first glance Atkinson Grimshaw's *The Rector's Garden* (Pl. 2) produces the impression of a realistic picture. The rectory overgrown with ivy, the garden path leading to a round bed of boxwood, the flowers and shrubs are captured in minute detail and, in their seclusion, contribute to the suggestion of an idyllic sanctuary. Even the presence of a young woman attired in Victorian fashion would not occasion the search for symbolic meaning had the artist not placed the figure alongside a prominent grouping of white lilies to the right of the centre. The parallel positioning of the lilies and the young woman recalls the composition of Albert Moore's symbolic portraits. It is not difficult to guess the emblematic implications of the flowers which she is grasping with her right hand. Once the painter's intentions have become clear, we realize that the entire scene is structured around this floral emblem. The central group of lilies is repeated in a second group in the left middle and a third in the right background, emphasizing an underlying emblematic pattern in an otherwise realistic work of art.

Similarly, in the section of Woolner's *My Beautiful Lady* entitled 'Her Garden', the reader seems to encounter a straightforward realistic description of the garden.[90] But the lilies, conspicuous among the garden setting as in Arthur Hughes's painting *The Tryst*, are removed from everyday reality from the beginning because the ideal beloved refers to them as 'Radiant spirits robed in white'.[91] The awareness of the symbolic overtones of one's own gestures is widespread among late romantic figures and explains the theatrical quality of many works in the period.

In poetry, as in all literature, the conflict between symbolist and realistic elements often remains latent due to the inherent possibilities for conveying symbolic relationships; in painting, however, the conflict emerges quite openly and entails various compromises, like those typical for the use of flower emblems in Collins's *Convent Thoughts* (Pl. 3). The emblematic relationship between the lilies and the chaste nun would go unnoticed because the other details are depicted with equal accuracy and vividness. In order to clarify his intentions the artist has decorated each side of the golden frame with a lily standing out in relief, repeating the realistic flower emblem in a stylized parallel. The middle of the frame carries the inscription 'Sicut Lilium' which further underlines the emblematic meaning.

2 Atkinson Grimshaw, *The Rector's Garden*

3   Charles Allston Collins, *Convent Thoughts*

The handling of the garden motif provides a number of instructive examples of the central problem of Victorian art, the endeavour to impart a symbolic meaning by means of realistic representation. Unlike the selective typologies in Hunt's paintings[92] which require the viewer to establish the emblematic meaning of every particular detail, Millais's *The Deserted Garden* immediately evokes an overall emotional atmosphere. There are numerous parallels in literature which attest to the importance of the deserted garden as a fixed iconographical motif for the expression of the late romantic sensibility.[93] Among them are Swinburne's symbolist interpretation of a real garden in 'A Forsaken Garden' and Nerval's transformation of the garden into symbolic scenery in *Aurélia*. The garden planned by human hand becomes a symbol of the transience of all things; the 'dense, hard passage' barred with 'a girdle of brushwood and thorn' embodies the irretrievable loss of past love, the impossibility of returning to a time when the garden was not yet deserted.[94] Nerval, too, gives an accurate description of the garden,[95] and the lady in his novel clasps the long stem of a hollyhock as Woolner's ideal beloved or the Victorian woman in Grimshaw's painting held the lily. Here, however, the gesture does not emphasize an intentional allusion to a flower emblem, but marks the beginning of a mysterious process of identification, in the course of which the garden takes on the appearance of the beloved.[96] As the transfiguration progresses, the beloved fades away and the separation becomes final; 'le jardin avait pris l'aspect d'un cimetière'.[97] By transferring events to the level of visionary dream, Nerval was able to attain a convincing fusion of symbolist and realist elements and avoid the conflict between typological interest and photographic accuracy which plagued the Pre-Raphaelitism of the Hunt school.

A number of Pre-Raphaelites, it must be admitted, surpassed the artistic achievement of paintings like Hunt's *The Scapegoat* or *The Hireling Shepherd* and poems like Woolner's 'Emblems'.[98] In the sonnets 'Lovers' Walk' and 'Winged Hours' Rossetti integrates an aesthetic position orientated on Hunt's principles and outlined in 'St Luke the Painter'[99] into a new kind of symbolic experience by making subtle and sensitive use of the possibilities inherent in language as a poetic medium. Thus, the solutions he finds to a major problem of Pre-Raphaelitism are still acceptable to a modern reader. All too often we forget the ramifications of the differences in artistic media for the problem of symbolism. The specific dilemma of Hunt's paintings illuminates the advantages language offered Rossetti in *The House of Life*. Imagery constitutes the central means of expression for overcoming the conflict between symbolist and realist tendencies.

Holman Hunt surely would have captured the raindrops of 'A Dark

Day'[100] in minute detail, but he would not have been able to endow them with the symbolic overtones which the poet Rossetti achieved in a prevailing atmosphere of 'gloom'. The effect of the alternative copula 'or' linking the two brief similes at the end of the octave in 'The Morrow's Message' ('As of old leaves beneath the budding bough / Or night-drift that the sundawn shreds away')[101] demonstrates how, in the medium of poetry, a vivid scene can be cancelled just as quickly as it is conjured if it detracts from the symbolic purport of the realistic description. While the conception of spring 'as a girl sails balanced in the wind'[102] in the poem 'Barren Spring' could easily be rendered in the visual arts, the inversion of the spring theme originally inspired by flower emblems can only be attained in poetry:

> Behold, this crocus is a withering flame;
> This snowdrop, snow; this apple-blossom's part
> To breed the fruit that breeds the serpent's art.

In the finest poems of the sonnet cycle *The House of Life* Rossetti succeeds in conveying the specific late romantic state of spiritual and emotional suspension, which Nerval has so aptly described as 'l'épanchement du songe dans la vie réelle'.[103] In this fusion of inner and outer experience the Pre-Raphaelite accuracy of detail becomes an integral element in the landscape of the soul.[104] From its introduction as an ingenious simile in the first line ('Each hour we meet is as a bird') to the melancholy tone of the last line,[105] the bird metaphor serves as the structuring principle in the sonnet 'Winged Hours'. As a result of this *tour de force*, in the sestet the persuasive imagery is in danger of culminating in abstract diction when it suddenly acquires a new and shocking intensity: 'wandering around my life unleaved, I know / The bloodiest feathers scattered in the brake'. It is a sign of Rossetti's virtuosity that a single detail, although carefully incorporated in a complex and elaborate pattern, can still impart such suggestiveness.

Here, we also find the roots for Hopkins's theory of inscape.[106] While Holman Hunt cannot overcome the discrepancy between his photographic realism and the typological meaning affixed to it, Hopkins experiences both natural details and religious symbols with equal intensity and, in poems such as 'Spring' or 'Pied Beauty', is able to integrate them in homogeneous artistic wholes. This is all the more astonishing since Hopkins is not only a precursor of modernism but, as his symbolizing commentaries show, no less a Victorian than Holman Hunt or Ruskin: 'I do not think I have ever seen anything more beautiful than the bluebell I have been looking at; I know the beauty of our Lord by it. Its inscape is mixed of strength and grace.'[107]

Rediscovering allegory

In a letter dated 23 January 1855, Rossetti makes reference to his illustrations for the edition of the Moxon Tennyson. He had decided in favour of 'The Vision of Sin' and 'The Palace of Art', because, as he notes, they treat subjects 'Where one can allegorize on one's own hook on the subject of the poem without killing for oneself and everyone a distinct idea of the poet's.'[108] His assumption that the Victorian predilection for allegory is one of the main reasons behind 'the upshot of illustrated editions'[109] seems of interest because he refers to what was to become a dominant concern with the late romantics: the interrelationship of the arts. It would be of little use to apply a concept of allegory based on medievalist studies such as those by de Lubac or Lewis in analysing the allegorical literature of the late romantics. What Rossetti envisions is a subjective allegorical interpretation. Edgar Allan Poe's rather contradictory evaluation of allegory is of interest here because it is fairly characteristic of the nineteenth century. Poe retracts his statement 'In defence of allegory . . . there is scarcely one respectable word to be said'[110] in a modification symptomatic for the rise of the new symbolist kind of poetry: for if 'judiciously subdued, seen only as a shadow or by suggestive glimpses'[111] he finds allegory wholly acceptable. Baudelaire, in *Les Paradis Artificiels*, uses the terms *symbole, analogie, correspondance* and *allégorie* concurrently without making any clear distinctions because he is less concerned with allegory as a formal principle than as an inner experience:

L'intelligence de l'allégorie prend en vous des proportions à vous-même inconnues; nous noterons, en passant, que l'allégorie, ce genre si spirituel, que les peintres maladroits nous ont accoutumés à mépriser, mais qui est vraiment l'une des formes primitives et les plus naturelles de la poésie, reprend sa domination légitime dans l'intelligence illuminée par l'ivresse.[112]

In the hashish trance analogies, correspondences and allegories have lost their abstract character. Rossetti's, Poe's and Baudelaire's comments on allegory, despite their differences, are all equally relevant examples of various endeavours in the nineteenth century to adapt the allegory as a mode of expression for a new sensitivity.

Rossetti and his contemporaries had encountered the short allegory and stylized personification in the sonnets and canzoni of Cavalcanti, da Lentino and other authors translated in *The Early Italians* and they were familiar with allegory as informing the structure of long poetical works from Dante's *Divina Commedia*[113] or Spenser's *The Faerie Queene*. Keats, the idol of many Pre-Raphaelites, had introduced them to Spenser's work[114] and it is in fact his influence that causes numerous writers to misinterpret *The Faerie Queene* as a collection of 'purple

patches' (and not as a 'continued allegory') until the end of the nineteenth century.[115] As late as 1902 Yeats's essay on Spenser shows how
far the turn-of-the-century attitude is from Lewis's modern understanding of allegory. Yeats discovers 'A visionary strangeness and intensity'
in Bunyan's comparatively simple story and also refers to the author of
the *Romance of the Rose*, who pretends that the adventures originally
came to him as a vision. It is characteristic of Yeats's symbolist approach
to allegory that he considers Dante's visionary poem the fulfilment of
allegorical literature as such. Seen from this perspective it becomes clear
why Spenser's rational and functionalized use of allegory remains
foreign to him.[116]

Although allegory as a comprehensive structural principle does not
find widespread acceptance among the late romantics, allegory as a symbolic mode tallying with the fashion of typology retains a certain attractiveness. *The Faerie Queene* is particularly popular. Shields, for instance,
designs a cycle of *Faerie Queene* illustrations for Cheltenham College,[117] and Crane illustrates Spenser's allegorical poem in the taste of
the nineties.[118] James Thomson's (B.V.) discussion of Ruskin's critical
remarks about Speranza's 'anchor of hope'[119] is characteristic of the
peculiar Victorian interest in allegory and also offers considerable insight
into Thomson's own allegorical poems. Considering the fact that the
Victorians turned to allegory because of their own typological outlook,
it is understandable that Bunyan seemed to meet their expectations more
fully than Spenser.[120]

The rediscovery of allegory involves a striking preference for personification in late romantic poetry, a device enabling the poets to create
brief allegorical scenes. In the works of the great romantics, personification had already begun to undergo a process of transformation which
continues in the second half of the nineteenth century.[121] Francis
Thompson, in his essay on Shelley, not only relates Shelley, Crashaw and
Collins but links their personifications to the allegorical figures of
Spenser:

Crashaw, Collins, Shelley – three ricochets of the one pebble, three jets from
three bounds of the one Pegasus! Collins's Pity, 'with eyes of dewy light', is near
of kin to Shelley's sleep, 'the filmy-eyed', and the 'shadowy tribes of mind', are
the lineal progenitors of 'Thought's crowned powers'. This however, is personification, wherein both Collins and Shelley build on Spenser.[122]

The inner affinity between allegory as a principle of form and a poetry
of correspondences becomes obvious when Thompson explains Shelley's
personifications not as products of his 'vivifying power over abstractions' but of his experience of universal harmony.[123] Yet what came to

Shelley with the immediacy of an intuition becomes the object of arduous endeavours for the late romantic symbolist.

The works of James Thomson are particularly revealing for the study of late romantic allegory because almost all his poems contain allegorical elements. Within his *œuvre*, from 'The Doom of a City' (1857) and 'A Real Vision of Sin' (1859) to 'The City of Dreadful Night' (1870–4) and 'Insomnia' (1882), it undergoes numerous modifications, giving an impression of the changing nature of allegory throughout the period. While in 'Shelley' (1860) and 'The Dead Year' (1861), allegory is still the traditional means of hymnic expression, in 'The Naked Goddess' (1866–7) it serves the didactic commendation of a natural and spontaneous life, foreign to Thomson himself and therefore eminently desirable. Despite its title, the colloquial tone and realistic depiction of details in 'A Real Vision of Sin' initially dissuade us from considering it a symbolist poem; however, the anthropomorphic landscape[124] and the accumulation of revolting elements reaching cosmic dimensions ('the earth and the sky were a-rotting slow')[125] create an eschatological atmosphere and the tormented dying couple assumes representative features.

In 'To Our Ladies of Death' (1861), which belongs to the genre of the allegorical portrait, three different types of existence after death are embodied (Our Lady of Beatitude, Our Lady of Annihilation, Our Lady of Oblivion). The lyric speaker turns first to the positive, then to the negative and, finally, in a kind of synthesis addresses the third, Our Lady of Oblivion. Thomson's symmetrical arrangement of the figures bespeaks the symbolist tendency to form groups of symbolic portraits and to design poem-cycles. The attributes with which the figures are adorned (wings, swords, chalice, palm branch) derive from the allegorical tradition, although here they acquire a strange suggestiveness and lose the directness of strictly functionalized allegory. Whether the flaming chalice contains the burning poison of despair or that of destructive self-analysis is relatively unimportant; what matters is that it bathes the figure (Our Lady of Annihilation) in a ghostly and mysterious light ('whose light / Burns lurid on thyself').[126] The same holds true for the allegorical figures themselves. The fact that Our Lady of Beatitude and Our Lady of Annihilation leave the impression of monumental sculptures cannot be satisfactorily explained from the allegorical tenor of their names, but from James Thomson's symbolist liking for colossal monuments, which also led him to adapt Dürer's *Melencolia*. Similarly, the fragile beauty of the third figure (Our Lady of Oblivion) does not convey a clearly defined allegorical meaning but suggests a complex state of feeling comparable to that elicited by Rossetti's early symbolic portraits.[127]

Thomson, who presumably suffered from chronic sleeplessness as a result of his alcoholism, has, like Rossetti and Davidson, described this experience so typical of the late romantics in the form of an allegorical poem entitled 'Insomnia'. The passing hours appear as a procession of shadowy figures that, in turn, mercilessly keep watch at his bedside. As the protagonist becomes increasingly nervous, the allegorical figures take on other features, revealing that they not only embody the hours of the night, but also the mental states of the lyrical self. The same transformation of the allegory from an 'objective' structural principle into a 'subjective' means of expression is noticeable in Thomson's major work 'The City of Dreadful Night'. Even in this long allegorical poem Thomson's pessimism does not allow the development of a 'continued allegory' in Spenser's sense; allegory as a comprehensive structure is replaced by a series of interchangeable allegorical episodes which are repeatedly interrupted by reflection. To cite just one example, the crawling figure in section XVIII, in spite of its similarity to the personifications of the vices in *The Faerie Queene* ('A haggard filthy face with bloodshot eyes'),[128] is not a true allegorical figure but the projection of one aspect of the protagonist's experience. Like most personifications in 'The City of Dreadful Night', the brutish human being, in his agonizing and absurd 'search for things past', does not typify abstract virtues or vices, but embodies a peculiar state of mind of the late romantic individual. In this modified form of allegory, a strange oscillation between symbolic indefiniteness and allegorical definiteness arises and, together with the equally bewildering juxtaposition of visionary and realistic features of the landscape, creates the disconcerting effect of 'The City of Dreadful Night' and many late romantic works.

The same lack of coherence that modern scholars find fault with in Thomson's allegorical poem had previously been criticized by Rossetti in the poems of Thomas Gordon Hake as well as by Swinburne in Solomon's *A Vision of Love Revealed in Sleep*:

Read by itself as a fragment of spiritual allegory, this written 'Vision of Love revealed in Sleep' seems to want even that much coherence which is requisite to keep symbolic or allegoric art from absolute dissolution and collapse . . . Even allegory or prophecy must live and work by rule as well as by rapture; transparent it need not be, but it must be translucent.[129]

Conflicting tendencies gradually become apparent in the late romantic allegories themselves and in the theoretical writings of the period. On the one hand, Swinburne rather surprisingly demands what Rossetti terms 'consequent clear-headedness', a feature which particularly recommended the allegorical mode to the Victorians; yet, on the other hand, both authors harbour a secret liking for the suggestiveness of Maeterlinck's or Burne-Jones's symbolism. If 'fog' signifies the 'utter destruction' of allegory, then 'twilight' seems to be its 'true atmosphere'.[130]

As the title suggests, *A Vision of Love Revealed in Sleep*[131] by the minor Pre-Raphaelite Simeon Solomon belongs to the genre of visionary literature. Modelled on literary examples like Dante's *Divina Commedia*, it describes the progression from a state of absolute spiritual despair through *purgatorio* to the final *unio*. Solomon has clearly endeavoured to give his work a certain continuity. Therefore the speaker, accompanied by the soul, is always visible. Between the different visions he pauses to interpret them with the assistance of his guiding soul, who offers advice and prepares him for the event to follow. A certain sense of unity is evoked by the all-important love theme, the visionary atmosphere and the time motif, which runs through the work like an *ostinato*, either in direct allusions or various emblematic embodiments. In spite of these recurring themes and motifs the essential 'thread of union'[132] seems to be missing and, since the individual episodes have developed into independent tableaux, no 'continued allegory' in the traditional sense can evolve.[133] If we attempt to summarize Solomon's prose allegory in outline form, the result is not the description of a progressively unfolding plot but a sequence of titles reminiscent of a catalogue for paintings of ideas from the schools of Watts, Stuck or Crane. The composition is structured in cyclical arrangement and decorative symmetry, following principles governing the visual arts, rather than the discursiveness of verbal art. Thomson's apocalyptic poem and Solomon's stylized, Pre-Raphaelite prose allegory demonstrate that in the late romantic period it had become impossible to unite abstract values in coherent aesthetic systems. Even in those rare instances when the allegory appears in longer poems, it no longer functions as a comprehensive literary scheme but only as the shaping power behind loosely connected symbolic episodes. The preference for single personifications and short allegories and the frequency of symbolic portraits in poetry and painting should be seen in this context. In light of the fragmentation of the allegorical course of events in 'The City of Dreadful Night' and the emblem-like, almost statuesque, short scenes in *A Vision of Love Revealed in Sleep*, the striking interest of English as well as French poets in allegorical paintings and sculpture is worthy of our closer attention. Baudelaire's 'Le Masque' (Statue Allégorique dans le goût de la Renaissance), 'Une Gravure Fantastique' or 'Danse Macabre' seem to participate in the same tradition as Rossetti's *Sonnets for Pictures*, Payne's poems to Solomon's *Sleepers and One that Watches* and 'A Farewell' and J. A. Symonds's cycle 'Four Pictures by Burne-Jones'.

Picture-poetry and the problem of the emblem

Throughout the centuries the question of the interrelationship of the arts has always been an issue in the realm of aesthetics. For the nineteenth century it becomes a predominant concern; the romantic belief in the affinities between the arts and the Victorian penchant for typological interpretation converge in the development of new modes of expression. Swinburne and Symons had interpreted Blake's 'illuminated' poetry as being expressive of the romantic and symbolist conviction in the inter-relationship of all arts. Beyond the works of this painter–poet the Pre-Raphaelites were fascinated by the 'painterliness' of the 'Eve of St Agnes' as well as by the transposition of paintings, sculptures and vases into the language of poetry ('Ode on a Grecian Urn'). Not only Keats,[134] who was the first to express the poetic interest in the visual arts in a manner characteristic of the nineteenth century, but also Words-worth, who had written poems such as 'The Last Supper by Leonardo Da Vinci' and 'Before the Picture of the Baptist, by Raphael', have to be seen as precursors of a movement of inordinate significance for late romantic art. Conversely, William Turner, the painter later idolized by Ruskin, discovered in poetry much more than a vague source of inspira-tion for his paintings.[135] Turner's practice of selecting appropriate quotations from Milton, Byron, Pope, Gray and Thomson to adorn the reproductions of his paintings in exhibition catalogues or of composing commentaries in lyric form (e.g. 'For the Picture *Narcissus and Echo*') becomes an established procedure with Pre-Raphaelites and their suc-cessors,[136] though with typical late romantic modifications.

The idea of a close relationship between painting and poetry has decisive consequences for the works of art; the poetic texts gradually renounce their subordinate position in the exhibition catalogues and advance to the frames of the pictures (Holman Hunt, *Early Britons Sheltering a Missionary from the Druids*)[137] and finally to the canvas itself (Rossetti, *Proserpina*, Pl. 7). Whistler's famous *bon mot* – 'Rossetti, take out the picture and frame the sonnet' – reflects somewhat ironically the excessive emphasis on this aesthetic relationship among many of his contemporaries. Picture poesies vary considerably depending upon the talents of the individual author and the treatment of the particular painting. In addition to works like Lewis Carroll's 'The Finding of Christ in the Temple' (Hunt), Laurence Housman's 'Autumn Leaves' (Millais) and Arthur Symons's 'The Temptation of Saint Anthony' (after a design by Felicien Rops) which follow the subjects of the paintings and accentuate or divine a moral lesson from them,[138] there are just as many examples that take up the fashion on the surface but use the painting as a general pretext for their own reflections.[139] Not surprisingly, the references to the titles of paintings cited in the original versions of such poems often are omitted in later reprints (e.g. Payne).

It is symptomatic that the interpreting poems – as, for example, Swinburne's 'Erotion', that like Payne's 'Sleepers and One that Watches', goes back to a drawing by Solomon – often take the form of a dramatic

monologue comprising a self-analysis and an analysis of the painting
by the lyric speaker or a dialogue between the speaker and the poet. Lee-
Hamilton's sonnets 'On an Illustration in Doré's Dante' and 'On
Mantegna's Drawing of Judith' constitute a unique variation in the genre
of picture poesies; here the poet seems to refer to the paintings for the
sole purpose of rejecting and replacing their contents with an interpretation of his own: 'No, Heaven is not like this'[140]; 'No, no, not such was
Judith, on the night / When in the silent camp, she watched alone, / Like
some dumb tigress . . .'.[141] Interestingly enough, in his volume *Imaginary Sonnets* Lee-Hamilton draws upon historical events – ranging from
'Henry I to the Sea' (1120) to 'Napoleon to a St Helena Leaf' (1820) –
in a similar interpretative manner.

In Rossetti's *Sonnets for Pictures* we find the whole spectrum of
poems modelled on paintings. He includes in his own collection
paraphrases and comments on his own paintings as well as his highly subjective reinterpretations of paintings by other artists; for instance, the
mood-poem entitled 'For an Allegorical Dance of Women by Andrea
Mantegna'. Bell Scott's remarks on the illustrations for his *Poems* (1875)
aptly describe this last type of picture poesy: 'rather pictorial analogues
to the sentiments and meaning of the poems than direct representation'.[142] From Morris's poems 'The Tune of the Seven Towers' and
'The Blue Closet', which have only a pseudo-medieval atmosphere in
common with Rossetti's early watercolours, to Symons's empathetic
étude ('For a Picture of Watteau') this subjective type appears in a
multitude of variations. The widespread popularity of the picture poesy
is witnessed in the fact that even before Shrewsbury, an aesthete like
Gray and the symbolist Rimbaud dedicate poems to Millais's *Ophelia*
(Pl. 4).[143] This and other similar instances open a new dimension for
our understanding of Pre-Raphaelitism.

Encouraged by the theoretical writings of Ruskin and Pater,
Baudelaire and Swinburne, the poetry–painting relationship flourishes
within the context of a general enthusiasm for the arts which, curiously
enough, links the Victorian middle class with aestheticist literati. From
Bayliss' verses on 'La Sainte Chapelle' and 'Chartres Cathedral' to
Symonds's 'For One of Gian Bellini's Little Angels', titles like *The
Painter-Poets* or *Picture Poesies*[144] appear in bewildering abundance,
suggesting that the inclination to write poetry on paintings had developed
into a fully-fledged movement. In all likelihood, however, the Victorians
were less captivated by the incongruities and distortions arising from the
transposition of one art into another than their inherent convertibility.

The pronounced tendency of the period to describe and, above all, to

4   John Everett Millais, *Ophelia*

JOHN GRAY
On a Picture

Not pale, as one in sleep or holier death,
Nor illcontent the lady seems, nor loth
To lie in shadow of shrill river growth,
So steadfast are the river's arms beneath.

Pale petals follow her in very faith,
Unmixed with pleasure or regret, and both
Her maidly hands look up, in noble sloth
To take the blossoms of her scattered wreath.

ARTHUR RIMBAUD
Ophélie

Sur l'onde calme et noire où dorment les étoiles,
La blanche Ophélie flotte comme un grand lys,
Flotte très lentement, couchée en ses longs voiles.
On entend dans les bois lointains des hallalis.

Voici plus de mille ans que la triste Ophélie
Passe, fantôme blanc, sur le long fleuve noir;
Voici plus de mille ans que sa douce folie
Murmure sa romance à la brise du soir.

interpret works of the visual arts is in accordance with the general late romantic interest in emblematic literature of the sixteenth and seventeenth centuries. It is hardly coincidental that Rossetti, in his criticism of Hake's *Madeline and Other Poems*, points out 'His style, at its most characteristic pitch, is a combination of extreme homeliness, as of Quarles or Bunyan'[145] and, in his review of *Parables and Tales* by the same author in 1873, emphasizes 'the same impression as the old verse-inscribed Emblems of a whole school of Dutch and English moralists'.[146] Such statements and a score of works which, on the basis of their titles, fall within the emblematic tradition are typical of the nineteenth century.[147] An age intent upon the re-establishment of allegory and delighting in experiments with flower emblems was bound to be attracted to Quarles as well as Spenser, Bunyan or the Early Italians. It is possible to trace a direct line from the dedicatory poem 'To Francis Quarles' published in *Sacred Emblems* (1828)[148] – the age of Keble – to comments and allusions to allegorical literature by Rossetti and his generation[149] and to Grosart's complete edition of Quarles (1880–1).

This continuous preoccupation with emblematic literature also has its impact on the symbolist tendencies of the period. Alongside Johann Abricht's *Divine Emblems Embellished with Etchings on Copper, after the Fashion of Master Francis Quarles* (1838), which directly refers to the great poet, there are works like Mrs Alfred Gatty's *A Book of Emblems* (1872), G. S. Cautley's *A Century of Emblems* (1878) and Neale's *Emblems for the Young*. Although, strictly speaking, it is not an emblem book but 'simply a collection of parables illustrated with engravings',[150] Neale's book sheds considerable light on the mode of thinking in the nineteenth century. In the preface to *Shakespeare and the Emblem Writers* (1869), Henry Green summarizes major aspects of the late romantic understanding of the emblem:

In one sense every book which has a picture set in it, or on it, is an emblem-book . . . and when to Tennyson's exquisite poem of *Elaine* Gustav Doré conjoins those wonderful drawings which are themselves poetic, he gives us a book of emblems; – Tennyson is the one *artist* that out of the *gold* of his own soul fashioned a *vase incorruptible*, – and Doré is that *second artist* who placed about it ornaments of beauty, fashioned also out of the riches of his mind.[151]

Here a direct connection is established between the emblem books and the illustrated, interpretative works of the nineteenth century, indicating how far the Victorian emblem has diverged from its original conception. The rediscovery of traditional forms involves typological thinking, a flair for the archaic and a penchant for decoration already anticipating *art nouveau*. The analysis of a few picture poesies of the period shows, however, that the eclectic, often playful handling of emblematic elements and the didactic interpretation of paintings of ideas gradually develop into a genre in which emblem and allegory become mysterious images for experiences of the innermost soul.

This is confirmed by representative picture poesies of the period. In *A Sonnet* (Pl. 5) Rossetti achieves an integration of text and illustration in the manner of emblem books from Alciat and Whitney to Peacham and Quarles. As we already know from his remarks on Hake's poetry, Rossetti was well acquainted with Quarles, Bunyan and the Dutch emblematic school. In an explanatory letter to his mother he comments on the design[152] and outlines the emblematic implications of *A Sonnet*, proving how consciously he makes use of the tradition. Baudelaire, otherwise so different from his Pre-Raphaelite contemporary, betrays similar inclinations when he bases his poem 'L'Amour et le Crâne' on an emblem by the Dutch artist Hendrik Goltzius (1558–1617).[153] By no means is this an exception; between 1859 and 1866 Baudelaire commissioned a series of emblematic designs[154] for *Les Fleurs du Mal* and *Les Epaves* as well as for a luxury edition scheduled to appear on the occasion of the London World's Fair. He found the idea for these illustrations in Langlois as 'décoration de quelque livre d'heures ou de quelque recueil de moralité' (p. 101). Baudelaire's editor, Poulet-Malassis, provided Bracquemont with a list of the Latin names of the vices to be emblematically represented as 'flowers of evil': '. . . et comme vous êtes plutôt spirituel que botaniste, allez-y bravement sans vous occuper de Linné' (p. 106). Yet Bracquemont's sketches were such a disappointment that Baudelaire, impatient and angry, advised Poulet-Malassis to have Bracquemont produce a facsimile of Langlois's original print: 'Ces fleurs étaient absurdes. Encore aurait-il fallu consulter les livres sur les analogies, le langage des Fleurs, etc.' (p. 109). Statements such as these demonstrate that Baudelaire was well versed in analogical thinking and the tradition of flower emblems. We may clearly assume that the title of his most famous work, *Les Fleurs du Mal*, has its roots in this literary fashion even though the image 'flowers of evil' is governed by Baudelaire's basic conviction in an inversion of values and the poems collected in the volume seem to have nothing in common with the pretty and playful Victorian language of flowers.

A number of seemingly insignificant details suggest that the rediscovery of the emblematic tradition in France and England has to be considered within the broader context of symbolist tendencies. Félicien Rops, for example, known for symbolist works such as *The Temptation of St Anthony, Mors Syphilitica* or the sphinx on the title-page of *Les Diaboliques*, also submitted a design for *Les Epaves* inspired by the woodcut in Langlois which is an outstanding example of symbolist emblematic art of the nineteenth century. It is a telling coincidence that Green, in the preface to his *Shakespeare and the Emblem Writers*, also

5 Dante Gabriel Rossetti, *A Sonnet*

mentions Langlois,[155] to whom Baudelaire owes the idea of decorating the title-page of *Les Epaves* with an emblematic design.

The epigraph preceding Simeon Solomon's allegorical prose poem − 'Until the day break / And the shadows flee away, Song of Songs' − serves as a lemma for the subsequent description 'Day . . . lulled to Death in the all embracing arms of Night'[156] and its pendant 'Day . . . seated on his throne'.[157] Similarly, the unique theme and structure of Wilde's *poème en prose*, 'The Artist', only become transparent if analysed in light of the vestiges of the emblematic tradition in nineteenth-century paintings of ideas. Unable to find the bronze necessary for his new statue, the artist is forced to melt down and recast one of his earlier artworks. Significantly enough, Wilde reduces the two sculptures to their symbolic essence, their titles acting as epigraphs: 'And out of the bronze of the image of *The Sorrow that Endureth for Ever* he fashioned an image of *The Pleasure that Abideth for a Moment*.'[158] J. A. Symonds also models some of his poems on the structure of the traditional emblem, first describing the icon − in this instance Burne-Jones's cycle *Fortune, Fame, Oblivion, Love* − and then adding a summarizing moral interpretation in the final couplet:

> Captains and kings are fastened to her wheel,
> Which turns and turns; while she, close-veiled and blind,
> Thrusts her lean arm athwart them . . .
> . . .
> For God who all things made, to Fortune gives
> Power to subdue the mightiest man that lives.[159]

The influence of the emblematic tradition was far-reaching and of lengthy duration. As late as 1911 a Harrold Johnson,[160] under the title *The House of Life*, produced 'poetic translations' of the ideas inherent in Watts's allegorical paintings and met with Watts's fullest approval: 'I have had many literary and poetical translations of my pictures sent to me from time to time[161] but I may say that none have seemed to me so much in keeping with the work as your "House of Life".'[162] There is no question that the close relationship between poetry and painting (cf. Johnson's poem on 'Hope'[163] with Watts's painting [Pl. 6]) results from the symbolic objectives of Watts's own interpretative art.[164] Yet even an author like Johnson must have felt that the late romantic relationship of the sister arts cannot be reduced to thematic affinities alone, for he hoped to complete the effect with a musical version: 'The author trusts that he has succeeded in demonstrating the kinship of the two sister arts of painting and poetry. And he also entertains the hope that a musical rendering may yet be forthcoming'.[165] Apart from paintings of ideas, favoured topics for interpretation are mythological subjects and medieval or Renaissance pictures of saints, well suited to late romantic tastes because

6   George Frederick Watts, *Hope*

Hope

Now in the twilight
Of night, or of dawning,
Wistful and desolate,
Awed by the vastness,
Blindfold with mystery,
Not daring to fathom
The sweep of the systems,
The depth of the blue;

Weary of knowledge
That goadeth and saveth not,
Hope, with her lyre,
Yearning and listening,
Toucheth the string,
The string that remaineth,
Heareth the music
The music that lingereth:
Is it the tremor
Of night or of dawn?

(Harrold Johnson, *The House of Life. Interpretations of the Symbolical Pictures of the Late G. F. Watts*, Ln. 1911, 26, *Hope*) of their cryptic iconography. For Walter Pater and the two women poets writing under the pseudonym Michael Field, Da Vinci's and Veneto's well-known portraits[166] take on the same mystical and symbolic connotations expressed in Rossetti's 'Aspecta Medusa' and in Swinburne's description of Michelangelo's study of a woman's head: 'her mouth crueller than a tiger's, colder than a snake's and beautiful beyond a woman's'.[167]

The picture poesies of the period mirror the vacillation between emblematic representation in the sense of traditional allegories or typologies and that of an expressive symbolism. Rossetti understands Botticelli's *Spring* from the melancholy mood which inspired his own sonnet 'Barren Spring' or Beardsley's *Withered Spring* (Pl. 10), as a 'masque of a long-gone New Year's festivity'[168] or as one of 'the dead springs that takes its secrets into the grave'. The same atmosphere pervades Field's poem ('Venus is sad among the wanton powers'),[169] yet both poets strive to give an accurate description of the painting and repeat its iconographical structure exactly from the group Aurora, Zephyrus, Flora on the right above the dancing graces to the figure Hermes in the left half of the picture, underlining the implied movement from East to West, the symbolic region of death:

> And with those feathered feet which hovering glide
> O'er Spring's brief bloom, Hermes the harbinger.[170]

> The God that teaches Shadows to descend,
> But pauses now awhile, with solemn lip
> And left hand laid victorious on his hip.
> The triumph of the year without avail
> Is blown to Hades by blue Zephyr's gale.[171]

Only if it is in line with their interpretative intentions and suits their thematic purposes do the late romantic poets follow the iconography of a painting. For instance, Baudelaire, in 'L'Amour et le Crâne', provides a close depiction of Goltzius's emblem, yet his interpretation departs from the dominant *Quis Evadet* theme of the original to become a late romantic death wish:

> J'entends le crâne à chaque bulle
>   Prier et gémir:
> – 'Ce jeu féroce et ridicule,
>   Quand doit-il finir?'[172]

As another poem by Baudelaire, 'Sur le Tasse en Prison d'Eugène Delacroix', makes clear, the change in subject-matter dictates a change in the emblematic mode of representation. If Tasso is indeed 'emblème', he is so in a very different sense from Sisyphus in Whitney's emblem book.[173] Tasso, not a mythological but an historical figure, can create a much more subjective impression since he embodies the painful existence of the artist so traumatically experienced by Baudelaire himself: 'Voilà bien ton emblème, Ame aux songes obscurs, / Que le Réel étouffe entre ses quatre murs!'[174] Although the iconographical significance of Mantegna's painting is not difficult to determine and the Ruskin generation – which sees or invents types and emblems everywhere – exhibits an amazing ingenuity in discovering deeper meanings, Rossetti refrains from presenting a clear interpretation in his sonnet 'For an Allegorical Dance of Women by Andrea Mantegna' (In the Louvre), apparently intending to cloak the original meaning in darkness. While in his sonnet 'For Spring by Sandro Botticelli' (In the Academia of Florence) he follows the iconographic details of the painting, Mantegna's painting, so obvious in its allegorical meaning, becomes the cryptic image[175] of an emotional and spiritual state, the symbolic expression of a late romantic mood:

> It is bitter glad
> Even unto tears. Its meaning filleth it,
> A secret of the wells of Life: to wit: –
> The heart's each pulse shall keep the sense it had
> With all, though the mind's labour run to nought.[176]

The symbolic portrait

Symbolic portraits are widespread in late romantic painting and poetry and include works such as Gautier's 'Niobé'[177] and Sandys's portrayal of Cleopatra described by Swinburne.[178] Above all the term immediately brings to mind Rossetti's paintings *Pandora* or *Astarte Syriaca*, *Sibylla Palmifera* or *Proserpina*, paintings dominated by a single female figure incorporating mythological elements with certain features of the artist's real-life models. Rossetti underscores the symbolic implications of these figures by furnishing them with traditional emblematic attributes; for instance, the pomegranate held in Proserpina's hand (Pl. 7), the lute alluding to the sirens in *A Sea-Spell*, the apple and arrow in *Venus Verticordia*. In addition to this 'emblematic' symbolism there is that of psychological configurations such as Lilith's pose before a mirror, reflecting in the self-sufficient beauty and cruelty of the *femme fatale* male frustrations and anxieties. Occasionally, for example in *Fiammetta*, the specific symbolic meaning of the figure compels the painter to invent new emblems, which, lacking traditional associations, call for poetic explanation:

Along her arm the sundered bloom falls sheer,
                    . . .
Life shaken and shower'd and flown, and Death draws near.
                    . . .
While she, with reassuring eyes most fair,
A presage and a promise stands; as 'twere
On Death's dark storm, the rainbow of the Soul.[179]

Together with the more obvious emblems which impart the meaning of the individual painting Rossetti employs a second idiosyncratic type of symbol: the mysterious look, the sensual, voluptuous mouth, the luxuriant hair, the affected gesture of the hand, the awkward pose of a solitary figure in a grove. Recurring in many paintings with little variation, these later symbols are suggestive of the painter's own sensual, emotional and spiritual state. Both iconographical schemes reflect the vacillation between a typological and expressive symbolism, between an objectively given and a personal, suggested meaning.

At first glance *La Bella Mano* appears to be a superficial, somewhat overcrowded *intérieur* scene with two pages attending a lady who is washing her hands as a pretence for displaying their beauty. One would even feel inclined to consider it a coincidence that the basin has the same shape as the seashell from which the goddess alights in Botticelli's *Birth of Venus* had not Rossetti alluded to this connection in the sonnet:

O Lovely hand, that thy sweet self dost lave
In that thy pure and proper element,
Whence erst the Lady of Love's high advent
Was born, and endless fires sprang from the wave.[180]

The sonnet which Rossetti, in pursuit of typological explicitness, has placed in the upper right-hand corner of the canvas of his *Proserpina* painting (Pl. 7) directly refers to the myth.[181] In the painting itself, however, the only reminiscence of the myth – perceptible to the viewer schooled in iconography – is the pomegranate. The central figure herself, identified by carrying it in her hands, symbolizes no longer Proserpina but the same sentiments embodied in *Day Dream*.

What distinguishes the individual painting is less the symbolized spiritual state than the intensity in its depiction. The line 'tow'rd deep skies, not deeper than her look, / She dreams'[182] in the sonnet 'Daydream' characterizes Proserpina's state of mind; equally well, her late romantic experience – 'Afar from mine own self I seem . . . and listen for a sign'[183] – does not essentially differ from that in *Day Dream*. And who would deny that the following lines from 'Astarte Syriaca' could not with the same right appear in both of these sonnets?

7 Dante Gabriel Rossetti, *Proserpina*

And from her neck's inclining flower-stem lean
Love-freighted lips and absolute eyes that wean
The pulse of hearts to the sphere's dominant tune.[184]

These melancholy feelings of frustration, unorthodox states of spiritual awareness, yearnings for the identification of body and soul derive from individual problems as well as from the philosophical perplexities of the age. They are still discernible in certain aspects of the poems, while in the paintings they have been integrated into cohesive symbolic textures.

The great variety among symbolic portraits indicates that it was a medium congenial to the expression of the spiritual needs of an entire period. While Rossetti favours figures from classical mythology, Swinburne prefers to invest 'historical' figures like Cleopatra and Faustine with qualities that transcend the dimensions of their reality or, as in the case of Dolores and Hesperia, invents new mythical figures altogether. By means of ingenious montages Pater and Gautier, in their descriptions of works of art, attempt to produce the same impression of indefinite symbolism evoked by such figures as *Astarte Syriaca* or *Venus Verticordia*. Just as Pater transforms the *Mona Lisa* into a symbolic figure by incorporating St Anna and Leda, Helena's mother, Gautier designates Niobé the 'mother of the seven sorrows' and visualizes her seated upon Mt Athos and Calvary. Pater's extension of time into the unreality of myth ('She is older than the rocks among which she sits')[185] corresponds to Gautier's extension of space ('Quel fleuve d'Amérique est plus grand que tes pleurs?').[186]

Dante Gabriel Rossetti

Proserpina
(For a Picture)

Afar away the light that brings cold cheer
Unto this wall, – one instant and no more
Admitted at my distant palace-door.
Afar the flowers of Enna from this drear
Dire fruit, which, tasted once, must thrall me here.
Afar those skies from this Tartarean grey
That chills me: and afar, how far away,
The nights that shall be from the days that were.
Afar from mine own self I seem, and wing
Strange ways in thought, and listen for a sign:
And still some heart unto some soul doth pine,
(Whose sounds mine inner sense is fain to bring,
Continually together murmuring,) –
'Woe's me for thee, unhappy Proserpine!'

(The text on the canvas is that of the Italian version)

The stylized portraits of the Italian Renaissance lent themselves well to symbolist interpretations, as becomes obvious from Pater's and Field's descriptions of the *Mona Lisa* and from the lines which Katherine Bradley and Edith Cooper (Michael Field) dedicate to Bartolommeo Veneto's female portrait in the Städel museum in Frankfurt. Apparently the poem follows Huysmans's description of the same painting,[187] particularly in its characterization of the young woman as a courtesan. Although the two poets do succeed in capturing the minutest details of Veneto's portrait, by transferring them to a different context they alter the tenor of the painting. They imagine the young woman, with aestheticist care, selecting the details to figure in her portrait, destined to give immortality to all those transient things. With a refinement of taste recalling Des Esseintes she searches for simple flowers contrasting with her own complex nature:

> Forth to the field she goes and questions long
> Which flowers to choose of those summer bears;
> She plucks a violet larkspur, – then a columbine appears
> Of perfect yellow, – daisies choicely wide;
> These simple things with finest touch she gathers in her pride.
> Next on her head, veiled with well-bleachen white
> And bound across the brow with azure-blue,
> She sets the box-tree leaf and coils it tight
> In spiky wreath of green, immortal hue;
> Then, to the prompting of her strange, emphatic insight true,
> She bares one breast, half-freeing it of robe,
> And hangs green-water gem and cord beside the naked globe.[188]

If the green box-tree wreath seems an emblem of the immortality achieved by the young woman in the work of art, the contrived arrangement of bared breast and green gem[189] prompted by a 'strange, emphatic insight' develops into an expressive symbol of her decadent ambiguity: 'In perfect, still pollution smiles'.[190]

In his essay on Leonardo Da Vinci, Walter Pater draws a comparison between *La Gioconda* and Dürer's *Melencolia* which is of considerable interest for the question of symbolic portrait and personification: 'In suggestiveness, only the Melancholia of Dürer is comparable to it; and no crude symbolism disturbs the effect of its subdued and graceful mystery.'[191] In truth he is just as enraptured with the suggestive power of Dürer's celebrated allegorical figure as his contemporaries, but in contrast to Yeats, who accepts the use of emblematic attributes for underlining symbolic implications,[192] Pater prefers the indirect and restrained suggestiveness which he finds in the *Gioconda* portrait. While in poetry personification rarely loses its abstract character, in painting it can acquire visual qualities that go beyond the immediate function of depiction and the directness of the allegory. To Gautier, Thomson, Nerval or Pater, Dürer's engraving does not illustrate an abstract idea like one of Ficino's four temperaments; instead, as Nerval's 'El Desdichado' implies, it appeals to their sensitivity through imaginative association: 'et mon luth constellé / Porte le soleil noir de la Mélancholie'.[193]

The portrayals of the four seasons in late romantic painting and poetry are particularly instructive examples of the transition from the conventional personification or allegorical figures to the symbolic portrait. Burne-Jones paints the seasons as four women (Pl. 8 and Pl. 9), each of whom is immediately identifiable by her attire and attributes.[194] But apart from these external features the four women bear a striking resemblance to one another: all are young, all have the same meaningful look in their eyes and, comparable to Rossetti's portraits, are embodiments of something more than the actual seasons, namely, a certain melancholic yearning of the artist himself.

This impression can be confirmed from still another *Spring* by Burne-Jones. The picture shows a female figure half-turned toward the viewer clad in a gown with Botticellian gathers and a waving veil, who moves, floating rather than walking, from the right toward the left corner of the canvas. In the background italianized buildings give way to a forest landscape. Holding the veil in her right hand and pointing with the outspread fingers of her left to the foreground, the woman looks into the distance seeming to foretell a fateful prophecy with resigned composure. Although there is a pattern of flowers and tendrils around her bare white feet, these natural details are not sufficient to identify the figure as the personification of spring. She could just as easily represent the evening or an angel mourning the fall of man. The emphasis on the movement and the awkwardness of the pose heighten the enigmatic nature of the painting.

Like Rossetti's sonnet 'Barren Spring', Beardsley's *Withered Spring* (Pl. 10) diverges from the traditional associations connected with spring through an inversion of the implications. Both the appearance of the central figure and the details of the surrounding scenery are governed by the devastation wreaked by the emblematic figure of the storm at the top of the picture. It is difficult to determine the precise meaning. Sexual implications are unmistakable yet are fused with the suggestion of a more general experience of transience and frustration. In the centre of the picture the half-hidden epigraph, 'ars longa', reminds us of the emblematic tradition, and in stating the aestheticist credo ironically evokes the missing and final half of the adage, 'vita brevis', Beardsley's true theme. However, Beardsley's drawing does not convey this idea in the way sixteenth- and seventeenth-century emblems illustrate an abstract subject, but communicates it as the mood of a late romantic soul.

8 Edward Burne-Jones, *Spring*

9 Edward Burne-Jones, *Autumn*

Spring am I too soft of heart
Much to speak ere I depart
Ask the summer tide to prove
The abundance of my love

Laden autumn here I stand
Worn of heart and weak of hand
Nought but rest seems good to me
Speak the word that sets me free

This manner of rendering the seasons is not merely a peculiarity of the
Pre-Raphaelites and their successors in the nineties; it has numerous
parallels in continental art, among them Puvis de Chavanne's paintings
on seasons and Böcklin's *Autumn Thoughts* (Pl. 11). The autumn poems
by Laurence Housman, Le Gallienne and Lord Douglas as well as the
personification of summer in Verlaine's 'Allégorie', a sonnet translated
into English by Wratislaw, have to be seen in conjunction with this tradition. The title *Autumn Feeling* or even *Autumn Thoughts*, which Böcklin
tellingly chose for his painting, would have been appropriate for Lord
Douglas's autumnal ode, since the allegorical figure of autumn is only
of importance as an embodiment of the melancholy feelings of the
speaker:

> Thou sombre lady of down-bended head
>
> . . .
>
> Give me thy empty branches of the biers
>
> . . .
>
> Thy falling leaves to count my falling tears.[195]

The preference of the age for the allegorical figures of the four seasons
can probably be explained from the fact that they can be transformed
into symbolic portraits with relative ease; less precise by definition, they
allow for a subjective suggestiveness difficult to attain in personifications
like justice and faith because of their more precise connotations. A
myriad of poems on personifications of individual months, days or times
of the day appearing at the same time seem to confirm this impression.
Poems like Olive Custance's 'The Autumn Day', 'April Twilight', 'The
Lingering Day', 'Twilight', 'Autumn Night', 'Fantasy' ('Dusk and the
darkness sisters twain') or 'A Rainy Day' are all examples of this
tendency.

> The Spirit of the day is there
> At my window, wild and white
> With her large eyes full of light,
> And the dawn dews in her hair,
> She has slain the demon Night,
> But its shadows haunt her yet,
> And she cannot quite forget
> The black terror of the fight.
>
> . . .
>
> Such sadness broods about her
> This beautiful, sad day.[196]

'A Rainy Day' and Dowson's 'My Lady April' mark two poles of a richly
varied genre. Custance's poem is dominated by a personification which,
due to the emotional implications, has lost its abstractness and become

10   Aubrey Beardsley, *Withered Spring*

a late romantic symbol full of melancholy allusiveness. The Lady April of Dowson's sonnet, on the other hand, has developed into a figure reminiscent of the ideal beloved and related to the portrayals of spring by Burne-Jones and Beardsley.

> Dew on her robe and on her tangled hair;
> Twin dewdrops for her eyes; behold her pass,
> With dainty step brushing the young, green grass,
> The while she trills some high, fantastic air,
> Full of all feathered sweetness: she is fair,
> And all her flower-like beauty, as a glass,
> Mirrors out hope and love: and still alas!
> Traces of tears her languid lashes wear.
>
> Say, doth she weep for very wantonness?
> Or is it that she dimly doth foresee
> Across her youth the joys grow less and less,
> The burden of the days that are to be:
> Autumn and withered leaves and vanity,
> And winter bringing end in barrenness?[197]

As a symbolic portrait 'April', who already senses the dead leaves of autumn and the foreboding barrenness of winter, is of particular significance. In the perfect *fin de siècle* beauty of Dowson's poem, a period aware of its own decadence and yearning for the youthful innocence of the Early Italians finds its due expression.

Dominant personifications

> She stands as pale as Parian statues stand;
> Like Cleopatra when she turned at bay,
> . . .
> Her face is steadfast toward the shadowy land,
> For dim beyond it looms the land of day:
> . . .
> She stands alone, a wonder deathly white.[198]

The striking impact of the symbolic portrait on the late romantic personification, both in form and content, is mirrored in Christina Rossetti's poem 'A Soul'. As a consequence of its favoured status in late romanticism, the allegorical scenery tends to transform itself into a landscape of the soul. Both in Rossetti's 'Hand and Soul' and Solomon's *A Vision of Love Revealed in Sleep* an allegorical figure of the soul accompanies the protagonist as his patron saint: 'I am an image, Chiaro, of thine own soul within thee. See me, and know me as I am.'[199] Chiaro's 'moral allegory of peace', a painting of ideas, proves to be a devastating

11   Arnold Böcklin, *Autumn Thoughts*

failure when the picture is splashed with the blood of warring parties;
only when he depicts his own soul does he achieve a convincing work of
art. The painting, which bears the inscription 'Manus Animam pinxit,
1239' in one corner,[200] is infused with the same kind of symbolism
prevalent in the works of Burne-Jones and Simeon Solomon:

> The picture I speak of is a small one, and represents merely the figure of a
> woman, clad to the hands and feet with a green and grey raiment, chaste and
> early in its fashion, but exceedingly simple. She is standing: her hands are held
> together lightly, and her eyes are earnestly open. . . . You knew that figure, when
> painted, had been seen; yet it was not a thing to be seen of men.[201]

Since the *Psychomachia* of Prudentius abstract values, moral faculties
and the soul itself have been the subject of innumerable representations.
What distinguishes the late romantic personification of the soul from its
traditional conception is not only its pre-eminent position or its specific
romantic introspectiveness but its philosophical foundations. In an age
increasingly dominated by the relative spirit the soul was destined to lose
its assured ontological status. Pater's new understanding of the soul in
a period that tended 'to regard all things and principles of things as
inconstant modes or fashions', modifies that of Hadrian and inspires the
controversial interpretations of Pound ('Blandula, Tenulla, Vagula') and
Eliot ('Animula'); the soul has become a mysterious organ of inner
experiences (*Animula Vagula*)[202] that can only be represented in vague
allegorical contours:

> O Princess prisoned in a house of pearl,
> Strange little princess that I call my soul . . .
> Silent you stand and listen all day long
> With smiling parted lips, for you have heard
> The far faint fluting of that fairy bird
> That weaves enchantments with its magic song . . .[203]

In canto IV of James Thomson's 'The City of Dreadful Night' the protagonist meets a mysterious, vaguely familiar figure, who reminds him
of his dead beloved but, at the same time, seems to be a personification
of hope. During the course of the encounter the speaker realizes that a
strange process is taking place within himself: 'I was twain / Two selves
distinct that cannot join again.'[204] A similar experience is the subject of
Rossetti's sonnet 'He and I'. The figure designated as 'he' proves to be
a new self, whom the lyric speaker attempts to analyse in elaborate
reflections.[205] Expressed in these poems is a central experience that also
becomes increasingly prominent in other literatures (Baudelaire's
'L'Héautontimorouménos'). A passage from Nerval's *Aurélia* confirms
this with an allusion to the wraith or *Doppelgänger* motif of German
romanticism:

Par singulier effet de vibration, il me semblait que cette voix résonnait dans ma poitrine et que mon âme se dédoublait pour ainsi dire, distinctement partagée entre la vision et la réalité. Un instant, j'eus l'idée de me retourner avec effort vers celui dont il était question, puis je frémis en me rappelant une tradition bien connue en Allemagne, qui dit que chaque homme a un double, et que, lorsqu'il le voit, la mort est proche.[206]

Rossetti has also taken up this motif in his painting *How They Met Themselves* (Pl. 12). In English-language literature it makes its appearance in Poe, then in the works of his English admirers, the Pre-Raphaelites and contemporaries (Bell Scott) and epigones (Bourke Marston, Payne, O'Shaughnessy) and the poets of the nineties (Lee-Hamilton, O'Sullivan, Sidney R. Thompson).[207]

In addition to its impact on the allegorical representation of the soul, the experience of the doubling self influences other personifications which, in the absence of an objective moral order, arise from the subjective states of the crisis-ridden mind. As a result, contrary to the richly differentiated world of medieval allegory, in late romantic poetry we find a relatively limited number of closely related allegorical figures that derive from a central problem of the age – life in an alien and hostile world and the attempt to escape it. From Payne to the young Yeats sorrow[208] remains the protagonist's – and the reader's – tedious companion. It is accompanied by a pallid beauty marked by death or the maid Quiet.[209] Flitting hope slowly approaches the grave. Love, once the radiant and glorious sovereign for the Early Italians, is mortally wounded or even dead[210] in the poetry of Symonds, Bourke Marston, O'Shaughnessy and their contemporaries. Death itself lovingly prepares a final repose for the fatigued decadent soul.[211] The shadowy figures move slowly or stand quietly like statues and silently bow their beautiful pale heads.[212] Almost always enveloped in a veil-like robe, giving them an air of mystery, they appear lost in thought or stare into the distance as though awaiting a portentous message. While the meanings of traditional allegorical figures are clearly recognizable in their attributes, the late romantic embodiments of hope, love, death and the soul rarely assume the character of unmistakable entities. The almost stereotypical use of such adjectives as 'white' or 'pale'[213] makes it even clearer that these personifications differ only in nuance and all embody related aspects of the same basic emotional and spiritual state.[214]

Symmetries and cycles in late romantic poetry and painting

Allegorical representations of the four seasons are not only favourites with the Pre-Raphaelites because they lend themselves readily to subjective interpretation, but also because of their stylistic potential. The

personifications of seasons, days or hours tend toward the composition
of groups which, in turn, can be arranged in decorative symmetries and
cycles (cf. Pl. 8, Pl. 9).[215] These structural patterns gain in importance
as Victorian allegory evolves into a poetry of static tableaux and the symbolic portrait becomes a prevailing mode of expression.

> One flame-winged brought a white-winged harp player
> Even when my lady and I lay all alone;
>   . . .
> Then said my lady: Thou art Passion of Love
> And this Love's Worship: both he plights to me . . .[216]

> He bade his soul rise upward
> And stand on her window-sill.
> It rose in a straight blue garment,
> When owls began to call:
>   . . .
> He bade his heart go to her,
> When the owls called out no more;
> In a red and quivering garment
> It sang to her through the door.[217]

In Rossetti's 'Passion and Worship' and Yeats's 'Cap and Bells' the
personifications share the atmosphere of artificial simplicity typical of
the Pre-Raphaelite cult of love. They are also related in their use of
decorative colour patterns ('flame-winged . . . white-winged'; 'straight
blue . . . red and quivering garment'). The contrasting colours
(red–white; blue–red) produce a much stronger effect than the abstract
ideas they are meant to illustrate. Passion and worship, soul and heart
are but aspects of an overall atmosphere and could be complemented by
many other personifications had not the grouping in contrasting pairs
proved so effective.[218] A similar procedure can be noted in a poem by
John Davidson ('Insomnia') with rather different thematic concerns:

> The Seraph at his head was Agony;
> Delight, more terrible, stood at his feet:
> Their sixfold pinions beat
> The darkness, or were spread immovably.
> Poising the rack.[219]

Here the symmetry depends upon the positioning of the allegorical
figures at the head and foot of the sleepless figure stretched out on the
'golden rack'. Although by definition the two personifications are
opposed, they appear to be related ('Agony – Delight more terrible'),
suggesting that Davidson is less interested in conveying the precise meaning of the figures than the stylized atmosphere they evoke when, in the
'olive-light of chrysoprases dim', they beat or spread their sixfold
pinions over the golden rack.[220]

12 Dante Gabriel Rossetti, *How They Met Themselves*

By means of symmetrical arrangements Davidson achieves in 'Insomnia' the same enigmatic suggestiveness that James Thomson, in his poem of the same title, evokes through enumerative descriptions of the shrouded, shadowy figures embodying the hours which stand like basalt columns at the bedside of the sleepless protagonist. In its very precision, the use of numbers (for example, the number three in Thomson's 'To Our Ladies of Death') has a mysterious effect and helps to create the same suggestive ambience produced by the symmetrical patterning of personifications that we find in Lord Douglas's pendant poems 'Night Coming Into a Garden' and 'Night Coming Out of a Garden'. Even in a poem like Baudelaire's 'Les Deux Bonnes Sœurs', although a less extreme example, this structural principle remains clearly noticeable. In the final tercet Baudelaire underlines the parallelism of the two allegorical figures – 'La Débauche et la Mort' – by assigning them emblematic plants, poisonous myrtle and black cypress. The symmetry also implies a certain symbolic affinity beyond that inherent in the actual concepts.[221]

The widespread tendency to arrange paintings and poems in cycles and decorative groups also extends to the symbolic portraits in Swinburne's 'The Masque of Queen Bersabe' and O'Shaughnessy's *An Epic of Women*. Equally worthy of mention in this respect are the voices of pride, hatred and the flesh in Verlaine's 'Les Voix', the curses of the dead and – illustrating again the use of specific numbers in the allegorical schemes – the responses given by the four boards of the coffin lid in Swinburne's 'After Death', as well as the seven lute strings and the three men in 'A Ballad of Life' or the 'four loves' in 'A Year of Love'.

> The seven strings were named accordingly;
> The first string charity,
> The second tenderness . . .

> There were three men with her, each garmented
> With gold and shod with gold upon the feet.[222]

> There were four loves that one by one,
> Following the seasons and the sun,
> Passed over without tears and fell
> Away without farewell.

> The first was made of gold and tears,
> The next of aspen-leaves and fears,
> The third of roseboughs and rose-roots,
> The last love of strange fruits.[223]

It is not difficult to trace a continuous line from 'there the Loves a circle go' in Yeats's 'The Two Trees' to the procession of days in Bourke

Marston's 'A Vision of Days',[224] the special forms of personification attesting to continuities in the literary and artistic tastes and aspirations from 1850 to 1900. Still, the underlying motives are far from identical. While Olive Custance presumably visualizes dusk and darkness as two allegorical sisters for suggestive and decorative purposes, Watts's *Love and Death* and Laurence Housman's 'Love and Life' clearly use personification to express abstract themes.[225] Similarity of effect in the use of personification by no means renders this differentiation superfluous. Anthithesis and enumeration obviously belong to the rhetorical tradition; the parallel and sequential arrangements of personifications cited above, however, primarily pursue visual effects and no longer convey abstract ideas. Although at the time widespread in literature, the symbolic portrait and the description of allegorical sculpture are, strictly speaking, non-literary forms. Similarly, the penchant for groups, cycles, symmetrical and decorative enumerations is closer to the spirit of visual than verbal art.

In order to portray various and changing aspects of the *Fortuna* theme, Burne-Jones had to combine unity with diversity, which he did by creating a cycle of paintings. A similar cyclical structure is recognizable in Rossetti's 'Willowwood' sonnets and in the two sonnets entitled 'Newborn Death' where he contrasts the child 'Death' and its older siblings 'Love, Song, Art' by placing them in two separate scenes.[226] Cyclical patterning is employed in late romantic art and poetry for decorative and allusive rather than discursive and abstract purposes. As larger contexts are divided into smaller independent scenes, details can stand out with greater intensity and vividness. Apart from that, the elements of separateness and connectedness in a cycle together produce a secret tension that appealed to the late romantic imagination.

Personification and its contexts

Among the poems published in Evelyn Douglas's *Selections from Songs of a Bayadere and Songs of a Troubadour* in 1893 we find a poem entitled 'The Black Troubadour', which on the basis of plot, stanza form and other formal elements like repetitions belongs to the genre of the ballad.[227] As the ballad unfolds, however, it becomes clear that the main character, a troubadour, personifies sin: 'In sable feather and cloak of gloom / Stands Sin, the troubadour'.[228] After the heroine has fallen prey to this suitor's seductive charms, he becomes the embodiment of death.[229] The ballad has been transformed into an allegorical poem. Verlaine's allegorical ballad 'Le Chevalier Malheur', translated by John Gray in *Silverpoints*, confirms that 'The Black Troubadour' is not an exception. Under the influence of symbolist tendencies this genre common-

ly associated with realistic figures, dramatic situations and epic objectivi-
ty evolves into a mode of expression for subjective experiences.

Far more important for major literary developments are the
endeavours of the young Yeats and his contemporaries to introduce and
integrate personifications into a realistic context. As is often the case, a
minor poem furnishes the best example. Edwin J. Ellis's 'At the Hearth',
included in the first *Rhymers' Book* in 1892, opens on a somewhat
poeticized but essentially realistic situation. Two lovers are sitting at the
hearth: 'The kettle sang beside the bars / A tender ballad soft and
low.'[230] Suddenly Time enters the concretely depicted fireside scene,
preparing for the appearance of other personifications, Love and Pity.
None of these figures achieves the independence and vividness of those in
The Faerie Queene because the real persons — the lyric speaker and his
bride — are always present and observe the personifications, embodiments of their own experiences, with an awareness typical of the
decadent age. The tenor of the allegorical event reflects late romantic
tastes: Pity offers the sentimental solution to the conflict between Time
and Love. Significantly, the allegorical figures open a new dimension to
the realistic couple: in their solemn presence the two lovers appear
removed from the world of everyday reality. In his thematically related,
well-known poem 'When You are Old' Yeats, on the other hand, avoids
an obtrusive use of personifications and, allowing sufficient space for the
development of realistic elements, succeeds where Ellis failed. The personification of love in his poem emerges convincingly from a realistic
situation and, without impairing its concreteness, transforms it into a
new symbolic context:

> When you are old and grey and full of sleep,
> And nodding by the fire, take down this book,
> . . .
> And bending down beside the glowing bars,
> Murmur a little sadly, how Love fled
> And paced upon the mountains overhead
> And hid his face amid a crowd of stars.[231]

Given the important role of personification in the French symbolist
movement,[232] parallels in the works of Rossetti and Swinburne are of
particular significance. Like Thompson, who refers to Shelley's use of
personification, Pater mentions the 'really imaginative vividness . . . of
. . . personification'[233] in the works of Rossetti. In many ways Pre-
Raphaelite personification was in line with the usage which Rossetti and
his friends had discovered in the works of the Early Italians. The summarizing identification of love and death in Rossetti's 'Death-in-love',
the use of personification in monologues and dialogues or as elements of
an ornate style of argumentation,[234] for instance, are well-known

devices from the rhetorical tradition. In contrast to the abstract qualities
of eighteenth-century poetic diction, the Pre-Raphaelite personification
frequently takes on a surprising intensity. Even in the otherwise
straightforward speech in Wilde's 'Apologia' there are instances of Swinburnean allegory which suddenly emit an unexpected vividness: 'To have
walked hand in hand with Love, and seen / His purple wings flit once
across thy smile'.[235] The result is an impression of heterogeneity that in
turn contributes to the rather mannered character of the poem. Rossetti's
sonnet 'Vain Virtues', however, demonstrates that there is a formal principle at work here that ideally can lead to convincing representation. The
rhetorical question at the beginning instantly provokes an apocalyptic
scene culminating in the intense concentration of horrifying details:

> What is the sorriest thing that enters Hell?
> None of the Sins, – but this and that fair deed
> Which a soul's sin at length could supersede.
> 　　　. . .
> Night sucks them down, the garbage of the pit,
> Whose names, half entered in the book of Life
> Were God's desire at noon. And as their hair
> And eyes sink last, the Torturer deigns no whit
> To gaze, but yearning, waits his worthier wife,
> The Sin still blithe on earth that sent them there.[236]

Sonnets like 'Known in Vain', 'Lost on Both Sides', 'The Sun's Shame
II' or 'Pride of Youth' illustrate that the 'imaginative vividness' Pater
praises in Rossetti's poetry is largely the result of a kind of staging typical
of Pre-Raphaelite painting and not so much of the use of strikingly
realistic details:

> Even as a child . . .
> 　　　. . .
> Even so the winged New Love smiles to receive
> Along his eddying plumes the auroral wind
> Nor, forward glorying, casts one look behind
> Where night rack shrouds the Old Love fugitive.[237]

The structure of the simile emphasizing the difference of signifier and
signified, the length of the comparisons and the abstractness of the content,[238] all impede the fusion of concrete imagery and allegorical
figures. Thus the motivation behind Rossetti's decision to incorporate
realistic details (a child . . . sorrow; cowslip, corn-poppy, etc.) does not
seem to arise from a desire for integration, but from a manneristic
delight in flaunting the incompatibility of the two levels.

Among the allegorical poems of the Pre-Raphaelites we also find a
particular type characterized by a prettified quality unthinkable for a
writer like Baudelaire.

I found Love sleeping in a place of shade,
And as in some sweet dream the sweet lips smiled;
Yea, seemed he as a lovely, sleeping child.
Soft kisses on his full, red lips I laid,
And with red roses did his tresses braid;
Then pure, white lilies on his breast I piled,
And fettered him with woodbine sweet and wild,
And fragrant armlets for his arms I made.[239]

This quality can still be found in a poem like Wratislaw's 'A Summer's Love' where the basic Pre-Raphaelite features take on the air of Elizabethan songs:

Between blue June and red July
Love gat him golden wings to fly;
With ringing feet and singing mouth
He fled toward the scented south;
He fled and fell in ambush there
Amid my lady's coiling hair.[240]

Christina Rossetti's 'An End', the concluding piece in the first issue of *The Germ*, displays the same playful ingenuity ('Love, strong as Death, is dead')[241] inherent in the question-and-answer game of Yeats's 'The Cloak, the Boat, and the Shoes'. Similarly, in Le Gallienne's 'Green Silence' stylized imagery contributes to the impression of refinement:

Silence, whose drowsy eyelids are soft leaves
And whose half-sleeping eyes are the blue flowers,
On whose still breast the water-lily heaves,
For all her speech the whisper of the showers.[242]

Such contrived awareness could not remain without influence on the emotions. In many of Christina Rossetti's poems as well as in Payne's 'A Song of Dead Love' it leads to a strong sentimental quality expressed in the nostalgia for a realm of quiet and shadows:

Love, strong as Death, is dead.
Come, let us make his bed
Among the dying flowers:
A green turf at his head;
And a stone at his feet,
Whereon we may sit
In the quiet evening hours.
He was born in the spring
And died before the harvesting.[243]

What distinguishes the personifications in *The House of Life* from those in *Les Fleurs du Mal* is – apart from the obvious unevenness in quality – the fact that they mark almost diametrically opposed reactions to the crisis in the relationship to reality. In the stylized world of Rossetti and Bourke Marston embodiments like those of ennui, prostitution or hatred[244] have become impossible. Baudelaire's personifications encompass a much wider range of subjects and develop a richer, more dynamic imagery. The vision of hope as 'a bat erring along the walls with timid wings and striking its head against rotting beams', the image of pleasure fleeing 'like a sylph into the wings of the theatre', and the description of self-accusation reproaching itself for having 'bowed down before colossal, bull-headed stupidity'[245] all attest to Baudelaire's willingness to confront a reality which the Pre-Raphaelites try to escape.

3 The impact of symbolist tendencies on late romantic poetry

Poet and poetry

The symbolist tendencies discussed in connection with the conception of the symbol and the typological and allegorical literature of the period were bound to influence the language of late romantic poetry. For the poet, acutely aware of the complexities of modern existence and forced to withdraw into his inner self, the question of how to grasp and impart this elusive 'world it sees so steadily within'[1] becomes an all-important issue. Marking the transition to an expressive symbolism, the increasing preoccupation of the introverted poet with his own states of mind and his art is indicated in the abundance of poems like 'The Poet' (Field), 'The Dead Poet', 'To a Silent Poet' (Douglas), 'The Songspinner' (Custance) or 'L'Art' (Gautier), 'La Muse Malade', 'La Muse Vénale' (Baudelaire), 'L'Art Poétique' (Verlaine) or in the equally frequent use of the poet and his work as a metaphor.

> The nightingale is like a poet's soul,
> She finds fierce pains in miseries that seem.[2]

> As is the Poet to his fellow-men,
> So mid thy drifting snows, o snowdrop, Thou.[3]

For Alfred Lord Douglas, the poet is a seer of 'hidden things',[4] who has the gift to discover 'under the common things the hidden grace'[5] and to transform the world into a 'magic land'. This *Elévation*, invoked by Baudelaire and mentioned again and again by the English late romantics,[6] cannot be clearly defined. In Baudelaire's poem it is realized in a mystical soaring movement and in the ability to understand 'sans effort / le langage des fleurs et des choses muettes';[7] in Payne's 'Evocation' it culminates in the encounter with the ideal beloved in the 'golden zones of mystery'[8] and in Evelyn Douglas's 'The Priest of Beauty' or O'Shaughnessy's 'A Priest of Beauty' it serves as the basis for a morbid cult of beauty.

Having been divested of their philosophical orientation, many central concepts of late romantic poetics remain unclearly defined, the idea of beauty being a case in point. Keats's equation of beauty with truth, which O'Shaughnessy valiantly attempts to sustain,[9] has lost its validity for Laurence Housman; the two ideas no longer seem interrelated and have grown less and less precise in meaning: 'For truth is that which without knowledge dwells / And Beauty that which beyond Nature is.'[10] Wilde's pointed remark signals the end of this development: 'Beauty has as many meanings as man has moods. Beauty is the symbol of symbols. Beauty reveals everything, because it expresses nothing.'[11] Not least because of this very vagueness beauty becomes the object of late romantic visionary aspirations.

In spite of the indeterminate nature of beauty, however, a surprising consistency is recognizable in the attitude of the poet towards it. In Baudelaire's 'La Beauté', a sonnet translated by Lord Douglas, beauty exerts the dangerous fascination of a *femme fatale*, appearing as a 'sphinx incompris' and, like the main figure in Gautier's 'Symphonie en Blanc Majeur', uniting 'un cœur de neige à la blancheur des cygnes'.[12] The mystical experience of beauty, which ultimately leads to a new sense of form, is a difficult and bewildering affliction for Baudelaire,[13] an 'exquisite malady of the soul'[14] for O'Shaughnessy. 'La Destruction', like Symonds's later poem 'Perdition', combines the aesthetic element with a kind of diabolism and inverted religiosity. Significantly, O'Shaughnessy, who suffered from feelings of depravity throughout his entire life, translated this poem by Baudelaire into English. Through this agonizing 'Nostalgie des Cieux', as O'Shaughnessy entitles one of his poems, the poet estranges himself from the world and from his fellow man:

> But I am weak among them, cannot seem
> Full-hearted in their life, with many a look
> I wound them or repel . . .[15]

The duality of the poet, embodied by Baudelaire in the image of the albatross,[16] is also the theme of Michael Field's 'A Poet'. Here the world mocks the poet and 'as from a dullard turns annoyed', while the poet 'ever set apart . . . / waits the leisure of his god's free heart'.[17]

Neither the English nor the French poets of the period tire of emphasizing their élite position. If, as Gautier describes, the poet stumbles 'à chaque pas sur les chemins du monde',[18] this awkwardness arises from his otherwise sublime ability since 'Of dreamland only he is citizen',[19] appearing to the world as a 'pure visionary'.[20] The basic attributes of the poet – 'no common man, strange heart, magic mask, mysterious man, wistful smile, lips . . . Sibylline'[21] – coincide with the general symbolist tendencies of an age which sees in 'Virgil, magician and poet' the perfect embodiment of its ideals.[22] Viewed from this perspective it is no longer surprising that, apart from the ironic jester figure typified by Wilde, Beardsley and Beerbohm, the artists of the nineties tend to be in-

ordinately earnest. The almost priestly solemnity noticeable in the art of
the nineties is already discernible in many Pre-Raphaelite works and cannot therefore be dismissed as a consequence of French influences.

Less essential but nonetheless pertinent attributes are explicable in
terms of the symbolist poet, for instance, his 'complicated state of
mind',[23] his readiness to yield to transports of ecstasy[24] or his penchant
for brotherhood esotericism, all of which are caricatured by Gilbert and
Sullivan as being 'perceptively intense and consummately utter'.[25] The
state of depression as well as the cultivated and blasé air of listlessness
and fatigue treated by Symons and Wratislaw in poems under the title
'Satiety' or by Douglas in his rather mundane imitation of 'Ennui' are
a natural aftermath of moments of ecstasy.

> My thoughts soared up like larks into the morning,
>
> . . . .
>
> And saw the whole world like a ball of fire
>
> . . . .
>
> What is there left?[26]

Amidst the stifling orderliness of everyday Victorian life the disharmony
between reality and the imaginary world of the poet is felt all the more
deeply. Attacking Rossetti and his school for their 'sick indifference to
the things of our own time, and a spurious devotion to whatever is
foreign, eccentric, archaic or grotesque',[27] the critic from *Macmillan's
Magazine* raises a problem that the poets themselves recognize. Authors
like Lee-Hamilton, Symons or the young Yeats by no means accept their
isolation with satisfaction or consider it an ideal situation, yet a number
of poets see their unsought seclusion as a fatal and unavoidable outcome
of their contemplative way of life.

Arthur Symons has dealt with this question in the 'Prologue' to *Days
and Nights* (1887) and in the cycle *The Brother of a Weed* (1907). The
remarks of an author whose theoretical and literary contributions to
symbolism are more extensive than those of most English contemporaries seem of particular interest in this context. Although Symons
urged his fellow poets to select their subject-matter from the realm of
everyday life 'where cities pour / Their turbid human stream through
street and mart',[28] even after the turn of the century he is − contrary to
Yeats − unsuccessful in integrating a convincing and relevant vision of
reality into his own poetry. There is no question that Symons also suffered from his carefully cultivated aristocratic isolation, a situation
which eventually led him to assume the pose of a Franciscan monk in an
attempt at escapism:

> I will get down from my sick throne where I
> Dreamed that the seasons of the earth and sky,

> The leash of months and stars were mine to lead,
> And pray to be the brother of a weed.[29]

While many English writers of the late nineteenth century share Baudelaire's feeling of alienation in an unfeeling, increasingly banal world, their reactions are markedly different. Unlike the obsessive dreams and nightmares in *Les Fleurs du Mal*, which always retain some connection with reality, the narcissistic self-reflections of an esoteric soul destroy the metaphysical import of many late romantic visions before they actually develop:

> Safe in my golden room of thought,
> I hear outside the rush and sweep
> Of travel wearied wings of sin:
> . . .
> My musings are with visions fraught.[30]

In 1900 Symons, who lived until 1945 yet never relinquished his *fin de siècle* ideals, wrote the poem with the revealing title 'The Loom of Dreams' in which the thematic complex 'poet – reality – dreamland' finds its definitive expression. Secluded from the world in his tiny room, the poet imagines himself the ruler of imaginary stars, lands, continents and seas, creating a fictitious world to replace the real one. His question 'For what is the world but what it seems?',[31] can, despite its extreme formulation, be seen to derive from the romantics' subjective view of life, particularly as expressed in the works of Blake. It is hardly a coincidence that Symons quotes Blake's well-known letter to Dr Trussler at great length in his own book on the poet:

But to the Eyes of the Man of Imagination, Nature is Imagination itself. As a man is, so he sees. As the Eye is formed, such are its Powers. You certainly Mistake when you say that the Visions of Fancy are not to be found in This World. To Me This World is all One continued Vision of Fancy or Imagination, and I feel Flattered when I am told so.[32]

The comment 'To Me This World is all One continued Vision of Fancy or Imagination' makes it possible to trace a direct link to Yeats's startling remark: 'Solitary men in moments of contemplation . . . make and unmake mankind, and even the world itself, for does not "the eye altering alter all"?'[33] The different strains converge in Yeats's essay 'The Symbolism of Poetry'. After referring to O'Shaughnessy's poem 'We are the Music Makers', he cites the final lines from the second poem of Francis Thompson's sonnet sequence 'The Heart', later to be included in his anthology *The Oxford Book of Modern Verse* (1892–1935):

> Our towns are copied fragments from our breast;
> And all man's Babylons strive but to impart
> The grandeurs of his Babylonian heart.[34]

The outer world is nothing but an image of the inner world. As a result of the functionalization of reality, symbols lose an independent existence of their own, blurring the distinction between the historical Babylon and the late romantic city of dreams. In 'The Song of the Happy Shepherd' Yeats goes even further; here it appears questionable whether a world exists at all outside the poetic imagination.[35]

From such an interpretation of reality it is easy for the poet to escape into an imaginary world of dreams.

> This is the mansion built for me
> By the sweating centuries;
> Roofed with intertwined tree,
> Woofed with green for my princelier ease.
> Here I lie with my world about me,
> Shadowed off from the world without me.[36]

This refuge described by Thompson, like Olive Custance's 'garden of all dreams and ecstasies',[37] is the poet's favourite dwelling-place, yet it still bears a strong resemblance to the Pre-Raphaelite bower. Possessed by the same desire as the French symbolists, the English late romantic poets design their own fictitious worlds; their landscapes of vague yearnings and futile hopes, however, do not yet engender the city of art achieved in the 'Byzantium' poems of the mature Yeats. Even when the poet conspicuously places himself at the centre of his dream landscape (as in O'Shaughnessy's 'Palm Flowers'), identifying it as a work of his own making, it is quite clear that the English writers lack the poetic talents which so masterfully evoked the imaginary world of 'Rêve Parisien'.

> O that land where the suns linger
> And the passion-flowers grow
> Is the land for me the Singer:
> There I made me, years ago,
>
> Many a golden habitation,
> Full of things most fair to see;
> And the fond imagination
> Of my heart dwells there with me.[38]

Such visionary objectives bring about a new understanding of language and form unthinkable for the romantics before 1832 or for the Victorians: '. . . you cannot give a body to something that moves beyond the senses, unless your words are as subtle, as complex, as full of mysterious life, as the body of a flower or of a woman'.[39] At the same time the late romantic artists seem to be well aware of the perils inherent in the new emphasis on form. Lee-Hamilton portrays the artist obsessed with form as a modern alchemist who, like King Midas in classical mythology, turns everything into gold and thereby causes his own downfall.[40] Francis Thompson feels the sterile 'predominance of art over inspiration'[41] in his own age as compared to the poetry of Shelley. While Oscar Wilde, consistent with the principles expounded in Pater's 'Style' essay, proclaims that 'all fine imaginative work is self-conscious and deliberate',[42] Thompson remains bound to his romantic heritage with its ideal of immediate inspiration, and criticizes the confining, destructive effect of the new sense of form. Not until the time of Yeats does the late romantic achievement of linking the 'Latin love of beauty' with the visionary tendencies of the indigenous romantic tradition gain general recognition.[43] The call for a mode of expression befitting the 'vision within'[44] is central to Pater's essay 'Style', and even in minor poets like Payne and Douglas the tension between ecstasy and form, between the vagueness of late romantic aspirations and the restrictive precision of representation plays a crucial role.[45]

Apart from its essayistic formulation Wilde's idea of the 'Critic as Artist' undoubtedly derives from the view Baudelaire expresses in his 'Tannhäuser' essay: 'tous les grands poètes deviennent naturellement, fatalement, critiques'.[46] Yet the fact that so many English poets have recourse to French poetics is only fully comprehensible when considered within the context of parallel tendencies prevailing in the English literature of the period, for instance in the meticulous formal sophistication of The House of Life. Rossetti, who as early as 1857 had criticized Whitman in a letter to Allingham, and rejected 'poetry without form' as a contradiction in terms,[47] praises the new sense of form in O'Shaughnessy's collection of poetry Epic of Women.[48] The Academy review of Epic of Women, however, while showing a full awareness of the movement's goals and practices, is evidence of a less favourable general response to it.

Influences to which we should be inclined to refer it are those of a section of the French Romantiques, Baudelaire and Gautier at their head, who set themselves, with a conscious purpose of art, and with an immense care for the technical execution, finish, and symmetry of their art, to give expression to remote phases of super-subtle feeling or perverse imagination, to produce fantastic and demoralized spiritual exotics of the finest colour and perfume.[49]

The image of the poet as goldsmith or gem-cutter and his work as gem or intaglio appears as the characteristic expression of the new poetics. Frequently used to convey the conscientious workmanship and new feeling of form in the poetry of Douglas[50] and countless other writers of the nineties, this image can be traced back not only to Gautier and Baudelaire but to Rossetti as well.[51] French influences merge with indigenous traditions in England in the rise of a new sensitivity and the endeavour to find new modes of expression.

In the postscript to Appreciations, an essay primarily known for its attempt to differentiate between the concepts of classical and romantic art, Pater defines what he considers to be the main task of poetry in his age: 'For the literary art, at all events, the problem just now is, to induce order upon the contorted, proportionless accumulation of our knowledge and experience.'[52] From Rossetti and O'Shaughnessy to Douglas and the young Yeats the period abounds in poems expressing the same conviction: 'What escapes decay? / A certain faultless, matchless, deathless line.'[53] If the visionary aspirations and the aristocratic ineffectuality affected by so many late romantic poets seem foreign to us today, we should not forget that the concepts of *poeta doctus* and *poeta faber* dominating Pound's and Eliot's poetics have their roots in this generation which, unsettled by philosophical crises, found a certain solace in form. Erudition and a critical awareness of form are cited as essential qualities of the poet in Pater's essay 'Style' and in *Marius the Epicurean*,[54] and it is in these terms that Yeats discusses Lionel Johnson in his *Autobiographies*.[55] But while Pound and Eliot are later to use their knowledge of medieval or Metaphysical poetry to create a new poetic relationship to reality, discovering literary allusions as a means of organizing the incoherent flow of impressions, Lionel Johnson sees the Gregorian chant and Latin hymn as a possibility for erecting 'the impenetrable barrier of beautiful style'[56] between his art and reality. Pater, who admires Rossetti for his 'sustained impressibility towards the mysterious conditions of man's everyday life',[57] is equally approving of his strivings for symbolist perfection in form. Against Coleridge's organicist understanding of form he develops his modern theory of form being the result of conscious craftsmanship.[58]

The problem of genre

Villiers de l'Isle Adam's *Axël* and the plays of Maeterlinck and Yeats reveal that symbolist tendencies are not limited to poetry alone, although the poem is, of course, the true medium for the evocation of the innermost soul. If drama, by nature the more extroverted genre with distinct outlines and a strong emphasis on action, is used to convey inner experiences, its generic traits tend to disappear. The broad spectrum of complicated poetic forms,[59] the declining popularity of the long poem together with the preference for painting and music poems demonstrate that the borderlines of the lyric genre have become as blurred as those of other literary forms in the late romantic period. Contrary to Coleridge ('Christabel') or Keats ('Eve of St. Agnes'), who were captivated mainly by the atmosphere of the medieval world, the Pre-Raphaelites and their successors are attracted by its characteristic literary forms. Before Banville, Rossetti looks back to Villon ('The Ballad of Dead Ladies') and translates the stylized, ornate poetry of the Early Italians. Swinburne experiments widely, with 'Hendecasyllabics' and 'Sapphics' and with the Chaucerian ballad. As Baudelaire had earlier and Symons and Wratislaw will later, he also uses the litany form, following a movement which culminates in Lionel Johnson's Latin hymn 'Satanas'. Late romantic epigones including Payne, Dobson and Gosse, familiar with the works of Charles d'Orléans and his contemporaries through Banville, write madrigals, virelays, rondels and double ballads[60] and – like the Verlaine of *Fêtes Galantes* – even develop a liking for the rococo.[61] Wilde who, like Dowson and the young Joyce, tries his hand at the villanelle, summarizes this 'aesthetic eclecticism' with the following *bon mot* in 'Pen, Pencil and Poison': 'All beautiful things belong to the same age.'[62]

The adaptation of the most divergent historical styles is an outcome of the growing preoccupation with form and the attempt to transcend the limits of temporality through aestheticism. Yeats's appreciation of Dobson's and Lang's *études* in the old style – with their rejection of Victorian 'externality'[63] – indicates their importance for the development of symbolist tendencies:

but a new poetry, which is always contracting its limits, has grown up under the shadow of the old. Rossetti began it, but was too much of a painter in his poetry to follow it with a perfect devotion; and it became a movement when Mr Lang and Mr Gosse and Mr Dobson devoted themselves to the most condensed of lyric poems, and when Mr Bridges, a more considerable poet, elaborated a rhythm too delicate for any but an almost bodiless emotion, and repeated over and over the most ancient notes of poetry.[64]

This combination of a modern sensitivity with traditional and established forms described by Yeats is documented by numerous examples from contemporary poetry. Even the villanelle in Dowson's works can be termed a functional form inasmuch as its preciseness prevents the late romantic moods from dissipating and gives expression to them through numerous sound repetitions. Joyce's description of the young artist writing the 'Villanelle of the Temptress'[65] with its wide range of late romantic motifs offers revealing insight into the final phase of the movement. From his account of the process of poetic creation in *A Portrait of the Artist as a Young Man* we gain a general impression of how the villanelle, revived by Dowson and his contemporaries for its challenging formal difficulties and archaic character, is adopted as a form conducive to conveying the symbolist inspiration.

Along with the rediscovery of strict and traditional forms the late romantic predilection for experiment has an impact in quite a different realm. Due to the author's visionary motivations, prose, the established medium of action, description and reflection, is made to undergo a process of lyricization in many works like De Quincey's 'The Daughter of Lebanon' and 'Dream Fugue', James Thomson's 'A Lady of Sorrow' or Solomon's *A Vision of Love Revealed in Sleep*. This anticipates Wilde's and Dowson's *Poems in Prose* as well as the dream prose on the passage of time in Virginia Woolf's *To the Lighthouse*. Although Eliot's prose poem 'Hysteria' may have been directly inspired by Laforgue, there can be no doubt that Wilde's and Dowson's *Poems in Prose* are grounded in the tradition of De Quincey, Thomson and Solomon and constitute an English parallel to the French genre of prose poems from Baudelaire to Gabriel de Lautrec. The implicit symbolist impulse comes to light in Baudelaire's dedication of *Petits Poèmes en Prose* to Arsène Houssaye:

Quel est celui de nous qui n'a pas, dans ses jours d'ambition, rêvé le miracle d'une prose poétique, musicale sans rythme et sans rime, assez souple et assez heurtée pour s'adapter aux mouvements lyriques de l'âme, aux ondulations de la rêverie, aux soubresauts de la conscience?[66]

Although the lyrical flow of this prose would seem to contradict the strictness of form advocated at the time, the fact that Baudelaire wrote *Les Fleurs du Mal* as well as *Petits Poèmes en Prose* and that Dowson makes use of the villanelle alongside the prose poem proves the contrary. The peculiarity of this poeticized prose, which prompts Pater, in 'Style', to refer to 'imaginative prose . . . as the special art of the modern world',[67] manifests itself strikingly when Yeats, by a simple change in the typographical arrangement, effortlessly transforms the *La Gioconda* passage in Pater's 'Da Vinci' essay into a poem.[68]

While the tendency toward strictness in form unquestionably arises as a reaction against the Victorian preoccupation with content, with what Yeats called 'externality',[69] the dissolution of stanza forms and verse patterns reflects the search for a new medium to express the subtle and complex shades of inner experience. Both impulses, incompatible though they may appear, are but different aspects of the same phenomenon, the quest for intensity: 'il est de certaines sensations délicieuses dont le vague n'exclut pas l'intensité'.[70] Originally a quality referring to content, intensity is a prominent and enduring feature of the late romantic sensibility, informing the erotic experiences portrayed in Morris's 'Guenevere' as well as the edifying, didactic personifications in Shields's decorations for the chapel of the Duke of Westminster.[71] Swinburne's lavish praise of Rossetti's poetry for being 'so intense in aim, so delicate and deep in significance'[72] brings various poetic situations to mind: the lovers' encounter in 'Silent Noon', the frightening intensity in the facial expressions of the wraith figures in 'Willowwood' and the experience of frustration in 'Heart's Hope' ('. . . intense / As instantaneous penetrating sense, / In Spring's birth-hour, of other Springs gone by'[73]). In 'The Two Dreams'[74] Swinburne combines the same intensity with a specifically Pre-Raphaelite weariness to impart the strange fusion of spiritual and erotic elements so typical of the age.

Allusions in parodies like Gilbert and Sullivan's *Patience* – 'I am soulfully intense'[75] – prove how widespread the conception had become. Earlier Dobson had recognized the close connection between the struggle for intensity and the visionary objectives of the symbolists in his attack against the Pre-Raphaelitism of the Rossetti school:

> Men may prate
> Of their ways 'intense' and Italianate, -
> They may soar on their wings of sense and float
> To the *au delà* and the dim remote.[76]

It is in conjunction with the particular late romantic experience of time that intensity becomes a formal quality. The reduction of the flow of experiences to isolated moments in Rossetti and Pater demands a concentrated mode of representation: 'Not width but intensity is the true aim of modern art.'[77] The ground seems to have been laid for Wilde's summary of Pater's convictions largely by Poe, whose rejection of the long poem[78] is not only a consequence of his affective poetics but also a reaction against the didactic heresy[79] and the result of a peculiar striving for 'supernal beauty' that appealed to the late romantics.[80]

Wilde's belief that the 'very concentration of vision and intensity of purpose which is the characteristic of the artistic temperament is in itself a mode of limitation'[81] coincides with the rising predominance of the sonnets,[82] from Rossetti's *The House of Life* to the literary *études* of his epigones Douglas and Lee-Hamilton. One of the most noticeable features of the period is the profusion of 'sonnets on the sonnet'[83] in which authors attempt to define or capture the tension between their spiritual aspirations and melancholy frustrations, between intensity in form and vagueness of mood.[84] The fascination of the decadents with their own complicated emotions together with Pater's conception of the moment cause 'mood' to become a key word in late romanticism. This concept of mood is of particular interest in literary history because it establishes a connection between Wordsworth's 'spots of time' and Joyce's 'epiphanies' and provides a basis for understanding a dominant aspect of symbolist poetry.

'For what is Truth? . . . in matters of art, it is one's last mood',[85] Oscar Wilde's aestheticist interpretation of truth, is directly derived from Pater's conviction 'that the momentary, sensible apprehension of the in-

dividual was the only standard of what is or what is not'.[86] In the flow
of aesthetic experience thought and emotion fuse and can only be
registered by the senses, not apprehended by the intellect:

Art is a passion, and, in matters of art, Thought is inevitably coloured by emotion, and so is fluid rather than fixed, and, depending upon fine moods and
exquisite moments, cannot be narrowed into the rigidity of a scientific formula
or a theological dogma.[87]

But by giving shape to the moments the artist conveys the impression of
a unique aesthetic permanence: 'To create, to live, perhaps, a little while
beyond the allotted hours, if it were but in a fragment of perfect expression'.[88] The artistic capturing of the wide range of human moods constitutes the only order and permanence which the relative spirit allows:

The moods of men! There I find my subject, there the region over which art rules
... I declare that every poem is the sincere attempt to render a particular mood
which has once been mine, and to render it as if, for the moment, there were no
other mood for me in the world.[89]

While the mood remains a rather vague idea in Symons's preface to
London Nights, in Wilde's 'The Critic as Artist' it acquires the specific
implications rendering it essential to symbolist poetics. In accordance
with the symbolist ideal of contemplatio, Wilde's 'Critic as Artist' deals
'not with life's physical accidents of deed or circumstance, but with the
spiritual moods and imaginative passions of the mind'.[90] All elements
of form contribute to the conveyance of this late romantic spirituality.
Rhyme, for instance, is 'not merely a material element of metrical
beauty, but a spiritual element of thought and passion also, waking a
new mood'.[91] Admittedly, many poems of the time are concerned with
reproducing moods that merely reflect external impressions, but there
are no clear boundaries between the purely impressionistic and the purely
symbolist mood-poem. Marius, the hero of Pater's novel, proceeds from
discriminating and subtle observations and gradually approaches a
'peculiar' mood which he tries to record in the chapter entitled 'The Will
as Vision' and which hardly differs from the 'mystic moods' in AE's
poem 'Symbolism'.

But for once only to have come under the power of that peculiar mood, ... to
have apprehended the great ideal, ... left this one particular hour a marked point
in life never to be forgotten.[92]

Now when the spirit in us wakes and broods,
Filled with home yearnings, drowsily it flings
From its deep heart high dreams and mystic moods.[93]

Arthur Symons, who had dealt with the concept of mood in the prefaces to both his volumes of poetry published in 1896, reconsiders it in his book on Blake, giving it a new and revealing dimension:

By *states* Blake means very much what we mean by *moods*, which in common with many mystics, he conceives as permanent spiritual forces, through which what is transitory in man passes, while man imagines that they, more transitory than himself, are passing through him.[94]

Here Symons's argumentation obviously follows that of Ellis and Yeats; in the introduction to their edition of Blake appearing in 1893 they had adopted Blake's idealistic understanding of the symbol and interpreted the history of the universe as a history of moods. For Yeats and Ellis the cosmos is a 'symbol of the infinite thought which is in turn symbolic of the universal mood we name God'.[95] From poetic genius emerges 'first, a bodiless mood, and then a surging thought, and last a thing'.[96] Far more significant for the development of literary ideas than this rather esoteric theory is the underlying conviction that the outer world is but a reflection of an inner world of moods. This fundamental late romantic belief is expressed in countless poems, be it in Thompson's line 'Our towns are copied fragments from our breast'[97] or O'Shaughnessy's 'With wonderful deathless ditties, / We build the world's great cities.'[98] The imaginary landscape and the idealized woman – the themes of many mood-poems – are projections of the poet's own mind based on this idealistic pattern. In his essay 'The Moods', written two years after the publication of the edition of Blake, Yeats designates the mood the decisive criterion for all poetry: 'Literature differs from explanatory and scientific writing in being wrought about a mood, or a community of moods, as the body is wrought about an invisible soul.'[99]

The vast spectrum of mood-poems mirrors the diversity of their philosophical sources. Although Bourke Marston entitles one of his sonnets 'A Mood', he does not succeed in conveying the mood itself, but refers to the widespread contemporary pessimism in a purely abstract way. O'Shaughnessy, however, is quite successful in evoking the atmosphere of the ecstatic moment through an elaborate scheme of synaesthesia in *Music and Moonlight*. Rossetti, in 'Sudden Light',[100] does not yet achieve the perfect translation into sound which qualifies Verlaine's 'La Lune Blanche' as a masterpiece of mood-poetry, yet the adaptation of the song form and the suggestive reiteration of selected rhyme words betray the same endeavour to invoke the ambience of the central epiphany. In 'Chanson Sans Paroles' with its concise rhyme scheme (abbab), Dowson combines a lulling monotony with rhythmic flexibility to place the reader under the spell of the visionary experience:

In the deep violet air,
  Not a leaf is stirred;
  There is no sound heard,
But afar the rare
  Trilled voice of the bird.

Is the wood's dim heart,
  And the fragrant pine,
  Incense, and a shrine
Of her coming? Apart,
  I wait for a sign.[101]

The visual quality of imagery is just as important as musicality for the conveyance of a mood. In Olive Custance's poem 'Peacocks', subtitled 'A Mood', the image of the peacock — suggestive of beauty and misfortune — gradually develops into an embodiment of the speaker's own moods, to whom the handsomeness of her lover appears as a challenge to fate.

In gorgeous plumage, azure, gold and green,
They trample the pale flowers, and their shrill cry
Troubles the garden's bright tranquillity.[102]

Most mood-poems tend to be rather short and are structured around one central image; as this image develops thematically it becomes expressive of the particular mood. This concentration on a single image and the mood evoked by it is already noticeable in Rossetti's 'Woodspurge' and signals the beginnings of a new poetry which reached its peak with the imagists. What distinguishes poems like Hulme's 'Above the Dock' or Pound's 'In a Station of the Metro' from late romantic mood-poems is a shift in emphasis, whereby the lyric speaker becomes superfluous and the image and the mood it symbolizes are alone relevant.[103]

Late romantic mood-poetry — as in Olive Custance's 'A Mood'[104] — deals with the states of mind of a lyrical self. Starting from the perception of an outer world, it withdraws into an inner dreamland, unable to bear the bitter transience of time. The deserted terrace in Dowson's 'Saint Germain-En-Laye' and the garden in Verlaine's 'Après Trois Ans' are more than places full of memories; they become symbolic scenery, embodiments of moods. Titles like 'Langueur', 'Spleen' or 'Ennui' are indicative both of a refined sensitivity and a pronounced mental passivity. Curiously enough, this passivity is accompanied by the demand for stimulants and heightened perception (sexual perversions, opium, absinthe) leading to abnormal, trance-like states as described in Dowson's prose poem 'Absinthia Taetra' or O'Sullivan's 'Malaria'.

> Hot air that takes away control
> From all my body's nerves, and falls
> Like scented water through my soul.
> Miasmas spread like perfumed palls.[105]

At first glance these moods appear to be fundamentally different from the mystical experience Yeats describes in 'The Moods', but if considered within the context of contemporary spirituality, which was manifest in a general yearning for ecstatic moments rather than in specific visionary features, it is obvious how alike these seemingly different moods are:

> Time drops in decay,
> Like a candle burnt out
>   . . .
> What one in the rout
> Of the fire-born moods
> Has fallen away?[106]

Yeats's 'The Valley of the Black Pig' and 'The Travail of Passion', although rather special variations, nonetheless belong to the genre of the mood-poem. Not only do they comply with the postulate of intensity being 'a moment's monument', and 'memorial from the Soul's eternity',[107] they also represent moods expressive of a secularized transcendence.

Late romantic diction

The difficulty in defining the symbolist mode of expression arises from the fact that it develops in conjunction with widespread eclectic tendencies and a general change in style.[108] Although stylistic devices such as archaic rhyme schemes, compound forms and clusters of alliterations only fully achieve symbolist effects within the context of specific literary works, such as Rossetti's sonnets, for instance, we can better appreciate their contributions to the overall effect by first considering the variants individually. The Pre-Raphaelites use archaic diction − or what they take to be archaic diction − in a continuation of the romantic tradition of medievalism, in order to render their dream world as authentically as possible. To this purpose they generously sprinkle their verses with phrases like 'In midst whereof, shaped heartwise, God wot, shameful wise,'[109] and 'Give Ye good hap',[110] employing a 'medievalizing' diction to express their pseudo-medieval ideals:

> She was a maiden of most quiet face,
> Tender of speech, and had no hardihood
> But was nigh feeble of her fearful blood;
> Her mercy in her was so marvellous.[111]

In the evocation of a medieval atmosphere, a new sensitivity to words can be detected which was unknown to the romantics. The litany of names in Morris's 'Golden Wings', characteristically imitated in Gray's nineties' poem 'Les Demoiselles de Sauve', is, thematically speaking, non-functional, yet it suggests a distinctly medieval ambience and a mystic experience that could not be conveyed in strictly rational language.

> O Miles and Giles and Isabeau,
> Fair Ellayne le Violet,
> Mary, Constance fille de fay!
> Where is Jehane du Castel beau?[112]

Rossetti envisions this symbolism of sound in 'The Blessed Damozel' when he describes the names of the five handmaidens of Mary as 'five sweet symphonies'.[113]

Archaic forms alone do not produce a symbolist effect, particularly not in the sense of Mallarmé, but are often instrumental in conjuring up an unrealistic, disorientating atmosphere. Rossetti uses such forms and occasionally even has recourse to single medieval words like 'wayfaring', 'malisons' or 'suitservice' to express personal and modern experiences in *The House of Life*, yet rhyme words are his preferred means of archaization: 'solicitous – thus, compel – favourable'; 'recall – memorial, head – garlanded'.[114] Similar rhymes occur in the poems of Lionel Johnson and other writers of the nineties.[115] Poets like Thompson ('Epilogue to The Poet's Sitter; wherein he Excuseth Himself for the Manner of the Portrait') and Yeats (e.g., 'He Bids his Beloved be at Peace') also choose to allude to the symbolic event of their poems in stylized titles.

Determining the function of these medievalisms is a relatively simple matter, since the period abounds in parallel stylistic tendencies, among them Swinburne's preference for biblical language: 'Make thee soft raiment out of woven sighs'; 'Clad about with sand'; 'clothed with pity'.[116] The presence of both biblical and medieval language in a great number of Swinburne's poems proves that they are not contradictory but rather complementary features concurring in the same intense though indeterminate suggestiveness:

> Behold, my Venus, my soul's body, lies
> With my love laid upon her garment-wise[117]
>
> Soiled, without raiment, clad about with sand.
> . . .
> Trodden as grapes in the wine-press of lust,
> Trampled and trodden by the fiery feet.[118]

'Laus Veneris' is governed by the inversion of traditional religious and erotic conventions. Although Swinburne diligently seeks to devise appropriate modes of expression for this, he only succeeds in constructing a synthetic language consisting of a number of heterogeneous elements. Biblical and medieval phrases are combined with rhetorical patterns, alliterative groupings and recurring images in a Swinburnean diction which does not adequately serve either the contents of the poem or the actual experience of reality: 'language, uprooted, has adapted itself to an independent life of atmospheric nourishment'.[119] In literary history this tendency for style to become an end in itself is a phenomenon typical of decadence and the eclecticism that goes with it. If viewed within the context of symbolist tendencies, it constitutes an attempt to convey the same esoteric themes and motifs that Baudelaire, Mallarmé and Verlaine discovered in their endeavours to transcend the banality of reality. But Swinburne's poetic genius did not prove equal to the difficult task of inventing a style congenial to the new visionary inwardness.

In most of the poems in Swinburne's *Poems and Ballads* the prevailing fusion of spiritual and erotic elements is formulated in a rather direct manner, causing the central concepts of body and soul to stand out obtrusively amidst the sterile, artificial language. The impression of refinement arising from the medievalist and biblical phrasing in many late romantic poems is the consequence of an 'excessive care in word-selection',[120] which more often than not chooses the rare in preference to the appropriate word. Francis Thompson, who himself adorned his poems with words like 'usufruct; day-fall's carcanet; green cymar; caerule empery' and upon one occasion even admitted 'my figured descant hides the simple theme',[121] seems to be a competent judge of the situation.

The vocabulary is derived from the most diverse sources but the motivation prompting these authors to search for the 'stunning-word' (Rossetti) is the same, and the same effects are produced whether, following Gautier's advice, they pore over dictionaries or, like Lionel Johnson, immerse themselves in the language of religious poetry and in the poetic diction of the eighteenth century; whether, emulating Wilde, they unearth exotic and suggestive word formations (Tragelaphos, Abana and Parphar)[122] or, in line with Swinburne's 'Masque of Queen Bersabe',[123] compile catalogues of strange-sounding names ('Aholibah, Abihail, Azubah, Aholah'). In Pater's novel, Flavian is described as an 'indefatigable student of words' and the 'golden book' that he and Marius study is 'full of the archaisms and curious felicities in which that generation delighted, quaint terms and images'.[124] In conjunction with the Pre-Raphaelite revival of archaisms, Swinburne's adaptation of biblical language and Thompson's preference for ornate vocabulary,

Pater's generation acquires a new insight into the properties of language as a medium: 'Product of a myriad of various minds and contending tongues, compact of obscure and minute association, a language has its own abundant and often recondite laws.'[125] This medium is only available to the poet who is both a 'lover of words' and a 'scholar'. Not only Eliot's 'Waste Land' or Pound's *Cantos*, but Thompson's mannered poetry and numerous lines in *The House of Life* remain inaccessible to the general reader.

Words and word combinations like 'undesecrate', 'dark Paraclete', 'steely soul of ice'[126] by which Lionel Johnson attempts to convey his fashionably sombre Catholicism presuppose a new sensitivity to language as described for the first time by De Quincey in the remarkable fascination and associations which the words 'Consul Romanus' evoke in his opium-induced dreams.[127] Baudelaire, in *Les Paradis Artificiels*, has dealt with a similar experience of the heightening of language:

La grammaire, l'aride grammaire elle-même, devient quelque chose comme une sorcellerie évocatoire; les mots ressuscitent revêtus de chair et d'os, le substantif, dans sa majesté substantielle, l'adjectif, vêtement transparent qui l'habille et le colore comme un glacis, et le verbe, ange du mouvement, qui donne le branle à la phrase.[128]

The impact of this new consciousness of language is still noticeable in Joyce's *A Portrait of the Artist as a Young Man*. The transition from superficial acoustic effects ('The ivy . . . whines and twines') to a symbolist verbal sensitivity developing new associations by exploiting etymological possibilities would be unthinkable without the late romantic 'excessive care in word selection' (Francis Thompson).

His own consciousness of language was ebbing from his brain . . .

> The ivy whines upon the wall,
> And whines and twines upon the wall,
> The yellow ivy upon the wall,
> Ivy, ivy up the wall.

Did anyone ever hear such drivel? . . . Yellow ivy; that was all right. Yellow ivory also. And what about ivory ivy? The word now shone in his brain, clearer and brighter than any ivory sawn from the mottled tusks of elephant. *Ivory, ivoire, avorio, ebur.*[129]

Rossetti had a penchant for words not quite as unusual as many examples in Wilde's 'The Sphinx' but exuding an air of rareness and refined erudition (encomiast, solstice, halcyon).[130] However, this impression of strangeness often tends to arise from uncommon combinations of everyday terms — 'exquisite hunger; hungering thrill; debatable borders of the year'[131] – rather than from the use of rare words. Apart from an overall stylizing effect this sort of diction serves little function[132] in the works of Pre-Raphaelite epigones such as Bourke Marston and Payne or occasionally even in those of Rossetti himself; yet in the finest sonnets of *The House of Life* it convincingly conveys the symbolic implications. The unexpected phrase 'untuneful bough' which appears together with 'wingless skies' in Rossetti's 'Winged Hours', for example, successfully condenses the sonnet's pervasive bird imagery[133] in a sombre metaphor.

Along with esoteric modes of symbolic expression such as archaistic phrases and 'stunning words' the Latin titles gracing many late romantic poems are worthy of mention. This tendency surfaced in Gautier's 'Caerulei Oculi', Verlaine's 'Crimen Amoris' and in Baudelaire's 'Duellum', 'Franciscae meae laudes' and 'Sed non satiata'; it can also be found in the works of their English contemporaries Rossetti ('Aspecta Medusa'; 'Retro me, Sathana!') and Swinburne ('Anima Anceps', 'Satia te Sanguine'). Transmitted by epigones like Payne ('Silentia Lunae') and Douglas ('Amoris Vincula'), it reaches its culmination in Dowson's poetry ('Ad Domnulam Suam', 'Amor Umbratilis') and lingers on in the fashionable imitations by Wilde ('Amor Intellectualis') and A. Symons ('Stella Maligna').[134] In keeping with the contemporary love of eclecticism their origins are many and varied. Two sources are immediately recognizable: the traditions of classical Latin poetry and of Latin church hymns. While late romantic poets turn to Latin poetry in search of formal precision ('Non sum qualis eram bonae sub regno Cynarae', Dowson;[135] 'Arma Virumque', L. Johnson), they borrow from Latin hymns in accordance with their spiritual needs and ritualistic inclinations ('Mater Liliarum', Symons; 'Te Martyrum Candidatus', L. Johnson). This latter tendency leads to the revival of Latin hymnic poetry with strikingly new contents ('Franciscae meae laudes', Baudelaire; 'Satanas', L. Johnson). In the nineties the esoteric quality engendered by the mannered combination of medievalisms, biblical expressions, 'stunning words' and Latin titles becomes even more pronounced through the dedication of the poems to initiated friends.

A poetry which strives for the adequate expression of moods is forced to renounce discursive language for a language of suggestion. The poetic tradition offers a wide range of modes of expression, among them alliteration, assonance and internal rhyme, which the late romantics adapt in unorthodox variations and unusual concentration. Very often the same technique fulfils different or even opposing functions. In their use of alliteration, for instance, Rossetti and Lionel Johnson sometimes combine musical effects with an intellectual punch-line: 'The bliss so long afar, at length so nigh . . . Where one shorn tress long stirred the longing ache' – 'The hinting tone, the haunting laugh'.[136] Both authors also share the same liking for word and sound repetitions to stress the 'mystical' tone of their concluding lines ('Fire within fire, desire in deity' – 'Lonely, unto the Lone I go; / Divine to the Divinity'[137]). The alliteration in 'Thy longing leans across the brink'[138] from Lionel Johnson's 'Vinum Daemonum', on the other hand, conveys a more visual and sensuous quality, comparable to the diction of Swinburne's *Poems and Ballads*:

> Laughs low for love's sake and the words he saith.
> For she lies, laughing low with love; she lies,
> And turns his kisses on her lips to sighs,
> To sighing sound of lips unsatisfied.[139]

Since Swinburne uses this sort of alliteration in very different poems without any distinction as to its function, it tends to become a prominent but non-functional component of an autonomous diction.

Although in *The House of Life* alliterations occur in similar abundance, they produce a less mannered effect because Rossetti goes to great lengths to make them expressive of each particular mood. In the 'Willowwood' sonnets, for instance, he skilfully evokes the mystical atmosphere of the Pre-Raphaelite symbolic landscape through the deliberate and subtle tuning of sounds, startling compound forms, the leitmotif-like repetition of words, alliterations, assonances and internal rhyme:

> O ye, all ye that walk in Willowwood,
> That walk with hollow faces burning white;
> What fathom-depth of soul-struck widowhood . . .[140]

In the superior sonnets of Rossetti's cycle *The House of Life* these sound patterns open a new dimension of symbolic suggestiveness and the sestet of 'Nuptial Sleep' can still elicit praise from the modern reader:

> Sleep sank them lower than the tide of dreams,
>   And their dreams watched them sink, and slid away.
> Slowly their souls swam up again, through gleams
>   Of watered light and dull drowned waifs of day;
> Till from some wonder of new woods and streams
>   He woke, and wondered more: for there she lay.[141]

Apart from the richly diversified sound structures themselves, their combination with numerous other elements, such as compound forms, for example, imparts the impression of a new poetic language.

> . . . at her touch they shone
> With inmost heaven-hue of the heart of flame.

Till the tempestuous tide-gates flung apart
Flood with wild will the hollows of thy heart.[142]

Rossetti's virtuosity lies in the careful preparation for the climax of his poem and the strategic use of the compound forms.

Gilbert and Sullivan's parody of compound forms like 'heart-hungry' or 'heart-whole'[143] in *Patience* confirms the importance of this stylistic device in English literature from Rossetti to Yeats. Obviously Rossetti and Yeats, Poe and Payne often conceived compound forms as complex units of sound and therefore linked them through alliteration, assonance or a combination of the two techniques; 'cloud-control; soul-sequestered' (Rossetti); 'pearl-pale; dew-dropping' (Yeats); 'love-light; heart-histories' (Poe); 'wide-winged; soul-semblance' (Payne).[144] Frequently these compound constructions act as a nucleus for entire systems of alliterations and assonances structuring the immediate and even the broader context.

Now many memories make solicitous
The delicate love-lines of her mouth, till lit . . .[145]

. . . that world of white
With drooping wings and winter-saddened eyes.[146]

. . . a woven world-forgotten isle
Where people love beside the ravelled sea.[147]

The compounds are of further interest in terms of their lexical content. In Bourke Marston's 'The Soul's Pregnancy' ("'Tis that the pain-wed soul is conscious of / Some in-wombed child of spiritual good'),[148] they contribute to the intended cryptic touch. In Rossetti's 'Love-sweetness' the compound of the title suggests a specific experience of love while the compound adjective 'cloud-girt' stresses the esoteric effect of the noun 'wayfaring'.[149] The most widespread of these compounds are those in which one component is further qualified by a second, more expressive one, adding to the strained and cloying effect of the Pre-Raphaelite language: 'blossom-spread' (Payne); 'rose-winged' (Rossetti); 'joy-environing' (Bourke Marston); 'wise-tongued' (Yeats).[150] Within the context of the individual poem, however, this type of compound merely sustains the generally stylized atmosphere. It comes as no surprise that Yeats eliminated many of these compounds when later revising his early poetry; unlike his precursors he had come to recognize the perils of decorative formulae.

Of much greater significance for the study of symbolist tendencies is a type of compound linking two concepts of similar intensity ('wind-warm space'; 'osier-odoured stream')[151] in order to convey the complex late romantic sensitivity. This refined sensitivity manifests itself in synaesthetic combinations of perceptions as well as in the fusion of tenor and vehicle, and of inner and outer senses: 'Roses . . . gave out, in return for the *love-light* / Their odorous souls' (Poe); 'Against the red throb of its [Heaven's] *sunset-heart* / I laid my own to beat' (F. Thompson).[152] Compound forms were one of the favourite devices as they combined concentration and intensity with complexity and ambiguity, thus coming close to fulfilling the spiritual and artistic ideals of the time. With their unusual lexical combinations compound forms above all facilitated the rendering of moods and dream states wavering between eroticism and spirituality.[153] The striking prevalence of compounds incorporating the words 'soul' or 'love' reflects the attempt to find adequate means of expression for a new kind of experience: 'Love-light' (Poe); 'love-breath', 'soul-wrung implacable close kiss' (Rossetti); 'soul-centred' (Dowson).[154] In compounds such as 'soul-sequestered' and 'soul-stilled face' (Rossetti)[155] the relationship between the two elements remains intentionally ambiguous and obscure.

An eminently conscientious craftsman, Rossetti often uses compound forms to encapsulate the thematic and metaphorical structure of an entire poem in a single concise formulation. In 'Mid-rapture' the compounds underline the identification of the 'love-world' of the octave with the vision of heaven ('Light circled in a heaven of deep-drawn rays') in the sestet.[156] The light imagery in the octave of 'Soul-light' at first appears to grasp no more than a glimpse of the external landscape ('at the end of some deep avenue / A tender glamour of day'). At the end of the octave, however, it turns out to be 'Soul-light', suggesting the fusion of eroticism and spirituality implied in the compound title:

> Such fire as Love's soul-winnowing hands distil
> Even from his inmost ark of light and dew.[157]

Payne's 'Silentia Lunae' illustrates how the compound forms affect a whole context, combining with other stylistic devices to blur the contours of the world of the senses, and mirroring the moods of the late romantic self:

>   and thereupon the mirrored lights
> Of the soft stars shone out like petal-whites
> Of gold-heart lilies, floating waveringly
> Upon the moon-silences . . .
>   . . . we have steeped our love by-past
> In the white peace of night . . . we have cast
> Our twinned souls out with kisses and with tears
> Upon the flooding moon.[158]

Aspects of late romantic imagery

The reader who encounters a new sensitivity expressed in verses like Swinburne's 'The scent and shadow shed about me make / The very soul in all my senses ache'[159] will find it difficult to reconcile this phenomenon with the equally strong inclination for rationally calculated effects. A natural response is to dismiss Swinburne's elaborate rhetorical patterning and Rossetti's conceits as secondary and casual embellishments. If the individual lyric contexts are taken into account, however, a more balanced view of such devices emerges. At first glance the image 'And her breast's secrets peered into her breast' in Rossetti's 'The Love-letter' seems to arise from a sheer delight in manneristic abstruseness, yet upon closer consideration, it proves to be an integral part of the poem's pervasive metaphorical structure:

> Warmed by her hand and shadowed by her hair
> As close she leaned and poured her heart through thee,
> Whereof the articulate throbs accompany
> The smooth black stream that makes thy whiteness fair . . .[160]

Starting with a physical detail the imagery is gradually transformed through an intellectual process. Unlike the stricter stylization in the poetry of the concettists, it is characteristic of Rossetti's art that he has no difficulty in returning to the concretely visualized scene ('Sweet fluttering sheet, even of her breath aware'), before introducing another mannered metaphorical pattern ('silent song') that culminates in the vision of 'married music in Love's answering air'.

Not always is such a complete fusion of intellectual and sensuous aspects achieved. In poems like Swinburne's 'Fragoletta', imagery is replaced by rhetorical formulae like 'The son of grief begot by joy? / Being sightless, wilt thou see?'[161] and the predominant impression remains one of intellectual ingenuity comparable to that found in Symons's *études* in the style of the concettists.

> Death in her lilied whiteness lives,
> The shadow of Death's eternal lust
> After the delicate flesh that gives
> The life of lilies to the dust.
> Ah, if thy lust my love forgives,
> Death, spare this whitest flesh that lives![162]

Despite the somewhat questionable quality of their literary output, it was of great importance for the development of modern poetry that the late romantics persistently strove for a 'unification of sensibility'[163] in their imagery. Although the cleverly contrived metaphors in Laurence Housman's poem on the dead beloved[164] hold little appeal for a modern reader, his return to the mannerist tradition illustrates how, after 1850, a new poetic sensitivity arises that was unknown to Keats or the Wordsworth of *The Prelude*. In their attempt to reintroduce the role of the intellect into poetry, authors like Lionel Johnson look back to the poets of the seventeenth century:

> The ardour of red flame is thine,
> And thine the steely soul of ice:
> . . .
> Apples of ashes, golden bright;
> Water of bitterness, how sweet!
> Oh banquet of a foul delight,
> Prepared by thee, dark Paraclete![165]

At the same time their choice of words[166] is intended to appeal to the reader emotionally. The result is a strange tension between the traditional imagery and its new spiritual implications.

Rossetti's poems 'The Birth-bond', 'Known in Vain' and 'Lost on Both Sides' are each structured as one comprehensive simile, the vehicle developing in the octave and the tenor in the sestet.[167] The comparison itself is devised with such ingenuity that it requires the reader's fullest concentration to keep the intended meaning in mind. The imagery, more intellectual than visual from the very beginning, loses the emotional quality of romantic metaphors and imparts a 'sensitivity of a cultivated intellectual type'.[168] As it turns out, this kind of sensitivity is not incompatible with posing and the development of sentimentality.

Thus for Alfred Douglas the nightingale 'is like a poet's soul / She finds fierce pain in miseries that seem' – 'Nay, she weeps not because she knows sad songs, / But sings because she weeps.'[169] How this attitude affects imagery and diction becomes obvious from other sonnets in the same group ('A Triad of the Moon'). Douglas dedicates the octave of the second sonnet to the nightingale and her 'sighful song':

> That she should so devise to find such lore
> Of sighful song and piteous psalmody,
> While Joy runs on through summer greenery,
> And all delight is like an open door.
> Must then her liquid notes for evermore
> Repeat the colour of sad things, and be
> Distilled like cassia drops of agony,
> From the slow anguish of a heart's bruised core?

After the obtrusive patterning of the second line with its alliterations, parallelisms and rare words ('piteous psalmody'), the two following lines create a short allegorical scene typical of many Pre-Raphaelite poems. Unusual imagery and elaborate synaesthesia contribute to the stylizing effect of the second quatrain. The mannered metaphor of the distilled drops of cassia, cleverly linking the 'liquid notes' of the first line in the second quatrain with the 'slow anguish of a heart's bruised core' of the last line, is symptomatic of the self-conscious sensitivity of the poet.

The ideal of intensity also leads to new forms of synaesthesia.[170] Baudelaire's very conscious use of analogies in 'Correspondances' is an elucidating example of the significance that synaesthesia acquires in connection with symbolist tendencies.[171] What the romantics perceived as sensuous forms are regarded by late romantics primarily as rational combinations. This hardly seems justified if we think of Swinburne's 'The silence as music, thy voice as an odour that fades in a flame'[172] or 'Blows with a perfume of songs',[173] lines in which synaesthesia evokes a mood blurring the contours of the real world. However, the deliberately arranged rhetorical passages in 'Hesperia' as well as the carefully contrived synaesthesia in the poetry of Rossetti, Francis Thompson and John Davidson confirm the initial impression of greater intellectual awareness and purposeful metaphorical design.

In Rossetti's 'Mid-rapture' the rhetorical figure of the opening lines and the ensuing catalogue of beauty gradually lead into the heart of a mood-poem at the beginning of the second quatrain. This effect is mainly achieved through the synaesthetic structuring of imagery.

> whose voice attuned above
> All modulation of the deep-bowered dove,
> Is like a hand laid softly on the soul;
> Whose hand is like a sweet voice to control
> Those worn tired brows it hath the keeping of.[174]

While the transition from the acoustic ('attuned . . . above . . . dove') to the tactile perceptions seems to appeal solely to the senses, the subsequent inversion of the same movement demonstrates the intellectual awareness and 'art' governing the structuring of this imagery. In his sonnet 'Silent Noon' Rossetti uses the synaesthesia 'visible silence'[175] in a similarly sophisticated way. Silence, as a symbol of fulfilment, determines the mood of the poem.

Many examples of synaesthesia in late romantic poetry take the form of an oxymoron. The artistic awareness dictating such patterning is also noticeable in another type of imagery even more obvious in its fusion of intellectual and sensuous elements. Abstractions like Night, Love or Silence are placed in realistic descriptions, as in Payne's lines on the 'madonna of his dreams' and help to concentrate the dreamlike atmosphere in a thematic focus. The ensuing tension between abstract and visual qualities echoes the tension arising from the correspondence of the different perceptions:

The night was fragrant as a violet
With perfume of the early bloom of love;
The silence hovered o'er us, like a dove
Of peace, and in the ferns the brook did fret
Its stones to music.[176]

With minor poets like Payne this results in forced comparisons ('Silence
. . . like a dove of peace') producing a stylizing effect but never reaching
the density of symbols. In other cases, such as Francis Thompson, the
synaesthetic linkage of perceptions does not develop on a suggestive level
but constitutes a cleverly contrived rhetorical crossover to the visionary
theme of the poem:

But the superior seraphim do know
None other music but to flame and glow.
                    . . .
At the rich odours from her heart that rise
My soul remembers its lost Paradise . . .[177]

Rossetti, in 'Heart's Compass', employs the same combination of music
and fire metaphors − reminiscent of the religious imagery of the seventeenth century − as Francis Thompson, and in so doing confirms the
close relationship between the new sensitivity and the search for a
language going beyond that of the romantics:

Whose unstirred lips are music's visible tone;
Whose eyes the sun-gate of the soul unbar,
Being of its furthest fires oracular.[178]

During the nineties the importance of synaesthesia remains undimin-
ished, yet under the growing French influence an interesting stylistic
development takes place. In the works of writers like Symons and
Wratislaw, synaesthesia of the Swinburne–Rossetti type continues to
exist, side by side and sometimes even in combination with synaesthesia
of the French symbolist variety. The final lines of Wratislaw's 'Orchids'
display such a mixture of styles. Here we find not only French influences
but elements of Pre-Raphaelite diction ('A shrine of loves . . . A temple
of . . . sorrows') and personifications like sorrow and sin integrated in
a synaesthetic scheme ('in clamorous orchestra of hues, / The palette of
your perfumes'):

A shrine of love that laugh and swoon and ache,
A temple of coloured sorrows and perfumed sins.[179]

John Davidson's experiments with synaesthetic forms are of even
greater significance for the English tradition. Two basic types of
synaesthesia stand out in his poetry. The first, in 'Yuletide', arises from

his attempt to create an impressionistic fusion of perceptions connected with the discovery of the city motif:

> And tossing bells
> Of stealthy hansoms chime
> With silvery crash
> In radiant ways
> Attuned and frozen up
> To concert pitch.[180]

The second variant, developed with particular finesse in 'Bartlemas', imitates romantic models[181] but surpasses these sources in its systematic widening and patterning of synaesthetic relationships. In the section entitled 'A Threnody Celebrating the Fall of the Leaf' the opening lines twice proceed from a reference to the nightingale's song, establishing a vertical correspondence between its melody and the stars:

> No longer the nightingales chant
>   To the silvery pulses of night,
> That echo the measure and grant
>   Responsal of starry delight.
> No nightingales longer descant
>   To the stars as they throb with their light.[182]

Without abandoning the vertical relationship the poem moves to a horizontal correspondence when the 'dye of the autumn', then perfume, light and 'ruby and pearl' enter into a synaesthetic union with the 'throng of the silences':

> In the Forest the silences throng:
> No throstle, no blackbird devout
>   As the seraphim mingle their song,
>   With perfume entangle the light
>   And powder the woodland with pearl,
> Nor usher the star-stricken night
>   With incense and melody rare;
>   The song-thrush devout and the merle
> No longer enrapture the air
>   With concord of ruby and pearl . . .

Through formulations like 'stellar reply' and 'sidereal echoes' the poem returns to the scheme of vertical correspondences. Such expressions and the meticulously planned patterns of synaesthesia are characteristic of Davidson's earnest, if not always successful, endeavours to develop a language befitting the new sensitivity.

With many late romantic poets the striving for intensity entails a mannered and sophisticated handling of imagery, regardless of whether this imagery is realistic or mythological in origin:

By what word's power, the key of paths untrod,
Shall I the difficult deeps of Love explore,
Till parted waves of song yield up the shore
Even as that sea which Israel crossed dryshod.[183]

Rossetti's far-fetched comparison of the beauty of his beloved to the genius of Homer, Dante and Michelangelo ('Genius in Beauty')[184] as well as the revival of the lodestar[185] metaphor have to be seen in connection with this tendency.

In view of these intellectual metaphors and other literary parallels between the seventeenth and the nineteenth[186] centuries, one feels inclined to assume that the imagery of the French symbolists and the English late romantics can be related to the Metaphysicals in the 'essential quality of transmuting ideas into sensations, of transforming an observation into a state of mind'.[187] However, the group of poets classified under the general and rather problematic term 'Metaphysical' is as diversified as the group of late romantic poets discussed in this book, so that it is only viable to trace affinities between individual authors. Dante Gabriel Rossetti's imagery at times recalls that of Donne, while the devotional poetry of his sister Christina seems more in the vein of George Herbert. Francis Thompson's lyrics have already been likened to those of Crashaw by his contemporaries.[188] Once the comparisons leave the safe ground of direct influence, however, numerous problems arise. As with the revival of the principle of correspondence, the obvious affinities should not obscure the fundamental differences. The purpose of such studies suggested by Payne's poem 'With a Copy of Henry Vaughan's Sacred Poems' or Le Gallienne's remarks on Gray,[189] for instance, should be to determine the specific features in the late romantic lyric which would go unnoticed without the comparison to Metaphysical poetry.

Swinburne, writing about the religious 'designs' by his friend Simeon Solomon, praises 'the burning mysticism and raging rapture' of the 'Teresa' hymn;[190] what he has in mind is the same visionary intensity – 'rapturous ethereality' – which causes Francis Thompson to designate Crashaw, and not Donne, the most important of the Metaphysical poets.[191] This quality is hardly the most important attribute of Metaphysical poetry in the eyes of Eliot and his generation, but it seems all-important for an understanding of late romantic literature. Characteristic of a transitional movement like late romanticism is that Francis Thompson enjoys the Metaphysicals for their 'frank toying with imagery' and finds their poetry echoed in Shelley, but unequivocally prefers the great romantic because of his 'passionate spontaneity':

The Metaphysical School, like Shelley, loved imagery for its own sake: and how beautiful a thing the frank toying with imagery may be, let 'The Skylark' and 'The Cloud' witness . . . The Metaphysical School failed, not because it toyed with imagery, but because it toyed with it frostily . . . So you may toy with imagery in mere intellectual ingenuity, and then you might as well go write acrostics: or you may toy with it in raptures, and then you may write a 'Sensitive Plant'.[192]

To evaluate Thompson's statements properly requires a close study of his own imagery. His handling of metaphor seems much more closely related to the art of the concettists than to the romantic lyric and leaves no doubt that he admires the spontaneity of Shelley as a feature which his own work lacks. Symons, in his criticism of Thompson, seems to confirm this assumption, underlining both the affinities and differences between his contemporary and the seventeenth-century poets. As Symons points out, much in Thompson's poetic representation of detail appears vague, although 'closely copied from that which was fantastically precise in Crashaw, Donne, Vaughan'.[193] His 'lack of reticence'[194] together with his longing for immediacy link him to his romantic predecessors, while the arrestation of his poetic spontaneity and his manneristic 'verbal intelligence' producing 'a splendour of rags and patches'[195] are characteristic of the new poetic language hovering on the brink of modernity. Thompson, of course, was unaware that what he describes as outstanding features of Crashaw's metaphysical poems are equally characteristic of numerous poems from Rossetti to John Gray and Davidson, not to mention those he had written himself:

He has, at his best, an extraordinary cunning of diction, cleaving like gold-leaf to its object. In such a poem as 'The Musician and the Nightingale' the marvel of diction becomes even too conscious; in the moment of wondering at the miracle, we feel that the miracle is too researched . . .[196]

In the sestet of Rossetti's 'The One Hope' ingenuity merges with a late romantic mood in a way that seems characteristic of the period:

> Ah! when the wan soul in that golden air
> Between the scriptured petals softly blown
> Peers breathless for the gift of grace unknown, –
> Ah, let none other written spell soe'er
> But only the one Hope's one name be there, –
> Not less nor more, but even that word alone.[197]

While the involved allusions to the modified Hyacinthus myth (neither Apollo's lament, nor the name of his dead favourite inadvertently slain at the discus match, but just the single word 'hope' is to be written on the flower petals) place these verses among mannerist poetry, the image of the 'wan soul', 'breathless' in typically Pre-Raphaelite fashion, peering 'for the gift of grace unknown', belongs to the genre of the late romantic mood-poem.

Accompanying a strong tendency toward stylization, the ingenious selection and patterning of imagery in the works of many of these poets give rise to ornate and mannered metaphors like 'Her breasts are like white birds' and 'The breath of kindred plumes against his feet'.[198] This combination also leads to the creation of another type of imagery in which stylization fuses with great subtlety of perception:

> Sky like smoked mother-o'pearl,
> Dim background for bare trees
> That lift against it stained twig traceries.[199]

Pre-Raphaelites like Rossetti, Swinburne and Simeon Solomon as well as poets of the nineties like Gray and Douglas frequently adopt biblical imagery or diction to heighten the impact of their verse.

> Large lovely arms and a neck like a tower[200]
> [Thy neck is like the tower of David builded for
> an armoury, Song of Solomon 4.4; Thy neck is as
> a tower of ivory, 7.4]

> I see her breasts,
> Pricked out with lamps they stand like huge black towers[201]
> [I am a wall, and my breasts like towers, Song of Solomon 8.4]

The appropriation of imagery from the Song of Solomon results from the same stylistic intentions which motivate the highly artificial, sometimes grotesque images in the works of Wilde, Gray or Wratislaw.

> Those violet-gleaming butterflies that take
> Yon creamy lily for their pavilion
> Are monsignores.[202]

In the poetry of John Davidson stylizing and distorting elements appear in disconcerting proximity. The imagery in the first stanza of 'A Frosty Morning' strongly recalls the 'gold bar of Heaven' from which Rossetti's Blessed Damozel leans out.[203] Later in the poem, however, when the 'diamond-dust of rime' settles upon 'rail and tramway rust', the spirit of a new and modern poetry is announced, appearing even more vividly in the lines 'like gongs the causeys clamoured, / Like drums the asphalt beat'. In 'Yuletide', too, decorative elements[204] are prominent, but the distorting effects are even more noticeable than in 'A Frosty Morning'. Imagery in the lines 'Each lamp-lit gorge by traffic rent / Asunder, / Ravines of serried shops / By business tempests torn'[205] already anticipates the mannered urban metaphors in 'The Love Song of J. Alfred Prufrock' or 'Rhapsody on a Windy Night'. Eliot does not go into the formal aspects of his imagery but he explicitly acknowledges 'my debts to John Davidson . . . I also had a good many dingy urban images to reveal'.[206] It can scarcely be coincidental that in this same preface to Davidson's poetry the poet of 'The Waste Land' also mentions James Thomson B.V., the author of 'The City of Dreadful Night'.

After the contrastive use of 'dingy urban images' and stylized metaphors in 'Yuletide', Davidson develops a cosmic vision:

When the winds list
A fallen cloud
Where Yellow dregs of light
Befouled remain,
The woven gloom
Of smoke and mist,
The soot-entangled rain
That jumbles day and night
In city and town,
An umber-emerald shroud
Rehearsing doom,
The London fog comes down.
But sometimes silken beams,
As bright
As adamant on fire,
Of the uplifted sun's august attire,
With frosty fibrous light
Magnetic shine
Of happier dreams
That abrogate despair
When all the sparkling air
Of smoke and sulphur shriven,
Like an iced wine
Fills the high cup
Of heaven.[207]

Among the late romantics John Davidson, the indefatigable experimenter with poetic language, is perhaps the poet most important to the rise of the modern lyric. He resorts to ornate expressions ('sun's august attire'), searches for 'stunning words' ('abrogate despair'), experiments with synaesthesia, invents new forms of imagery and in 'Thirty Bob a Week', a poem singled out by Eliot, he discovers the poetic possibilities of colloquial speech. In 'Yuletide' he tries out the short line, and in parts of 'Bartlemas' combines synaesthesia with repetitions imitated from Poe to create a language suitable to the nature of the mood-poem.

Cosmic imagery appealed to the late romantic desire for intensity and allowed for visionary amplification. In Baudelaire's 'Le Couvercle' the sky resembles the black lid of a 'grande marmite / Où bout l'imperceptible et vaste Humanité'[208]; in Thomson's 'The City of Dreadful Night' the visionary speaker watches the sun burn out, leaving 'a bleeding eyeless socket red and dim'.[209] During the late nineteenth century, cosmic imagery recurs in countless variations. While the suggestion of vast expanses ('the curled moon / Was like a little feather / Fluttering far down the gulf')[210] emphasizes the unbridgeable distance between the lyrical self and the ideal beloved in Rossetti's 'The Blessed Damozel', in O'Sullivan's poetry it becomes the projection of late romantic nightmares:

> All down the valley of the universe,
> Through firmaments to where the tall stars end,
> The terror lurks, and stabs us like a curse.[211]

In *Les Paradis Artificiels* Baudelaire describes the effects of opium on human perception; familiar and trivial objects are transformed into a 'monde d'inspirations, une procession magnifique et bigarrée de pensées désordonnées et rhapsodiques'.[212] A similar process occurs in the visionary imagery of English late romantic poetry, not due to the use of laudanum, opium or alcohol but because the author projects his own perplexities and anguishes onto the world around him and makes nature and cities the apocalyptic reflections of his own soul.

The fact that before Eliot a number of poets in the nineties, obviously under the influence of the French, created imagery unthinkable for Tennyson ('The daisies' leprous stain' – 'Every lamp I pass / Beats like a fatalistic drum'[213]) has generally led critics to overlook the corresponding indigenous English tradition. A detailed study of the imagery in the poetry of Bailey, Dobell and Alexander Smith, those authors known as the 'Spasmodic School' since Aytoun's parody, would doubtless confirm that their mannerisms and distortions signal the advent of a new poetic language. As Tennyson does in 'The Charge of the Light Brigade', Dobell depicts an episode from the Crimean war in his poem 'Grass from the Battle-Field', and although it is a rather minor work, it is of some relevance here due to its unique modes of representation. The first-person narrator observes the events of the battle, the advance of the troops, the agonizing death of a soldier from the vantage point of a grassy mound. The world of battle is only presented in segments but the details stand out with an unnatural precision. At one point his attention is riveted on the boots of a soldier rushing past: 'I saw the wrinkles of the leather grain, / The very cobbler's stitches, and the wear / By which I knew the wearer trod not straight.'[214] This rendering of detail recalls the intensity of Pre-Raphaelite art. As the description of a sparrow picking at the saliva of a dead horse makes clear, however, Dobell's intentions governing the selection of incidents and details are radically different from those of Holman Hunt's typologies.

The intensifying effect of a limited perspective is further heightened by mannered imagery. In the portrayal of a dying officer Dobell focuses his attention on one hand, combining the exact reproduction of its movements with contrasting imagery that ultimately overpowers it.

> Betwixt thy blades and stems
> There fell a hand,
>
>   . . .
>
> Idly, one by one,
> The knots of anguish came undone,
> The fingers stretched as from a cramp of woe,
> And sweet and slow
> Moved to gracious shapes of rest,
> Like a curl of soft pale hair
> Drying in the sun.[215]

Dobell's conscious workmanship shows all too clearly in the many forced comparisons and in the carefully constructed tension between the minute depiction of detail and the exaggeration of gigantic visions: 'As if the plain were iron, and thereon / An iron hammer . . . As a dead giant'.[216] The inordinate length of the poem, numerous elements of the diction and, above all, the unconcealed sentimentality (the hand of the dead soldier is grasped by his beloved, who, a kindred sister of Florence Nightingale, has searched for him on the battlefield) all classify 'Grass from the Battle-Field' as a second-rate Victorian work of literature. Yet the perspectivist mode of presentation and the precise rendering of details reveal a quite modern sensibility and signal the rise of a new poetic language in mid-nineteenth-century England.

Symbolist tendencies and the interrelationship of the arts

In the late nineteenth century the time-honoured theme of the inter-relationship of the arts becomes once again a central theme in poetic theory and practice.[217]

> The ear receives in common with the eye,
> One beauty, flowing through a different gate;
> Melody is its form, and harmony
> Its hue; the arts so interpenetrate,
> And all reciprocally sympathize,
> For all at first from one foundation rise.[218]

These lines from Allingham's narrative poem 'The Music Master' outline the late romantic idea of the relationship between the arts, which is based on theories of the imagination like the one developed by William Blake. Emphasizing that 'le meilleur compte rendu d'un tableau pourra être un sonnet ou une élégie',[219] Baudelaire attempts to translate the impression *Tannhäuser* left on him into the 'Correspondances' sonnet of the *Wagner* essay, 'de rendre avec les paroles la traduction inévitable que mon *imagination* fit du même morceau, lorsque je l'entendis pour la première fois'.[220] What distinguishes his motivations from the mannerists' delight in ingeniously relating the unrelated is the conviction that the essence of a work of art cannot be grasped by rational interpretation but can only be transposed into the language of another art belonging to the same realm of imagination.

During the final phases of a movement under the spell of Wagnerian music,[221] John Davidson establishes a direct connection between Wagner's union of music with literature and Rossetti's association of painting and poetry:

Literary criticism implies a contradiction in terms. It is impossible to give an account of one art except by another . . . Wagner gave a more or less successful account of his endeavour and meaning in music by the medium of another art, Literature namely . . . Rossetti was able to employ two arts as the complements of each other in a very special way . . .[222]

The anti-rational element in the romantic concept of imagination constitutes a main source of late romantic mysticism, which in turn provides the spiritual background for a new, comprehensive, symbolist world-view embracing the idea of the interrelationship of all arts.

C'est l'imagination qui a enseigné à l'homme le sens moral de la couleur, du contour, du son et du parfum. Elle a créé au commencement du monde, l'analogie et la métaphore.[223]

If the Trinity were not revealed, I should nevertheless be induced to suspect the existence of such a master-key by the trinities through which expounds itself the spirit of man. Such a trinity is the trinity of beauty – Poetry, Art, Music . . . So absolutely are these three the distinct manifestations of a single essence that, in considering the general operation of any one of them we consider the general operation of all.[224]

In the course of the nineteenth century the theory of the connection between the arts, like the concept of the symbol itself, undergoes a process of transformation; although difficult to schematize it can be approximately defined by looking at its early and final forms. The romanticists were fascinated with the interrelationship of the arts because they yearned for a world-view rendered harmonious by the unifying power of the imagination. Allingham stresses this relationship in 'The Music Master' by following the lines dealing with the harmony between the arts with a stanza relating this belief to the harmony in nature: 'Nature is one, and Art is also one, – / The Sun of nature and the Moon of Art'.[225]

Baudelaire's 'Richard Wagner et *Tannhäuser* à Paris', too, has its roots in this idea. Comparing his own sonnet 'Correspondances' with the poetic prose descriptions of the *Tannhäuser* music by Liszt and other contemporaries, he declares 'que la véritable musique suggère des idées analogues dans les cerveaux différents',[226] deriving this conviction from a world order of 'complexe et indivisible totalité' expressed in a comprehensive system of synaesthesia and the reciprocal analogy of all things.

The romantic vision of an all-encompassing system of universal analogies is the driving impulse behind Wagner's ideal of the *Gesamtkunstwerk* as well as Liszt's 'musical paintings' and symphonic poems;[227] from Mallarmé to Yeats – who significantly mentions Nerval, Maeterlinck and Villiers de l'Isle-Adam in this context – this conception lingers on in the motif of 'the new sacred book, of which all the arts . . . are beginning to dream'.[228] For the early romantics the belief in a harmony between the arts led to an understanding of music merely as a more expressive form of language and to a disregard for its sensuous qualities as a medium in its own right. The late romantics, however, came to emphasize the structural aspects of music and, in accordance with the law of dialectics, the romantic conviction of the inner affinity of all arts ultimately engenders the exact opposite: the development of a new insight into the specific nature of each individual art. While Francis Thompson continues to stress the unity in the trinity 'Poetry, Art, Music', Pater, in his Giorgione essay, criticizes this position, arriving at the modification central to late romantic aesthetics:

It is the mistake of much popular criticism to regard poetry, music, and painting . . . as but translations into different languages of one and the same fixed quantity of imaginative thought . . . a clear apprehension of the opposite principle – that the sensuous material of each art brings with it a special phase or quality of beauty, untranslatable into the forms of any other, an order of impressions distinct in kind – is the beginning of all true aesthetic criticism.[229]

Before formulating his famous dictum 'All art constantly aspires towards the condition of music'[230] he consistently quotes Lessing's *Laokoon*[231] and passes on to Wagner's ideas, also well known in France from Baudelaire's 'Richard Wagner et *Tannhäuser* à Paris'.

But although each art has thus its own specific order of impressions, and an untranslatable charm, while a just apprehension of the ultimate differences of the arts is the beginning of aesthetic criticism; yet it is noticeable that, in its special mode of handling its given material, each art may be observed to pass into the condition of some other art . . . by which the arts are able, not indeed to supply the place of each other, but reciprocally to lend each other new forces.[232]

Oscar Wilde recognizes in Wagner's, Pater's and Baudelaire's concept of the 'limitations in art' the basis for a new understanding of art that corresponds to his own experience of beauty as a mystery.[233]

This, also, is the explanation of the value of limitations in art. The sculptor gladly surrenders imitative colour, and the painter the actual dimensions of form, because by such renunciations they are able to avoid too definite a presentation of the Real . . . It is through its very incompleteness that Art becomes complete in Beauty, and so addresses itself, not to the faculty of recognition, not to the faculty of reason, but to the aesthetic sense alone . . . You see, then, how it is that the aesthetic critic rejects these obvious modes of art that have but one message to deliver, and having delivered it become dumb and sterile, and seeks rather for such modes as suggest reverie and mood.[234]

Here Wilde follows a tradition that can be traced back to Swinburne. Within the context of his essay on the art of Simeon Solomon, Swinburne interprets the 'boundary lines of the several conterminous arts . . . less as lines of mere distinction than as lines of mutual alliance'. To Wilde the 'mystery in all beauty' lies in the incompleteness of the individual arts, yet to Swinburne it arises from 'The subtle interfusion of art with art, of sound with form, of vocal words with silent colours.'[235]

For a generation that found in the mood-poem its appropriate mode of expression, the deficiencies of poetry – 'being of all the arts most closely cognate to the abstract intelligence'[236] – could only be compensated by borrowing from the other arts. The Pre-Raphaelites discovered early the pictorial quality in Keats ('The next Keats must be a painter', Rossetti)[237] and Poe's brilliant acoustic effects. Hence the rejection of an abstract, conceptual language is as characteristic of the English poets in the nineties as of the French symbolists. Yeats's description of symbolic experience reflects this tendency. Proceeding from the sensuous foundations of art ('all sounds, all colours, all forms'),[238] he unites them in a synaesthesia dominated by Platonic music imagery embodying the resolution of the tension between diversity and unity: 'and when sound, and colour, and form are in a musical relation, a beautiful relation to one another, they become, as it were, one sound, one colour, one form, and evoke an emotion that is made out of their distinct evocations and yet is one emotion'.[239]

The rising awareness of the importance of style expressed in Pater's novel *Marius the Epicurean* and his essay 'Style'[240] mirrors the refinement of a decadent age and furnishes new impulses for the reciprocal borrowing among the arts. Le Gallienne, like so many of his contemporaries, addresses the question of decadence in his review of Gray's collection of poetry *Silverpoints*, touching upon another aspect of the problem:

In what does decadence consist? In a self-conscious arrangement of 'coloured' vowels, in a fastidious distribution of accents, resulting in new and subtler harmonies of verse – say some. In the choice for themes of disease and forbidden things generally – . . . The real core of decadence is to be found in its isolated interests . . . Its recent development almost entirely confines its outlook on life to the colour-sense. It puts men and dead game on the same basis – of colour. . .[241]

One reason behind the literary assimilation of elements from painting is the antipathy to Victorian didacticism. Many late romantics believe that poetry can only free itself from the impact of Victorianism by borrowing from other arts like music and painting, arts characterized by non-conceptual qualities and by structural principles independent of thematic ideas. What constitutes an issue of criticism for Le Gallienne becomes a poetic principle for Wilde: 'The highest art rejects the burden of the human spirit.'[242] The late romantic belief in the unique status of the arts could only be realized by turning away from reality. Like Wilde, who excludes the realms of nature and everyday life from poetic experience, the young Yeats defines art from an esoteric anti-position: 'Art is art because it is not nature.'[243] To the escapist generation the arts seem to be closely interrelated because of their remoteness from life: 'The conception of making a prose poem out of paint is excellent. Much of the best modern literature springs from the same aim. In a very ugly and sensible age, the arts borrow, not from life, but from each other.'[244]

The pronounced interest in the visual arts is immediately evident in the titles of late romantic collections of poetry. Yet even here the variety of approaches within this general tendency is easily recognizable. Laurence Housman's *Green Arras* evokes the same colourful world of Pre-Raphaelite medievalism found in Morris's *Guenevere*, while Gray's *Silverpoints*, Wratislaw's cycle *Etchings* or the 'Brush and Chisel' section in Lee-Hamilton's *Sonnets of the Wingless Hours* only hint at the analogy between these artistic techniques and the poetic handling of language. Titles of volumes like Gautier's *Emaux et Camées* and Payne's *Intaglios* or the poems 'A Cameo' (Swinburne), 'To a Greek Gem' (Plarr), 'Le Panneau' (Wilde),[245] 'Le Jeune Homme Caressant sa Chimère (For an Intaglio)' (Symonds) directly invoke the Parnassian ideal of gem-carvers and engravers. Wilde's 'Le Réveillon' and Arthur Symons's collection *Silhouettes* including 'Pastel: Masks and Faces', recall, like Verlaine's *Aquarelles* with its poem entitled 'Green', the somewhat listless *fin de siècle* art of Charles Condor – so tasteful in his decoration of fans – more strongly than the paintings of the French Impressionist school. The vast differences between 'In the Key of Blue' (Symonds), 'Symphony in Yellow' (Wilde) and 'Symphonie en Blanc Majeur' (Gautier),[246] poems which, on the basis of their titles combining elements of music and painting, would seem to be closely related, indicate the wide range to be found within music and colour poetry.

Oscar Wilde's love of precious stones and metals has repeatedly been cited as symptomatic of his mannered delight in decoration. The longing for sensuous profusion already noticeable in Keats intensifies in the late romantic period, giving rise to the poignant desire to replace the ugliness and banality of the industrial age with an exotic and opulent world of art. This basic impulse quite naturally undergoes rich and manifold modifications. While in the poetry of the Pre-Raphaelite epigone Payne precious jewels conjure up a melancholy atmosphere of escape into an ideal world ('Soft sapphire and pale amethyst / And every tender mystic hue / Of emblem'd sadness'),[247] in Wilde's 'The Sphinx' they heighten the surface effect of brilliant splendour.[248] In Evelyn Douglas's 'The Palace of Pleasure' their sole purpose is to underline the foreignness of the sultry *intérieur* scenes; in O'Shaughnessy's 'The Daughter of Herodias' they serve to emphasize the aesthetic and spiritual implications of the dance motif.

For Charles Baudelaire pearls and precious stones become a central and complex symbol. Not only do they exercise an eroticizing effect ('La Chevelure') but, contrasted with the nakedness of the beloved ('Les Bijoux'), they help to create the same world of artificiality and unnatural beauty as marble and metal do in 'Rêve Parisien'. Jewels also symbolize in 'Les Bijoux' the synaesthetic fusion typical of late romantic sensitivity ('Ce monde rayonnant de métal et de pierre . . . où le son se mêle à la lumière')[249] and aid the transformation of the central female figure into a symbolic portrait in 'Avec ses Vêtements Ondoyants et Nacrés'. It is obviously under the influence of Baudelaire that Symonds ('Le Jeune Homme Caressant sa Chimère') uses jewels and precious stones to describe the metamorphosis of his *femme fatale* into a 'nature étrange et symbolique'.[250]

Plarr continues this tradition in 'The Goddess of the Islanders' by assigning a special symbolic meaning to each individual stone: 'each stone is sentient, and half human, / A passion or a crime'.[251] This poem illustrates how in English literature a transition from Parnassian precision to symbolic suggestiveness takes place, corresponding to the shifts within Baudelaire's *Les Fleurs du Mal*. The soulful eyes of the symbolic figure are no longer attracted by the brilliance of diamonds and gold but by the subdued shine of precious and semi-precious stones with their rich spectrum of colours and mysterious intensity.[252] Plarr's verses make it quite clear why the opal more than other gems enjoyed immense popularity at the time. In 'Opals' Arthur Symons expounds upon the symbolic meaning of the gem, but in far more detail than the poetic quality of the poem actually allows:

My soul is like this cloudy, flaming opal ring.
The fields of earth are in it, green and glimmering,
The waves of the blue sky, night's purple flower of noon,
. . .
And as the opal dies, and is reborn the same,
. . .
So must my swift soul constant to itself remain . . .[253]

All these examples of the aestheticist interest in precious stones appear in a new light if one bears in mind that parallel tendencies are noticeable in the Victorians. It is presumably as a consequence of the contemporary interest in geology shown by Ruskin as well as by ecclesiastic apologists and their opponents that C. W. King and H. Emanuel published their two authoritative Victorian works on gems and precious stones.[254] In both books scientific objectives are combined with cultic associations and historical information serving as the basis for the symbolic interpretation of the stones. For Christina Rossetti, who, to judge by her commentary on the Apocalypse (*The Face of the Deep*) and her devotional calendar of saints' days (*Called to be Saints*), was familiar both with lapidaries and with studies like those of King and Emanuel, precious stones acquire the clarity and concision of religious emblems. However, for Arthur Symons ('Opals', 'Rubies') who continues a tradition deriving from the enumerative catalogue of precious stones in *Mademoiselle de Maupin*, they become suggestive symbols of an expressive symbolism. The importance that Wilde attaches to precious stones in his description of an antique statue cannot only be attributed to *Emaux et Camées* but also to the late romantic striving for precision and strictness of form and the eclecticist delight in ornamentation:

The sculptor hewed from the marble block the great white-limbed Hermes that slept within it . . . With enamel or polished jewels he gave sight to the sightless eyes . . . All subtle arts belonged to him also. He held the gem against the revolving disk, and the amethyst became the purple couch for Adonis, and across the veined sardonyx sped Artemis with her hounds.[255]

In Pater's novel the role of the sculptor, gem-cutter and goldsmith in late romanticism receives particular emphasis. Marius sees 'that touch of the worker in metal' as the model for all art because of 'a certain firmness in outline'[256] and the skill and conscientious craftsmanship it requires. There are only three things that appeal to the protagonist in Gautier's *Mademoiselle de Maupin*: 'l'or, le marbre et la pourpre, éclat, solidité, couleur',[257] the same qualities which, in *Marius*, lead the work of the jeweller and gem-cutter to become a metaphor for the perfect literary work of art: 'Like jewellers' work! Like a myrrhine vase! admirers said of his writing.'[258] The inordinate significance of this special relationship between the arts and literature for symbolist aesthetics is further demonstrated by the imagery in Yeats's Byzantium poems; in 'Sailing to Byzantium' the art of the goldsmith is a symbol of immortality, in 'Byzantium' it is the embodiment of the aesthetic power that subjects 'all complexities of mire and blood' to the principles of order inherent in art.[259]

Rossetti, in a letter to O'Shaughnessy, praises the awakening appreciation of craftsmanship that the Elizabethans had taken for granted and considers the parallels with painting and sculpture as inspiring a new consciousness of form.[260] O'Shaughnessy himself takes up this formal aspect of the interrelationship of the arts in his remark on the cycle 'Thoughts in Marble', deriving from it the outlines of a somewhat modified theory of *l'art pour l'art*:

I wish to provide against the series of poems which I have associated with the art of sculpture being judged from an erroneous point of view. My artistic object is gained if, in them, I have kept strictly within the lines assigned to the sculptor's art, an art in which I have as yet failed to perceive either morality or immorality. They are therefore essentially thoughts in marble, or poems of form and it would therefore be unjustifiable to look in them for a sense which is not inherent in the purest Parian.[261]

Admittedly, O'Shaughnessy's poems are a rather minor literary achievement, yet they are deserving of our attention because they reflect the poet's endeavour to express experiences characteristic of the symbolist tendencies. The naked blonde beauty in 'Living Marble', whose pose and significance recall 'Les Bijoux', is contrasted with the barbarian and primitive seductiveness of the Negress in 'Black Marble'.[262] In 'Paros' the poet is represented as a sculptor,[263] and the figure described in 'Carrara' becomes the embodiment of an aesthetic spirituality:

> my effigy is grown
> Passionless, speechless through the postured stone
> That holds one changeless meaning in its pose.[264]

O'Shaughnessy's poet posing as a sculptor calls to mind the protagonist in *Mademoiselle de Maupin* for whom 'toutes ces figures de femmes' are nothing but 'symboles de couleur et de linéament'.[265] This tendency to transform women into works of art,[266] present in many writers of the age, is a mode of stylization enabling them to transcend the transience and triviality of life. The tradition lives on in a work as late as Eliot's 'La Figlia Che Piange'.

Originating in the tension between the reality of life and the ideality of art, O'Shaughnessy's poetic sculptures are a counterpart to Burne-Jones's *Pygmalion* cycle in their attempt to represent this dominant contemporary dilemma. The hero's reflections in *Mademoiselle de Maupin* leave no doubt that the image of the poet as sculptor cannot satisfactorily be explained merely in terms of the Parnassian interest in the plasticity of form:

Ce que je fais a toujours l'apparence d'un rêve . . . Les figures prennent un air surnaturel et vous regardent avec des yeux effrayants. Aussi, par une espèce de réaction instinctive, je me suis toujours désespérément cramponné à la matière, à la silhouette extérieure des choses, et j'ai donné dans l'art une très grande place à la plastique. – Je comprends parfaitement une statue, je ne comprends pas un homme; où la vie commence, je m'arrête et recule effrayé . . . Le phénomène de la vie me cause un étonnement dont je ne puis revenir.[267]

The influence of the visual arts on literature is far too complex to be reduced to the influence of sculpture alone. Numerous late romantic poets are inspired by paintings, and the effect of colour becomes a major theme and structural pattern in the poetry of the period. Two different types of colour schemes are easily distinguishable in English late romantic poetry. The clear and intense shades of the blue, gold, red and green of Pre-Raphaelite medievalism – 'At each pant shows some fiery hue / Burns gold, intensest green or blue'[268] as Woolner describes a bird in *My Beautiful Lady* – are the predominant impressions in Morris's *The Defence of Guenevere* and many poems from Swinburne[269] to Lord Douglas, Wilde, O'Shaughnessy, Wratislaw, Davidson and Yeats:

Alice the Queen, and Louise the Queen
Two damozels wearing purple and green.

In a gold and blue casket she keeps all my tears.
But my eyes are no longer blue, as in old years.[270]

While this Pre-Raphaelite colouring still persists in literary works, the attraction of more delicate colours and subtler hues is discovered under the influence of Whistler ('The Thames nocturne of blue and gold / Changed to a Harmony in grey')[271] and Conder (grey, white, yellow, gold).[272] The eclectic poets of the age have no difficulty in using both colour systems simultaneously or combining them. Quite often it is less the colours themselves that differ than their mode of integration within the context of an individual poem. The late romantic poets attached considerable importance to colour because, being a non-rational means of representation and appealing exclusively to the visual faculties, it allows for the development of new structural principles and patterning schemes.

In their assessment of the handling of colour in the works of William Morris some critics have been misled by the temptation to draw a distinction between the decorative and symbolic use of colour. If one expects an exact correspondence between a colour and the meaning ascribed to it, as expounded by Swinburne in 'Tebaldeo Tebaldei's Treatise of Noble

Morals', then all of Morris's poems seem to be 'frankly essays in colours'.[273] However, if we consider the suggestive relationship between the individual colours and their symbolic implications, a great number of the poems from the *Guenevere* volume appear in a different light. Baudelaire clearly does not have the purely decorative use of colour in mind when, in his essay 'De La Couleur', he states, 'On trouve dans la couleur l'harmonie, la mélodie et le contre-point',[274] going on to quote E. T. A. Hoffmann, in whom we find one of the sources of the tradition of colour symbolism in poetry from Morris and Swinburne to Gould Fletcher and Vernon Watkins.

J'ignore si quelque analogiste a établi solidement une gamme complète des couleurs et des sentiments, mais je me rappelle un passage d'Hoffmann qui exprime parfaitement mon idée, et qui plaira à tous ceux qui aiment sincèrement la nature: 'Ce n'est pas seulement en rêve, et dans le léger délire qui précède le sommeil, c'est encore éveillé, lorsque j'entends de la musique, que je trouve une analogie et une réunion intime entre les couleurs, les sons et les parfums.'[275]

The colours of things created are all of them virtues; thus the colour of red is love, and the colour of green is pity, and colour of purple is nobleness of mind, and the colour of blue is desire of good things, and the colour of black is heat of heart and singleness of courage, and the colour of white is the freedom of the senses and the soul, and the colour of yellow gold is the true and faithful appetite of affection which when it is once crowned will never abdicate or decay.[276]

The quoted passages outline the two major types of late romantic symbolism. Morris uses phrases like 'green hope' and 'white fear' and, like Rossetti in 'Passion and Worship' or Yeats in 'The Cap and Bells', arranges colours symmetrically to reinforce the allegorical scheme of the works: 'And one of these strange choosing cloths was blue. / Wavy and long, and one cut short and red'.[277] At the same time he strives to establish colour patterns informing the entire structure of poems in order to give them added symbolic suggestiveness.

Morris's 'Golden Wings'[278] belongs to the genre of the narrative poem or ballad, but lacks, however, a clearly defined plot. Elements of plot are only briefly brought in for the purpose of creating an atmosphere. Due to the absence of any continuous narrative, new structural principles have to be invented. Morris discovers them in a colour scheme which he implements as a leitmotif. *Gold* is suggestive of Jehane's longing for her faraway lover: 'the colour of yellow gold is the true and faithful appetite of affection'.[279] However, by occasionally using this colour in realistic descriptions ('A red roof gold-spiked over it'),[280] Morris avoids an excessively obtrusive symbolism. For the same reason *red*, the colour linked with Jehane's death as a result of unfulfilled love, does not only appear in many scenes but is developed contrapuntally against the gold theme. In one instance — the red apples at the beginning of the poem contrasting with the green ones at the end — it even acquires a positive meaning. *Green*, initially combined with red, is central to the description of the setting but loses these idyllic connotations in the course of the poem and ends up conveying negative associations. *Red-white*, the colours of Jehane's family coat-of-arms, used for pictorial effects at the beginning, gradually turns into a negative symbol, since it is her familial relationship that ultimately thwarts her union with the golden knight. *Red-white* thus becomes a second counter-theme which sets off the predominant *gold-red* motif in the style of a musical composition. Other colours (*blue*, *white*, *grey* and *yellow*) are introduced sporadically as contrasting elements and their significance can only be inferred. In the final stanza of the poem, from the whole spectrum of colours only *green* remains, a symbol of frustration and decay: 'The apples now grew green and sour; The green weeds trailing in the moat'.[281]

J. A. Symonds's 'In the Key of Blue' is an extreme example of the influence of painting on poetry and an experiment which, despite the poet's explanations, did not escape the criticism of contemporary reviewers.[282] The poem comprises seven studies on the colour blue, which, inspired by Whistler's colour arrangements, vary the basic shade by changing the complementary colours: (1) black and blue; (2) blues and white; (3) blues and brown; (4) pink and blue; (5) blues and gold; (6) blues and green; (7) blues and red. In the final section Symonds tries to depict the young Venetian who had served as his model as more than a mere accessory figure by granting him 'more actual and kindly human sympathies'.[283]

> How blue you were amid the black,
> Lighting the wave, the ebon wrack!
> The ivory pallor of your face
> Gleamed from those glowing azures back
> Against the golden gaslight; grapes
> Of dusky curls your brows embrace,
> And round you all the vast night gapes.[284]

Symonds's studies in subtly modulating hues of colour supplement the Pre-Raphaelite contribution to the late romantic genre of colour poems marked by the clustering or contrapuntal arrangement of clear colours. They also establish a link to the colour symphonies of Gould Fletcher and the delicate colour effects of the Imagist School even to be found in Pound's *Cantos*. For the problem of symbolism itself 'In the Key of Blue' is only of passing interest. In contrast to a poem like Gould Fletcher's 'Irradiations', where the vacillation between optic and acoustic perceptions, enhanced by elaborate imagery, serves as the basis for a symbolist experience of nature, Symonds's 'In the Key of Blue' seems exclusively concerned with the analogy to painting and with refined observations. However, reflecting on his experiment Symonds by chance hits upon the principle which is just the starting point for many symbolist poems:

> Nevertheless, something may still be pleaded in favour of verbal description. If it be sufficiently penetrated with emotion, it has by its very vagueness a power of suggestion which the more direct art of the painter often misses.[285]

This tradition of colour poems lives on well into the twentieth century. They generally start from a decorative pattern – 'Art begins with abstract decoration', as Wilde phrases it[286] – then, with remarkable persistence although by very different means, transcend the level of visual perception in an attempt to express the symbolist spirituality. Four poetic symphonies in white – Gautier's 'Symphonie en Blanc Majeur', Swinburne's 'Before the Mirror', Gould Fletcher's 'White Symphony' and Vernon Watkins's 'Music of Colours' can provide a general impression of the wide range of late romantic colour poems.

Gautier endows his 'Symphonie en Blanc Majeur' with a symbolic dimension from the very outset by focusing on the whiteness of the mythical 'femmes-cygnes' that, according to the 'contes du Nord', swim upon the Rhine.[287] The majority of the poem is dedicated to the description of one of these mythical women 'Qui chez nous descend quelquefois'; the series of comparisons, however, does not produce a visual effect but evokes a poetic atmosphere. With their wealth of associations (e.g. 'de quelle hostie et de quel cierge'; 'le duvet blanc de la colombe')[288] and suggestiveness ('Le vif-argent aux fleurs fantasques . . .') these comparisons lead beyond the purely external visual quality which Symonds never transcends in his impressionistic *étude*. In their allusiveness the images convincingly prepare the ground for the poem's symbolist conclusion in which the white female figure is associated with Séraphita and becomes 'la Madone des neiges' and a 'Sphinx blanc', hiding 'de blancs secrets gelés' behind the 'implacable blancheur' of her white breast.

Like Gautier in his 'Symphonie en Blanc Majeur', Swinburne in his poem 'Before the Mirror', written for Whistler's painting *The Little White Girl, Symphony in White No. 11* (1864) (Pl. 13), strives to render the impression of complete whiteness by means of metaphor, which, being a means of expression particularly suited to poetry, allows him to visualize this idea and, at the same time, to translate it into the symbolic. If the central image of the white rose – together with the snowdrop and the snow dominating this symphony in white – does not possess the

13   James MacNeill Whistler, *The Little White Girl: Symphony in White No. 11*

visual power and evocativeness so characteristic of Gautier's symphony, the intention to transpose the effect of whiteness into a symbol nonetheless remains unmistakable. In the second section where Whistler's young girl appears as the lyrical speaker, Swinburne uses the mirror − tellingly alluded to in the title − to introduce the late romantic wraith motif, changing the little girl in white found in Whistler's impressionistic painting into a symbolist portrait, embodying both self-sufficient, ethereal beauty and the melancholy experience of temporality:

> Come snow, come wind or thunder
>   High up in air,
> I watch my face, and wonder
>   At my bright hair;
> Naught else exalts or grieves
> The rose at heart, that heaves
>   With love of her own leaves and lips that pair.[289]

While the sensuous qualities of Swinburne's imagery are so weakly developed that one occasionally loses sight of the colour white as a leitmotif, quite the opposite is true of Gould Fletcher's 'White Symphony'. Here the symbolic implications are in danger of being overwhelmed by a bewildering preponderance of impressions and, in contrast to the Parnassian restraint of Gautier's poem, of dissolving into diffuse suggestiveness. Gould Fletcher obviously recognized this peril and, at the end of the first section, tries to resolve the problem by moving from the enumeration of impressions into a litany of abstract concepts. He is more successful in achieving his symbolist objectives in the final section of the poem when he contrasts the different shades of white with the darkness of the graves and the red lightning.

> Under the glare of the white-hot day,
> Under the restless wind-rakes of the winter,
> White blossom or white snow scattered,
> And beneath them, dark, the graves.
>
> Dark graves never changing,
> White dream, drifting, never changing above them:
> O that the white scroll of heaven might be rolled up,
> and the naked red lightning thrust at the smouldering earth![290]

Like Gould Fletcher but unlike Gautier and Swinburne, Vernon Watkins opens his poem 'Music of Colours − White Blossom' with realistic observations. By making these impressions the starting point for complex intellectual imagery right from the beginning, he keeps the element of realism in check even though it recurs repeatedly throughout the poem.

White blossom, white, white shell; the Nazarene
Walking in the ear; white touched by souls
Who know the music by which white is seen,
Blinding white, from strings and aureoles,
Until that is not white, seen at the two poles,
Nor white the Scythian hills, nor Marlowe's queen.[291]

Yet in all the modulations of his difficult religious and mythical imagery, which encompasses Solomon's lilies as well as the figure of Leda, the colour white remains the foundation of the symbolic structure, culminating in the contrasting image of the black swan.

From Gautier's 'Symphonie en Blanc Majeur' to Vernon Watkins's 'Music of Colours – White Blossom', colour effects are again and again connected with musical concepts, and thus bespeak the late romantic conviction in the interrelationship of all arts. These poetic expressions of the twofold relationship figure among many endeavours in all the arts to establish cross-relationships between them. Whistler is not the only artist to give his paintings musical titles. Watts calls one of his paintings *Fugue*;[292] one of Beardsley's drawings bears the title *A Nocturne of Chopin, Ballade III, Op. 47* (Pl. 14) and even carries a line of musical notation comparable in function to the texts on the canvas or frame of Pre-Raphaelite paintings. Conversely, Liszt composes musical works for paintings by Raphael and Kaulbach, and Debussy, who in turn sets Rossetti's 'The Blessed Damozel' to music,[293] also writes compositions for Japanese woodcuts (*Estampes*). Mussorgsky's *Pictures from an Exhibition* and Rachmaninov's *Etudes Tableaux* also contribute to this tradition.

Wagner, Beethoven, Schumann, Dvořák,[294] Brahms to a certain extent and above all Chopin count among those composers who on the basis either of their works or their artistic personae exerted a particular fascination on late romantic poets in England. In O'Shaughnessy's *Music and Moonlight*, Chopin and his music function as a leitmotif, which, synaesthetically fused with the descriptions of the colours and jewels of an exotic landscape, leads to an aesthetic and mystic climax. Oscar Wilde gives an account of the effect of Chopin's music on the late romantic listener[295] and Thompson explicitly establishes an analogy between the poetic works of Coleridge, Shelley, and Keats and the nocturnes of Chopin, claiming that 'such analogies between masters in the sister-arts are often interesting'.[296] In an age which found its most fitting literary genre in the mood-poem and also displayed such brilliancy and refinement of taste, the veneration of Chopin is thoroughly understandable. To judge from the countless allusions to the composer and his music, the idolization of Chopin is just as widespread as the Wagner cult. There are references to the Polish composer not only in the poetry of

Chopin. Ballade III Op 47

14   Aubrey Beardsley, *Chopin, Ballade III Op. 47*

Bourke Marston, O'Shaughnessy and Symons,[297] but even in parody form in Eliot's early poem 'Portrait of a Lady':

> We have been, let us say, to hear the latest Pole
> Transmit the Preludes, through his hair and finger-tips.[298]

Although the late romantic conception of music is unthinkable without that of the romantic tradition, it has, of course, undergone considerable modifications. Gray's poem 'Sound', which systematically tries to render the specific sounds of fifteen different musical instruments, is doubtless a *tour de force* and a typical product of the decadent delight in experimentation. The insertion of parodic music imagery in Lionel Johnson's 'A Decadent's Lyric' presupposes the timbre of late romantic spirituality: 'Ardour and agony unite; / Desire, delirium, delight':[299]

> Her body music is: and ah,
> The accords of lute and viola!
> When she and I
> Play on live limbs love's opera!

Symons's 'Music and Memory' (1891) with its carefully developed metaphorical structure, contrived synaesthesia and mannered phrasing is an equally representative example.[300]

For Yeats symbolic metaphor is the mode of poetic expression which comes nearest to perfection because it is 'the most subtle, outside of pure sound';[301] even earlier Wilde has stressed the increasing predominance of the analogy between literature and music in his theoretical writings, replacing the poetics inspired by Gautier's 'L'Art'[302] with a conception of poetry advocated by Verlaine's 'Art Poétique':[303]

Modern life is complex and relative; those are its two distinguishing notes: to render the first we require atmosphere with its subtlety of *nuances*, of suggestion, of strange perspectives; as for the second we require background. That is why sculpture has ceased to be a representative art and why music is a representative art.[304]

While the allusion to nuance calls to mind Verlaine's 'Art Poétique', the combination of literature and music seems to derive from Pater's discriminating remarks in 'Style'. Behind Pater's analogy between prose and music lies the principle discussed at length in 'The School of Giorgione', that 'all arts aspire to the condition of music' since in music the tension between form and content finds its ideal resolution. The relationship between music and poetry, like that between the visual arts and poetry, involves a variety of elements. While Pater's understanding of music in the Giorgione essay is primarily coloured by the new sense of form, in Wilde's 'The Critic as Artist' the focus is on the symbolist element in this relationship: 'This is the reason why music is the perfect type of art. Music can never reveal its ultimate secret.'[305]

In this emphasis on the 'ultimate secret', the same quality is being cited as was postulated by Poe in the term 'suggestive indefiniteness'. Not only Poe's repetition of single words and entire lines but also the refrains of many Pre-Raphaelite ballads conjure an indeterminate musical suggestiveness. The refrain, of course, constitutes a traditional element of the ballad genre, yet this fact hardly provides a full explanation for the special forms and functions it acquires in poetry from William Morris to Alfred Douglas. Together with other musical borrowings, colour patternings and the enigmatic use of precise numbers, the suggestive sound repetitions of the refrain create late romantic moods. In Morris's 'Two Red Roses Across the Moon', for instance, it is largely due to the refrain with its musical and visual elements and numerical symbolism – repeated in the title – that the ballad acquires a symbolic dimension and comes close to being a mood-poem. The slightly varied repetition of single lines in Swinburne's 'August'[306] has a similar effect:

> There were four apples on the bough,
> Half gold half red, that one might know. (stanza 1)

> There were four apples on the tree,
> Red stained through gold, that all might see. (stanza 3)

> There were four apples on the tree,
> Gold stained on red that all might see. (stanza 10, final strophe)

In the late romantic endeavours 'to take back from music what poets had lost to it'[307] rhyme and rhythm gain new significance:

> Rhyme, that exquisite echo which in the Muse's hollow hill creates and answers its own voice; Rhyme, which in the hands of the real artist becomes not merely a material element of metrical beauty, but a spiritual element of thought and passion, also, waking a new mood, it may be, or stirring a fresh train of ideas, or opening by mere sweetness and suggestion of sound some golden door at which the Imagination itself had knocked in vain.[308]

> The purpose of rhythm, it has always seemed to me, is . . . to keep us in that state of perhaps real trance, in which the mind liberated from the pressure of the will is unfolded in symbols.[309]

Besides these general, often indirect influences of music on poetry, not without significance for literary history, there are numerous music poems directly inspired by musical compositions or by musical principles and techniques, poems comparable to the picture poesies of the same period. Far more important than Payne's Wagner poems or Wratislaw's poems based on the plots of specific opera scenes[310] are verses like Payne's 'Cadences 1. (Minor); 2. (Major)' or Wratislaw's 'A Minor

Chord' which fashionably allude to the predominant mood in their musical titles. In *Airs for the Lute* Arthur Symons attempts to transpose the impression that the music of Thomas Morley and John Dowland left on him into the language of poetry, rendering the elaborate musical structures of the Elizabethan composers through rhyme schemes, versification and the deliberate selection of words.[311] Symons also makes use of musical conceptions in 'The Andante of Snakes', combining them with the snake motif in mannered imagery intended to convey the experience of beauty and repulsion, art and nature.

The most perfect fusion between music and poetry is achieved in prose poems like De Quincey's 'Dream Fugue' suggestive of musical structures. Two types of music poem can be distinguished in this category: those inspired by actual musical compositions (O'Shaughnessy, 'The Heart's Question; Chopin's Nocturne, Op. 15, No. 3'), and those masquerading as fictitious musical compositions (J. A. Symonds, 'An Improvisation on the Violin; Sonata quasi una fantasia'), constituting a parallel to descriptions of fictive paintings so popular in the period.[312] John Todhunter, a little-known and relatively minor poet, is worthy of mention in this context. In the preliminary remarks to his 'Poems on Musical Themes' published in the *Selected Poems by John Todhunter*, we find a statement that holds true not only for Todhunter's own 'Poems on Musical Themes' but for numerous contemporary music poems as well: 'These poems are not meant to be paraphrases in verse of the music that suggested them. They are merely records of a listener's moods, phantasies inspired by the emotional spirit of each composition . . .'[313]

Upon closer consideration it becomes evident that in a number of instances the affinity between the individual poem and its original source is deeper and considerably more complex than might be assumed from Todhunter's remark. While in O'Shaughnessy's 'Charmed Moments' (Chopin's Nocturne, Op. 37, No. 1) the Parnassian character of the imagery ('The sky is a brilliant enamel; / The sea is a beautiful gem')[314] does not fit the song-like simplicity of the 'Nocturne' nor the monotonous ductus of the verses do justice to Chopin's subtle agogics, in 'The River' (suggested by the Fifteenth Prelude of Chopin) Bourke Marston is more successful in translating musical structures into poetry. By reiterating the main components of the central phrase 'The river flows forever'[315] as the rhyme words in all six stanzas, he masterfully imitates the technique of musical variations and comes close to reproducing the melody of the piano piece in D flat major, Op. 28, often called the 'Raindrop' Prelude. Todhunter, in his verses for Beethoven's *Appassionata*,[316] follows the sonata as closely as is possible in another medium. From the three-part form to the individual details, he strives to find poetic equivalents, making it easy to recognize the musical source behind the introduction of the main theme and the development of the counter-theme in the first part and even in the repetition and variation of specific motifs. Compelled as a poet to envisage thematic correspondences, Todhunter identifies the first theme as the sibyl motif, the second as swan or ship motif:

> Through night's vast voiceless gloom a Sibyl cries
> To man's heart some apocalyptic word,
> Which falters on her tongue; then wailing flies
> Like an affrighted bird.
>   . . .
> Yet back she comes once more; . . .
>   . . .
> A Swan, a Royal Bark, it fights the waves
> Of sudden storm.

The same endeavour to model the poem on its musical source governs the second 'movement' which Todhunter attempts to reproduce through alterations in the tempo ('Then faster throbs'), the introduction of a new motif ('And now young spirits of joy ensky the theme') and a final reprise. His poem comes closest to Beethoven's sonata in the transition between the second and third movements, yet even in the finale the analogy is sustained:

> A judgment trumpet for the souls of men
> It seems, as now the solemn chords outring,
> Ere seeking a full close, it sinks: and then
> Discords, like sudden clash of swords encountering!

The modern reader who has difficulty approaching these late romantic imitations of music will not find it any easier to appreciate those poems presented as imaginary musical compositions. Yet from the perspective of an escapist mysticism – visible in O'Shaughnessy's 'A Duet: Piano and Violoncello' and in *Music and Moonlight* – music recommends itself as a non-conceptual medium to convey the nostalgic yearnings to transcend one's hostile and banal surroundings, to express the inexpressible and to come together with a kindred soul in a moment of ecstasy. It is for this reason that, in 'A Duet: Piano and Violoncello', two musical instruments – and not two human figures – are communicating with each other.[317]

In O'Shaughnessy's poem the influence of musical elements is restricted to thematic aspects alone. Symonds, who had meticulously attempted to translate techniques of painting into the verse of 'In the Key of Blue',[318] introduces musical structure as a principle of poetic form. He entitles one of his poems 'Tema con Variazioni', opening it with a 'Prelude' and closing it with a 'Finale', even attempting to imitate the variations in musical tempo by metrical alternation. How carefully and conscientiously Symonds works can be deduced from his handling of these musical transpositions; the central theme is only introduced in the last three of the 'Prelude's' six stanzas, immediately preceding the section entitled 'Tema':

> stanza 4: A wild swan's note of Death and Love in one.
> stanza 5: Love burned within his luminous eyes, and Death
> Had made his fluting voice so keen and high;
> stanza 6: The wail, the dirge, the dirge of Death and Love.

It is not until the first part of the main section that the theme is clearly defined. While in the 'Prelude' the pairing of love and death is intended to appear rather casual, in the four four-line stanzas of 'Tema' it becomes the main theme and is developed in parallel and contrapuntal arrangements: stanza 1 – 'Love came . . . blood-red flowers'; stanza 2 – 'Death came . . . lily white'; stanza 3 – 'Love's red, red roses fell'; . . . 'Death's lily flourished well'; stanza 4 – 'Love wept, but Death was true'. Following this order, in the ensuing five variations the first three stanzas are dominated by love, the last two by death. It would be far too time-consuming to describe the subtle and mannered musical analogies in 'Variations' in detail; this brief outline suffices to show how concerted Symonds's efforts were to transfer and imitate musical principles of composition.

Poetically speaking, Symond's music poem is perhaps as unconvincing as his colour compositions in the style of Whistler. Yet this rather sceptical evaluation should not lead us to underrate the importance of these musical poems for the development of modern poetry with its lyric masterpieces like *The Cantos* and *Four Quartets*; the techniques which essentially remain eclectic experiments for O'Shaughnessy and Symonds become integral structural components of modern poetry for the generation of Pound and Eliot, of Wallace Stevens and William Carlos Williams.

4 The imaginary landscape

In October 1855 Christina Rossetti created a poetic landscape with the revealing title 'Cobwebs' that is characteristic of the imaginary world of the English late romantics:

> It is a land with neither night nor day,
> Nor heat nor cold, nor any wind nor rain,
> Nor hills nor valleys: but one even plain
> Stretches through long unbroken miles away.[1]

This landscape cannot be described in a direct manner but only defined by an enumeration of negated elements from the real world, giving it the quality of an unreal and symbolic place ('No future hope, no fear for evermore'). The sister of the great Pre-Raphaelite obviously shares Gautier's nostalgic longing for a universe 'à part qui ne ressemble en rien / A notre monde à nous'. However, the context proves that this affinity is not attributable to a direct influence. The world Gautier designs in 'Albertus ou L'Ame et le Péché' (1832) is a Parnassian world of art 'Où tout parle aux regards, où tout est poétique, / Où l'art moderne brille à côté de l'ancien',[2] a far cry from Christina Rossetti's shadowy land of oblivion.

The sources of the imaginary landscape in such an eclectic age as the nineteenth century are as richly varied as its different forms and implications. Whether they hark back to the *locus amoenus*, the medieval *hortus conclusus* or the mythological gardens of the Renaissance, whether they favour allegorical or realistic settings, they are all subjective landscapes originating from the tendency 'of projecting moods into scenery until landscape becomes a symbol'.[3] There can be little doubt that the landscapes of the English romantics serve as the models during the period between 1832 and 1900, yet in line with the more selective late romantic taste only a limited number of these models are adopted. Blake's and Coleridge's 'construction[s] of imaginary worlds'[4] live on in the works of Poe and the French symbolists as well as in those of the Pre-Raphaelites. It is the fantasy landscape of *Alastor* and the exotic world of Coleridge's opium dreams, the romanticized gardens and bowers of the Spenserian tradition in Keats's 'Endymion' that inspire the develop-

135

ment of the imaginary landscape in late English romanticism. The following study of landscape depiction among minor poets of the nineteenth century is intended to increase our awareness of a tradition ranging from the poetry of the romantics to Eliot's 'The Waste Land', Auden's 'Paysage Moralisé' and the Byzantium poems of Yeats.[5]

The late romantic experience of time

The imaginary landscape of the late romantics arises from their specific experience of time. As early as the works of Rossetti the moment constitutes the dominant form of experience.[6] In the memory it becomes a place of refuge; in the act of experiencing, it is a 'sensuous culmination'.[7] More acutely aware of its ephemerality than its duration, Rossetti can only find a temporary oblivion in the moment: 'His frustration lay in the fact that no moment, however intense, really gave the sense of escape from self that he desired.'[8]

As a consequence of the reduction of time to single moments, poems like Rossetti's 'The Blessed Damozel' or Dobson's 'A Song of Angiola in Heaven' emphasize that the heavenly beloved experiences time quite differently from her bereaved lover left behind on earth:

> From the fixed place of Heaven she saw
> Time like a pulse shake fierce
> Through all the worlds.[9]

> And in her clear cheek's changeless red
> And sweet, unshaken speaking found
> That in this place the hours were dead,
> And Time was bound.[10]

The longing of many late romantic poets to transcend temporality through the ideality of a Pre-Raphaelite heaven or in ecstatic moments of human existence[11] results from their special relationship with the past. This experience of time is one of the reasons for the creation of distant dream worlds. Titles like 'Lost Days' (Rossetti), 'Lost Years' (Lee-Hamilton), 'Love's Lost Days' (Bourke Marston), 'The Spectre of the Past' (O'Shaughnessy) and 'Haunted Life' (Payne) point to the same problem that is later to concern the young Yeats. For him 'Words alone are certain good' because it is a 'cracked song that Chronos sings'.[12] In Rossetti's 'A Superscription' the lyric speaker – who presents himself as 'Might-have-been', 'No-more', 'Too-late', 'Farewell'[13] – embodies the relationship between a threatening past and momentary escape. It is not 'the rose-winged hours' of ecstatic love which await the lyrical self in 'The Soul's Sphere' but rather that last

Wild pageant of the accumulated past
That clangs and flashes for a drowning man.[14]

Only against the background of this particular awareness of time is it possible to appreciate the full meaning of a line like 'The peace of time wherein love dwelt',[15] which captures the essence of Swinburne's Pre-Raphaelite idyll 'August'.

In Poe's 'Dreamland' the traveller is haunted by 'Sheeted Memories of the Past', in Rossetti's 'Willowwood' the protagonist encounters 'mournful forms, for each was I or she, / The shades of those our days that had no tongue' (cf. Pl. 12) and in Austin Dobson's 'A Song of Angiola in Heaven', they are 'shrouded shapes of yesterday'.[16] William Allingham portrays the same theme without the use of personification, in a seemingly realistic scene. In 'Evening Shadows'[17] a small boy scrapes moss from a tombstone, and as the letters become visible again, he recognizes the inscription as his own name. With sad resignation the child looks into the future, the adult into the past. A similar feeling of frustration informs Bourke Marston's sonnet significantly entitled 'Buried Self'.[18] The protagonist roams through places from his past and sits down beside the grave of his own buried self, where he converses 'with other ghosts of vanished days' and enjoys the sad sweet glance of his deceased self, a sentimental and ultimately superficial pose. In the twilight of winter days the lyrical speaker ponders things past ('My Ghosts') and in Bell Scott's 'Seeking Forgetfulness' – interesting to compare with his brother's drawing *Self-Accusation* – he is hounded by a horde of forms of his past self.[19]

The range of variations on this theme is illustrated by a poem like O'Shaughnessy's 'The Great Encounter':[20]

My old aspiring self, no longer Me –
Came up against me terrible, and sought
To slay me with the dread I had to see
His sinless and exalted brow.

This depressing experience explains the late romantic yearning for timelessness. Yet the protagonist in Payne's 'Westering Hope',[21] with a symbolic gesture towards the West, admits that this can only be achieved in death.

Anglo-French parallels are as clearly identifiable in the experience of time as in the vision of imaginary landscapes. The central figure in Baudelaire's *Les Paradis Artificiels*, who already displays traits of the modern literary hero, suffers from the same painful awareness of a wasted life which afflicted his English contemporaries: '. . . nous irons . . . jusqu'à admettre des fautes anciennes, et, ce qui doit en résulter dans une nature facilement excitable, sinon des remords positifs, au moins le regret du temps profané et mal rempli'.[22]

It is under the influence of this attitude towards time that the late romantic landscape develops its characteristic features. Sidney R. Thompson's 'The Land of Might-Have-Been'[23] and J. A. Symonds's 'Oblivion'[24] are two excellent examples. In the garden with its brook of oblivion 'Where remembrance hath no sting' all transient loves and joys are assembled and transformed into flowers of an eternal spring. Besides this idyllic location shaped by escapist longings there is another, equally prevalent, type of landscape which symbolizes the threatening aspects of temporality. Payne's sonnet 'Buried Cities',[25] like Poe's 'The City in the Sea', takes up the ancient Veneta myth and depicts an eerie vision of the past. From a dream boat floating on the sea of past time, the horrifying 'cities of the past' are visible in the ocean's depths, St Elmo's fire raging in their streets in the form of the vain hopes of the lyrical self.

Arthur Symons's poem 'Laus Stellae' proves that this harrowing experience of time is not restricted to Rossetti and his Pre-Raphaelite epigones Payne and Bourke Marston. In the third section entitled 'Stellae Anima Clamat', Stella, observing her reflection in the mirror, contemplates the effects of temporality: 'Oh, what sad ghosts her mournful memory raised − / Ghosts of the days that pass and are in vain.'[26] Pre-Raphaelite influences combine with those of Baudelaire and Verlaine in the works of Symons − the well-known exponent of French literature − and of many English late romantics. A good illustration of this two-fold influence is also to be found in the first of six sonnets 'To Olive' by Lord Douglas. On the gloomy judgment day of memory 'The timid ghosts of dead forgotten days . . .'[27] appear. Since Douglas had translated numerous poems by Baudelaire − not only poems like 'Harmonie du Soir', 'Le Balcon' and 'La Beauté' but also 'Recueillement' − it seems neither possible nor appropriate to determine whether his poem derives from the English or the French tradition.

> Vois se pencher les défuntes Années,
> Sur les balcons du ciel, en robes surannées;
> Surgir du fond des eaux le Regret souriant.[28]
>
> The old lost years in worn clothes garmented
> And see regret with faintly smiling mouth.[29]

What can be ascertained is that the experience of time − regardless of any qualitative differences − is a common feature helping to explain the mutual interest of English and French literati of the age.

Although laments of the late romantics emerge from rather diverse biographical events, they find in the theme of the tragic transience of time a common pattern, as becomes apparent in the popularity of the motif from Christina Rossetti's 'Dreamland'[30] to 'The White Birds' of the young Yeats.[31] In 'Cease Smiling, Dear' from the volume *Verses* (1896), Dowson attempts to escape from the imminent threat of temporality into an idyllic garden setting: 'Here in thy garden, through the sighing boughs, / Beyond the reach of time and chance and change'.[32] The prevailing atmosphere of the prose poem 'Absinthia Taetra' in the collection *Decorations* (1899), however, is one of disillusioned resignation in the face of the terrifying yet inescapable ascendancy of time, the opening line also serving as the conclusion: 'Green to white, emerald to opal: nothing was changed'.[33]

This particular experience of time results from the consciousness of living in a decadent age. What determines the conception of time in 'L'Horloge' is the knowledge 'J'ai plus de souvenirs que si j'avais mille ans' and the ensuing nostalgia for uncultivated naiveté[34] shared by English and French authors alike, by O'Shaughnessy ('The Glorious Lady') as well as Gautier ('Melancholia' fragments):

> O then there were great sins of course;
>   Men were worse
> Some ways no doubt; at any rate
>   Men were great . . .[35]

> Ah! quelle différence, et que près de ces vieux
> Nous paraissons mesquins.[36]

At the end of a century described by Wilde – on the basis of Darwin's and Renan's criticism – as a turning-point in history, a century marked by the triumph of the 'relative spirit'[37] over established metaphysical principles, the late romantics, cast back upon temporality as the determinative human experience, are confronted with revolutionary developments in science and culture, the consequence of which we are only beginning to comprehend today. Under the impact of this crisis, the romantic idea of the organic growth and decay of culture finds its final, negative form in the late romantic feeling of decadence. As most of the English poets of the time lack the spiritual and poetic power to apply new principles of order to their world of absolute temporality, they withdraw from society and reality. But even in the seclusion of their idyllic refuges, they continue to be haunted by the 'lost Days' of their squandered or guilt-ridden past.

The garden – a favourite Pre-Raphaelite refuge

In William Morris's 'King Arthur's Tomb', a subject also known through Rossetti's painting, Launcelot thinks back upon his days of love with Guenevere: 'In the old garden life, my Guenevere / Loved to sit still among the flowers . . .'[38] Nor has Guenevere herself forgotten the 'quiet garden walled round every way' which she too perceives as a mirror of her own emotions. The garden becomes a favoured setting in Pre-Raphaelite poetry because it offers seclusion from the world within the realm of nature. This aspect holds a new fascination for poets as well as painters of the time, like Hunt, Millais and Collins, who paint out of doors in the attempt to capture the scenery as accurately as possible for their paintings.

> I was right joyful of that wall of stone
> That shut the flowers and trees up with the sky.[39]

The enclosed garden in *The Defence of Guenevere* clearly originates in the medieval *hortus conclusus*. What prompted Morris to adapt this topos was, apart from the Pre-Raphaelite longing for shelter and seclusion, the idyllic features already inherent in it in the Middle Ages. The grove where the lovers in Rossetti's 'The Blessed Damozel' hope to meet the Virgin Mary and her five handmaidens weaving 'the birth-robe for them / Who are, just born, being dead',[40] belongs to this tradition.

Between 1850 and 1900 this basic type appears in numerous variations. Occasionally, as in Symonds's 'Dreamland', with its 'cool translucent stream', it displays features of the *locus amoenus*; without exception it is a refuge from the world, a spot of peace 'For no storms assail the garden'.[41] After the idyllic grove scene in 'The Blessed Damozel' it comes as no surprise that the heroine in Dobson's 'A Song of Angiola in Heaven' (1868) also experiences heaven as 'a garden place'.[42] While it is difficult to decide whether the imaginary garden in which Rossetti and his successors hope to find the fulfilment of their erotic dreams is located in this life or the life to come, for Francis Thompson the image of the garden clearly becomes the location for a transcendental experience.

> Secret was the garden,
> Set i' the pathless awe
> Where no star its breath can draw.
> Life, that is its warden,
> Sits behind the fosse of death. Mine eyes saw not, and I saw.[43]

Distinguishing this garden from that of the Pre-Raphaelites is its relationship to Calvary (stanzas XIV and XV) and Mt Ararat (stanza XIII). Just as important as the Christian variant of the motif is the pantheist interpretation in O'Shaughnessy's *Music and Moonlight*. While Eucharis plays Chopin, her soul embarks on a mystical journey and unites with the soul of the composer. The lotus blooms and in a 'glittering inner

garden full of hues / And liquid singing'[44] a mystical union between
phoenix and aloe comes to pass, a situation which seems to anticipate the
ecstatic moment in Eliot's first quartet:

> And the pool was filled with water out of sunlight
> And the lotos rose quietly, quietly,
> The surface glittered out of heart of light.[45]

Undoubtedly the rose-garden in 'Burnt Norton' has different symbolic
implications, and a number of elements in its description (box circle and
drained pool) can readily be explained in terms of concrete events from
Eliot's own life, but the tendency to make the garden the setting for
ecstatic experiences derives from the late romantic interpretation of the
motif.

In the light of the broader literary context other Pre-Raphaelite variations of the late romantic landscape acquire new and increased importance. Particularly worthy of mention is the motif of the orchard, the
favourite Pre-Raphaelite refuge after 1850. In one of the many Pre-
Raphaelite poems in his notorious *Poems and Ballads* (1866), Swinburne
describes the place where his beloved dwells, whom he introduces as
'Madonna Mia' in the fashion of the Early Italians:

> Under green apple-boughs
> That never a storm will rouse,
> My lady hath her house
> Between two bowers.[46]

The orchard is not always painted in these pale hues. In 'August'[47]
Swinburne lends it the lavish sensuousness of Keats's autumn landscape
and through the colourful depiction of details it becomes the place where
he expects the fulfilment of his erotic dreams.

A typical example of the use of the orchard motif in the late romantic
period is the ballad 'On a Whitsunday Morn in the Month of May'. Its
author is John Orchard, a relatively unknown writer, who also produced
the 'Dialogue on Art' published in the same issue of *The Germ*. His
ballad is as revealing for the cultural background as his discourse on art
is for Victorian poetics, for Lord Thomas's decision to marry his
mother's maid on account of her chastity illustrates the idealistic system
of values as well as the changing social structures from which it arises.
At all points the poet attempts to maintain a close relationship between
the love scene and the surrounding scenery:

> He gave her a kiss, she gave him twain
> All beneath an apple tree.[48]

The orchard particularly recommended itself as a motif because it allows
for a Pre-Raphaelite depiction of nature. In Symonds's garden ('In

Dreamland') the yellow quinces – like the golden red apples in Swin-burne's 'August' – stand out luminously from the garden twilight, and the boughs of the fruit trees form a natural bower.[49] With its associa-tions of sensuous profusion, of intimacy and silence, the orchard provides the ideal framework for the erotic atmosphere peculiar to the Pre-Raphaelites: 'Save words like sighs and swimming eyes / No utter-ance they found'.[50]

If we recall the human figure lost in the vastness of Caspar David Friedrich's landscapes, it becomes clear why the Pre-Raphaelites create a landscape that offers the protection of an *intérieur*. The untenability of the romantic harmony with nature, symbolically announced in Friedrich's paintings, induces the Pre-Raphaelites to withdraw into a garden landscape that seems strangely artificial in its photographic rendering of detail and anticipates the final turn to a landscape of art. No wonder the poets of the nineties continue to employ the orchard motif. O'Sullivan uses it in a contrapuntal arrangement with the convent theme:

> The apples dropping from the trees,
> A smell of apples in the air,
> As I lay in the orchard there.
>
>   . . .
>
> Through convent casements opened wide
> There floats the praise of Holy God; –
> Of Jesus Christ who our earth trod.[51]

The whispering of the orchard, a 'soft earthvoice', becomes a symbol of temptation countering the asceticism and piety of convent life. Presumably it is this sensual trait in conjunction with the biblical allusion to the temptress with the apple which prompts Rossetti, in the fragment 'The Orchard-pit', to transform the scenery of Pre-Raphaelite idylls into a landscape of terror:

> Piled deep below the screening apple-branch
> They lie with bitter apples in their hands:
> And some are only ancient bones that blanch . . .[52]

Interesting as this variant may be, it remains an exception among the otherwise consistently positive implications of the motif. Numerous poems written in the nineties – Theodore Wratislaw's 'A Summer's Love' is a case in point – are more in line with its traditional use. The 'Summer's Love' scene is set 'Beneath green shade of apple-boughs'[53]; the poem's diction as well as the adjectives of colour and the archaisms confirm this as a typically Pre-Raphaelite refuge. In the poem with the revealing title 'Her Tryst', Wratislaw's attempts to integrate event and scenery (the lover walks 'Into her tangled orchard close') eventually lead to the rather forced metaphor 'She moved her neck and little face, / An apple on a stately tree'.[54] Wratislaw's first collection of poetry, *Love's Memorial* (1892), is quite characteristic of the literary situation in the nineties; translations of poetry by Gautier and Baudelaire appear side by side with verses inspired by the Pre-Raphaelites, illustrating how English poets endeavour to assimilate French influences without denying their own tradition.

In John Gray's *Silverpoints*, for instance, we find a similar combination of French and English influences. The volume includes translations from Baudelaire, Verlaine and Mallarmé along with poems like 'Les Demoiselles de Sauve' in which Gray continues the Pre-Raphaelite tradition ('Beautiful ladies through the orchard pass').[55] But while Gray's poem never reaches beyond the level of literary bric-à-brac, Dowson, in 'Yvonne of Brittany', succeeds in making a final and convincing contribution to the Pre-Raphaelite tradition of the orchard motif. With his flair for formal perfection, he conceals the very conscious patterning of the motif behind a pose of ballad-like naiveté. His skilful mirroring of the stages of a frustrated love through subtle changes in 'actual' and imagined orchard scenery make this poem a masterpiece of *fin de siècle* literature:

I

In your mother's apple-orchard,
Just a year ago, last spring:
Do you remember, Yvonne!
The dear trees lavishing
Rain of their starry blossoms
To make you a coronet?
. . .

IV

In the fulness of midsummer,
When the apple-bloom was shed,
Oh, brave was your surrender
Though shy the words you said.
. . .

V

In your mother's apple-orchard
It is grown too dark to stray,
There is none to chide you Yvonne!
You are over far away
There is dew on your grave grass, Yvonne![56]

The intense wish for peacefulness and freedom from the galling awareness of temporality which leads the Pre-Raphaelites to seek refuge in the
garden and under the leafy canopy of the orchard also prompts them to
search for places offering even greater seclusion, such as groves and
bowers, within their ideal landscape. These Pre-Raphaelite bowers undoubtedly derive from the bowers of Spenser and their medieval sources,
although in many of the nineteenth-century variants the affinity is difficult
to recognize. For Rossetti the bower is the place where the beloved dwells
('The Song of the Bower') and, above all, the place where the lovers meet,
far away from the perils of the world. Like many writers of the period,
Rossetti uses the designations 'bower' and 'grove' interchangeably, since
both symbolize a similar state of mind.[57] His sonnet 'Sleepless Dreams' is of
particular interest because in it the grove, a metonym for the ecstatic fulfilment of love, is contrasted with the thicket, symbolizing frustration.[58]

The Pre-Raphaelite epigones carry on their predecessors' search for a
place 'remote from the world's throng'.[59] Payne describes the scenery in
'The Light O'Love' as 'this wood-deep' and 'thick-bowered in a little
sun-screened space'.[60] The continuity in the use of the motif is evident
in the fact that both Payne and the young Swinburne refer to the
secluded bower simply as a 'place', defining it afterwards in a stylized,
Pre-Raphaelite description:

> A place of woven flowers and singing winds,
> Jewelled with moss . . .[61]

O'Sullivan's 'Serenade' is an instructive example of the motif complex
'garden – orchard – bower' and the relationship between the Pre-
Raphaelites and the poets of the nineties.

> O My Love, in this ravishing garden of dreams,
>
> . . .
>
> Under trees that are crusted with odorous gems:
> 'Tis the time to go wistfully straying,
>
> . . .
>
> We are mad for the warmth of thy body that warms,
> And a breathless embrace in the soft-cushioned bowers.[62]

The study of the scenery and landscapes in the poetry of the Pre-
Raphaelites explains why in Hughes's painting *The tryst* as well as in
many of Rossetti's symbolic portraits (e.g., *The Day Dream*, *A Sea
Spell*, *Fiammetta*) the figures do not so much appear in front of a
background of blossoms and foliage as within a bower-like *intérieur*. The
obsessive desire for shelter and protection motivating the frequent use of
the bower also leads to another variant of the motif. Besides the voluptuous, sensual mouth and soulfully deep eyes it is above all the luxuriant
hair of the Pre-Raphaelite woman that characterizes so many paintings

of the period. The sestet of Rossetti's 'Love's Lovers' illustrates the wider context surrounding the use of the hair motif, later to be so strikingly developed in the poetry of the young Yeats:

> Therefore Love's heart, my lady, hath for thee
> His bower of unimagined flower and tree:
> There kneels he now, and all-ahungered of
> Thine eyes grey-lit in shadowing hair above,
> Seals with thy mouth his immortality.[63]

For Rossetti the cascading hair of the Blessed Damozel becomes the symbol of a real or imagined encounter with the beloved ('Surely she leaned o'er me − her hair / Fell all about my face . . .'); for Dowson it is a sheltering canopy that, like the bower, serves as a refuge for the lovers:

>   Cover me
> In the deep darkness of thy falling hair:
> Fear is upon me and the memory
> Of what is all men's share.[64]

Yeats devises an astonishing number of variations of the motif in his early poetry. During the ecstatic moment in 'The Travail of Passion'[65] the erotic aspect of protective love fuses with a mystic religiosity. The request 'O women, bid the young men lay / Their heads on your knees, and drown their eyes with your hair', in his praise of the beloved[66] displays the influence of Pre-Raphaelite poses equally visible in the guilty memories of frustrated love.[67] In 'The Heart of the Woman' the beloved, yielding to passion, expresses her belief that 'The shadowy blossom of my hair / Will hide us from the bitter storm'.[68]

Interestingly, the particular combination of erotic and escapist elements characterizing the Pre-Raphaelite motif complex 'garden − orchard − bower' is also essential to the depiction of the hair motif in the early Yeats. In both the garden and the hair motif, the symbolism of refuge is tied to the special experience of time treated at the outset of this chapter. For the peace which the lyric speaker in 'He Bids his Beloved Be at Peace'[69] hopes to find for himself and his beloved under the sheltering veil of her hair is identical with the 'peace of time' which Swinburne seeks in the seclusion of his orchard bower: the transcendence of time and suffering in the moment of love.

The shadowy land

The Pre-Raphaelite landscape is not the only symbol of the late romantic tendency to flee from an oppressive reality. Very often the land of dreams itself is only vaguely outlined while the nostalgic longing to

reach it constitutes the dominant theme of the poem. Such poems of
departure are important for the understanding of late romantic symbolic
landscapes because they draw attention to the principles underlying the
many variants. Yeats's famed refrain 'I would that we were, my beloved,
white birds on the foam of the sea'[70] continues a tradition already
noticeable in Swinburne's 'Hesperia':

> Let us take to us, now that the white skies thrill with a moon
> unarisen,
> Swift horses of fear or of love, take flight and depart and not
> die.[71]

It is not the image of the bird alone which makes Christina Rossetti's
melancholy wish − 'If I had wings as hath a dove, / If I had wings that
I might fly'[72] − appear like an anticipation of the poem from Yeats's
collection *The Rose*; the impulse that induces both writers to employ this
image is the same: 'For the world's more full of weeping than you can
understand'.[73]

Occasionally the lyric speaker is seized by doubts whether a departure,
an escape into a 'green land' is at all possible: 'How should we reach it?
Let us cease from longing; let us be at peace.'[74] The idyllic orchards and
bowers, embodiments of the fulfilled Pre-Raphaelite love, would not be
an adequate setting for this experience. The late romantics are thus compelled to develop new types of symbolic landscapes better suited to the
conveyance of their hopeless yearnings, their scepticism and fatigue:

> I wish there were a fairy boat
> For you, my friend, and me.
>   . . .
> But ah where is that river
> Whose hyacinth banks descend
> Down to the sweeter lilies
> Till soft their shadows blend
> Into a watery Twilight? −
> And ah where is my friend?[75]

The wish to set out for an ideal world dominating the first stanza, a land
'where we should not care for all the past', gradually dissolves together
with the syntactic structure and the contours of the landscape in the last
stanza. Neither the poet nor the reader knows the exact location of this
river but the steady descent towards a twilight world suggests Acheron
and Lethe rather than the brooklet of the *locus amoenus*:

> Life, of thy gifts I will have none,
> My queen is that Persephone,
> By the pale marge of Acheron,
> Beyond the scope of any sun.[76]

Christina Rossetti, too, knows that land in the West 'where sunless rivers weep / Their waves into the deep'.[77] The meaningful pose in 'A Soul' – 'Her face is steadfast toward the shadowy land'[78] – is as characteristic of the poetry of the period as the expression of erotic fulfilment in a Pre-Raphaelite bower. In fact, Dowson's exhortation to depart for the realm of the dead – 'Let us go hence, somewhither strange and cold, / To Hollow Lands'[79] – seems to arise from the same desire as the withdrawal into the Pre-Raphaelite garden or fairyland, as is indicated by the fact that between 1850 and 1900 poets begin to use elements of the Pre-Raphaelite idyll to describe their land of shadows. In Lord Douglas's 'The Garden of Death', modelled on the mythological and allegorical gardens of the Spenserian tradition,[80] death appears as an embodiment of love, taking possession of all things in their first bloom to preserve their unspoiled innocence[81] and, reflecting a deep-rooted romantic anguish, to protect them from a hostile reality. In spite of being a land of autumn and the setting sun, the country visualized by Payne in 'Indian Summer'[82] is the place where love finds the consolation denied it in real life, and it appears as an idyllic landscape inscribed with the 'legend Peace'. The 'Sad but very sweet' music of golden rain captures perfectly the atmosphere of this symbolic landscape. Like Poe's 'City in the Sea', Payne's city is situated in the West.[83] Veiled hope listens to the sad murmurings of the sea while the lovelorn thoughts of the lyric speaker roam the quiet streets of this Hesperia. There is a strong note of sentimental eroticism that distinguishes Payne's city from Poe's 'strange city lying alone / far down within the dim West'[84] where the late romantic motif of the dead city first displays the features antici-pating Baudelaire's 'Rêve Parisien' and Rodenbach's *Bruges-la-Morte* as well as Christina Rossetti's 'The Dead City' and 'The City of Dreadful Night' of James Thomson.[85] In their search 'for aye some pale and shadowy land of sweet and delicate sadness'[86] the Pre-Raphaelites seem less motivated by the aspiration to an ideal than by their longing to escape from reality. The unspoken conviction that it is ultimately impossible to escape a hostile world deprives such yearnings of their élan, producing an intermediate state of sweet sadness which is equally removed from suffering and fulfilment alike. Again and again the poems circle around this sterile experience, until it becomes little more than a calculated aestheticist pose.

Significantly, in this strange state of mind the differences between sleep and death are effaced. Bourke Marston's[87] land of sleep, for in-stance, has the same features as the land of death. Conversely, Dowson's 'A Requiem' is a poem to peacefulness rather than a dirge.[88] Relatively rare are poems like O'Shaughnessy's 'The Cypress' in which the pro-tagonist, with quiet horror, imagines himself following the ivory bird into the gloomy land of the cypress.[89] The verses that Olive Custance dedicates to the strangely fascinating 'Song-Bird' seem more in line with the English late romantic ideal. The bird with the flame-coloured plumage comes 'from that grey city fair . . .', bringing a reassuring message that frees the lyric speaker from all the toils of this world.[90]

The only landscape appropriate for this experience is one of forgetfulness: 'Among the poppies by the well / Of Lethe where I weary lay'.[91] Accordingly, from Swinburne to Dowson this landscape of shadows and oblivion only displays vague contours and never acquires the highly visual qualities of the Pre-Raphaelite orchard. It is a place 'where the world is quiet',[92] 'the silent valley'.[93] Not surprisingly, James Thomson chooses the third figure – the Lady of Oblivion – in 'To Our Ladies of Death' as his patron saint. The hidden land where she prepares a place of rest for those suffering in this toilsome world is located within the same realm as Swinburne's 'Garden of Proserpine' and Dowson's 'silent valley':

> Passionless, senseless, thoughtless, let me dream
> Some ever-slumbrous, never-varying theme
> Within the shadow of thy Timeless land.[94]

The exotic landscape

'''L'un d'eux, nommé Paul, voulut me reconduire chez moi, mais je lui dis que je n'entrais pas.'' – ''Où vas tu?'' me dit-il. ''Vers l'Orient!'''[95] The Orient: this is not only the destination of Nerval's real-life or imaginary journeys but the goal of an entire movement in the cultural history of the nineteenth century. By 1835 its popularity has become so widespread that Gautier, with the self-irony of the French *homme de lettres*, defends a somewhat far-fetched metaphor in *Mademoiselle de Maupin* with the remark: 'C'est égal, nous la conservons par pur orientalisme'.[96] A common interest in exotic forms and contents explains many of the striking parallels between French and English literature. The influence of Coleridge's 'Kubla Khan', De Quincey's *The Confessions of an English Opium Eater* and Tennyson's 'The Lotos-Eaters' on Baudelaire is as well known as similar French influences on Wilde.[97]

Between 1845 and 1849 Sir Austen Henry Layard, the English archaeologist and diplomat, undertook a series of archaeological excavations in Nineveh and Baghdad. Dante Gabriel Rossetti's 'The Burden of Nineveh'[98] is only one of many examples betraying the lively interest which the English public took in the finds.[99] Although Rossetti's poem does not yet depict a symbolic landscape it is of interest since, like

Gautier's 'Nostalgies d'Obélisques',[100] it anticipates elements of exoticism not fully developed until later in the century. What connects the two otherwise so different writers in these poems is their experience of the discrepancy between the past greatness of the pagan idol or the obelisk and the banality of their present surroundings, between the richness of an exotic world and the coldness of a modern city, between the cultic significance of the monuments and the Victorian didacticism with which they are now considered.

It is this experience of difference which prompts the late romantics to choose the exotic world as one of their symbolic landscapes. After Darwin the romantic longing for ideality lingering on in the imaginatively impoverished industrial world becomes more difficult to satisfy in the spirit of Wordsworthian simplicity and the natural surroundings of the Lake District. The decadent sensibility demands more refined and complex attractions, calling for the invention of artificial or at least exotic landscapes. As demonstrated by the art world of 'Rêve Parisien' with its 'Babel' and 'des Ganges' and the imitations by Baudelaire's English admirers, the artificial and the exotic landscape have similar forms and symbolic implications:

> Orange and purple, shot with white and mauve,
> Such in a greenhouse wet with tropic heat
> One sees these delicate flowers whose parents throve
> In some Pacific island's hot retreat.
> Their ardent colours that betray the rank
> Fierce hotbed of corruption whence they rose
> Please eyes that long for stranger sweets than prank
> Wild meadow-blooms and what the garden shows.[101]

Wratislaw prefers orchids to 'wild meadow-blooms' because of their exotic origin and because they are grown 'by man's careful art'[102] ('Hothouse Flowers'), that is, because they are products of art rather than nature. In this atmosphere of cultivated exoticism they symbolize what simple meadow and garden flowers cannot convey, a condition of dangerous and beautiful decay modelled on *Les Fleurs du Mal*.

The relationship of the exotic landscape to Pre-Raphaelite scenery is not as immediately evident as its affinity with the world of art. 'The Burden of Nineveh' is, after all, the only poem by Rossetti which is directly connected with exoticism. However, in the works of the Pre-Raphaelite epigones the affinities become more clearly perceptible. In Payne's 'Light O'Love', for instance, the poet's personified days tell 'Stories of Ind and Orient skies / and of vast cities',[103] a rather unexpected occurrence in the midst of a Pre-Raphaelite setting. Lee-Hamilton's sonnet 'In the Wood of Dead Sea Fruit' depicts a forest reminiscent of Rossetti's 'Willowwood' that only bears the bitter fruit of frustrated hopes,[104] yet in the final line he contrasts it vividly with Ophir, the legendary source of King Solomon's gold and precious stones, and Golconda, once famous for its palaces, mosques and diamond-cutters, these exotic places becoming symbolic of wasted opportunities. Such a poem as Francis Thompson's 'The Mistress of Vision', already mentioned because of its juxtaposition of different types of landscape, is also interesting in this context because the beloved, who, in keeping with the Pre-Raphaelite tradition, still dwells in a bower, conjures up the exotic city of Cathay in her visionary song.

> So fearfully the sun doth sound
> Clanging up beyond Cathay;
> For the great earthquaking sunrise rolling up beyond Cathay.[105]

It is on account of their remoteness from everyday reality that the exotic world and the Pre-Raphaelite garden became favourite late romantic settings. No less important than certain functional similarities are the distinctive features of the several types of landscape. The vague contours of an indefinite land of shadows as well as the precious rendering of so-called natural details[106] suggest the poetic and spiritual insecurity of the successors to the great romantics, while the fully developed exotic landscape reflects the desire for sensuous richness. 'Dreamland', by John Barlas, marks the final stage in the replacement of the Pre-Raphaelite by the exotic dreamland:

> Hast not sailed in dreams upon a mystic river
> Through caverns, and through mountains, and through palaces?
> Seen the sun-rays fall, the moon-beams quiver,
> On the roofs of Tripolis and Fez:
> > . . .
> Or on waters, black and turbid as the Stygian,
> Ebon gloom 'mid many a square colossal shaft,
> Carved with symbols of a huge religion,
> Hideous gods that leer with hate and craft . . .[107]

At first sight, the recurrence throughout the poem of the adjective 'mystic' and the vision of a dreamland both seem to link Barlas's poem to the Pre-Raphaelite tradition. Unlike Rossetti, however, in whose works 'mystic' appears as a vague cliché signifying 'the *au delà* and the dim remote',[108] Barlas lends the word a new meaning, evoking frightening associations of cruel cults. There can be little doubt that what Barlas attempts to capture and define in the word 'mystic' is the kind of experience described by Wilde in 'The Sphinx':

> You whispered monstrous oracles into the caverns
> of his ears:

With blood of goats and blood of steers you taught
   him monstrous miracles.
White Ammon was your bedfellow! Your chamber was
   the steaming Nile!
And with your curved archaic smile you watched
   his passion come and go.[109].

The modern reader occasionally suspects that the generation of Renan placed the Christian revelation in question because they had inappropriate expectations of it. However, what remains indisputable is that rationalist criticism and apologetics alike left the deeper religious needs of the time unsatisfied. These spiritual impulses unacceptable within the framework of traditional church doctrine manifest themselves outside orthodox religion and constitute an essential element of European symbolism. Rossetti's playful experiments with religious forms are one response, Baudelaire's blasphemous inversions and negative spirituality another reaction to this problem. The horror and fascination of atrocious cults, which Wilde and his contemporaries connect with the experience of exotic worlds,[110] have to be seen within the context of these unorthodox religious aspirations. Significantly, the initiation of the speaker in O'Shaughnessy's 'The Disease of the Soul', to whom the secrets of the world are revealed through a 'mystical malady of the soul',[111] takes place in an exotic setting:

Mine were the odorous bowers
On Tiber river and Nile;
The orgies of fabulous hours . . .

The exotic landscape evoked by John Barlas is 'Dreamland' in the sense of De Quincey's nightmarish visions. As in *The Confessions of an English Opium Eater* it is the ancient, mysterious cults of Asia and Egypt and not the barbarous myths of Africa which held such a fascination for the late romantic writers:

No man can pretend that the wild, barbarous, and capricious superstitions of Africa, or of savage tribes elsewhere, affect him in the way that he is affected by the ancient, monumental, cruel, and elaborate religions of Hindostan. The mere antiquity of Asiatic things, of their institutions, histories, above all, of their mythologies etc., is so impressive, that to me the vast age of the race and name overpowers the sense of youth in the individual . . . nor can any man fail to be awed by the sanctity of the Ganges, or by the very name of the Euphrates . . . From kindred feelings, I soon brought Egypt and her gods under the same law.[112]

True to the spirit of decadence the ancientness of this foreign world is continually evoked in poems ranging from Rossetti's 'The Burden of Nineveh' and Gautier's 'Nostalgies d'Obélisques' to Wilde's 'The Sphinx':

> A thousand weary centuries are thine while I have hardly seen
> Some twenty summers cast their green for Autumn's gaudy
> liveries.[113]

Although highly exaggerated Wilde's comparison is understandable when considered as the product of a transitional age.

In De Quincey's *Confessions of an English Opium Eater* we find a plausible explanation for the frequent use of Asian scenery by late romantic authors: 'I am terrified by the modes of life, by the manner, by the barrier of utter abhorrence placed between myself and *them*, by counter-sympathies deeper than I can analyse.'[114] The phrase 'counter-sympathies deeper than I can analyse' suggests the psychoanalytical or archetypal quality of several features of the imaginary landscape, which future critics might consider worthy of further exploration. Not only does the exotic landscape symbolize the fear of the unknown; it can also become the embodiment of the striving for unlimited opportunities. Particular features in the description of the landscape show that this desire is no longer identical with the romantic yearning for infinity dominating the world of *Alastor*:

> Within, on couches rare, inlaid
> With rich mosaic blazonry
> In sandal-wood and ivory,
> Amid a rosy-tinted shade,
> And curtained with fair tapestry,
> Bright girls lay panting with their dreams . . .[115]

The sensuous opulence of the *intérieur* in Evelyn Douglas's 'The Palace of Pleasures' vividly illustrates why Wilde and his generation prefer Keats among the romantic poets.[116] At the same time it establishes a link between the English Keats tradition and certain aspects of Baudelaire and Gautier, which Wilde himself points out: 'Like Gautier, I have always been one of those "pour qui le monde visible existe".'[117] Even though in English poetry the exotic setting rarely attains the sophistication and stylization of Baudelaire's 'Rêve Parisien', the preference for the visual arts so prevalent in the literature of both countries does come to light. In O'Shaughnessy's *Music and Moonlight* the changing scenery, which gradually takes on exotic features, becomes a landscape of art where the soul of Eucharis, the pianist, is united with the soul of Chopin:

> The yellow flood grew narrow, and the shore,
> Closing steeply on them, more and more
> Loomed with tremendous temples, marble massed
> On marble, water-steps and peristyles,
> . . .

And then they entered long and winding aisles,
The amber water beating with soft stress
Slim lurid pillars, through whose long defiles
They floated: deepest luxuries and calms
Immeasurable and perfumes filled those ways.[118]

The exotic landscape can almost imperceptibly change into an equally unreal underwater landscape, a fact betraying their deeper affinities as symbols of underlying psychological or spiritual experiences. Admittedly, the 'realm in the sea' does not yet possess the qualities of a symbolic cipher for the unconscious as in the final phase of French symbolism. This is confirmed by a poem like Lee-Hamilton's 'Sunken Gold' in which sunken treasure obviously embodies frustrated hopes and missed opportunities. Nevertheless, Lee-Hamilton's attempts to create a deep-sea landscape with its associations of riches and mysterious perils remain significant as an example of the early English variants of the motif.[119]

What distinguishes Baudelaire's use of exotic motifs from that of Wilde, Barlas or Symonds is the depth of his imagination no less than his artistic discipline. In Wilde's 'The Sphinx'[120] the superficial delight in the display of exotic opulence – which Baudelaire controls by the stylizing effect of banishing all 'végétal irrégulier' – leads to the long litanies of exotic elements. Three of the five stanzas in Barlas's 'Dreamland', all introduced by the random copula 'or', never go beyond the enumeration of far-away place names (Tripoli, Fez, Nile, Ganges, China, Japan). And the attraction of the age-old culture of the Nile in Symonds's 'The Lotus-Garland of Antinous'[121] seems to lie exclusively in the opportunity it presents for displaying sensuous magnificence. The lack of reticence in the presentation of details corresponds to the apparent lack of design. Barlas doubtlessly intends the Ganges in 'Dreamland' to be more than a poeticized travel impression but this is not apparent in his mode of depiction. While in Baudelaire's 'Rêve Parisien' the plural form (Des Ganges) and the accompanying adjectives ('Insouciants et taciturnes, / Des Ganges, dans le firmament . . .')[122] have a non-realistic effect and are indicative of the symbolic function of the river image, in Barlas's poem this can only be surmised from its combination with other mystical and magic streams.

However, we should not allow these differences in quality to obscure the English and French parallels. As in Baudelaire's 'La Chevelure' and 'Parfum Exotique',[123] the encounter with the beloved in O'Shaughnessy's 'Palm Flowers'[124] evokes an exotic vision. In O'Shaughnessy's poem, too, it eventually develops into a symbolic landscape, although, contrary to Baudelaire's subtle fusion of landscape and love scene, the description seems to become autonomous and loses its symbolic suggestiveness. Quite the opposite proves true in Wratislaw's 'Frangipani': the exotic landscape conjured by the perfume is made too strictly subservient to its metaphorical function:

> Perfume! That lingerest round the throat,
> . . .
> Thou leavest on the languid skin
> . . .
> A spice of health that blossoms in
> Hot lands that tropic fragrance win
> From marvellous flowers and scented oil.[125]

'Frangipani' and 'Palm Flowers' nowhere achieve the unique combination of highly conscious form and authentic visual detail of 'Parfum Exotique', but the English poems undoubtedly share the same symbolist goals as the French masterpiece.

As the tropical scenery and other exotic motifs embody escape and infinite riches as well as danger and mystery,[126] they represent a far more comprehensive counter-world than the Pre-Raphaelite orchard or bower. In their ambiguity they mirror more complex states of mind, or – indebted to the tradition of De Quincey's *Confessions of an English Opium Eater* – suggest the enigmatic realm of the subconscious.[127] Baudelaire's 'Le Poison'[128] describes the poison flowing from the eyes of the beloved as being more potent than wine or opium, and in the 'luxe miraculeux' of its imaginary architecture goes back to the exoticism of Coleridge's 'Kubla Khan'. What Coleridge still designates a 'psychological curiosity'[129] becomes the focus of major interest for De Quincey and his successors on both sides of the Channel. As late as 1899, in one of Dowson's prose poems, the drinker, under the influence of absinthe, sees 'blue vistas of undiscovered countries, high prospects and a quiet caressing sea'.[130] To express the strangeness of exotic scenery as the effect of stimulants had become a literary fashion.[131] As Baudelaire notes, however, in *Les Paradis Artificiels*: 'le haschisch ne révèle à l'individu rien que l'individu lui-même'.[132] From this point of view, the ambiguity of the exotic landscape is seen above all as that of the late romantic imagination.

The landscape of terror

Just as the experience of time and the flight from temporality inspire the development of a characteristic type of Pre-Raphaelite refuge, the feeling of frustration, too, leads to the creation of a special kind of landscape-projection. Due to the effective Pre-Raphaelite strategies of suppression, however, it appears in only a relatively small number of poems, Rossetti's four 'Willowwood' sonnets being the best known among them. This sonnet cycle is of particular interest because it offers an insight into the techniques Rossetti employed in designing the symbolic landscape.[133] Taking up the traditional image of the willow tree, he expands and considerably modifies the emblem of forsaken love still used by Lewis Carroll ('The Willow Tree') in the manner of the old romances:

> She scarcely saw the gallant train:
> The tear-drop diamond dimmed her e'e:
> Unheard the maiden did complain
> Beneath the Willow-Tree.[134]

Christina Rossetti — although well acquainted with her brother's sequence of poems (see her poem 'An Echo from Willowwood', 1870) — in her own 'In the Willow Shade' (1882) follows the accepted and conventional usage as she had done in her earlier lines 'Under Willows' (1864):

> I sat beneath a willow tree
> Where water falls and calls . . .[135]

> Under willows among the graves
> She met her lost love, ah welladay![136]

If seen within the context of this tradition the full relevance of Rossetti's 'Willowwood' sonnets becomes clear. Through the introduction of mirror imagery the 'woodside well' acquires the character of a symbolic place where the speaker and the beloved, materializing out of the personification of love, enjoy one ecstatic moment of union. The willow trees lose their natural appearance and develop bizarre and threatening features, each flanked by the figure of a personified day from the speaker's wasted past, 'All mournful forms, for each was I or she, / The shades of those our days that had no tongue'.[137] Plants like 'tear-spurge' and 'blood-wort' with symbolic rather than botanical connotations underline the transformation of the willow-emblem into a symbolic landscape. The facial expressions of the figures ('with hollow faces burning white') roaming through the Willowwood reveal inner conflicts deeper than the sentimental pose of the 'lovelorn maid' so often found walking under willows bewailing her fate. It is not the land of death, with its promise of idyllic rest, but the realm of frustrated life, the 'Willowwood', which is the incarnation of the Pre-Raphaelite landscape of terror:

> Better all life forget her than this thing,
> That Willowwood should hold her wandering![138]

In Rossetti's poem 'The Portrait', reminiscent of 'Willowwood', the tree image once again appears more meaningful if we realize its psychological implications:

> In painting her I shrined her face
> Mid mystic trees, where light falls in
> Hardly at all . . .[139]

But the imaginery scenery of the portrait where the lyrical self has a most disconcerting encounter with 'many a shape whose name / Not itself knoweth'[140] is also the reflection of a real forest in which the self once found the fulfilment of his love. Memories of both scenes converge in a third, in which the protagonist experiences a painful epiphany:

> And as I stood there suddenly,
>   All wan with traversing the night,
>   Upon the desolate verge of light
> Yearned loud the iron-bosomed sea.[141]

The continuity of the literary tendencies from the Pre-Raphaelites through to the poets of the nineties is illustrated by Lionel Johnson's use of the willow motif. In 'A Dream' (1887) the lyric speaker, plagued by self-reproach, believes that an unhappy rival is leaving his place of rest ('Where the willowed water rounds / Each dim point with gentle grace, / Filled with windy, willow sounds')[142] in order to avenge the loss of his beloved. This idea leads to one of the transformations of the traditional motif so frequent in the period:

> The gray precincts water-worn
> Shiver at a sundering flame,
> On a vehement whirlwind borne
> Into the drear house of shame
> From the home of souls lovelorn
>
> He, love's melancholy saint
> Cloistered by the innocent plains
> Willow-bowered for true love's plaint![143]

The 'sundering flames' and 'vehement whirlwinds' provide the traditional abiding place of unhappy lovers with a spiritual dimension absent in other treatments of the motif.

Similar to Rossetti's use of the emblem of the willow, Lee-Hamilton opens a poem with the image of Sodom's apple, which, according to legend, is associated with the Dead Sea. 'The Wood of Dead Sea Fruit' evoked by this association is also related to Lake Avernus with its sinister connotations (the entrance to the underworld, grotto of the sibyl, grove of Hecate). Emerging from the water metaphor is the imagery of the

15   Giambattista Piranesi, *Carceri VII* (2nd state)

mirror, which, as in 'The Willowwood' sonnets, suggests a doubling and splitting of the personality:

> This is the pool which mirrors him who bends
> Over its stillness, such as once he was,
> Not such as now he is, in face and eyes.[144]

Lee-Hamilton's sonnet, which symbolizes the experience of frustration all too clearly, ends strikingly with the contrasting vision of two exotic places, Ophir and Golconda.

These legendary place names recall Gautier's 'architecture féerique' which, because of its richly suggestive symbolism, was particularly popular in the period:

> Dans la nature et dans l'art, je préfère, en supposant l'égalité de mérite, les choses grandes à toutes les autres, les grands animaux, les grands paysages, les grands navires, les grands hommes, les grandes femmes, les grandes églises, et, transformant comme tant d'autres, mes goûts en principes, je crois que la dimension n'est pas une considération sans importance aux yeux de la beauté.[145]

In this passage from the 'Salon de 1859' Baudelaire calls attention to a feature which characterizes many of his own poems as well as those of his contemporaries. The vision of gigantic rooms and constructions had, of course, been widespread in the visual arts since the beginnings of the romantic era and constitutes an interesting parallel to similar tendencies in literature. John Martin's *mezzotinto* illustrations to *Paradise Lost* are representative and explain why Piranesi's *Carceri* sequence (Pl. 15) exerted such fascination on his own and the following generation. Not surprisingly, it is De Quincey who establishes a connection between his own dream architectures and those of Piranesi described to him by the author of 'Kubla Khan':

> Many years ago, when I was looking over Piranesi's *Antiquities of Rome*, Coleridge, then standing by, described to me a set of plates from that artist, called his *Dreams*, and which record the scenery of his own visions during the delirium of a fever. Some of these . . . represented vast Gothic halls . . . Creeping along the sides of the walls, you perceived a staircase; and upon this, groping his way upwards, was Piranesi himself . . . and so on, until the finished stairs and the hopeless Piranesi both are lost in the upper gloom of the hall. With the same power of endless growth and selfreproduction did my architecture proceed in dreams.[146]

Dreamlike visions of colossal architectures also inform the spatial conceptions in Nerval's *Aurélia*: 'une sorte d'hôtellerie aux escaliers immenses'.[147] Its poetic expression in the fantastic journey of a mail-coach[148] through a cathedral that takes on gigantic proportions and becomes a necropolis is no less illuminating as regards the specific forms of the symbolic landscape than De Quincey's self-analysis in his *Confessions*: 'Space swelled, and was amplified to an extent of unutterable and self-repeating infinity.'[149]

Such visions of a permanently self-repeating expansion of space become the embodiment of specifically late romantic experiences. The unreal proportions of these immense sceneries underline their imaginary character. Faced with a reality determined by mechanistic and utilitarian principles, the dreamland − as a refuge − assumes gigantic dimensions. Contrary to the sublime alpine landscape, vastness and immensity no longer have an elevating effect but develop the frightening obsessive quality of the nightmare. As is so often the case, Edgar Allan Poe was one of the first to design these vast sceneries in the literature of the English-speaking world; they are characteristic of his 'Dreamland' lying beyond time and space:

> Bottomless vales and boundless floods,
> And chasms, and caves, and Titan woods,
> With forms that no man can discover
> For the dews that drip all over;
> Mountains toppling evermore
> Into seas without a shore . . .[150]

The protagonist in 'Ulalume' walks through 'an alley Titanic'[151] towards the dreadful confrontation. Apocalyptic elements of the landscape govern the evocation of imagery anticipating the desert scene in Thomson's 'The City of Dreadful Night':

> Enormous cliffs arose on either hand,
> The deep tide thundered up a league-broad strand;
> White foam belts seethed there, wan spray swept and flew;
> The sky broke, moon and stars and clouds and blue:
>   . . . on the left
> The sun arose and crowned a broad crag-cleft;
> There stopped and burned out black, except a rim,
> A bleeding eyeless socket, red and dim.[152]

Lines like these explain why James Thomson showed a particular interest in De Quincey, whose 'Suspiria de Profundis' he used as a source for his poem dealing with a similar spiritual situation ('Our Ladies of Death'). It is the vision of enormous landscapes of terror which links the two authors. Even before 'The City of Dreadful Night' Thomson evokes fantastic worlds in the prose poem 'A Lady of Sorrow'.[153]

Vast dimensions inform a very wide variety of late romantic landscapes, ranging from Evelyn Douglas's exotic countries to the shadowy land of the Pre-Raphaelite epigone Payne. The scenery in 'The Masque of Shadows'[154] with its 'white fantastic porticoes' and its colonnades

16   Thomas Cole, *The Titan's Goblet*

'prolong'd . . . / In maddening endless countlessness' has affinities not only with Thomson's city of terror[155] but also with Baudelaire's world of art.

This dreamlike expansion of space corresponds to the equally widespread preference for monumental figures, found, for example, in *The Titan's Goblet* (Pl. 16) by the American painter Thomas Cole. In the middle of a sublime mountain landscape an enormous goblet awaits the hand of a giant. The fantastic distortion is even further emphasized by the buildings at the brim of the goblet and the boats sailing on the surface of the water in it, all of which display the same proportions as the harbour lying at the foot of the mountain. Baudelaire's 'La Géante'[156] is one of the best-known examples of this phenomenon in poetry. Nerval's and Thomson's poetic adaptations of Dürer's *Melencolia* are also worthy of mention. The famous engraving of 1514 aroused considerable interest in the nineteenth century, not only as an expression of the 'naive' style which Gautier praised in the paintings of the Old German School[157] and Rossetti discovered in the Early Italians, but even more so as the embodiment of the same gloomy spirituality ('plein de rêverie et de douleur profonde')[158] that was to make 'mystic' a key word for the entire symbolist movement. Thus it comes as no surprise that the huge dream-figure in Nerval's *Aurélia* resembles the gigantic 'Mélancolie':

Un être d'une grandeur démesurée . . . il tomba enfin au milieu de la cour obscure, accrochant et froissant ses ailes le long des toits et des balustres . . . il resemblait à l'Ange de la Mélancolie, d'Albrecht Dürer.[159]

The fascination which Dürer's allegorical figure held for James Thomson is one of many indications of the English participation in the all-encompassing symbolist movement of the nineteenth century. Even in the fragment[160] which Dobell counts among Thomson's early works the poet refers to Melencolia as a colossal figure: 'She sits, a Woman like a Titaness.'[161] Her huge stature is likewise stressed in the final canto of 'The City of Dreadful Night':

An Image sits, stupendous, superhuman,
The bronze colossus of a winged Woman,
Upon a graded granite base foursquare.[162]

Comparable to the late romantic landscape itself, Melencolia, in Dürer's engraving still a well-integrated figure, grows in 'The City of Dreadful Night' to gigantic proportions, and, denying despair and the threat of time, reigns supreme over Thomson's landscape of terror:

Fronting the dreadful mysteries of Time,
Unvanquished in defeat and desolation.[163]

Monumental dimensions are an essential but not the sole stylizing feature contributing to the unreal atmosphere of the symbolic landscape. The remark made by Gautier's hero − 'J'aime ce qui dépasse les bornes ordinaires'[164] − also explains the accumulation of precious stones and metals as well as the strange petrified shapes which, together with gigantic dimensions, characterize this type of imaginary landscape:

C'est une architecture féerique qui n'a son égale que dans les contes arabes. Des entassements de colonnes, des arcades superposées, des piliers tordus en spirale, des feuillages merveilleusement découpés, des trèfles évidés, du porphyre, du jaspe, du lapis-lazuli, que sais-je, moi! des transparences et des reflets éblouissants, des profusions de pierreries étranges, des sardoines, du chrysobéril, des aigues-marines, des opales irisées, de l'azerodrach, des jets de cristal, des flambeaux à faire pâlir les étoiles, une vapeur splendide pleine de bruit et de vertige, − un luxe tout assyrien![165]

Given the contemporary penchant for exoticism the comparison with *The Arabian Nights* is hardly a coincidence. The other important point of reference, particularly as regards the precious stones, is the heavenly city of the book of Revelations.

Although the delight in precious stones characteristic of many poets of the nineties and their French masters has generally been considered a typical feature of aestheticism, a similar predilection may be discerned as early as the imaginary cities of certain Pre-Raphaelite texts. Christina Rossetti's 'The Dead City'[166] opens with a typically Pre-Raphaelite nature scene that suddenly turns into 'a desert drear and cold' where the protagonist enters 'A fair city of white stone', apparently a dead city. Strangely enough the palace towering above these uncanny surroundings is inspired by the heavenly Jerusalem of Revelations:

Golden was the turreting,
And of solid gold the base.

The great porch was ivory,
And the steps were ebony;
Diamond and chrysoprase
Set the pillars in a blaze,
Capitalled with jewelry.

At first glance the discrepancy seems to be due to the didactic intentions of the poem − the city's inhabitants have been transformed into stone statues because of their pride − but the real reason behind the usage of precious stones and metals which are normally associated with celestial beauty can only be surmised from parallels in contemporary literature. In Lee-Hamilton's sonnets 'The Wreck of Heaven' the motif has been developed more fully and carries radical connotations, which are nonetheless typical of the times:

I had a vision: naught for miles and miles
But shattered columns, shattered walls of gold,
And precious stones that from their place had roll'd, . . .
Through scattered chrysolite the blind wind moans;
And topaz moulders into earth at last.
And earth is the reality; its hue
Is brown and sad.[167]

Lee-Hamilton's sonnet sequence is keyed towards the claim that 'earth is the reality', a statement all the more remarkable in the light of the late romantic proclivity for escapism, but the detailed description of the New Jerusalem throughout two entire sonnets betrays the captivation in which the visionary city held him. This becomes even more apparent in a poem such as Bourke Marston's 'Love's Lost Pleasure-House';[168] the original religious implications of the city have disappeared, but the image of the city continues to be the setting for a Pre-Raphaelite experience of love.

Although Thomson's 'The Doom of a City' is not directly derived from the biblical source, it does display the same stylizing tendencies that prompted other writers to look back to the book of Revelation. As in Christina Rossetti's 'The Dead City' the petrification of the city-dwellers is depicted as a horrifying experience:

The whole vast sea of life about me lay,
The passionate, heaving, restless, sounding life,
. . .
Frozen into a nightmare's ghastly death.
. . .
Stark, strangled, coffined in eternal stone.[169]

For both poets the didactic aspect seems less important than the alarming impression of 'awful stillness' where 'life is frozen into a nightmare's ghastly death'. Like Christina Rossetti in her variation on the biblical passage, Thomson, too, attempts to attune the entire scenery of his poem to this situation:

Grand marble palaces and temples, crowned
With golden and radiant towers and spires,
Stood all entranced beneath that desert sky,
Based on an awful stillness.[170]

The eeriness of such lifeless and sterile magnificence recalls Baudelaire's 'Rêve Parisien', but Thomson's city does not become the embodiment of a world of art despite his ironic allusion to Keats's 'Ode on a Grecian Urn'. Having turned all humans into stone, the gods need no longer fear being harassed by their supplications:

> Lifted up from clay's corruption into marble firm and fair,
> Fear and shame and anguish stilled, every evil passion killed,
> Crooked forms and ugly faces grown transcendent works of art;
> While the grand or lovely mood of the fair and young and good
> Is beatified in beauty that can nevermore depart . . .[171]

Thomson comes as close to the European movement evident in 'Rêve Parisien' as was possible for a Victorian writer in the service of Bradlaugh's *National Reformer*. More informative for our discussion of the symbolist tradition in England than a comparison with Baudelaire's masterpiece is a brief glance at an earlier American example. Poe, like Thomson in 'The Doom of a City', does not yet develop a city of art but the same elements of stylization that lead to its final development are already clearly perceptible in 'The City in the Sea'. The strange, unreal character of this imaginary landscape is directly stated as well as being indirectly conveyed by mysterious light effects and reflections. In conjunction with aestheticist features[172] these elements produce the tension aptly evoked in the formulation 'hideously serene' which also characterizes the atmosphere of 'Rêve Parisien' and numerous poems of the period in England. The striving for a world of art reaches a climax in 'Ulalume' when Poe not only incorporates stylizing details but entire settings from Weir's paintings and Auber's ballet (*Le Lac des Fées*):

> It was hard by the dim lake of Auber,
> In the misty mid region of Weir —
> It was down by the dank tarn of Auber,
> In the ghoul-haunted woodland of Weir.[173]

All of these different landscapes have one essential feature in common: they are not related to real locations but are conceived as alternatives to reality. Their purely imaginary character allows the authors to endow them with the whole spectrum of symbolic implications. However, the following examples of the city motif demonstrate that similar effects can also be obtained by a combination of real and fictitious elements. With its lagoon and canal the city depicted in 'The City of Dreadful Night' intentionally conjures associations of Venice and is even referred to as Venice, yet the qualifying formulation 'Venice of the Black Sea'[174] indicates that it is an imaginary city on an allegorical sea. The tidal river leading to the ocean[175] is clearly reminiscent of the Thames near London, but when referred to again in canto XIX, it has become a symbolic river and 'is named the River of the Suicides'.[176] Numerous elements, including streets and bridges, cathedral and marketplace as well as certain figures (the minister or the speaker in canto VIII) gradually lose their realistic quality in the visionary atmosphere of the landscape of terror. This process begins as early as the first canto when the speaker

ponders how the city can best be described: 'The City is of Night; per-
chance of death, / But certainly of Night . . .'[177] The city, although it
disappears at night, is always present.[178] This insight develops into a
nightmare acquiring such vividness that it becomes impossible to decide
whether it is a dream or a real city.[179]

'The City of Dreadful Night' illustrates one of many possibilities for
transforming the city – a predominant aspect of nineteenth-century life
– into a symbol of states of mind.[180] This tendency is already
noticeable in Blake's *Jerusalem* where the names of contemporary London suburbs are combined with reminiscences of the Apocalypse:

> The fields from Islington to Marybone,
> To Primrose Hill and Saint John's Wood,
> Were builded over with pillars of gold;
> And there Jerusalem's pillars stood.[181]

Russell's poem 'The City'[182] proves that this was not a unique case
resulting from Blake's eccentricity. By incorporating Babylon and
Nineveh with their rich suggestiveness Russell, who sees with Blake's
eyes, transforms Dublin into the scene for moments of ecstasy.

How widespread this tendency became is demonstrated by many minor
examples of city poetry. In Le Gallienne's 'A Ballad of London' the
metropolis acquires a mythical dimension through its association with
the great and wicked cities of the past (Babylon, Rome, Sidon, Tyre):

> Paris and London, World-Flowers twain
> Wherewith the World-Tree blooms again,
> Since time hath gathered Babylon
> And withered Rome still withers on.[183]

The elaborate and mannered use of flower imagery further heightens this
effect. Realistic elements from London scenes are transformed and then
attributed to the realm of 'World-Flowers'. Thus the street lights in the
Strand are 'iron lilies', the coaches are 'like dragonflies, . . . With jewelled eyes, to catch the lover'. Even the social and moral aspect of the city
is incorporated into this imagery as a jungle-flower. From one of his
travel impressions of Venice, Arthur Symons, an adept *homme de
lettres*, devises an image of a city of art clearly modelled on 'Rêve
Parisien'.

> Water and marble and that silentness
> Which is not broken by a wheel or hoof;
>
>   . . .
> A city without joy or weariness
> Itself beholding, from itself aloof.[184]

Very often impressions become the symbol of the moods they have evoked; as a consequence, mannered images frequently tend to overwhelm the surface description of perceptions.

> The sun, a fiery orange in the air,
> Thins and discolours to a disc of tin,
>   . . .
> And, in the evil glimpses of the light,
> Men as trees walking loom through lanes of night
> Hung from the globes of some unnatural fruit.[185]

Lord Douglas, in 'Impression de Nuit, London', proceeds from light impressions that soon lead to a personification of the city; the original vision of London recurs but in a distorted form as the inner landscape of a giantess:

> And in her brain, through lanes as dark as death,
> Men creep like thoughts . . . The lamps are like pale flowers.[186]

The integration of realistic elements in the visionary landscape and the transformations of real places prove, in conjunction with the diversity of the purely imaginary scenery, that the symbolist tendencies are not limited to one kind of poetry. Indeed, their importance lies in the development of a broad spectrum of very different forms preparing the way for Yeats's Byzantium poems as well as for the apocalyptic scenery in Eliot's 'Prufrock', 'Rhapsody on a Windy Night' and 'The Waste Land'.

The allegorical landscape

Among the several nineteenth-century dream worlds, the allegorical landscape, rediscovered in connection with contemporary medievalism and the Neo-Renaissance, is of particular relevance to the symbolist movement. In accordance with their eclecticist tastes many authors turn to the most diverging sources and prototypes, adapting them in new and unconventional ways. Literary precedents are rarely as easy to identify as in Payne's 'The Garden of Adonis' with its direct allusion to 'Spencer's Faery [sic] Queene. The Legend of Britomart, VI, 29.'[187] As a link between traditional and modern allegorical sceneries (e.g. Auden), the late romantic variant is particularly deserving of attention.

The first stanza of Francis Thompson's well-known poem 'The Hound of Heaven' abounds in references to allegorical places: 'I fled Him, down the arches of the years; / I fled Him, down the labyrinthine ways / Of my own mind; / . . . Up vistaed hopes I sped; / And shot, precipitated / Adown Titanic glooms of chasmed fears.'[188] These various elements do not, however, grow into one homogeneous landscape but in all their concreteness ('I pleaded, outlaw-wise, / By many a hearted casement, curtained red, / Trellised with intertwining charities') remain components of separate allegorical situations. Even a poet like Baudelaire seldom gives an extended description of his imaginary settings, preferring to evoke them in minimal scenes. In 'La Destruction' the protagonist, led by a demon, suddenly finds himself 'au milieu / Des plaines de l'Ennui, profondes et désertes'.[189] But, while in Baudelaire the brief but suggestive allegorical sceneries serve as focal points, similar landscape elements in Thompson's poem have little or no real function and seem to arise from the same impulses which inspire the mannered imagery.

In long poems, such as Symonds's 'The Valley of Vain Desires' or James Thomson's 'The City of Dreadful Night', the same problem presents itself under a somewhat different guise. Symonds begins by explicitly stating his intention: 'This is an attempt to describe by way of allegory the attraction of vice that "fascinates and is intolerable", with its punishment of spiritual extinction or madness in this life . . .'[190] Despite such assurances it soon becomes clear that this is by no means an allegorical landscape like Bunyan's 'Slough of Despond' or 'The Doubting Castle' where all the details illustrate the underlying theme. What Symonds has created instead is a visionary landscape of terror in which certain allegorical elements contribute to the overall atmosphere and justify the poem's title. In James Thomson's 'The City of Dreadful Night' the relationship between tenor and vehicle, generally constant in traditional allegory, is marked by a peculiar vacillation. In some cantos the visual aspect of the imagery is strictly subservient to its theme; in others it takes on the suggestiveness of a symbol going far beyond its allegorical purpose. In yet other instances the reverse process takes place, the theme of the vision emerges more distinctly, and the imaginary landscape assumes the more definite shape of allegorical scenery:

> At length he pauses: a black mass in the gloom,
> A tower that merged into the heavy sky;
>   . . .
> Then turning to the right went on once more,
>   . . .
> He gazed and muttered with a hard despair,
> Here Love died, stabbed by its own worshipped pair.[191]

The wanderings of the protagonist through this scenery turn out to have an allegorical meaning, for the road upon which he follows the stranger continually turns to the right,[192] leading him in a circle. This circular movement and the clock ticking on without face or hands symbolically express the hopelessness of the situation.

Unlike these works by Thomson or Symonds with their combinations of diverse imaginary landscapes, O'Sullivan's 'The Houses of Sin' employs the allegorical landscape in a traditional sense. As in the medieval sources all allegorical locations are limited to the illustration of the theme:

> Till at a house where Avarice was writ
> In scarlet letters, he said: 'Get you in!
> This is the first house in the street of Sin . . .'[193]

O'Sullivan's verses reveal where the roots for the allegorical houses of love, life, death, sleep and dreams so prevalent in Pre-Raphaelite poetry are to be found. The house or mansion appealed to nineteenth-century authors above all because of its imaginary character which could be adapted to their own symbolist purposes. In fact, these houses were better suited than other symbolic scenery to the illustration of moral concepts and values, a goal attracting both painters of ideas like George Frederick Watts and Frederic Shields, and the Pre-Raphaelite poets. Minor Pre-Raphaelites, too, like Bourke Marston and Payne, seemingly had a predilection for these allegorical houses not only because of their medieval timbre but also because they were convenient stage props that could be put to diverse symbolist use without any undue exercise of the imagination, by simply changing the qualifying attributes.[194] In some instances the allegorical house is introduced to impart a spiritual dimension to an otherwise superficial description or, as in Olive Custance's 'Candle-Light', to give additional emphasis to a symbolic allusion:

> Roses with amber petals that arise
> Out of the purple darkness of the night
> To deck the darkened house of love.[195]

Dowson makes use of allegorical sceneries in order to keep his moods from evaporating by affixing them to one symbolic location. Unfortunately, he allows his settings too little concreteness to achieve this aim. The refrain 'By the waters of separation', [196] for example, appears in all five stanzas of 'Exile', supplying the poem with a formal pattern and a suggestive biblical ring, but not with any allegorical place that can be visualized. Very often these references to mythological or allegorical places lead to a new type of poetic diction, a tendency already beginning with *The House of Life*.[197]

Equally characteristic is the frequent combination of different types of landscape and the transition from real to allegorical scenery. Symonds's 'Anticyra',[198] for instance, is composed of several heterogeneous elements. The poem is structured around the personification of mortally wounded love, who travels through an allegorical place 'o'er the foam / Of tempest-stricken wishes!' This allegorical scene, however, is not developed much further; in its place Anticyra in Phokis is introduced, a spa popular in antiquity because of the indigenous hellebore plant and still in existence today. It is not long, though, before this real location vanishes, yielding to an imaginary landscape of peace and harmony 'on the blue billows of the mind'. The tendency of these allegorical settings to change into 'landscapes of the soul' is one of the most prominent characteristics of symbolist poetry.

The landscape of the soul

It would be contrary to the very nature of symbolism were one to insist on a strict borderline between allegorical landscapes and 'landscapes of the soul'. Instead, it is probably more rewarding to attempt a description of this type of symbolic landscape with its wide range of variations. This allows us to recognize the connection between works like Verlaine's 'Le Rossignol'[199] and Rossetti's 'Winged Hours' in which the bird metaphor informs the atmosphere and the structure of the poems.[200] It also calls attention to the affinity in the settings of otherwise such different poems as Baudelaire's 'Causerie' and Custance's 'The Inn of Dreams'.

> Mon cœur est un palais flétri par la cohue;
> On s'y soûle, on s'y tue, on s'y prend aux cheveux![201]

> My heart is like a lighted Inn that waits
> Your swift approach . . . and at the open gates
> White beauty stands and listens like a flower.[202]

Baudelaire evokes a miniature scene, exciting in its vividness and realism, while Custance chooses to place an allegorical figure in the foreground of her poem in the Pre-Raphaelite vein. However, both works share the image of the heart envisaged as symbolic scenery. The tendency not to use this scenery to render 'objective values' as in medieval allegory but to relate it to the mood of a specific lyric subject is one of the prominent features of the late romantic landscape of the soul:

> But in the secret cloisters of my soul
> A white flower sleeps upon a forest-pool.[203]

> And lead you, with wide questioning eyes,
> Within my soul's most deep alcove . . .[204]

Direct mention of the speaker's heart or soul is generally not even necessary to identify the scene as the world of inner experiences; the insertion of a possessive pronoun often suffices to mark the transition to an inner landscape or a landscape of the soul:

> Destroying waves break loud upon my strand,
> Wild winds and ruining blight infest my land:
>   . . .
> . . . my song-birds are all dead.[205]

Despite differences in quality, detail and national origin this type of imaginary landscape remains essential to symbolic representation in the late nineteenth century. A brief comparison of Rossetti's sonnet 'Nuptial Sleep' and Bourke Marston's epigonic attempt 'A Lake' is illuminating in this respect.

> Sleep sank them lower than the tide of dreams,
> And their dreams watched them sink, and slid away.[206]

> O Soul serene! like some fair placid lake
> That flows on silently 'neath day and night . . .[207]

While Bourke Marston imparts the impression of a landscape of the soul by directly addressing the soul and by devising an awkward simile, Rossetti uses the image of the floating souls to evoke an underwater landscape that in turn symbolizes the spiritual state of the lovers.

With its wealth of symbolic implications, the garden is the favoured type of landscape of the soul in the English and French literature of the period. The garden in Baudelaire's 'L'Ennemi' is undoubtedly an inner landscape even if not explicitly designated a 'garden in my soul'[208] as in Olive Custance's or Lord Douglas's poetry.

> Le tonnerre et la pluie ont fait un tel ravage
> Qu'il reste en mon jardin bien peu de fruits vermeils.[209]

> Within my soul are some mean gardens found
> Where drooped flowers are, and unsung melodies . . .[210]

Numerous gardens in the poetry of the Pre-Raphaelites and their epigones are immediately recognizable as landscapes of the soul because the lyric speaker or even the soul itself designs, plants or builds the garden, bower and 'pleasure-house' or, in another frame of mind, destroys them.

> Out of thy broken past
> Where impious feet have trod,
> Build thee a golden house august and vast.[211]

> I must pull down my palace that I built,
> Dig up the pleasure-gardens of my soul.[212]

From this limited appraisal it becomes obvious that the landscape of the soul — on the basis of its manifold variants alone — acquires special importance in the period. Alongside allegorical gardens too clearly governed by contrived ingenuity[213] to be convincing poetic contributions, we find the perfectly designed symbolic sceneries of 'Le Rossignol', 'L'Ennemi', and 'Nuptial Sleep'.

Anglo-French parallels are not only evident in the widespread popularity of the landscape of the soul but also in the tendency to create landscape metaphors. Baudelaire's 'L'Invitation au Voyage' may be considered a representative example. Since the imaginary world of this lyric poem is unquestionably a landscape of the soul, the speaker is able to compare it to his beloved: 'Au pays qui te ressemble'.[214] In line with the particular atmosphere of the poem in question Baudelaire reverts to different types of scenery.[215] A similar use of landscape imagery can be found in the francophile Symons,[216] as well as in contemporaries more strongly indebted to the English tradition. Laurence Housman, for instance, models the simile in his appeal to the dead beloved on the allegorical houses of the Pre-Raphaelites ('How like a vacant house I find you sweet')[217] while John Gray adapts the image of the Pre-Raphaelite orchard ('You are my magic orchard feof').[218] Given such affinities it is understandable why Verlaine's 'Clair de Lune' ('Votre âme est un paysage choisi'),[219] translated by Gray and O'Shaughnessy,[220] generated so much enthusiasm among the English late romantics.

Although rooted in romantic subjectivity, the landscape of the soul could only find its final expression in a late period of literary history. The replacement of romantic nature scenery by imaginary landscapes marks the first step in a development culminating in the conscious linking of these worlds with the self that designed them. Without the escapist tendencies of the Pre-Raphaelites and the poets of the nineties, the discovery of the symbolist 'world within' would be unthinkable.

5   The ideal beloved

Together with the late romantic vision of the imaginary landscape the creation of a specific type of female figure plays an important role in the transition from romanticism to modernism. It is with Poe and his Pre-Raphaelite successors that the ideal beloved acquires the features still recognizable in a character like the Laila of Robbe-Grillet's *L'Immortelle*. Once again, a comparison with parallels in other European literatures proves enlightening for our understanding of English literature during the period. Bearing in mind the collection of poetry which the Russian author Alexander Blok dedicates to his 'Lady Beautiful', the Pre-Raphaelite cult of women can no longer be considered a unique case.[1] The Seraphita motif serves as a representative example of this interrelationship.

Presumably inspired by Gautier's 'Symphonie en Blanc Majeur' or O'Shaughnessy's 'Seraphitus', Dowson discovers this type of ideal figure in Balzac's novel *Séraphita*, a work which also announces the symbolist interest in Swedenborg.[2] Gautier, in his preface to *Les Fleurs du Mal*, explicitly links Baudelaire to Balzac and his Swedenborgian theme, referring to 'la Séraphita-Séraphitus de Balzac, cette étonnante création'.[3] Thus it scarcely comes as a surprise that the 'Seraphita' sonnet counts as one of the three poems by Dowson that Stefan George translated into German. The international significance of the movement is confirmed by Hofmannsthal's early essays on Swinburne and Pater and the idealized woman of the late romantics,[4] who lived on in the ironic music-hall performance of the Barrison sisters, with their complicated and strange child-like appeal so typical of the Beardsley generation.[5]

Moreover, these essays call attention to various elements inherent in the female symbolic figure participating in this broader European tendency. In his Swinburne essay, Hofmannsthal emphasizes artificiality as the woman's outstanding trait, indicating an inner affinity between figures such as Rossetti's Blessed Damozel and Pater's Mona Lisa:

It is due to the sophisticated and unique appeal of this technique that it keeps reminding us of works of art and that its very subject matter is a beauty stylized and transfigured by art: the beloved is dressed in the glorious colours of the Song of Solomon, with fantastic attributes, which mysteriously and so cleverly instil the eeriness of love into the soul. . . . or the beloved is painted as the childlike masters of the Quattrocento paint her, sitting on a small narrow bed, with a short-stringed lute in her delicate fingers or a red and green psalter: or she appears standing in the dark like the white women in Burne-Jones with pale foreheads and opaline eyes.[6]

Balzac's — and after him Dowson's — Séraphitas not only share features of the hermaphrodite[7] but also of the madonna. More surprisingly perhaps, even the *femme fatale* seems to be related to this female cult figure although her relationship to her less scandalous sister has so far gone unnoticed. Nevertheless, their concurrent appearance in numerous works of the period — Swinburne's 'Dolores' and 'Hesperia', Rossetti's 'Soul's Beauty' and 'Body's Beauty', for instance — already suggests their basic complementarity as figures symbolizing psychological or spiritual longings.

The *femme fatale* as symbolic figure

The central figure in James Thomson's 'A Lady of Sorrow', 'in obedience to subtle inward impulses, or perhaps to imperious agencies from without, which she can neither resist nor control, is perpetually suffering transformation'.[8] These metamorphoses reflect the multiplicity of her symbolic nature. In the first section the Lady of Sorrow resembles Rossetti's Blessed Damozel,[9] but only as long as the lyrical self 'was found worthy to be comforted with angelic communion'[10] does she appear to him in the glory of transfiguration. In the second section, assuming the character of a *femme fatale*, she turns herself into a siren, luring the protagonist into the labyrinthian depths of the sea and, as in Swinburne, taking the form of a panther.[11]

After Praz's detailed analysis of the psychological impulses governing the *femme fatale* type, a possible next step would be to study her as a symbolic form. Swinburne and O'Shaughnessy, like their French contemporaries, exhibit a striking preference for figures that have acquired a certain literary notoriety:

> O all ye Messalinas of old time —
> Ye Helens, Cleopatras, ye Dalilahs,
> Ye Maries, ye Lucrezias, Catharinas — [12]

This enumeration in O'Shaughnessy's 'A Troth for Eternity', somewhat amusing to a modern reader, is doubtless intended to lend a new dimension to the purely temporal situation of a jealous lover conversing with his knife before murdering his beloved.[13] It is the intention to make the *femme fatale* a symbol of general psychological impulses that prompts many authors, including O'Shaughnessy (*An Epic of Women*)[14] and

Swinburne ('The Masque of Queen Bersabe'), to design entire sequences of closely related symbolic portraits. The montage in Pater's famous portrait of Mona Lisa can also be explained in these terms: 'And as Leda, / Was the mother of Helen of Troy / And, as St Anne, / Was the mother of Mary'.[15] Above all, the clever handling of the mythological and Christian analogy furnishes the prose poem which opened Yeats's anthology with the essential quality of a symbolic portrait. A similar technique is noticeable in the envoi of Swinburne's 'A Ballad of Life', where the writer endows the Pre-Raphaelite vision of a medieval lady[16] with the *femme fatale* associations of the name Borgia. His miracle play 'The Masque of Queen Bersabe' illustrates the interplay of diverging stylizing tendencies. Together with notorious temptresses (Herodias, Cleopatra, Messalina), Swinburne cites exotic names (Aholibah, Abihail, Azubah, Aholah, Ahinoam, Atarah, etc.) full of vague suggestiveness.

The forms and stylistic devices employed in the creation of symbolic portraits are many and varied. In 'Faustine', Swinburne, with a sado-masochistic flair typical of the times, imparts a mythical aura to an already legendary figure. Thomson ('The City of Dreadful Night') falls back upon a work of art − Dürer's *Melencolia* − for inspiration, yet, by integrating it into a new scenic context of monumental proportions, invests it with symbolic implications fundamentally different from its original meaning. Visions of Circe, Eva-Lilith and Loreley fuse in Rossetti's fragment 'The Orchard-pit'; 'the ravishing eyes of Death' as opposed to 'Life's eyes . . . gleaming from her forehead fair' conjure memories of grotesque allegorical artworks from the Renaissance but at the same time confirm that this is very much a new type of symbolic figure in its own right.[17]

English as well as French poets often employ similar techniques to achieve this effect. Like Baudelaire,[18] Swinburne compares his *femme fatale* to the madonna and, following the tradition of Mariolatry, addresses Dolores as 'Our Lady of Pain' and Hesperia as 'Our Lady of Sleep'.[19] In 'The Destroying Angel' Arthur Symons stresses the quasi-religious traits of the *femme fatale* popular with many symbolist writers.[20] Even with a minor poet like Wratislaw the adaptation of religious elements is obviously not just a mannered or bizarre pose, but an attempt to express a new spirituality through the inversion of orthodox beliefs.

> Lilith or Eve, I was before the flood,
> And Eden grew the palace of my sin
> > . . .
> Kissing my mouth he saw that ill was good,
> Lust was Love's brother, Vice to Virtue kin.[21]

Such unorthodox religious ideas inform the conception that the mythical woman has been individually created by God (O'Shaughnessy, 'Creation')[22] or is herself divine in nature: 'For thou art eternal beyond dispute, infernal / A fair Woman with no heart in her great eyes, / As all day thou sittest at thy silvern mirror, / Alone in the great skies'.[23] Reminiscent of Rossetti's symbolic portraits, she embodies godlike self-sufficiency. Silently brooding, lost in the contemplation of her own beauty, she combs her hair before the mirror while all things pass by her reflection unnoticed. The precious stones with which Plarr adorns the figure have an allegorical meaning ('each stone is sentient, and half human, / A passion or crime')[24] and underline her symbolic character. In their sterile beauty they reinforce the impression that the goddess, like a statue, observes the islanders' suffering with rigid indifference.

O'Shaughnessy's poem 'To a Young Murderess' is of greater interest to a modern critic for its stylizing elements than its perverse content, so fashionable at the time:[25]

> Fair yellow murderess, whose gilded head
> Gleaming with deaths; whose deadly body white,
> Writ o'er with secret records of the dead . . .[26]

The diction, the unnatural colour of hair and body and, above all, the emphasis on inner tension ('her tranquil eyes, that hide the dead from sight') all suggest the treachery and inhuman quality characterizing so many symbolic figures of the period. Gautier's 'Caerulei Oculi' conveys the siren's artificiality through the Latin title, mannered imagery and numerous literary allusions,[27] a tendency beginning in Poe's 'Ulalume' where imaginary landscapes are evoked by references to works of art.

A brief discussion of the Helen of Troy motif offers supplementary examples of stylistic devices found in portrayals of the *femme fatale*. Her vampire-like appearance, identified by Praz in the Helens of Moreau, Samain or Pascoli,[28] is not the only striking feature of the type. Another aspect comes to light in Rossetti's ballad 'Troy Town'; here the two-part refrain and the central image 'heart's desire' repeated in the fourth line of each stanza, the diction as well as the rhyming techniques, all contribute to the sense of pseudo-medieval naiveté appropriate to the poem's basic situation.[29] As in 'The Blessed Damozel' the tension between erotic subject-matter and idealizing form evokes a peculiar atmosphere of artificiality:

> See my breast, how like it is;
> > (*O Troy Town!*)
> See it bare for the air to kiss!
> Is the cup to thy heart's desire?

> O for the breast, O make it his!
>   (*O Troy's down,*
>   *Tall Troy's on fire!*)[30]

The *femme fatale* motif is kept in the background while interest is focused on an erotic ritual, Helen imploring Venus in mannered language to grant the fulfilment of her love. The forced analogy in the imagery contrasts with the very intentional simplicity in the flow of the verses.

> Each twin breast is an apple sweet.
>   (*O Troy Town!*)
> Once an apple stirred the beat . . .

Swinburne had already objected to such representation of the best-known *femme fatale* figure in connection with Rossetti's painting *Helen of Troy* (1863), where, except for a few details, 'there is little to suggest that "daughter of the gods divinely fair" for whom the towers of Ilium were sacked'.[31] Her preciosity notwithstanding, Rossetti's Helen clearly belongs within the tradition; a similar case is that of the esoteric Pre-Raphaelite beauty in 'Eden Bower' who is no less a *femme fatale* than Lilith, the 'stunner' of 'Body's Beauty'.[32]

It is typical of the national variations of this European movement, which achieved its maturest expression in French literature, that the English poets choose to concentrate on minor events in their treatment of the Helen motif. O'Shaughnessy, for instance, depicts the love and the ensuing catastrophe as a memory of the heroine who now longs to return to Lacedaemon and, in characteristic Pre-Raphaelite manner, suffers under the weight of the past.

> She looked upon the great sea rolled between
> Herself and Lacedaemon: but the Past,
> The sins and all the falseness that had been
> Seemed like an ocean deeper and more vast.[33]

Wilde's 'Serenade', in a certain sense a pendant piece to 'Troy Town', focuses too on a minor incident, Paris waiting for Helen to flee with him. The same medievalism that is present in Rossetti's ballad[34] gives Wilde's Helen an air of artificial naiveté absent from Symons's description modelled on French examples.

> For any woman to endure:
> That beauty and that heavy hair,
> That flesh so pure to the impure,
> The impure that mock her in the streets
> And follow her to the market-place.
> O Helen of the sensual heats . . .[35]

The English literary variations on the *femme fatale* motif are neither as scandalous nor as widespread as those in France. Apart from a few obvious instances based on the authors' biographies (Swinburne) or Francophile inclinations (Symons, Wratislaw, etc.), the *femme fatale* is a less characteristic trait of English aestheticism than the ideal beloved.

Despite the persona Wilde carefully cultivated as a Parisian *homme de lettres*, 'The New Helen' and many other works seem more obviously indebted to the English tradition than to French influences. Unlike the medieval atmosphere in 'Troy Town' and 'Serenade' which gives rise to the artificial quality Hofmannsthal had noticed in Swinburne, the stylizing elements in 'The New Helen' are used to transform the Homeric heroine into a symbolic figure. The rhetorical questions at the outset prepare for her final apotheosis, achieved by means of the imagery, the use of legendary or mythical places names and by various literary allusions.[36] This transfiguration is intricately planned and implemented in the Helen–Venus montage and the imagery from Marian litanies ('Lily of love, pure and inviolate! Tower of ivory! red rose of fire!'). Although certain aspects of the *femme fatale* motif continue to be perceptible, the figure is no longer the exclusive embodiment of lust but now also 'The incarnate spirit of spiritual love'.

While the poem itself is hardly convincing, Wilde's conscious intention to portray Helen as a symbol of spiritual love sheds considerable light on poems such as Yeats's 'The Rose of the World'.[37] As in Pater's portrait of Mona Lisa, the symbolic nature of Yeats's heroine, already suggested by the title, is underscored by the combination of figures from different mythological spheres: in Pater's case, classical antiquity and the Bible, in that of Yeats, classical antiquity and Irish mythology. The traditional features of the *femme fatale*, particularly the sexual aspects so strongly emphasized during the nineteenth century, disappear almost completely, while the spiritual implications gain in prominence. A similar development is visible in Yeats's 'The Sorrow of Love', a poem clearly related to 'The Rose of the World' through the metaphor of 'red mournful lips'.[38] The introduction of the Helen figure in the second of the three stanzas illustrates her central role. In the title and the image of the 'red mournful lips' the eroticism of the original motif lingers on, but the enigmatic young woman is not, strictly speaking, a *femme fatale*. Instead she embodies the awareness of the tragic threat which is inherent in beauty and essential to human existence.

The ideal beloved: the biographical background

In the ideal beloved, a type of stylized portrayal which enjoyed greater popularity in England than the *femme fatale* did, literary and biographical elements co-exist in a peculiar fusion. Rossetti's 'The Blessed Damozel' is an excellent example of the interaction between literary and real influences. The first version of the poem, the Pierpont Morgan Ms. of 1847, was written long before his relationship with Elisabeth Siddal and her tragic death, and can therefore be exclusively attributed to literary sources like the Early Italians. Later versions, however, include more and more biographical details, making it virtually impossible to distinguish between 'poetic myth'[39] and biography, between fiction and reality. In this respect 'The Blessed Damozel' is by no means an isolated case. Several other works in the same period, marked by a similar literary patterning of biographical elements, suggest that this is but another expression of the inclination for aestheticist poses and symbolic portraits.

Among the unpublished treasures of the Bodleian library is the manuscript of a translation of Novalis's 'Hymnen an die Nacht' made by James Thomson B.V. in 1865. Even if we take into consideration Thomson's particular interest in foreign poetry, his preoccupation with Novalis seems rather puzzling. Thomson presumably came across the name of the German romantic in Carlyle's 'Novalis' essay of 1829 but then pursued further studies on his own.[40] Because of his role as a cultural mediator, Carlyle evidently felt compelled to introduce this 'mystical German' to English-speaking readers, although the 'veiled, almost enigmatic character'[41] of Novalis's works always remained foreign to him. Thomson was obviously motivated by deeper impulses than the urge to broaden his literary background, since Carlyle's essay on the mystic German romantic could scarcely have made him attractive to a Victorian follower of the radical reformer Bradlaugh. There can be no doubt that the reason behind Thomson's fascination with Novalis is the biographical parallel. Thomson, whose child bride (Matilda Weller) died at the tender age of fourteen, clearly saw an analogy between his own situation and Novalis's relationship to Sophie von Kühn. The English writer's obsession with the biographical parallel – despite Carlyle's criticism[42] – is evidenced in the anagram Vanolis (Novalis) which he combines with an allusion to his idol Shelley (Bysshe) in the pseudonym B.V. and, above all, in the idealizing vision of the beloved in his works.

In the brief introduction to his Novalis translation we find ample evidence of Thomson's intentions to transform Sophie (Matilda) into a stylized symbolic figure along the lines of the contemporary Beatrice cult:

Written by Novalis (Friedrich von Hardenberg) in the August of 1797, when he was in his twenty-sixth year, about six months after the death of his Beatrice,

Sophie von Kühn, who died when just fifteen years old. She was his betrothed: he first met her when she was about thirteen.[43]

Thomson's personal relationship to Matilda Weller, whom he met in Ireland in 1851 and whose early death in 1853 so completely shattered him that he refers to it repeatedly throughout his literary career, cannot be exclusively evaluated in terms of straightforward literary biography.[44] Indeed, it is not the loss of the beloved while still a child, but rather the fact that Novalis and Thomson transform their relationships to the deceased beloved into a cult, which is significant for literary history. Similar tendencies are noticeable in the works of E. A. Poe, Dante Gabriel Rossetti, and Ruskin.

The night celebrated by Novalis in his hymns brings back his beloved. In the ecstatic vision of the night the lover's spirit sees her transfigured face.[45] Thomson depicts the same theme in another cycle, 'Four Points in a Life' (1858). In the stillness of the night the eyes of the dead beloved follow the lover, penetrating with their purifying effect the 'cavernous darkness'[46] of his soul.[47] Although the second poem is entitled 'Marriage', this union remains a dream which can only be fulfilled in his fervently awaited death ('Parting'). In the fourth poem of the cycle the lover already believes that he is 'At Death's Door' and, as in Novalis's 'Hymnen an die Nacht', is allowed a glimpse of the heavenly splendour. Like Rossetti's Blessed Damozel, Thomson's beloved appears in her full glory. Thinking about her abiding in heaven, the lover asks himself, in 'Mater Tenebrarum', the disconcerting question: '. . . is her soul as her body which long / Has mouldered away in the dust . . .?'[48] The motif of the dead beloved necessarily raises the question of immortality. Although the lover reassures himself that the pure soul of his deceased beloved is immortal, the underlying question is no less agonizing than the one which the lyric speaker asks the raven in Poe's famous poem.[49]

It is in 'Vane's Story' that Thomson has dealt with the motif of the dead beloved in the greatest detail. This poem has long been judged an uneven and unconvincing work by critics because they have not taken the numerous allusions to Heinrich Heine into account. Closer analysis confirms that Thomson does indeed imitate the ironic, often farcical, style with which he was well acquainted in the poetry of the German.[50] Again like Rossetti's Blessed Damozel, Thomson's dead beloved is worried about her imperfect lover still revelling in the 'slough of sin', and she asks him: 'And have you no firm trust in God . . . ?'[51] He answers in the mocking tone of Heine's poems, indicating that he is not anxious to enter heaven, '. . . that bland *beau monde* the sky / Whose upper circles are so high'.[52] In her reply, however, the beloved takes up the same tone and laughs at Vane's anti-religious remarks. In some instances the dead beloved appears as a pert and cheerful maiden, in others, as a Pre-Raphaelite saint whose kiss resembles a cultic gesture rather than an expression of earthly love.

Of major importance for the tradition of the dead beloved is Thomson's endeavour to translate his relationship to Matilda Weller into symbolic language. Even in 'Vane's Story', a work marked by Heine's influence and literary allusions, alternating between visionary and burlesque features, the same tendencies are visible as in 'The City of Dreadful Night', where the transformation of biographical material achieves the form most characteristic of Thomson's art, becoming part of an allegorical scene. In the desert from canto IV of 'The City of Dreadful Night', the protagonist encounters a woman carrying a lamp. Upon her appearance, the refrain 'no hope could have no fear',[53] thus far repeated without alteration, undergoes a decisive change: 'Hope travailed with such fear',[54] and the reader is prompted to interpret the woman as an allegorical figure, perhaps that of hope. At the same time, the self divides into two halves, one looking on as the other is embraced by the woman and carried off into the sea. The beloved has been transformed into a symbolic figure in this scene and 'takes with her when she parts from him his better half, leaving only the worse alive on earth'.[55]

Given this idealization of the beloved by Thomson, the cult which Ruskin created around Rose La Touche no longer appears as a simple coincidence. Similar to the montage technique used in symbolic portraits, Ruskin draws upon a number of different sources to achieve the stylization of his former drawing pupil. Rose's refusal to greet him seems prefigured in the scene from the *Vita Nuova* painted by Rossetti; the *Roman de la Rose* served as his other great model since it enabled him to establish the etymological implications of the name Rose in the medieval style. Ruskin's identification of Rose with the St Ursula of Carpaccio typifies the aestheticist tendency to represent the beloved as a saintlike symbolic portrait. The uncanny mixture of the typological and the pathological in Ruskin's effort to subject life to literary patterns becomes apparent from his autobiographical remark: 'I went crazy about St Ursula and the other saints . . . But the doctors know nothing either of St Ursula or St Kate, or St Lachesis – and not much else of anything worth knowing.'[56] Taken at face value such a remark can be explained as an attempt by Ruskin to prove his soundness of mind as well as to articulate his deep-rooted aversion to the modern science which placed his anachronistic world-view in question. What his doctors – and a number of modern literary critics – failed to recognize, however, is that the Rose–St Ursula cult is simply another manifestation of Ruskin's emblematic tendencies previously mentioned in conjunction with the nineteenth-century evolution of the symbol. From his late lecture 'The

Pleasures of Truth', the connection between the stylization of the real beloved and the contemporary typological tastes and — even more importantly as regards symbolist form — the relationship to the litany-like arrangements and the montage technique in Pater's portrayal of Mona Lisa become strikingly evident.

No one knows who she is or where she lived. She is Persephone at rest below the earth; she is Proserpine at play above the ground. She is Ursula, the gentlest and the rudest of little bears; a type in that, perhaps of the moss rose, or of the rose spinosissima, with its rough little buds. She is in England, in Cologne, in Venice, in Rome, in eternity living everywhere, dying everywhere, the most intangible yet the most practical of all saints . . .[57]

The nineties see the continuation of the most diverse modes of stylization ranging from the young Yeats's cult of women to Lionel Johnson's adaptation of archaic forms. Johnson's 'The Last Music' is not an elegy on the death of an actual beloved one but an aesthetic *étude* in the elegaic tradition.[58] The entire situation — the idealization of the long-dead beloved and the attitude of the speaker who assumes the pose of the mourning lover — is fictitious and contributes to the evocation of an elegiac mood. Dowson's 'Adelaide' poems, on the other hand, are based on the idealization of a real person. Although in the eyes of many of the poet's friends the 12-year-old Adelaide Foltinowicz, a restaurant-keeper's daughter, was 'a most infelicitous Laura or Stella', Dowson approaches her, in Symons's words, with 'a sort of virginal devotion, as to a Madonna'.[59] It is of considerable relevance to the question of English symbolism that Yeats, in 'The Trembling of the Veil', touches upon this tendency towards stylization in connection with Dowson's religiosity.

Dowson's poetry shows how sincerely he felt the fascination of religion, but his religion had certainly no dogmatic outline, being but a desire for a condition of virginal ecstasy. If it is true, as Arthur Symons, his very close friend, has written, that he loved the restaurant-keeper's daughter for her youth, one may be also certain that he sought from religion some similar quality, something of that which the angels find who move perpetually, as Swedenborg has said, towards the dayspring of their youth.[60]

The child

What the previous examples of stylized portrayals all have in common, be they biographical or literary in nature, is the childlike quality of the ideal beloved.[61] Historically speaking, the late romantic cult of the child[62] is derived, of course, from the romantic ideal of the child as we find it in the works of Blake and Wordsworth. A direct link can be traced back from Wilde's interpretation of Christ as the precursor of romanticism because 'He took children as the type of what people should try to become'[63] to Wordsworth's vision of the child as 'Seer blest! / On whom those truths do rest / Which we are toiling all our lives to find'.[64] Francis Thompson's essay on Shelley illustrates the late romantic variation as well as the continuity of the theme:

> We of this selfconscious incredulous generation, sentimentalize our children, analyse our children, think we are endowed with a special capacity to sympathize and identify ourselves with children; we play at being children. And the result is that we are not more child-like, but our children are less child-like . . . Know you what it is to be a child? . . . it is
>
> > To see a world in a grain of sand,
> > And a heaven in a wild flower . . .[65]

Although the author still cites Blake's memorable lines, his comparison of the contemporary cult of children with the idyllic tendencies of 'effete French society before the Revolution' reveals that with the evolving sensibility in the nineteenth century the implications of the child as a literary motif have also undergone fundamental changes. What separates Thompson's own *Poems on Children* from Blake's *Songs of Innocence* is not only the decadent consciousness and idealist urges of his generation but also the prior systematic study of children by the Victorians and the ensuing loss of immediacy. Thompson refuses to see that the shift in emphasis he so ardently espouses remains within the scope of the very movement he criticizes. The development of the child motif is ultimately subject to a fatal dialectic; its conscious use as a counter-symbol increasingly divests it of the emotional and spiritual impulses it is intended to embody.

In 'Poems on Children', which opened the collection of Thompson's poetry published in 1893, various aspects of this problem come to light. The childlike beloved in 'Daisy' appears hand in hand with the personification of Innocence, and the speaker assumes the pose of a child: 'Two children did we stray and talk / Wise, idle, childish things'.[66] 'Wise' is a typical Pre-Raphaelite concept and designates the curious combination of artificial naiveté and profundity so often expressed in the deep, 'soulful' eyes of Rossetti's and Burne-Jones's figures. The number and nature of the love tokens[67] also suggest the contrived simplicity and ballad-like archaisms of the Pre-Raphaelites. At the very moment when this love approaches fulfilment, the face of the beloved takes on that well-known, Pre-Raphaelite expression of simultaneous wistfulness and pensiveness, which accompanies the withdrawal from the actuality of the present to a nostalgic no man's land: 'She looked a little wistfully, / Then went her sunshine way'. The scene is characteristic of the Pre-

Raphaelite tension between eroticism and repressive idealistic counter-forces.

In 'The Poppy' the impossibility of a union is evident from the very beginning. Between his hands and those of the child the speaker senses 'twenty withered years'.[68] The flower which the child bride gives to him can be none other than the poppy symbolizing dream or oblivion. To understand these poems fully it seems appropriate to recall the biographical background, Thompson's relationship to the children in the Meynell family. Subconscious yearnings, in part directed towards the mother and beyond any hope of realization for Thompson, are expressed in the playful, uncle-like pose ('I am but, my sweet, your foster-lover').[69] Occasionally the erotic element is completely absent in his representation of the child motif; for example, in the pseudo-naive idyll of heaven, 'The Making of Viola',[70] or in 'To Monica Thought Dying', a poem closely related to the motif of the dying child so popular in the nineteenth century.[71]

The complex assimilation of half-articulated wishes, inhibitions and compensations is reflected in a poem like 'To Olivia'. Here the lyric speaker longs to love her, but his *fin de siècle* consciousness warns him: 'Love's the ambassador of loss'.[72] His assertion 'I fear to love thee' can similarly be explained in terms of the guilt complexes in Pre-Raphaelite poetry that intensify into an agonizing experience of depravity in the nineties. The innocent child as ideal beloved represents a kind of complement and counterweight to the desires and anxieties embodied in the *femme fatale*.

In the second section of 'Sister Songs', a poem abounding in mannerisms, the underlying reasons for the late-nineteenth-century modification of the child motif come to light. Once again, the basic situation is the poet's guilty pose known from 'To Olivia': 'how . . . shall I come / To plead in my defence / For loving thee at all', yet here it is his plight as an aestheticist poet rejected by the rest of the world that serves as an explanation: 'I who can scarcely speak my fellows' speech, / Love their love, or mine own love to them teach; / A bastard barred from their inheritance'.[73] The image of the birds, which only sing as long as they have not achieved the fulfilment of their yearnings, suggests why he is destined to remain alone.[74] The child bride – in this respect comparable to the hermaphrodite motif – symbolizes a love not endangered by its possible consummation. For this reason the poet is able to envision the Meynells' daughter as the incarnation of that 'bodiless paramour'[75] who, simultaneously present and distant, evokes the ambivalent state of love and sorrow informing poetry such as his own.

'Sister Songs' also demonstrates the complementary relationship between the *femme fatale* or Medusa[76] and the child bride, the two polar figures of the late romantic vision of woman. The fact that the image of woman appears split in this way would seem not only to indicate male sexual inhibitions but also the more complex social and cultural disturbances of the period as well.

Dowson's poems addressed to his child bride again raise the question of real and stylized biographical elements. A number of remarks made by Yeats and other contemporaries place Dowson's Adelaide-cult in its proper perspective: 'he was full of sexual desire . . . Sober, he would look at no other woman, it was said, but drunk, desired whatever woman chance brought, clean or dirty.'[77] His sexual drives produce guilt feelings which are repressed and later superseded by the vision of the beloved.[78] The sentimentality inherent in Dowson's poems on and to children confirms what a disastrous effect this erotic conflict has on the late romantic sensibility. Dowson, like Ruskin, watches the child mature and 'the glory of her childhood change'[79] with considerable alarm. A fear of the end to the idyll is common to these two authors, otherwise so different:

> Little lady of my heart
> Just a little longer
> Be a child: then, we will part
> Ere this love grow stronger.[80]

The close connection between the realm of shadows and the erotic atmosphere of the Pre-Raphaelite garden corresponds to the tendency to link the death motif and the motif of the child bride. Death, which preserves the child from defilement by life, also redeems the weary *fin de siècle* self from his guilt-ridden life.

The different variations of the child motif reflect the diverging aspects of the late romantic sensibility. While the naive tone in Olive Custance's 'Mélisande' together with the death motif allows for a specifically aestheticist blend of eroticism and mysticism,[81] Lionel Johnson recognizes in his 3-year-old cousin, whom he calls 'A queen of lilied Arcady, / Or Lady of Hesperides', the opportunity to transfigure poetically a banal reality:

> The ugliness and uproar seem
> To soften, at a child's pure dream.[82]

We should not forget, however, that in Lionel Johnson's case it is his carefully cultivated decadent attitude[83] which leads him to admire the child and which distinguishes his 'Lines to a Lady upon Her Third Birthday' from Wordsworth's 'Characteristics of a Child Three Years Old'. Behind Johnson's celebration of the child's naiveté lies his conviction 'That life is a ritual'.[84]

At this point, parallels in *Marius the Epicurean* also come to mind. For Pater, too, the child embodies 'a perpetual age of gold',[85] producing an elevating effect on even the simplest of parents by introducing them to 'the world's refinement'.

I see daily, in fine weather, a child like a delicate nosegay, running to meet the rudest of brickmakers as he comes from work. She is not at all afraid to hang upon his rough hand: and through her, he reaches out to, he makes his own, something from that strange region, so distant from him, yet so real, of the world's refinement.[86]

This aestheticist aspect can only be fully understood within the broader philosophical context, well demonstrated in the twenty-sixth chapter of the novel where Pater again takes up the child motif. The funeral scene during which one of the children from Cecilia's household is buried reveals that the generation that discovered the child as a touching symbol of its aspirations was aware that such hopes are vain illusions. The child, who on an earlier occasion had been erroneously supposed dead, had inspired a reawakening of religious belief in the small community 'through the light of mere physical life glowing there again'. But now the child is truly dead. Although the other children push away the grave-diggers, chanting the psalm *Laudate Pueri Dominum*, for Marius the scene represents 'The failure of some lately born hope or purpose of his own . . . he felt that he too had had to-day his funeral of a little child.'[87]

The dead beloved

'What pleasure, what happiness proffers thy Life, that can outweigh the ecstasies of Death? Does not all which inspires us wear the hue of Night?'[88] This quotation, taken from Thomson's translation of Novalis, reveals that a fascination with death characterizes both romantic and late romantic literature. Nerval's *Aurélia* (1854–5), a work in which the death and burial of the beloved inspire the lover's mystic visions, exemplifies the French parallels. In 'Love in Tears' Vincent O'Sullivan portrays the situation so typical of the period 'where I for my dead love did sadly crave'.[89] Another of his poems, 'The Voice of the Winds', offers a general impression of the wide range of variations and implications associated with this theme. The bereaved lover asks each of the four winds the same fateful question concerning the whereabouts of the deceased beloved, as in Poe's 'The Raven', and receives four different answers. Quite often a flair for the macabre merges with a tendency for idealization in the depiction of the dead beloved:

In cheerless churchyard by crumbling tomb –
Dank and heavy and fraught with gloom –
She stands . . .[90]

The best-known formulation of this theme is, of course, Poe's: 'The death, then, of a beautiful woman is, unquestionably, the most poetical topic in the world – and equally it is beyond doubt that the lips best suited for such a topic are those of a bereaved lover.'[91] The first version of 'Romance' (1831) provides one possible explanation why 'the death of a beautiful woman . . . is . . . the most poetical topic in the world'. Here major aspects of the late romantic sensibility come together in the theme of the deceased beloved: 'I could not love except where death / Was mingling his with Beauty's breath'.[92] Poe's intense preoccupation with this issue in his theoretical and literary works anticipates Pater, who sees, in the 'desire of beauty quickened by the sense of death',[93] the essence of 'aesthetic poetry'. The same endeavour to transfigure reality which inspired the creation of imaginary landscapes motivates the contemporary preference for the motif of the dead beloved:

Of that transfigured world this new poetry takes possession, and sublimates beyond it another still fainter and more spectral, which is literally an artificial 'earthly paradise' . . . The secret of the enjoyment of it is that inversion of homesickness known to some, that incurable thirst for the sense of escape, which no actual form of life satisfies, no poetry even, if it be merely simple and spontaneous.[94]

As the title of O'Sullivan's 'The Verge' indicates, it is an extreme situation in which the poem's speaker here encounters his beloved. The midnight atmosphere of terror[95] seems the appropriate setting for his despair, yet when the beloved bends down to kiss her mourning lover, the ominous clouds vanish. Obviously modelled on Poe,[96] the experience is characterized by a combination of apparently contradictory features. The formulation 'terribly serene', reminiscent of the phrase 'hideously serene' in Poe's 'The City in the Sea', captures the new tension between spiritual and aesthetic elements which culminates in Baudelaire's negative religiosity and his *esthétique du laid*. In Arthur Symons's 'The Flames of Hell', a poem which marks the final stage of this development, the polarities beauty – death / beauty – sin appear with the deliberateness of shock effects:

Dead women, be my brides once more. Not Death
Shall be more amorous of you . . .[97]

Poems like Allingham's 'The Pale Image' or the section 'Of My Lady in Death' in Woolner's *My Beautiful Lady* are considerably more typical of the English branch of the movement. After giving a detailed description of the beloved on her bier, Allingham warns the lover: 'If you feed your loving eyes / . . . She shall come in deathly guise . . .'[98]

The horror and fascination of death, expressed in the *revenant* conception and made popular in Poe's 'Ligeia', are as characteristic of the dead beloved motif as the hope to be reunited with a 'Blessed Damozel'. In O'Shaughnessy's 'The Disease of the Soul' the speaker's narcissistic description of his ecstatic reunion with 'phantom loves' displays the aestheticist assimilation of originally heterogeneous elements:

> Its wan sad oval is fair,
> With each fallen angel's despair,
> And my lips have the languid complexion
> Of the phantom loves that they kiss.[99]

Considering the emphasis that Woolner, in the poem on his lady, places on an idyllic nature scene depicted with a Pre-Raphaelite attention to detail, the abrupt transition from the fulfilment of love to the death of the beloved comes as a surprise. If, however, the Pre-Raphaelites are seen within the framework of the late romantic movement, the fusion of an aestheticist idealization with the vision of death and decay ceases to be incongruous: 'My day-dreams hovered round her brow; / Now o'er its perfect forms / Go softly real worms'.[100] The fact that this ambivalent state of perfect beauty and horror is already a characteristic of Poe's ideal beloved confirms the significance of the American writer for literary history. His true achievement lies not so much in authentic poetic masterpieces as in the expression of a new sensitivity. 'Leonore' and 'The Sleeper' as well as 'Ulalume' and Thompson's 'Memorat Memoria' are all situated within this tradition. In Francis Thompson's poem, the encounter with a beloved of the *revenant* type turns into a confrontation with his guilty past. The shadowy figure of the girl[101] provokes the hero's self-accusation of having caused her division into the two figures of her past and present existence. In Dowson's treatment of the Ligeia theme the shadow of the dead Cynara[102] prevents the new love from coming to fruition, and in Thomson's 'The City of Dreadful Night' the cult image of the beloved absorbs the mourner's erotic devotion:

> The Lady of the images: supine,
> Deathstill, lifesweet, with folded palms she lay:
> And kneeling there as at a sacred shrine
> A young man wan and worn who seemed to pray . . .[103]

The penchant for sentimental self-observation and the melancholy delight in mourning a lost ideal lead the speaker to reflect further on the adopted pose:

> I kneel here patient as thou liest there;
> As patient as a statue carved in stone,
> Of adoration and eternal grief.[104]

The liturgical arrangement of the scene betrays the same sense of drama found in Rossetti's *Dante's Dream* and many other Pre-Raphaelite paintings.[105] The moving pose of the beloved on her bier and the display of 'soulful' and 'intense' emotions go a long way in explaining why the motif enjoyed such immense popularity.

> Now she is dead: her hands that wove in spells
> Around my life, my soul, my every sense,
> Are folded to her breast in soft pretence
> Of piety . . .[106]

From Swinburne through to Lionel Johnson,[107] the statuesque postures of the dead beloved and her mourning lover[108] symbolically express Poe's fusion of beauty and sadness. The transition from a cult of love to a cult of death[109] comes easily to the speaker in Swinburne's 'A Ballad of Death' because both are stylizing tendencies. Poems like Yeats's 'He Wishes His Beloved Were Dead'[110] confirm the deeper affinity between these apparent opposites. The lover's rather unusual wish arises from the symbolist desire for ideality; in death the imperfect traits of the beloved disappear and only her haloed icon remains. Yeats's emphasis on the redeeming qualities of death shows how closely he is related to the tradition well known through Rossetti's 'The Blessed Damozel' with its recourse to Dante and the other Early Italians.

The painful awareness of the elusiveness of ideal love also prompted Christina Rossetti to use the motif of the dead beloved in several of her poems. Her poem 'To the End'[111] closely approaches her brother's famous 'Blessed Damozel'. In her idyllic serenity the sainted heroine symbolizes the same escapism as that embodied in the Pre-Raphaelite land of shadows.[112] Although Christina Rossetti's poems do not count among Wilde's most important sources, a poem like 'Requiescat' could not have been written without her precedent:

> Tread lightly, she is near
>   Under the snow,
> Speak gently, she can hear
>   The daisies grow.[113]

As early as 1880, Harry Quilter, who criticizes Rossetti and his friends for their indifference to major problems of the times,[114] also recognizes the dead beloved as a dominant theme in the Pre-Raphaelites' poetry: 'Love interrupted by death is the main subject of the majority of the poems, sometimes even love dreaming of a possible reunion beyond the

grave.' The abundance of such poems as well as the range of their
sources strongly suggests that this theme reflects a more general spiritual
experience. The Early Italians constitute only one, although perhaps
the best-known source. Laurence Housman bases 'The Voice of the
Beloved' on the *revenant* type from the folk ballad;[115] James Thomson
models biographical events on Novalis' literary work 'Hymnen an die
Nacht'; Payne transforms the motif into a maudlin Victorian family idyll
('Hallow-Tide').[116] As can be seen from Le Gallienne's 'Love Platonic',
the pessimistic conviction that love can only be fulfilled in death, which
already informs Rossetti's *House of Life*, continues to be predominant
during the nineties:

> And the bright babe Death gave the Love he mated
> Shall leap to light and kiss the weeping past.[117]

Ironically enough, within this development, death loses its horror. Its
macabre traits are either subdued in the aesthetic fusion with beauty or
disappear completely. Death not only has a stylizing effect, it is itself
represented in a stylized manner.[118]

Admittedly, many of the cited poems do little more than document a
contemporary fashion, which itself is nonetheless of significance as
it reveals the spiritual concerns of the period. Thompson's view of
Christianity is too one-sided and the motif too widespread among non-
religious writers for him to be convincing in his attempt to derive the
dead beloved from the Christian tradition.[119] His argumentation,
however, opens new perspectives for the interpretation of otherwise
bewildering poems, like Dowson's 'Chansons Sans Paroles'.[120] The
transition from natural to liturgical imagery in many of these poems ('Is
the wood's heart, / And the fragrant pine, / Incense, and a shrine / Of
her coming?')[121] prepares the way for the redemptive experience with
which the poem reaches its climax.

The madonna

The almost indiscernible transfiguration of the dead beloved into the
madonna as well as the affinity with the child bride confirms the interrelationship of different aspects of the ideal woman. The encounter with
the deceased beloved in Dowson's 'Chansons Sans Paroles' is marked by
the same combination of erotic and religious elements found in his
rendering of the Seraphita motif so popular in European symbolism. In
the 'Seraphita' sonnet (the poem 'Seraphita-Seraphitus' published by
Flower constitutes a preliminary, though a minor study on the theme),
the ideality of the heroine informs the structure of the entire work.
Amidst the misery of the speaker's earthly existence, which is contrasted

with the 'serenity of thine abiding-place' in the octave, a reunion with the angelic figure seems an impossibility. Not until his downfall depicted in the sestet, 'when the storm is highest, and the thunders blare, / And sea and sky are riven', does he implore her to come to his assistance. During the course of the sonnet Seraphita undergoes a startling transformation; while the mystical union for which the lover yearns in the octave is distinctly erotic in nature, in the sestet he envisages the beloved in the protective attitude of a madonna:

> . . . O moon of all my night!
> Stoop down but once in pity of my great despair . . .[122]

This feature, recognizable in numerous poems including 'Vain Hope' and 'Impenitentia Ultima',[123] would be difficult to interpret were it not for the pronounced late romantic interest in Marian poetry. It is, of course, possible to account for poems like Francis Thompson's 'The Passion of Mary', 'Lines for a Drawing of Our Lady of the Night', 'Assumpta Maria' and 'Grace of the Way',[124] or the sonnet 'Our Lady of France'[125] by the convert Lionel Johnson, with references to the authors' Roman Catholicism. However, there are also similar poems by Dante Gabriel Rossetti (e.g. 'Ave'), not to mention Poe's 'Catholic Hymn' and Wratislaw's 'A Litany', 'Ave Maris Stella', 'Songs to Elizabeth'. The Marian poetry by Catholics and non-Catholics alike depicts the same basic situation: a suffering and outcast male speaker beseeches the ideal female figure to intercede on his behalf:

> Hear us at last, O Mary Queen!
> Into our shadow bend thy face . . .[126]

> Out of the cavern of my sin and pain
> My soul turns toward thee, star, my star, again.[127]

The inner affinity between late romantic Marian poetry and the symbolist preference for the madonna as the ideal female is not only visible in Arthur Symons's quasi-religious poems such as 'Mater Liliarum',[128] but also in the interest he shows for Verlaine's veneration of the Virgin Mary (e.g. 'Je ne veux plus aimer que ma Mère Marie') in *The Symbolist Movement in Literature*: '[Verlaine] abased himself before the immaculate purity of the Virgin.'[129] Many other writers, by no means as devout as Verlaine, turn to the figure of the Virgin Mary as a literary subject, prompting Henry Adams in *Mont-Saint-Michel and Chartres* and *The Education* (chapter xxv) to conceive of her as the embodiment of an archetypal pattern and to point out her relevance in cultural history. Earlier, in Gautier's oft-cited novel *Mademoiselle de Maupin*, the feminization of the late romantic world-view reflected in the madonna type is interpreted as one of the great cultural upheavals brought about by Christianity.[130]

La femme est devenue le symbole de la beauté morale et physique: l'homme est réellement déchu du jour où le petit enfant est né à Bethléem. La femme est la reine de la création; les étoiles se joignent en couronne sur sa tête, le croissant de la lune se fait une gloire de s'arrondir sous son pied.[131]

Nerval's blending of the Blessed Virgin with other mythical figures is typical of the period; the Christian connotations lose part of their original implications and St Mary is reduced to the female ideal. Thus Isis appears to him 'sous la figure de la Vénus antique, parfois aussi sous les traits de la Vierge des chrétiens'.[132]

Il me semblait que la déesse m'apparaissait, me disant: 'Je suis la même que Marie, la même que ta mère, la même aussi que sous toutes les formes tu as toujours aimée.'[133]

Her role as a madonna becomes more obvious in the novel's concluding vision where she not only grants forgiveness to the protagonist but – as is similarly implied in Dowson's 'Chansons Sans Paroles' – to the entire world.

Once again it is De Quincey who, acting as transmitter of cultural influences, introduces the beloved as madonna into English literature. In one of his 'Prose Phantasies' in the collection 'Suspiria de Profundis' he personifies the three sorrows, who stand in mysterious rapport with the goddess Levana, as 'Our Ladies of Sorrow' and explicitly designates the first, 'Mater Lachrymarum', a 'Madonna'.[134] James Thomson uses De Quincey's work as a source for his poem 'To Our Ladies of Death', retaining both the number of allegorical figures (three) and their madonna-like nature. These secularized madonnas share a sinister, almost demonic character with Swinburne's Dolores, 'Our Lady of Pain', and, like the *femme fatale*, constitute inversions of the ideal mother figure. Thomson's 'Mater Tenebrarum' demonstrates how the younger sister from De Quincey's prose work has fulfilled the demand of the 'Mater Lachrymarum', 'Suffer not woman and her tenderness to sit near him in his darkness';[135] she has deprived him of his child bride, whom he invokes in the same imploring tone as the lover in Dowson's 'Seraphita':

In the endless night, from my bed, where sleepless in anguish I lie,
I startle the stillness and gloom with a bitter and strong cry;
O Love! O Belovèd long lost! come down from thy Heaven above,
                    . . .
Or come as thou art, with thy sanctitude, triumph and bliss . . .[136]

The first section of Thomson's prose poem 'A Lady of Sorrow' depicts the granting of these supplications; just as in Rossetti's 'The Blessed Damozel', the beloved appears as patron saint, and, modelled on Beatrice, takes her lover by the hand and leads him through heaven. As in Rossetti's poem, as well as his sister's 'To the End',[137] Thomson's transfigured beloved still yearns for the unredeemed lover she has left behind on earth.[138] The striking similarity between so many details in the works of such different authors confirms that they are a product of the same late romantic sentiment: what these poems by Rossetti, Thomson and their contemporaries strive for is not the embodiment of a traditional metaphysics, but the expression of a new spirituality. Of course, it is far easier to capture this phenomenon *in abstracto* than in all its iridescent manifestations. A comparison of Francis Thompson's and Walter Pater's differentiations between Christianity and classical antiquity, a topic of much lively discussion due to the neo-hellenistic tendencies of the age, sheds a new light on the matter.

Both writers participate in the same movement, illustrating two different but related aspects in their outlooks, and both refer to one of its fundamental problems. In his criticism of neo-hellenistic tendencies, the Catholic Thompson sets out by contrasting ancient love lyrics with modern love poetry: 'compare the ancient erotic poets, delighting in the figure and bodily charms of their mistresses, with the modern love-poets, whose first care is to dwell on the heavenly breathings of their ladies' faces'.[139] The soulful eyes of the Pre-Raphaelite woman lead him to emphasize 'the indifference of the ancient singers to what in our estimation is the most lovely and important feature in woman, the eye!' Without regard for the essential differences between such poets as Dante and Rossetti, he explains ideal love as exclusively rooted in Christian ideas: 'The distance between Catullus and the *Vita Nuova*, between Ovid and the *House of Life*, can be measured only by Christianity.'[140] The love cult of the Early Italians unquestionably presupposes a Christian world-view, yet to interpret the *Vita Nuova* or *The House of Life* as typically Christian works requires Thompson's peculiar *fin de siècle* Catholicism, which ignores the radical differences between Rossetti's aestheticist cult of 'virginity' (Pl. 17)[141] − and the orthodox Christian concept of love. Even poems like 'A Carrier Song', 'Scala Jacobi Portaque Eburnea' and 'The Mistress of Vision' cause the modern reader to wonder whether Thompson's mystical religiosity stems from Christian belief or from a late romantic urge for ideality.

Pater, like Thompson, proceeds from the difference between classical antiquity and the Christian Middle Ages which he, too, views as the base for the development of a cult of love related to that of the Pre-Raphaelites. Although his position only represents a slight shift in

17   Dante Gabriel Rossetti, *The Girlhood of Mary Virgin*

accent, it is nonetheless revealing as regards 'aesthetic poetry' that Pater, the ritualist, so clearly distances himself from Thompson, the aestheticist Catholic. Provençal poetry, in his opinion, is 'a rival religion with a new rival cultus'. What the cult of love adopts from Christianity, according to Pater, is not its essence, as Thompson maintains, but its stance. Pater obviously has in mind the kind of attitude that ultimately leads to the development of the quasi-religious figure of the madonna in the aesthetic poetry of the period.

> The earthly love enters, and becomes a prolonged somnambulism. Of religion it learns the art of directing towards an unseen object sentiments whose natural direction is towards objects of sense.[142]

It is clear that poems like Woolner's 'My Beautiful Lady' and Rossetti's 'The Blessed Damozel' are typical rather than exceptional. In fact, parallels are also to be found in French literature. Gautier's 'Melancholia' fragment, for instance, displays surprisingly Pre-Raphaelite tastes; Italian Renaissance painting is rejected in favour of Dürer and the Early Italians: 'J'en excepte pourtant Cimabue, Giotto, / et les maîtres pisans du vieux Campo-Santo'.[143] Gautier's poetic reflections demonstrate that Rossetti's 'Blessed Damozel' belongs not just to the English Pre-Raphaelite School but also to an international movement extending from Gautier to Maeterlinck:

> J'aime les vieux tableaux de l'école allemande:
> Les vierges sur fond d'or aux doux yeux en amande.
> . . .
> Tout ce peuple mystique au front grave, à l'œil calme,
> Qui prie incessamment dans les missels ouverts,
> Et rayonne au milieu des lointains bleus et verts.[144]

While it is seemingly by chance that Gautier discovers in such paintings this type of stylized woman with her captivating air of religious innocence, O'Shaughnessy intentionally returns to the world of art as a source of inspiration. His clever introduction of a naive element at the beginning of *Epic of Women* creates an atmosphere of artificiality corresponding to the basic tendency for stylization evident in 'The Glorious Lady':

> I see you with the face they paint
>   For some saint
>   . . .
> Just such a saint as should have saved
>   My own soul.[145]

The striving to transcend one's own temporality through a madonna-like symbolic figure is the central theme in Rossetti's 'The Blessed Damozel',[146] O'Shaughnessy's 'The Glorious Lady'[147] and Dobson's 'A Song of Angiola in Heaven'.[148]

Another feature characteristic of the transfiguration of the beloved into a madonna is the use of elevating cosmic imagery, well known from the tradition of songs and poems in praise of the Virgin Mary:

> So high that looking downward thence
> She scarce could see the sun.[149]

> And lo, the Woman that these make
> Is more than flower, and sun, and skies![150]

> Whose soul looks downward from above
> Exalted stars, . . .[151]

> But know your hair was bound and wound
> About the stars and moon and sun.[152]

The recurring medieval features are the most striking devices of stylization and clearly establish the madonna-like beloved as an identifiable literary type. O'Shaughnessy, who describes his glorious lady folding her hands in a medieval manner,[153] suggests in his epigraph 'La gloriosa donna della mia mente' (cf. also Wilde's title 'La Bella Donna Della Mia Mente') where to find the source for this 'bella donna'. Rossetti and his contemporaries saw in Dante's *Vita Nuova* and the saints of medieval paintings[154] images of purity and perfection not in an orthodox religious but in an aestheticist sense. Just as the Virgin Mary acts as the mediator between her divine son and the sinner afraid to address him directly, the ideal beloved promises 'I'll take his hand and go with him / To the deep wells of light'.[155] This aspect acquires particular emphasis in the section 'My Lady's Voice from Heaven' in Woolner's poem: 'His message through my lips He sent / And on thy path His glory went / To guide thee to the blessed'.[156] In its fusion of the spiritual and the erotic, the icon of the madonna-like beloved constitutes an attempt to exorcize the Manichaean fear of the body. The ambiguity of the motif, however, indicates that the Victorian tension between an idealistic moral code and the demands of the flesh could not be convincingly overcome through the aestheticist compromise.

The same agonizing conviction that all erotic experience hovers between sexual excess and ideal love, reflected in the polarized types of the *femme fatale* and the madonna, also informs 'The Ballad of the Sinful Lover'. Le Gallienne accounts for the fact that the lover − like the speaker in Dowson's 'Cynara' − satisfies his sexual drives in a rather direct way ('he herded with the swine'), by reference to his grief over the death of the beloved. Consequently, the saintly beloved turns away from her 'sinful lover', symbolically illustrating the implicit themes of depravity and guilt:

> 'I know thee not', the saint replied,
> 'Thy sorrow is all changed to sin';
> And, moving towards a golden door,
> She turned away, and entered in.[157]

It is virtually impossible to determine how far 'The Ballad of the Sinful Lover' or the self-reproaches in Nerval's *Aurélia* are governed by a Christian understanding of sin: 'Je comprends, me dis-je, j'ai préféré la créature au créateur; j'ai déifié mon amour et j'ai adoré, selon les rites païens, celle dont le dernier soupir a été consacré au Christ.'[158] What many representations of the ideal and distant beloved reflect is a serious metaphysical and cultural dilemma, even though it is frequently concealed behind the mannered language of courtly love, as in Bourke Marston's sonnet 'Love's Yearning':

> Prayers have I, but no God, at need to call.
> Then in the absence of all Deity,
> Still show me, love, how I may serve thee best.[159]

The idealization of the beloved as a madonna entails another stylization: that of the bereaved earthly lover as someone — in the words of Psalm 130 — 'Crying out of the depths unto thee', the decisive difference being that these lovers do not cry unto the Lord but to their 'sainted' beloved. Bourke Marston's 'De Profundis' closely follows the psalm; Baudelaire, Thomson, Payne, Symons and others discover in this psalm a cultic source helping them to pattern their own experiences.

> Out of the depth, love, have I called to thee . . .[160]

> J'implore ta pitié, Toi, l'unique que j'aime,
> Du fond du gouffre obscur où mon cœur est tombé.[161]

The fact that these writers are all attracted by this particular psalm demonstrates that they are affected by the same cultural crisis, regardless whether, as in Johnson's case, it leads to conversion, or, as with Wilde[162] and others, to a secularized cultic pose. The same tendencies inherent in the cult of the beloved as a madonna are evident in Johnson's 'De Profundis'; the lover no longer dares to approach God directly and pleads for the intercession of the 'White Angels around Christ'. His way of imagining God's response to these supplications betrays a specific uncertainty and sentimentality resulting from the contemporary religious crisis and characterizing many poems of the waning nineteenth century addressed to God or to the ideal beloved.

Then, as He feels your chaunting flow less clear,
  He will but say: *I hear*
The sorrow of my child on earth! and send
  Some fair, celestial friend,
One of yourselves, to help me:
. . . who walk in darkness, far away
From your enduring day.[163]

In many of these poems this tendency to model personal feelings of
depravity on the outcry of the psalmist is little more than a pretext for
self-pity; in other cases it expresses a more profound longing for redemption arising from moral,[164] or, as in the psalm, spiritual impulses. There
are also poems in which the model of Psalm 130, briefly mentioned as
a topos of unworthiness (e.g. Rossetti's 'Equal Troth'[165]), is intended
only to enhance the madonna-like perfections of the beloved. Metaphors
of light and darkness are a typical mode of representation:

God knows I had no hope before she came,
And found me in the darkness, where alone
I sat . . .
She turned my night to day.[166]

The positioning of beloved and lover in Rossetti's painting *The Blessed
Damozel* (Pl. 18) symbolically represents the relationship between the
madonna and the *de profundis* or *out of the depth* motif: the
transfigured beloved is the subject of this 'altar painting' while the lover
is banished to the predella. This composition illustrates very well that the
beloved madonna is the counter-image or projection of the lover calling
'out of the depths' and transfiguring in her his own painful existence.
Despite his disproportionately small appearance, the bereaved lover constitutes the focus of the painting.

The immense popularity enjoyed by Dante's Beatrice during the period
is symptomatic of the same inclinations which lead to the portrayal of
the beloved as a madonna. Together with the well-known paintings and
poems by Rossetti (e.g. *Dante's Dream at the Time of the Death of
Beatrice* or *Beata Beatrix*) and his close friends, occasional poems like
Payne's 'Ad Dantem', his dedicatory lines 'Con un esemplare della
divina commedia', Le Gallienne's 'Beatrice' (For the Beatrice celebration
1890) or such fashionable renderings of the motif as Wilde's 'Vita
Nuova' and 'Madonna Mia' indicate the scope of the movement. Its cult-
like dimensions inspired Beardsley's caricature *Incipit Vita Nova* (Pl. 19)
as well as Bell Scott's satirical verses:

Ah, well for us 'tis not our part
In England's fresher, stronger air,
To shrine this saint-elected pair,

18 Dante Gabriel Rossetti, *The Blessed Damozel*

This mythologic, cleric dream,
Instead of Shakespeare . . .[167]

Bell Scott's admonitory reference to the indigenous tradition is of importance because of its implication that the Beatrice cult takes place within the aestheticist–symbolist branch of Pre-Raphaelitism, often criticized as an alien element in English literary tradition, without regard for the international impact of the motif. It is scarcely a coincidence that the protagonist's visions of the unknown beloved in Gautier's *Mademoiselle de Maupin* are inspired by works of art, the beautiful saints he admires in 'les vieux tableaux des maîtres':

je finissais par trouver que ces figures avaient une vague ressemblance avec la belle inconnue que j'adorais au fond de mon cœur; je soupirais en pensant que celle que je devais aimer était peut-être une des celles-là, et qu'elle était morte depuis trois cent ans.[168]

Beatrice, already a mythical figure in Dante's original,[169] was destined to have a special appeal for those authors who participated in the symbolist tendencies of the nineteenth century.[170] It comes as no surprise that Nerval, with the same literary consciousness that led Thomson to allude to von Hardenberg's (Novalis) child bride as 'his Beatrice',[171] sees his own love relationship as a re-embodiment of the *Vita Nuova*: 'Cette *Vita Nuova* a eu pour moi deux phases . . . et je me suis fait une Laure ou une Béatrix d'une personne ordinaire de notre siècle . . .'[172] The same qualities that fascinated Gautier and O'Shaughnessy in the saintly figures of the old masters prompted other authors of the period to turn back to the courtly poetry of the Early Italians. This portrays a cosmos in its own right, a cosmos of art, all the more attractive in an age of technical and economic upheaval that felt its known spiritual structures giving way. However, due to the relative spirit of the times, most writers and artists do not attempt to assimilate Dante's comprehensive world-view but, from Bourke Marston's 'In Heaven' and Payne's 'Madonna Dei Sogni',[173] to Le Gallienne's 'The Comfort of Dante', select from his work only what seems fitting for the expression of their own very subjective feelings. A late example, Symons's poem 'Beata Beatrix' (1900), tellingly illustrates how, in accordance with Rossetti's painting, Dante's relationship to Beatrice is used to transcend his own rather obvious love scene:

Lay your head back; and now, kiss me again!
Kneel there, and do not kiss me; . . .
So I have seen the face of Beatrice,
In pictures, dead, and in memory
Seeing the face of Dante out of heaven
O, out of heaven, when for my sake you lean,

19   Aubrey Beardsley, *Incipit Vita Nova*

Till not a breath of the world may come between
Our lips that are our souls . . .[174]

If the majority of the English Beatrice poems are only literary curio-
sities today, this is not due to the recurrent use of the symbolic figure but
to the poor quality of the poems. The late romantic adaptation of the
Beatrice figure so often remains unsatisfactory because few authors were
able to make it the authentic expression of their existential situation.
They apparently turn to this symbolic figure to escape their contemporary reality, and the medievalizing tendencies in their works become so
dominant that they conceal, rather than convey, the new sensitivity. For
Baudelaire, too, Beatrice is the incarnation of ideality, but the ironic in-
version of his title 'La Béatrice' (1855) into 'Le Vampire' shows that the
French poet sees the ideal beloved and the *femme fatale* as one being.
This mature but tragic view enables him to adapt the literary motif[175]

without escaping into no man's land, and to express convincingly the tension between reality and the ideal.

Idealism and aestheticism

In Rossetti's story 'Hand and Soul' the inner affinity between the various types and aspects of the aestheticist ideal stands out with almost exemplary clarity:

and sometimes, in the ecstasy of prayer, it had even seemed to him to behold that day when his mistress − his mystical lady (now hardly in her ninth year, but whose solemn smile at meeting had already lighted on his soul like the dove of the trinity) − even she, his own gracious and holy Italian art − with her virginal bosom, and her unfathomable eyes, and the thread of sunlight round her brows − should pass, through the sun that never sets, into the circle of the shadow of the tree of life, and be seen of God and found good.[176]

Here the beloved has the same childlike appearance as in the *Vita Nuova* or in the works of James Thomson, Ernest Dowson and Francis Thompson; like Dobson's Angiola she is removed from this world, and like Rossetti's Blessed Damozel, transfigured as a madonna. Although Chiaro still recognizes 'his mistress' in her, she is, at the same time, an embodiment of his 'gracious and holy Italian art', hence, an allegorical figure.[177]

Walter Pater has designed an imaginary portrait in 'Diaphaneité' that encompasses and complements the traits of the childlike, deceased and madonna-like beloved. Characteristically, Dante's Beatrice serves as his inspiration. In the concept 'Diaphaneité' Pater attempts to capture a quality that also distinguishes Gautier's vision of the ideal figure in *Mademoiselle de Maupin*:[178]

There are some unworldly types of character which the world is able to estimate . . . There is another type of character, which is not broad and general, rare, precious above all to the artist, a character which seems to have been the supreme moral charm in Beatrice of the Commedia. It does not take the eye by breadth of colour; rather it is that fine edge of light, where the elements of our moral nature refine themselves to the burning point. It crosses rather than follows the main current of the world's life.[179]

Despite a later reference to the principles of the *Imitatio Christi* − 'Sibi unitus et simplificatus esse'[180] − which Pater finds realized in 'Diaphaneité', it is evident that he does not have a traditional ideal of transcendence in mind. In an age dominated by the 'relative spirit', the 'Diaphaneité' portrait reflects the endeavour to transcend the surface values of an empiricist world-view in order to achieve the transparency of the material world essential to an expressive symbolism. 'The world has no sense fine enough for those evanescent shades'; 'It is a mind of taste lighted up by some spiritual ray within'.[181] Pater's observations on 'wistfulness' betray his relationship with Pre-Raphaelitism; 'wistfulness', a fundamental quality of numerous Pre-Raphaelite dream portraits in painting and poetry, becomes a symbol of the metaphysical experience of many late romantics. It is no longer the romantic longing 'after what is unattainable' and the hope of achieving it, but the feeling 'that there is so much to know'.[182] A contemplative attitude, not a directed and dynamic impulse, is the outstanding feature of the aestheticist idealism in 'Diaphaneité'. Dowson's prose poem 'The Princess of Dreams' realizes this combination of idealism and disillusionment so typical of the period. As in Morris's 'Rapunzel' there is a rescuing prince, but in the nineties his adventure is doomed to end on an ironic note.

But there are some who say that she had no wish to be freed, and that those flowers de luce, her eyes, are a stagnant dark pool, that her glorious golden hair was only long enough to reach her postern gate. Some say, moreover, that her tower is not of ivory and that she is not even virtuous nor a princess.[183]

Both qualities – the sceptical awareness of unrealizable aspirations designated as 'wistfulness', and the belief in artistic perfection ('its wistfulness and a confidence in perfection') – explain the strange sense of meditative stasis which pervades Pater's aestheticism and which he also projects onto Raphael's art: '[It] stood still to live upon himself, even in outward form a youth, almost an infant, yet surprising all the world. The beauty of the Greek statues is a sexless beauty.'[184] The comparison with the sexless beauty of Greek statues calls to mind the famous *Hermaphrodite Endormi* of the Louvre which Gautier ('Contralto') and, following his example, Swinburne ('Hermaphroditus') have poetically portrayed.

   Without a doubt there are psychological explanations for both the hermaphrodite figures of Simeon Solomon and the ideal beloved in Pre-Raphaelite poetry and art; however, Pater's 'Diaphaneité' portrait suggests that the emphasis on sexlessness is more than biographical coincidence. The sexlessness of beauty reflects a latent affinity between the hermaphrodite and many variants of the ideal beloved, and symbolizes a spiritual attitude, a state of ideal self-sufficiency. Given the scepticism implicit in aestheticist idealism, however, it is an ineffectual perfection. 'Here there is moral sexlessness, a kind of impotence, an ineffectual wholeness of nature, yet with a divine beauty and significance of its own.'[185] The generation of Pater discovers its ideal in the sterile beauty of art which allows them to forget the flow of existence, if only for a moment.

Pater's Platonism as expressed in his rather unorthodox interpretation of the Platonic world of ideas, a crucial impulse in the development of the late romantic concept of the symbol, had a parallel in the striking interest of the age in Platonic love, caricatured in Gilbert and Sullivan's *Patience* ('an attachment à la Plato for a bashful young potato'). Pater's 'Diaphaneité' portrait offers a new perspective for the understanding of the widespread fashion. Poems like Le Gallienne's 'Love Platonic'[186] and theoretical contributions like J. A. Symonds's essay 'The Dantesque and Platonic Ideals of Love'[187] demonstrate that the late romantic forms of Platonism have their root in the same tendencies which inspire the different types of the ideal beloved. The nineteenth-century pessimism informing Thomson's 'The City of Dreadful Night' and Gautier's *Mademoiselle de Maupin*[188] undermines the metaphysical base without which Platonism even in its romantic brand is not feasible. When the protagonist in Gautier's novel claims 'je n'ai aimé aucune femme, mais j'ai aimé et j'aime l'amour',[189] he is not describing the Platonic progress from the objects of the visible world to the world of ideas, but the unfulfilled and, in an age of increasing scepticism, essentially unfulfillable aspirations to a rather vague ideality.

The dominant experience of many contemporary poets – 'ce que je cherche n'existe point', with its special variant – 'j'aime ce qui dépasse les bornes ordinaires'[190] – explains the frequent appearance of the childlike, deceased or madonna-like beloved as well as the hermaphrodite motif, and also constitutes the basis for the special relationship between the ideal female figure and the *femme fatale*. What these two complementary figures (for instance Swinburne's Dolores and Hesperia) share over and above the psychological and spiritual content of their symbolism is a special kind of mythic aura and intensity of expression. The same holds true for 'quelque virginale créature',[191] the object of Gautier's and Rossetti's fervent dreams, and the equally fascinating siren in 'The Orchard-pit'. The woman in Gautier's 'Symphonie en Blanc Majeur' is an elucidating example of these 'affinités secrètes'. In the dazzling white of her ideality the polarity between madonna and sphinx is resolved:

> Des Groenlands et des Norvèges
> Vient-elle avec Séraphita?
> Est-ce la Madone des neiges,
> Un sphinx blanc que l'hiver sculpta.[192]

To comply with this striving for the intensity of an undefinable content the late romantics turn alternately to the visual arts and to poetry, restlessly experimenting with the possibilities of stylization inherent in the particular medium.

La beauté idéale, réalisée par les peintres, ne vous a pas même suffi, et vous êtes allé demander aux poètes des contours encore plus arrondis, des formes plus éthérées, des grâces plus divines, des recherches plus exquises . . .[193]

O'Shaughnessy's 'Marble' cycle reveals the very poet who continued the Pre-Raphaelite tradition in 'The Glorious Lady' and 'May' also attempting to transcend reality by representing his beloved as a statue.[194] Burne-Jones's *Pygmalion* cycle provides a close example from the sister art.

That the urge behind the motif of the artist at work does indeed derive from the aestheticist impulse towards a stylized mode of existence becomes evident from examples such as Rossetti's 'Of His Lady and of His Making Her Portrait'[195] in imitation of Jacobo da Lentino, where the lover adopts the pose of a painter in order to praise his beloved. The reader acquainted with this tradition of aestheticizing representation – which includes Francis Thompson's 'Her Portrait' or 'Epilogue to the Poet's Sitter' (Wherein he Excuseth himself for the Manner of the Portrait) and Yeats's 'He wishes for the Cloths of Heaven'[196] – may conceivably consider Rossetti's poem 'The Portrait', but certainly not the sonnet of the same title, as the chance product of a painter–poet:

> O Love! let this my lady's picture glow
> Under my hand to praise her name, and show
> Even of her innerself the perfect whole.[197]

Similarly, the naiveté of the child bride is a mode of stylization inspired by the *dolce stil nuovo*, which raises the erotic relationship above the banality of everyday reality, giving it a profound if rather vague meaning. There is little doubt that the strong impulse towards an increased degree of stylization constitutes a desperate attempt to react against an age governed by the principle of success.[198] Most frequently, however, the late romantic poets withdraw from worldly wisdom to abandon themselves, apparently oblivious to the course of events, to the specifically Pre-Raphaelite condition of languor.

> 'Tis the time to go wistfully straying,
> 'Tis the time for low singing and playing,
> 'Tis the time to forget all the wise have been saying,
>   . . .
> O my Love, we are faint in the soft velvet air.[199]

While in O'Sullivan's 'Serenade' the retreat from 'the wise' creates an atmosphere of sensuous rapture, in Yeats's 'The Cap and Bells' the handling of stylistic devices (personification, colours, symmetries, repetitions) evokes the archaic awkwardness which Rossetti and his friends had admired as an expression of innocence and naiveté in the art of Orcagna and Giotto. Even the Pre-Raphaelite nature scenes and nature imagery are geared to this cult of naiveté. Their obtrusive use in Woolner's *My Beautiful Lady* distinguishes his approach to nature from the romantic spontaneity and enthusiasm characterizing the Wordsworth generation.

As the madonna illustrates, the striving for stylization often helps to explain the use of religious ideas and metaphors. Here, not only such simple and obvious examples as Rossetti's 'The Blessed Damozel' and Dobson's 'Angiola' poems come to mind with their playful use of ritualist imagery, but also Yeats's 'The Rose of Peace' in which the idealized female figure appears as the symbol of the *coincidentia oppositorum*. Rossetti's technique of endowing the lady in his songs of praise with a more general philosophical meaning aims at a similar effect, although these remain attempts of rather limited merit:

> Sometimes thou seem'st not as thyself alone,
> But as the meaning of all things that are;
> A breathless wonder, shadowing forth afar
> Some heavenly solstice hushed and halcyon.[200]

The rather direct lines from 'The Housemaid' – 'About thy soft and odorous waist / I know what other joys are placed' – indicate that the mysticisms in Le Gallienne's 'Adoration' should not be overrated in their spiritual significance; for the most part they do not exceed their function as stylizing elements.[201]

Since aestheticism, in its most extreme form, does not allow for a spirituality beyond a contemplative attitude, the stereotype enumeration of beautiful features becomes a primary means of expression. For a generation enraptured by the sensuous richness and plasticity of Keats's poetry, this mode of representation taken from medieval models offered a welcome opportunity for the display of pictorial qualities. Apart from rare instances like Wilde's 'La Bella Donna Della Mia Mente', a poem in which the portrait of the ideal beloved, overwhelmed by mannerist details, serves only as an excuse for stylistic posing, the late romantics remain committed to the idealism inspired by Dante's Beatrice. Their longing for an unattainable dream world results in a peculiar combination of Platonic and Manichaean rather than Christian elements. An unconcealed or an indirectly acknowledged scepticism divests these idealistic impulses of the power they had in other eras of history, as evinced, for instance, in the works of Plato, Dante, and the great romantics.

Many late romantics escape from reality into Pre-Raphaelite Arcadia; some are successful in transcending the banality of life by replacing reality with the realm of art, but all without exception suffer from the social, psychological and spiritual awareness of having to adjust to a transitional age. The ideal beloved is the embodiment of the desire for redemption ensuing from this agonizing experience:

Au-dessus de ce noir amas de maisons lépreuses, de ce dédale infect où circulent les spectres du plaisir, de cet immonde fourmillement de misère, de laideur et de perversités, loin, bien loin dans l'inaltérable azur, flotte l'adorable fantôme de la Béatrix, l'idéal toujours désiré, jamais atteint, la beauté supérieure et divine incarnée sous une forme de femme éthérée, spiritualisée, faite de lumière, de flamme et de parfum, une vapeur, un rêve, un reflet du monde aromal et séraphique comme les Ligeia, les Eleonor d'Edgar Poe et la Séraphita-Séraphitus de Balzac, cette étonnante création. Du fond de ses déchéances, de ses erreurs et de ses désespoirs, c'est vers cette image céleste comme vers une madone de Bon-Secours qu'il tend les bras avec des cris, des pleurs et un profond dégoût de lui-même.[202]

6   Late romantic spirituality

As early as his first attempt to define the essence of symbolism[1] Arthur Symons raises the question of its specific spirituality. Quoting Ernest Hello he names a number of fundamental characteristics: 'Having desire without light, curiosity without wisdom, seeking God by strange ways, by ways traced by the hands of men; offering rash incense upon the high places to an unknown God, who is the God of darkness'.[2] The phenomenon is as difficult to explain from the perspective of enlightened agnosticism as from the standpoint of orthodox religion. However, given its prevalence in the poetic theory and practice of the period it can neither be dismissed nor ignored. Valuable insight into this 'sort of religion in which an eternal mass is served before a veiled altar'[3] is gained by a survey of those elements described as 'mystic, magic, religious, spiritual' in late romantic works.

Mysticism

'I speak often in this book of Mysticism': with these words in the preface to *The Symbolist Movement in Literature*[4] Arthur Symons identifies a central concern in late romantic literature. Remy de Gourmont's *Le Latin Mystique* (1890), a translation and study of religious and mystical literature of the Latin Middle Ages, suggests its sources. Endeavours to derive this mysticism from the tradition of the great Christian mystics, however, promise little success, as the following remarks by Oscar Wilde demonstrate. While in 'De Profundis' he refers to the contemporary longing for a new spirituality: 'I have grown tired of the articulate utterances of men and things. The Mystical in Art, the Mystical in Life, the Mystical in Nature, this is what I am looking for',[5] in 'The Critic as Artist' he declares: 'To us the *città divina* is colourless, and the *fruitio Dei* without meaning. Metaphysics do not satisfy our temperaments, and religious ecstasy is out of date.'[6] It would be premature to draw final conclusions from Wildean *bons mots* but there can be little doubt that *fin de siècle* weariness and the search for oblivion in enigmatic gestures are key impulses underlying this peculiar mysticism. Nevertheless, alongside Wilde's faddish views of mysticism,

207

there are also works like Maeterlinck's translation of Ruysbroeck's
L'Ornement des Noces Spirituelles which, as Symons emphasizes, shows
'how deeply he [Maeterlinck] has studied the mystical writers of all
ages, and how much akin to theirs is his own temper. Plato and Plotinus,
St Bernard and Jacob Boehm [*sic*], Coleridge and Novalis . . .'[7]
Symons is not disturbed by the heterogeneity of these writers, confirming
that like most of his contemporaries he is less concerned with traditional
Christian mysticism than with a mystical aura. Plato's inclusion among
the mystic writers is typical of Pater's generation. In *Marius the
Epicurean* Pater speaks of the study of music 'in that wider Platonic
sense' as a 'kind of religion – an inward, visionary, mystic piety'.[8]
Although the aesthetic nature of this 'mystic piety' is indisputable, it
would be misguided to dismiss it in all cases as unimportant or to qualify
it as a mere mystical pose. For a serious thinker like Pater the mystical
experience represents the 'pleasure of the ideal present, of the mystic
now'[9] and provides 'something to hold by amid the perpetual flux'.[10]

With the critical awareness no less part of him than the ability to evoke
dream visions, Nerval describes the metaphysical situation from which
this particular brand of mysticism arises:

Mais pour nous, nés dans des jours de révolutions et d'orages, où toutes les
croyances ont été brisées . . . il est bien difficile, dès que nous en sentons le
besoin, de reconstruire l'édifice mystique dont les innocents et les simples
admettent dans leurs cœurs la figure toute tracée.[11]

While the reasons for the contemporary association of aesthetic and
religious experience clearly lie in an opposition to post-Darwinian
science, a precise definition of the 'mystical' elements or an assessment
of their validity nevertheless remains difficult. O'Shaughnessy's poem
'Death', however, gives a representative example of a 'mystic
moment':

> I close my eyes and see the inward things:
>   The strange averted spectre of my soul
>   Is sitting undivulged, angelic, whole,
> Beside the dim internal flood that brings
> Mysterious thoughts or dreams or murmurings
>   From the immense Unknown.[12]

Late romantic mysticism encompasses both traditional religiosity and
new poses of a vague solemnity. Laurence Housman's *Spikenard, A
Book of Devotional Poems*, bearing George Herbert's line 'Love bade
me welcome' as an epigraph, stands in this respect alongside the collection of pseudo-mystical poems entitled *Whym Chow, Flame of Love*,
evocative of Beardsley's taste for the bizarre if not his brilliance. A handwritten remark[13] in the British Library copy of this esoteric volume

reveals that the two women poets united under the pseudonym Michael
Field employ the image of the Trinity in recollection of their dead Chow
Chow:

> O God, no blasphemy
> It is to feel, we loved in trinity,
> To tell Thee that I loved him as Thy Dove
> Is loved, and is Thy Own . . .[14]

In this grotesque instance, the meditations are rooted in Christian
beliefs[15] whereas the mysticism of Arthur Symons, his translations of St
John of the Cross notwithstanding, is closer to the spirit of Pater's 'Conclusion'. Yeats leaves no doubt about this when he writes: 'It seems to
me, looking backward, that we [Symons and Yeats] always discussed
life at its most intense moment, that moment which gives a common
sacredness to the Song of Songs and to the Sermon on the Mount, and
in which one discovers something supernatural, a stirring as it were of
the roots of the hair.'[16] What ultimately distinguishes Symons's
'spiritual' poems from the works of the great mystics is that they are not
governed by the clear and powerful desire for a reunion with God, but
by a love of mysticism *per se* and a spiritual flirtatiousness that can draw
inspiration from the most divergent of sources. While in 'Sponsa Dei'
erotic imagery in the manner of Richard of Saint Victor or Bernhard of
Clairvaux is employed to express the yearnings of a female mystic for the
bridegroom of her soul, in 'The Ecstasy' the diction inspired by the
mystical tradition serves to elevate a rather earthly love encounter.

One characteristic feature of late romantic mysticism is the aversion to
anything intellectual and the nostalgia for a religious naiveté which
Pater's 'relative spirit' had finally made impossible. Francis Thompson
has formulated the problem in the Prelude to his 'Ode to the Setting
Sun'. Neither his own religious convictions nor the historical situation
allow for a sun cult any more, yet he feels driven by a vague religious
impulse:

> For worship it is too incredulous,
> For doubt – oh, too believing passionate![17]

A strange unearthly mood characteristic of the period already pervades
the opening stanzas:

> The wailful sweetness of the violin
> Floats down the hushèd waters of the wind,
> The heart-strings of the throbbing harp begin
> To long in aching music: Spirit-pined,
> In wafts that poignant sweetness drifts, until
> The wounded soul ooze sadness.[18]

The sunset scene in Rossetti's sonnet 'The Hill Summit' also illustrates the difficulty of distinguishing between an indefinite air of transfiguration and a mystical experience. At first we seem to witness only a nature scene, but, as we read on, the ascent and descent and the sojourn on the peak in the fading sunlight impress us as symbolizing an emotional and spiritual state. Words like 'feast-day, altar, vesper-song, worshipper' and, above all, the fusion of nature observations and biblical echoes in the image of the burning bush ('Transfigured where the fringed horizon falls, − / A fiery bush with coruscating hair'[19]) increase the spiritual impact of the scene. Despite the transcendence inherent in such associations, however, the sun never ceases to remain a natural object. The lyric speaker is too preoccupied with his experiences of frustration to seek a spiritual counterpart in the sun. Like Rossetti's sonnet, AE's poem 'Dawn' displays the symbolic use of nature scenery ('Fire on the altar of the hills at last'[20]), the concentration on a visionary moment and the awareness of the inevitable descent. The crucial difference lies in the fact that the visionary self is granted the intimate union − 'that high companionship' − with the divine. Conversely, 'The Hill Summit' is pervaded by a sense of melancholy because the self never experiences ecstasy; it remains elusive, an unattainable aspiration.

Mystical tendencies are so widespread in late romanticism that even an outsider like Dr Thomas Gordon Hake can be assimilated into the movement on this basis. Critics, expecting literary influences due to his personal acquaintance with many Pre-Raphaelites, have been disappointed and have generally ignored his dark poetry. We know too little about the man who waited until late in life before following his poetic inclinations to determine to what extent 'the mesmeric phenomena' that Rossetti finds in his poetry are actually related to the occultism of the period. In any case, the mysticism apparent in a title like *Maiden Ecstasy* constitutes a major concern in Hake's works:

> Her eyes, that leap like fountains into day
> At sounds of joy, are to the sunlight blind,
> Yet through night splendours track their starry way
> And every planet find:
> Her soul inlaid with each familiar ray
> In colours of the mind.[21]

Hake's affinities with the Pre-Raphaelites lie more in his mystical bent than in specific themes and stylistic devices. What formed a central impulse in his work was for them merely one aspect of a pose that furnished Gilbert and Sullivan's satirical talents with unlimited material:

There is a transcendentality of delirium − an acute accentuation of a supreme ecstasy − which the earthy might easily mistake for indigestion. But it is not indigestion − it is aesthetic transfiguration! . . .

Mystic poet, hear our prayer,
Twenty love-sick maidens we.[22]

Neither the interchangeability of the concept 'mystic' with words like 'magic' or 'mysterious' as, for instance, in Bourke Marston's 'Love and Sorrow' ('many a mystic cave and magic grove'[23]) nor its stereotypical repetition as an epithet in Payne's 'Light O'Love'[24] ('mystic spell', 'mystic time', 'mystic unseen flowers') suggest that the mysticism in these poets was an authentic or powerful experience. In the imaginary setting of Payne's poem, which throughout depicts an inner land-scape,[25] the personified days compile treasures in a way that illustrates the aestheticist quality of this mysticism: 'some gem / Within the mystery of thought / Some pearl of hidden art, or caught / Some strange sweet secret'.[26] The reader never learns what is meant by 'mystery of thought', 'hidden arts' or 'strange sweet secret'. Instead he is put in a frame of mind provoking mysterious and rapturous associations which, the designation 'mystical' notwithstanding, does not grant religious fulfilment but escape from a spiritual crisis: 'Curtained with solitudes and fed / With drink of dreams; absolved of doubts and fears, / Our silence spirit-dumb'.[27]

It is above all this feature which establishes a continuity between the mysticism of the Pre-Raphaelites and that of O'Shaughnessy and the aesthetic movement. Differences emerge quite vividly in the replacement of the Pre-Raphaelite nature scene with the exotic landscape of art. In O'Shaughnessy's *Music and Moonlight* the love of precious stones already noticeable in Payne's 'Light O'Love' becomes a formative impulse and converges with the element of mystery or mysticism that in Wilde's view the artist is to intensify: 'he will look upon Art as a goddess whose mystery it is his province to intensify, and whose majesty his privilege to make more marvellous in the eyes of men'.[28]

Music produces 'wide soft illuminations of the soul'[29] in the pianist Eucharis, and Chopin guides her in a silvery boat over 'mystical melodious waves'. In gigantic temples priests await the mythic union of phoenix and aloe, which simultaneously signifies that of the musician with the spirit of the composer in death. This moment of 'intense transfigure-ment' is only possible through a kind of escapist renunciation similar in function to the ascesis of many mystics. The aestheticist nature of the spiritual experience informs the description of the setting, the Alhambra, where the gems are 'All joined in mystic utterance'.[30] This is the same unique beauty envisioned by Poe when he defines beauty as 'that intense and pure elevation of *soul* – *not* of intellect, or of heart'.[31]

There might the soul exalted make a home
With thought's lone rhapsody . . .[32]

What attracted both the English Pre-Raphaelites and the French symbolists perhaps more than anything else in Poe was his unusual fascination with a beauty at the brink of death. Its effect on Poe's strangely sensuous soul appealed to the frustrated idealism of an increasingly sceptical era. The symbolist mysticism emerged as a reaction to this dilemma.

Phrases in O'Shaughnessy's poem, such as 'exquisite desolation' and 'death came / In most refined way supernatural', confirm that this 'soul exalted' is no longer the soul of the Christian mystical tradition but is a specifically late romantic organ which distils a new spirituality from sublimated sensual temptations. True to the spirit of *fin de siècle* eclecticism, the philosophical contents of the mystic meditations vary from poem to poem. *Music and Moonlight* is dominated by a pronounced aestheticism, 'Palm Flowers' by a belated pantheism and 'Seraphitus'[33] by the Swedenborg tradition continued in England by Blake, in France by Balzac. The angel Seraphitus, who departs from heaven but cannot dwell on earth, symbolizes the liminal situation also expressed in Rossetti's and Yeats's motif of the door ('angel-greeted door', 'flaming door'[34]).

Since institutionalized Christianity seemed not to offer a satisfactory answer to the increasing scepticism and materialism of the age, many poets develop an unorthodox mysticism. However, as the mystical experiences are usually less intense and less frequent than their spiritual needs demand, the highly self-conscious generation attempts to produce spiritual experiences by artificial means. 'I take hashish with some followers of the eighteenth-century mystic Saint-Martin',[35] admits Yeats, and his friend Arthur Symons arrives at bizarre metaphysical insights at the end of a 'haschisch' poem:

> Who said the world is but a mood
> In the eternal thought of God?
> I know it, real though it seem,
> The Phantom of a haschisch dream
> In that insomnia which is God.[36]

Occult tendencies

The interest of late-nineteenth-century artists in occultism has to be seen in the historical context.[37] Estranged equally from the materialistic age and religious orthodoxy, but driven by vague spiritual desires, they display a half-serious, half-playful interest in occult practices and mystic systems: 'I ask who made the gold, and he says a certain Rabbi, and begins to talk of the Rabbi's miracles. We do not question him — perhaps it is true — perhaps he has imagined it all — we are inclined to accept every historical belief once more.'[38] What fascinates this generation about mysticism and occultism alike is the element of mystery, of something transcending the tangible, which, according to Wilde, is rapidly disappearing and, as he ironically remarks, is endangered particularly by the efforts of the Browning Society: 'Nowadays we have so few mysteries left that we cannot afford to part with one of them . . . where one had hoped that Browning was a mystic they have sought to show that he was simply inarticulate.'[39] Apart from in Yeats's case, direct occult influences in the line of Mme Blavatsky or Péladan cannot be identified in the artists discussed here. Nonetheless, a lively interest in occult phenomena has been documented by their biographers. Rossetti's participation in seances is an oft-cited example.[40]

Mesmerism and various other sorts of spiritualism appear widespread since the mid-nineteenth century, but William and Mary Howitt, the authors of a *History of the Supernatural*, are the initiators of the particular spiritist sittings frequented by Rossetti, Ford Madox Brown and Allingham.[41] The difference in reaction is characteristic of the contemporary attitude towards occultism. While Allingham dismisses it all as 'tiresome nonsense', Ruskin receives 'from Mrs A. (a society medium) . . . the most overwhelming evidence of the other state of the world'.[42] Ruskin exemplifies the spiritual stance of many contemporaries. He vacillates between the strict evangelism of his upbringing and the Victorian agnosticism represented by W. M. Rossetti; he exhibits an interest in saints, in line with the aesthetic–mystical Catholicism of the time, and is initiated into occult practices by Mrs Cowper-Temple.

What attracts Francis Thompson[43] and Aubrey Beardsley to *Virgilius the Sorcerer*, or Lionel Johnson ('Magic') to the figure of the magician is his opposition to the rational world around him: 'Because I work not, as logicians work / . . . Because by leaps I scale the secret sky, / . . . Therefore my name is grown a popular scorn'.[44] The solitude of the initiate, esoteric wisdom and powers make 'Virgil, magician and poet'[45] the ideal of the symbolist poet: 'Men pity me; poor men, who pity me! . . . I choose laborious loneliness'.[46] The magician's painful recognition of the futility of his incantation[47] reflects the same scepticism towards the occult spiritualism between 1850 and 1900 that is present in Beardsley's ironic depiction *Of A Neophyte, And How The Black Art Was Revealed Unto Him*. It is in a mysticism of the body that the tension between spiritual desires and critical awareness finds its most significant expression.

The spiritualization of the flesh

From Buchanan's Victorian attack[48] to Talon's modern interpretation of Rossetti's intentions[49] there has been no end to the discussion of the 'fleshliness' of Pre-Raphaelite art. A major critical stumbling-block lies in the strange combination of 'fleshliness' with a strong tendency towards mysticism. 'An ecstatic mingling of body and soul'[50] is often named as an essential characteristic, particularly with respect to Rossetti. The same 'spiritualization of the flesh'[51] also informs the works of Swinburne, O'Shaughnessy, and Arthur Symons.

Thanks to his familiarity with European symbolism Hugo von Hofmannsthal was one of the first to appreciate the Pre-Raphaelite spiritualization of the flesh. Emphasizing 'this beauty, necessary in its inmost self, such a perfect spiritualization of the body as it were that it affects us like the embodiment of the spiritual', he finds in this idealism, 'almost exactly the opposite of the abstract concept of beauty arising from the idealism of the German classicists . . .'[52] This is by no means the misinterpretation of a continental poet; Swinburne expresses similar ideas in his essay on Simeon Solomon, from whom he is later to distance himself out of a Victorian desire for respectability. Swinburne's view of the relationship between body and soul is all the more significant in that it illustrates the impact of the 'relative spirit', which causes the collapse of traditional ontological dichotomies and antinomies, and penetrates the centre of symbolist spirituality. In almost all of Solomon's paintings Swinburne sees 'the same profound suggestion of unity between opposites, the same recognition of the identity of contraries'.[53] Through an allusion to Baudelaire he attempts to emphasize the newness of this spirituality[54] and, as Arthur Symons will later do, seeks to situate Solomon in the mystical tradition: 'One whole class of his religious designs is impregnated with the burning mysticism and raging rapture of her [St Theresa's] visions.'[55]

In connection with the spiritualized corporeality of Solomon's hermaphrodites it is interesting that Walter Pater's treating of body and soul in *Marius the Epicurean* proceeds from Christian conceptions. Marc Aurel, who despises the body, is contrasted with Cornelius, a Christian for whom 'the body of man was unmistakably, as a later seer terms it, the one true temple in the world; or rather itself the proper object of worship, of a sacred service, in which the very finest gold might have its seemliness and due symbolic use'.[56] The seemingly minor shift of accent ('or rather itself the proper object of worship') signifies no less than the inversion of the Pauline concept of the body as the temple of the holy spirit, and thereby announces a fundamental motive in aestheticist mysticism. With his characteristic quietness, Pater develops one of the radical blasphemies of the time, the identification of body and soul:

The human body in its beauty, as the highest potency of all the beauty of material objects, seemed to him just then to be matter no longer, but, having taken celestial fire, to assert itself as indeed the true, though visible, soul or spirit in things.[57]

With Oscar Wilde, the new dogma of the unity of body and soul becomes a *bon mot* and part of the jargon of *l'art pour l'art*: 'It is not merely in art that the body is the soul. In every sphere of life Form is the beginning of things.'[58]

In this wider context, Rossetti's mystical 'fleshliness', too, appears in a different light. Although the 'conversion of body into spirit'[59] in Rossetti's 'Secret Parting' may be too sudden to convince the modern critic, this suddenness is clearly in keeping with the poet's original intentions. Placing the identification of body and soul at the end of the octave in both 'Secret Parting' and 'Heart's Hope', Rossetti gives it the impact of a shock effect that recalls the techniques of the Metaphysicals:

> And as she kissed her mouth became her soul.[60]

> Thy soul I know not from thy body, nor
> Thee from myself, neither our love from God.[61]

In 'The Kiss' he prepares from the start for the fusion of body and soul found in the formulaic final line: 'Fire within fire, desire in deity'.[62] In 'Love-Lily' he uses the allegorical name of the beloved and the image of the love-spirit born between her hands, brows and lips as an ideal base for the mystic union in the concluding verses:

> Whose speech Truth knows not from her thought
> Nor Love her body from her soul.[63]

The rhetorical quality in such lines lends itself to repetition and makes Rossetti's mysticism, except for such rare cases as 'Nuptial Sleep', appear inauthentic to the modern reader. All too often he employs ingeniously manipulated rhetoric where only a new language could have conveyed his new experience. The difference between Rossetti and Baudelaire, who introduces the symbolist movement in France, is not one of intention − the fusion of the sensual and the spiritual − but, as the 'Correspondances' sonnet attests, one of superior creative imagination.

Even if Rossetti had looked to contemporary France and not to the Early Italians for inspiration, the problem besetting English late romanticism would not necessarily have been resolved. The style of *Poems and Ballads* demonstrates all too clearly that Swinburne also lacked the specific power of the symbolist imagination to create a new language, and believed he had captured the essence of French symbolism in the adaptation of scandalous themes and shocking phrasing. The Victorians were as appalled by poems like 'Laus Veneris' and 'Dolores' as the French were

by *Les Fleurs du Mal*, yet Swinburne's attempts to dissolve the traditional polarity of body and soul through a new kind of spiritualized sensitivity, as in Rossetti, result more often than not in rhetorical tricks,
rather than in a genuine fusion:

> And all her body was more virtuous
> Than souls of women fashioned otherwise.[64]

In the better parts of poems like 'Laus Veneris', however, Swinburne
achieves this 'mysticism of the senses' through the interplay of imagery
and music.

Poems such as 'The One Desire' (1899), which betrays Rossetti's
influence on Arthur Symons, confirm that French themes and motifs
were adopted by English poets with great enthusiasm, because they had
gone through similar experiences, although without developing an
English equivalent. From the obtrusive chiasmus 'soul–body; body–soul'
in the first four lines of Symons's 'The One Desire' to the image 'light
or flame' and the direct statement of this relationship in the final line,
the striving to articulate mystical experiences through the clever handling
of abstract conceptions – following the precedent of *The House of Life*
– is exceedingly evident:

> If I think of your soul, I see
> Your body's beauty; and then
> I pray to your body again,
> And your soul answers me.[65]

Where Rossetti and Swinburne failed, success by authors like Symons
and Wratislaw was unlikely; in their poems the 'concreteness' of the
representation impedes the process of spiritualization:

> I feel the perfume of your hair,
> I feel your breast that heaves and dips,
> Desiring my desiring lips,
> And that ineffable delight
> When souls turn bodies, and unite
> In the intolerable, the whole
> Rapture of the embodied soul.[66]

Even a poetaster like Le Gallienne seems to have felt the discrepancy between mystifying jargon and sexual directness in much of English *fin de
siècle* poetry. As one who responded with equal fervour to the attractions of
Platonic love and the more earthly charms of pretty maids, he traced all the
unfortunate transfigurations of the flesh back to the baneful influence
of Huysmans. Entitling a collection of his poetry *English Poems* he takes
his fellow countrymen to task for their decadent taste ('I light my palace
with the seven stars / And eat strange dishes to Gregorian chants') and

then parodies the mysticism of the fleshly school and the decadent enjoyment 'of a new sin: / An incest 'twixt the body and the soul'.[67] In view of the many second-rate examples of fleshly mysticism, Le Gallienne's parody is refreshing. But the dichotomy he creates between 'healthy beast' and 'singing bird' shows that, veering between aestheticist posing and Victorian attitudinizing, Le Gallienne understood as little of Baudelaire's *esthétique du laid*[68] as of Rossetti's and Swinburne's mysticism of the flesh:

O let the body be a healthy beast,
And keep the soul a singing soaring bird;
But lure thou not the soul from out the sky
To pipe unto the body in the sty.[69]

While in Christian mysticism earthly eroticism appears as a metaphor for spiritual love, late romantic mysticism deliberately 'con-fuses' the two. A Christian *fin de siècle* author like Francis Thompson is only able to achieve the spiritualization of the flesh in a *concetto*-like compliment addressed to the beloved which is neither poetically convincing nor spiritually binding.[70] If we recall the symbolic implications of the ideal beloved, the 'meeting of spirit and sense'[71] can be interpreted as an attempt of the period to transcend the division symbolized in the *femme fatale* and the madonna.

Satan and sin

The profound spiritual crisis of the period is reflected in its striking fascination with Satan and sin.[72] The difficulty with the various literary works is to penetrate the ambiguities and to assess both the guilt feelings of the believers and the cultivated sinfulness of the apostates. Lionel Johnson's 'Satanas' continues in the tradition of Rossetti's 'Retro Me, Sathana!' but while the exhortation of the latter title does indeed inform the entire Pre-Raphaelite sonnet, the *fin de siècle* poem derives its special note from the author's obvious delight in outlining the devil's attraction ('Cor corrumpens suaviter') in a Latin hymn:

Ecce! Princeps infernorum
Rex veneficus amorum
Vilium et mortiferorum,
Ecce! regnat Lucifer.[73]

'Vinum Daemonum' and 'The Dark Angel'[74] exhibit a spiritual disposition strikingly similar to Baudelaire's ('C'est Satan Trismégiste / Qui berce longuement notre esprit enchanté'),[75] but in Johnson's 'The Dark Angel' the devil,[76] invoked by Baudelaire in 'Les Litanies de Satan', is fought off in accordance with the traditional theological system:

> I fight thee, in the Holy Name!
> Yet, what thou dost, is what God saith.[77]

Nevertheless the entire poem is so strongly marked by a preoccupation with the Satanic that the reference to the role of the tempter in the divine plan of salvation seems more like a theological afterthought. Yeats, who apparently witnessed Johnson's self-conscious Catholicism often enough, registers doubts in this respect: 'Did the austerity, the melancholy of his thoughts, that spiritual ecstasy which he touched at times, heighten, as complementary colours heighten one another, not only the Vision of Evil, but its fascination?'[78]

This duality is characteristic of the intense experience of living at the brink of the abyss in a pessimistic age. On the one hand there is Pater's acute awareness of evil — 'Surely evil was a real thing'[79] — frequently overlooked in interpreting his aestheticism; on the other hand we see Douglas ('The Legend of Spinello of Arezzo'), continuing a great romantic tradition, idealize the Devil. At night he comes and displays his *fin de siècle* beauty to the painter who had portrayed him as a monster:

> . . . one whose eyes were soft as beams
> Of summer moonlight, and withal as sad.
> Dark was his colour, and as black his hair
> As hyacinths by night . . .[80]

The anthology edited by O'Sullivan and his friends also proves that Rossetti and Lionel Johnson, Pater and Douglas all sought to express a more general sentiment of the times shared by English and continental poets alike. Barlowe's poem 'The Tempter', in which the Devil attempts to seduce women with precious stones, and L. Cranmer–Byng's 'The Devil's Bride'[81] reflect the tenor established by the translation of Baudelaire's 'La Destruction': 'The Devil stirs about me without rest'.[82] In one of the introductory stanzas of 'The Houses of Sin' — the cover was designed by none other than Beardsley himself — O'Sullivan accurately, if somewhat inexpertly, captures an essential feature of late romantic spirituality:

> Bleak days of idle sin with madness shod,
> Wishes scarce wished before they had an end,
> The fear of Satan, and the fear of God,
> Now with the ashes blend.[83]

The authors approach the spiritual crisis — 'All down the valleys of the universe . . . / The terror lurks, and stabs us like a curse' — in a variety of ways. Dante Gabriel Rossetti, one of the most talented among them, prefers to allude to an enigmatic transcendence. Characteristically, in 'Cloud and Wind' and 'Through Death to Love', this transcendence manifests itself in apocalyptic images, but these provide the love theme with the authenticity which in his other sonnets is so often undermined by stylistic mannerisms:

> Our hearts discern wild images of Death,
> Shadows and shoals that edge eternity.[84]
> Ah! in your eyes so reached what dumb adieu,
> What unsunned gyres of waste eternity?[85]

Francis Thompson discovers his solution in orthodox Catholicism, but only after a great spiritual struggle. The protagonist in 'The Hound of Heaven' flees endlessly ('Adown Titanic glooms of chasmèd fears') from a *deus malignus* before he at last comprehends that the 'gloom' is nothing but the 'Shade of His Hand, outstretched caressingly'.[86] Dowson, whose world-view is otherwise governed by vague nostalgia, attempts, in 'Impenitentia Ultima', to cope with the tensions between the secular cult of the madonna and the orthodox conception of God. Even though other poems betray a less definitive impenitence than this defiant title would suggest, the blasphemous conclusion to 'Impenitentia Ultima' displays the rebellious rhetoric well known in poetry since Swinburne's challenge to divine anger:

> Before the ruining waters fall and my life be carried under,
> And Thine anger cleave me through as a child cuts down a flower,
> I will praise Thee, Lord, in Hell, while my limbs are racked asunder,
> For the last sad sight of her face and the little grace of an hour.[87]

Huysmans defined sadism as a 'bastard of Catholicism' in order to emphasize that it presupposes a religion to be violated.[88] Similar tendencies among the English poets of the period come somewhat as a surprise. James Thomson attempts to overcome his religious despair[89] by adopting an atheist stance, but he presents his new creed within the context of a liturgical scene. The setting of canto XIV of 'The City of Dreadful Night' is a cathedral; a minister appears and, with a blasphemous reversal of Luke 1.10 ('I bring you good tidings of great joy, which shall be to all people'), introduces a series of negations of Christian conceptions:

> Good tidings of great joy for you, for all:
> There is no God; no fiend with names divine. . .[90]

The dominant impulse in black mass — a subject of considerable interest at the time[91] — is the inversion of the Catholic liturgy. Affinities with Baudelaire and Huysmans, Swinburne, Wilde and Wratislaw are immediately evident. In the following verses from Swinburne's 'Dolores', for example, we find the blasphemous inversion of attributes of the Virgin Mary, put together in a kind of negative Marian litany:

> O tower not of ivory, but builded
> By hands that reach heaven from hell;
> O mystical rose of the mire,
> O house not of gold but of gain.[92]

Since Swinburne's poetic abilities here are not commensurate with his striving for intensity, he cleverly develops a new poetic diction from lexical inversions: 'the shrine where a sin is a prayer', 'In a twilight where virtues are vices'.[93] The result with Swinburne and epigones like Wratislaw is a total 'revaluation of values':

> We shall see whether hell be not heaven.[94]
>
> Kissing my mouth he saw that ill was good,
> Lust was Love's brother, Vice to Virtue kin.[95]

Oscar Wilde, always aware of the latest literary trends, also makes a contribution to the movement. Although not exactly a paradigm of lyric excellence, the following lines from 'The New Helen' illustrate the close connection between the spiritualization of the flesh and the more far-reaching metaphysical confusion:

> Of heaven or hell I have no thought or fear,
> Seeing I know no other god but thee:
>   . . .
> The incarnate spirit of spiritual love
> Who in thy body holds his joyous seat.[96]

Swinburne observes in the artworks of Simeon Solomon 'the latent relations of pain and pleasure, the subtle conspiracies of good with evil, the deep alliance of death and life, of love and hate, of attraction and abhorrence'.[97] Clearly there are points of comparison not only with the protagonist's complacent remark in *Mademoiselle de Maupin* – 'J'ai perdu complètement la science du bien et du mal'[98] – but also with the even more disconcerting self-observation of the protagonist in *Aurélia*, who believes that exotic costumes and customs are producing profound changes in him: 'il me semblait que je déplaçais ainsi les conditions du bien et du mal'.[99] What distinguishes Baudelaire's 'A une Madone' from Swinburne's 'Dolores' or Wratislaw's 'Modern Friends'[100] is not the sadistic features or the corresponding religious blasphemies, both of which also characterize the English poetry of the period, but the imaginative power necessary to express such experiences in a convincing manner.[101]

When one has become aware of the spiritual pattern, the number of poems influenced by it turns out to be amazingly large. In 'White Lilies' Wratislaw delights in the contrast between the purity of the lilies and the depravity of the lady carrying them; in 'Sonnet Macabre', in the discrepancy between beauty and sin.[102] The same tendency is noticeable in the fashionable blasphemies of Arthur Symons, who calls a 'Juliet of a night' 'Stella Maris' and who praises God 'who wrought for you and me / Your subtle body made for love' in a poem entitled 'Magnificat'.[103] His adherence to the traditional religious context is often so exacting that the reader of 'The Twelve-Thorned Crown', for instance, only gradually recognizes that the metaphors of the Eucharist are intended to evoke the spiritualization of carnal love ('Woman, when in the sacrament I take / The bread, your body, and the wine, your kiss').[104]

The influence of Renan's *La Vie de Jésus* and Strauss's *The Life of Jesus* does not go the whole way in explaining the aestheticist and blasphemous elements in Wilde's Christ figure.[105] Statements like, 'The mere existence of conscience . . . is a sign of our imperfect development',[106] with their double-edged irony aimed at Christianity and Darwinism alike were probably intended to shock the upper middle class. Nonetheless, such *bons mots* are only fully understandable within the context of that 'revaluation of values' found in Gautier, Nerval and Baudelaire, as well as in Rossetti, Swinburne and Symons. Wilde's affinities with the ritualistic atheism in Thomson's 'The City of Dreadful Night' are as unmistakable as those with the aestheticist Catholicism in Huysmans's *A Rebours*:[107]

When I think about religion at all, I feel as if I would like to found an order for those who *cannot* believe: the Confraternity of the Faithless one might call it, where on an altar, on which no taper burned, a priest, in whose heart peace had no dwelling, might celebrate with unblessed bread and a chalice empty of wine. Every thing to be true must become a religion. And agnosticism should have its ritual no less than faith.[108]

What is only imperfectly rendered by Swinburne's stereotypical inversions, Wilde's paradoxes and Symons's blasphemies finds masterly expression in Beardsley's ironic drawings (Pl. 20):

He made two or three charming and blasphemous designs; I think especially of a Madonna and Child where the Child has a foolish, doll-like face, and an elaborate modern baby's dress; and of a Saint Rose of Lima in an expensive gown decorated with roses, ascending to Heaven upon the bosom of the

20   Aubrey Beardsley, *Saint Rose of Lima*

Madonna, her face enraptured with love, but with that form of it which is least associated with sanctity. I think that his conversion to Catholicism was sincere, but that so much of impulse as could exhaust itself in prayer and ceremony, in formal action and desire, found itself mocked by the antithetical image; and yet I am perhaps mistaken, perhaps it was merely his recognition that historical Christianity had dwindled to a box of toys, and that it might be amusing to empty the whole box onto the counterpane.[109]

Most English poets would have been unable to live and write on the basis of Mallarmé's 'empty transcendence'. Disillusioned by their own futile attempts at momentary escape and embarrassed at having attacked the old order without finding a new one, many turn back to religious orthodoxy or seek refuge in religious idylls. This attitude is exemplified in Yeats's 'The Lover Speaks to the Hearers of his Songs in Coming Days' where he half-seriously, half-jokingly implores the devout women to 'pray for all the sin I wove in song'.[110] An even more dramatic example is found in Verlaine's 'Crimen Amoris', in the fall of the demon who had promised a new spirituality without 'Conflit entre le Pire et le Mieux'.[111]

Religious escapism

In view of the central role of Satan and sin it is not surprising to see aesthetic and idyllic versions of Christianity emerge as concomitant and complementary forms. In *Les Paradis Artificiels* Baudelaire's protagonist, who displays all the traits of the modern literary hero, remarks 'L'idée de beauté doit naturellement s'emparer d'une place vaste dans un tempérament spirituel tel que je l'ai supposé.'[112] It is this particular quality of the 'tempérament spirituel' that causes Pater and many poets of the time to be so receptive to 'the beauty of holiness, nay! the elegance of sanctity'.[113] Under the threat of a chaotic world of fleeting impressions, the urge for more lasting structures of spirituality grows continually stronger. Pater finds this order in the 'wonderful liturgical spirit of the Church'[114] and, characteristically, in the mythologies which Flavian, too, admires. The reasons behind the particular attraction of the Catholic Church are more difficult to determine than might be expected. With its emphasis on ritual, on the symbolic and sacramental, Catholicism was bound to exert a powerful appeal on England in the wake of the Oxford Movement. Another important, sociological, reason emerges in *Marius the Epicurean*: 'The mere sense that one belongs to a system or organization has, in itself, the expanding power of a great experience; as some have felt who have been admitted from narrower sects into the community of the Catholic Church.'[115] Moreover, the highly developed symbolic language of such a system offers structuring principles and patterns for emotions and ideas. The doctrines of the Church do not constitute religious or moral responsibilities for the dilettante, who is all the more inclined to seek his aestheticist solace in this 'venerable system of sentiment and idea', as Pater calls it.

The nature of the relationship between the liturgical and aestheticist movements in the nineteenth century is reflected in Wilde's wilful misinterpretation of a quotation by Newman:

Forms are the food of faith, cried Newman in one of those great moments of sincerity that make us admire and know the man. He was right, though he may not have known how right he was. The creeds are believed, not because they are rational, but because they are repeated. Yes; Form is everything. It is the secret of life.[116]

To view Wilde's aesthetic understanding of the Mass in the right perspective and to recognize the formalism of the nineties as a specific form of late romantic escapism, we must recall his justification for seeking refuge in art: 'Because Art does not hurt us.'[117] In this sense he is thankful 'that the supreme office of the church should be the playing of the tragedy without the shedding of blood: the mystical presentation by means of dialogue and costume and gesture even, of the Passion of her Lord'.[118] Since Wilde does not experience a convincing 'vision of evil' in 'De Profundis', it is even easier for him to transform the celebration of the Eucharist zestfully into a vaguely religious spectacle marked by his typical mixture of piety and blasphemy.

While the liturgy doubtless has no orthodox Christian meaning for Pater, it clearly means more to him than an aestheticist game to be enjoyed with Des Esseintes's hypersensitive tastes. Ultimately the Mass appears to him as the expression of the 'permanent protest established in the world . . . against any wholly mechanical and disheartening theory of itself and its conditions. That was a thought which relieved for him the iron outline of the horizon about him, touching it as with soft light from beyond.'[119] The fact that Pater's protagonist in *Marius the Epicurean* has need of such reassurance betrays a spiritual openness rarely recognizable behind the ritualist poses of other contemporaries. However, the formulation 'soft light from beyond' also calls attention to the philosophical vagueness inescapable in the relativist nineties as well as to the religious tenuousness which distinguishes late romantic spirituality from that of Donne or Herbert. It is particularly in Pater's fumbling grasp of evil, no less intensely felt by him than by Baudelaire, that this becomes clear. His passiveness would never have allowed him to release a spiritual dynamics through the dramatic inversion of orthodox values in the manner of Swinburne. In Pater's eyes a sentimentally 'softened' world-view characteristic of the contemporary tendency towards religious escapism represents, if not a solution, then a viable alternative:

And what we need in the world, over against that evil, is a certain permanent and general power of compassion – humanity's standing force of self-pity.[120]

The idyllic features of Christianity already recognizable in the Cecilia episode of Pater's novel are most evident in Marian poetry and the motif of the convent, popular in England since the advent of Pre-Raphaelitism. Here, too, an attempt to differentiate between committed Christianity and aestheticist posing would not do justice to the phenomenon characterized by its mixture of motifs. O'Sullivan, for instance, has written numerous religious poems comparable in their seriousness to those collected in Verlaine's *Sagesse* volume.[121] Alongside such verses there is the idyllic and playful 'Hymn in May':

> In this soft month of May,
> Thou, little Queen Mary,
> Dost pass in the prairie
> And rub Thy white feet
> In the rain-grass . . .[122]

It is typical of contemporary religiosity that the speaker in 'The Peace of God', tortured by 'strange scarlet things of sin and flame' and sincerely longing for spiritual peace, even in this situation cannot do without a degree of precious phrasing. The same self-consciousness evident in 'sweet prayers carven curiously'[123] also affects his emotions and causes his personal situation to be apprehended in sentimental terms. In 'Nuns of the Perpetual Adoration' Dowson even projects the melancholy attitude of self-pity onto the nuns, who symbolize the opposite of the speaker's uncertain and troubled existence: 'Calm, *sad*, secure'.[124]

If we consider a poem like Austin Dobson's 'At the Convent Gate' in isolation, it might seem as though the description of peaceful convent life is exclusively intended to capture details with Pre-Raphaelite accuracy.

> Look, there is one that tells her beads;
> And yonder one apart that reads
> A tiny missel's page;
> And see, beside the well the two
> That, kneeling, strive to lure anew
> The magpie to its cage![125]

However, the similarities with other depictions in literature and the visual arts disclose the true impulses behind Dobson's portrayal of the convent motif.[126] Idyllic traits also dominate Charles Collins's painting *Convent Thoughts* (Pl. 3). Surrounded by flowers in the convent garden, a nun in a white habit is devoting her attention to a blossom in her right

21 John Everett Millais, *The Vale of Rest*

hand, disregarding the illuminated breviary in her left; water lilies and goldfish can be made out in the pool at her feet. Millais's *The Vale of Rest* (Pl. 21) displays the same minute depiction of detail yet, despite significant idyllic features, elegiac tones predominate. In the little convent graveyard one nun is digging a grave while the other, her hands folded in an obtrusive gesture of pious resignation and spiritual peace, soulfully turns towards an imaginary onlooker unable to avoid the message. In both paintings the scene, sealed off by a wall in the background, opens out abruptly towards the front; in *The Vale of Rest* the foreground is completely absent, in *Convent Thoughts* it is overshadowed by the prominence of the central figure, giving the viewer the same impression produced by Dowson's poem of looking into a sheltered world from the outside. The sense of shelter and seclusion of these locations together with that note of foreignness explains the attraction cloistered life had for O'Sullivan and his contemporaries:

> Dear God! this peace is sorely far
> From me, nor can I gather near.[127]

Dowson's poem 'Extreme Unction' further clarifies the situation of the late romantics who hope for 'sweet / Renewal of lost innocence'[128] in the last rites of the church, while romantics like Blake and Wordsworth experience the original state of innocence in the immediacy of nature. The desire for peace and the purification of the extreme unction are undoubtedly genuine, yet it is equally true that the 'roses of the world'[129] – in spite of their imminent decay – generally hold a greater attraction for the decadent generation. In 'Palm Sunday' Wratislaw has candidly if crudely broached the conflict.

> We knelt together humbly, she and I
> Before the red-stained East,
> To seek for mercy from our sin,
>
>   . . .
>
> Then like two slaves regaining liberty,
>
>   . . .
>
> Forgot what hearts had felt or eyes had seen.[130]

With unintended humour Arthur Symons ('A Vigil in Lent') depicts how a woman, kneeling before the image of the crucified Christ, prays to be forgiven for her sinful love, yet, upon hearing her lover's whistle outside, ends her prayer abruptly with the words: 'O let it be a very little sin' and 'Remember me in mercy; for I go'.[131] One would be inclined to pass over this minor poem without comment if its scheme had not elsewhere received so much interest and convincing artistic treatment at the time.

Aubrey Beardsley has twice dealt with the subject: in 1892, in the style of Burne-Jones, *The Litany of Mary Magdalene* and in 1894, in his own unmistakable style, *The Repentance of Mrs . . .* (Pl 22). Interesting for

The text within the illustration:

THE REPENTANCE
OF Mrs ....

22 Aubrey Beardsley, *The Repentance of Mrs . . .*

our discussion is the contrast between the repentant sinner in the left half of the drawing and the grinning figures in the centre, as well as the relationship in which these two groupings stand *vis-à-vis* the idealized figure near the right-hand edge, reminiscent of Solomon's languishing hermaphrodites. In the course of his amazing artistic sublimation, Beardsley intensifies the irony of the situation through the secularization of costume and scenery and the simplification of line. The remorseful Mrs . . . , wringing her hands, is no longer kneeling in front of a prayer desk but a lectern – with cloven feet.

Even in Beardsley, however, the awareness of the escapist quality in contemporary religiosity does not signify the abandonment of spiritual aspirations. Just as typical as his oft-mentioned death scene is his reaction to AE's criticism of *The Savoy*, in which Beardsley's piety and the pathos of the modern artist merge:

Yeats, I am going to surprise you very much. I think your friend is right. All my life I have been fascinated by the spiritual life – when a child I saw a vision of a Bleeding Christ over the mantelpiece – but after all, to do one's work when there are other things one wants to do so much more is a kind of religion.[132]

Beardsley's drawings, Beerbohm's caricatures and above all, Oscar Wilde's essays engender the impression of an epoch characterized by frivolous worldliness and superficial brilliance. These features are unquestionably present, though far less widespread than is ordinarily assumed. The melancholy tone of Dowson's one-act play *The Pierrot of the Minute* corresponds more intimately to the sentiments of the English late romantics than the ironic detachment of Beardsley's illustrations. Similarly, with their acknowledgment of the religious crisis, Dowson's 'Benedictio Domini' and Lionel Johnson's 'The Church of a Dream' are considerably more typical than Beardsley's malicious exposure of religious escapism. The benediction appears 'perfect and complete', but outside the church the world speeds headlong towards doom and destruction.[133] Significantly, it is an ageing priest who celebrates Mass in both of these poems, a symbol of the 'Church of a Dream',[134] of sweet hopes and 'melancholy remembrances'.

Religious imagery

'Your style is too much sanctified – Your cut is too canonical'[135]: this sarcastic allusion to religious imagery, from Gilbert and Sullivan's *Patience*, makes sense when seen in connection with the mystical and occult tendencies, the interest in Satan and sin and the escapist forms of spirituality provoked by this. With the evaporation of religious content, the forms themselves become favoured modes of expression for a

secularized idealism. The remaining religious associations are welcome to
the symbolists because of their mystic inclinations. However, the degree
to which this imagery conveys an authentic spiritual experience is not
always easy to assess.

In the following lines from poems by Rossetti, Bourke Marston and
Le Gallienne the religious images have been reduced to clichés exercising
only a vague, idealizing effect:

> When do I see thee most, beloved one?
> When in the light the spirits of mine eyes
> Before thy face, their altar, solemnize
> The worship of that Love through thee made known.[136]

> O Love! O lord of all delight and woe!
> . . . Still to thy chosen children thou dost show
> The marvellous, sacred images that glow
> Within thine inmost shrine where one deep flame
> Intense and clear, of colour without name,
> Lights still the carven altars where they bow.[137]

> So I, who were fain of your story
> To be its high-priest to the throng
> To embody the mystical glory
> In a great eucharistical song.[138]

All of these poems celebrate the beloved or love in religious metaphors;
the last example, however, differs slightly in nuance, since the word
'eucharistical' has more specific and thus more intense religious connotations than 'altar', 'worship' or 'sacred images'. The contrast with
'Lovesight' and 'Brief Rest' becomes even clearer in 'Love's
Redemption':

> O Thou who at Love's hour ecstatically
> Unto my lips dost evermore present
> The body and blood of Love in sacrament;
> Whom I have neared and felt thy breath to be
> The inmost incense of his sanctuary.[139]

The range and intensity of the eucharistic vocabulary enhances the
metaphorical effect of the lines themselves but not its structural function
within the sonnet. The blasphemous quality, in particular, produces the
impression of contrived handling and endangers the intended spiritualization of love. The last of Rossetti's 'Willowwood' sonnets, on the other
hand, successfully suggests a union of spiritual love in imagery that arises
naturally from the notion of the well with its unobtrusive sacramental
associations:

Only I know that I leaned low and drank
A long draught from the waters where she sank,
Her breath and all her tears and all her soul.[140]

If the following verses from Wilde's 'Quia Multum Amavi' can be explained in terms of the aestheticist tendency towards the transfiguration of the flesh, the introductory lines to Francis Thompson's 'Orient Ode' seem to evolve from the new theological understanding of the sacraments. Nonetheless, as a consequence of the ambiguity of the matter, such distinctions are somewhat arbitrary since the transitions are frequently imperceptible. Thompson's eucharistic metaphors, although their ritualism is not as bizarre as that of Wilde's imagery in 'The Burden of Itys',[141] are not directly related to the spiritual focus of the poem. It may be possible to attribute this to Thompson's mannerist style but such an explanation begs the more basic question raised by Yeats's remarks on Beardsley's religiosity.

Dear Heart, I think the young impassioned priest
When first he takes from out the hidden shrine
His god imprisoned in the Eucharist,
And eats the bread, and drinks the dreadful wine

Feels not such awful wonder as I felt
When first my smitten eyes beat full on thee.[142]

Lo, in the sanctuaried East,
Day, a dedicated priest
In all his robes pontifical exprest,
Lifteth slowly, lifteth sweetly,
From out its orient tabernacle drawn,
Yon orbèd sacrament confest
Which sprinkles benediction through the dawn;
And when the grave procession's ceased,
The earth with due illustrous rite
Blessed, – ere the frail fingers featly
Of twilight, violet-cassocked acolyte,
His sacerdotal stoles unvest –
Sets, from high close of the mysterious feast,
The sun in august exposition meetly
Within the flaming monstrance of the West.[143]

In late romanticism religious imagery is characterized by the oscillation between a ritualistic 'gourmandise'[144] and the serious attempts to revitalize traditional liturgical conceptions in the service of the new spirituality. One aspect surfaces in Yeats's 'He Remembers Forgotten Beauty', the other in 'The Travail of Passion':

The roses that of old time were
Woven by ladies in their hair,

> The dew-cold lilies ladies bore
> Through many a sacred corridor
> Where such gray clouds of incense rose
> That only God's eyes did not close.[145]
>
> When the flaming lute-thronged angelic door is wide,
> When an immortal passion breathes in mortal clay
> Our hearts endure the scourge, the plaited thorns, the way
> Crowded with bitter faces, the wounds in palm and side,
>   . . .
> Lilies of death-pale hope, roses of passionate dream.[146]

Equally prevalent – not only in Rossetti's works but also in those of his epigones – is the tension between the idealizing function of religious metaphors and the unmistakable tendency towards their blasphemous inversion. While in Bourke Marston's 'The New Religion'[147] the idealization of the beloved is the dominant theme, the same aspiration takes on blasphemous overtones in 'Saving Love' when Christ's words 'I am the Resurrection and the Life'[148] issue from the mouth of worldly love. In 'Unseen Worship' Bourke Marston intentionally juxtaposes the veneration of the 'sacred image of my past',[149] lying like a saint entombed in the nave of a cathedral, with the Christian cult of the cross. His poem 'A Terrible Suggestion' ('If, after all, there should be Heaven and Hell')[150] illustrates all too clearly that behind the irreligious use of religious imagery there are indeed metaphysical ramifications.

Parallels in spirituality and artistic sensitivity produce similar formal problems for late romantic poets in France and England. A comparison of Baudelaire's use of religious imagery with that of his English contemporaries reveals differences in quality rather than in content, which consists of the same blasphemous inversions and secularized modifications of Christian material. The translations from *Les Fleurs du Mal* by Payne, Gray, Wratislaw and Douglas confirm the impression one has of similarity in subject-matter and discrepancy in stylistic achievement. In Douglas's English version of 'Harmonie du Soir'[151] the visual qualities of the original are lost in the replacement of concrete similes by abstractions ('Le ciel est triste et beau comme un grand reposoir' – 'A Shrine of Death and Beauty is the sky'), the use of colourless auxiliaries ('are' for 'frémit') and the recourse to Pre-Raphaelite stereotypes ('sweet; dancing feet').

The snake, the sphinx, the dance, and the rose as symbolist images

In their attempt to express a new kind of spiritual experience late romantic poets have recourse not only to traditional religious metaphors, but also show a preference for certain secular images. Several of these are closely related to one another. Baudelaire and Symons as well as O'Shaughnessy, for instance, frequently connect the image of the serpent with that of the dance. A brief glance at O'Shaughnessy's handling of the motif in 'The Daughter of Herodias' helps to illuminate the subtler representations found in Baudelaire's *Les Fleurs du Mal*:

> . . . on croirait qu'elle danse
> Comme ces longs serpents que les jongleurs sacrés
> Au bout de leurs bâtons agitent en cadence.[152]

Trying to capture the seductive and dangerous lure of Salome's dance O'Shaughnessy compares her hair to snakes. The words of her song become 'singing snakes' and one of the devils, in the guise of the 'Serpent king of old',[153] coils himself behind Herod's throne. The combination of the concepts of the dance and the snake reflects their shared function as motifs complementing the erotic anxieties symbolized in the *femme fatale* type. However, poems such as Symons's 'The Serpent', in which both Helen and Lilith–Eve are invoked, demonstrate that the serpent 'that before good and evil were / guarded the apple'[154] also retains its own religious significance:

> Is it the serpent that looks through
> Those eyes of death and wantonness?
> Wise men and kings, beholding you,
> Shrink up to dust and nothingness.
> Is it the serpent in your eyes
> That is still lord in paradise?

It is in the nature of symbolist imagery that these motifs appear in indirect metaphorical form[155] as well as in the descriptions of realistic scenes. While Baudelaire makes subtle use of suggestive language, second-rate authors like Symons and Field tend to state their theme more directly, but what they have in common is the effort to capture in the snake image the same contemporary fears of something unpredictably dangerous, repulsive or evil:

> The lethargy of evil in her eyes − . . .
> . . . − a viper lies.

> Brooding upon her hatreds: dying thus
> Wounded and broken, helpless with her fangs . . .[156]

> They weave a slow andante as in sleep,
>
> . . .
>
> Ancestral angers brood in these dull eyes
> Where the long-lineaged venom of the snake
> Meditates evil.[157]

Thomas Gordon Hake, whose interest in the dark and enigmatic came to light in *Maiden Ecstasy*, portrays the mysterious death of an ancient snake-charmer, who falls prey to his own quarry. Although devoid of biblical connotations and *femme fatale* associations, 'The Snake-Charmer' displays the symbolistic atmosphere of the snake motif:

> His eyes are swimming in the mist
> That films the earth like serpent's breath;
> And now − as if a serpent hissed −
> The husky whisperings of Death
> Fill ear and brain − he looks around −
> Serpents seem matted o'er the ground.[158]

In images like the serpent or the sphinx which have evoked mysterious and meaningful associations since time immemorial a contemporary penchant for esotericism is clearly manifest. As a result of their wide popularity, however, these metaphors of the mysterious are exposed to the danger of being overused and becoming clichés.

The enigmatic character of the sphinx (reflected, for example, in the title of Crane's painting, *The Riddle of the Sphinx*) appealed to the era of the 'relative spirit' because of both its threatening uncertainty and the possibility for widely varying interpretations it presented. With Rossetti and his epigones the sphinx remains a consistent motif. However, the continuity of this motif offers in itself little insight into its specific implications in literature or the visual arts. Two major types can be identified. The sphinx in Rossetti's drawing the *The Question, or The Sphinx* (Pl. 23) or in Thomson's 'The City of Dreadful Night' belongs to the breed fairly common in the allegorical painting of ideas[159] and, from the perspective of a pessimistic agnosticism, personifies the metaphysical situation in which only the meaningless power of the material world is perceptible. The aestheticist sphinx of Moreau (*Oedipus and the Sphinx*, Pl. 24) is characterized by the ambivalence of erotic fears and desires. Only with the many divergent uses of the motif in mind can the basic features of the type be discerned. In one of Baudelaire's 'Spleen' poems, the source of Wratislaw's epigraph for 'The Mad Sphinx', several aspects of the sphinx motif come together in a single context:

> Désormais tu n'es plus, ô matière vivante!
> Qu'un granit entouré d'une épouvante,
> Assoupi dans le fond d'un Sahara brumeux!
> Un vieux sphinx ignoré du monde insoucieux,
> Oublié sur la carte, et dont l'humeur farouche
> Ne chante qu'aux rayons du soleil qui se couche![160]

In canto XX of 'The City of Dreadful Night' James Thomson describes a symbolic scene in which a sphinx[161] defeats first an angel, then a soldier

23   Dante Gabriel Rossetti, *The Question, or The Sphinx*

24　Gustave Moreau, *Oedipus and the Sphinx*

and then an unarmed figure. Numerous conjectures have been made about the episode, which is probably intended to illustrate the various historical attempts to grasp the mystery of being. A previously ignored section from 'A Lady of Sorrow' offers new clues to its interpretation. Here Thomson uses the image of the sphinx as the expression of his own philosophical orientation:

Fate the Sphinx in the desert of Life, whose enigma is destruction to all who cannot interpret, and a doom more horrible before destruction to him who does interpret; Fate which weaves lives only too real in the loom of destiny so mysterious, uncompassionate of their agonies in the process; Fate, God petrified; the dumb, blind, soulless deification of Matter.[162]

The intellectual background of minor Pre-Raphaelites becomes clearer if we recall that Bourke Marston, whose lyric *œuvre* reads like a variation on *The House of Life*, explicitly refers to the sphinx figure in a poem dedicated to B.V., 'Brother, and fellow-citizen with me / Of this great city (i.e. The City of Dreadful Night)':

Still glowers the Sphinx and breaks us with her might
Of unresponsive front. There is no light;
There is no hope; God, there is no salvation.[163]

For Rossetti the sphinx unquestionably embodies a similar experience; in the sonnet 'The Trees of the Garden' he fearfully asks the dead

...is it all a show, −
A wisp that laughs upon the wall? − decree
Of some inexorable supremacy
Which ever, as man strains his blind surmise
From depth to ominous depth, looks past his eyes
Sphinx-faced with unabashed augury?[164]

The Scottish painter–poet Bell Scott also exhibits a striking preference for the sphinx. In the first of two pendant poems entitled 'The Sphinx', he asks the blind poet Homer circling the monstrous figure in search of the meaning of life, 'Did it tell thee anything?';[165] in the second he finds the solution, through a legend earlier portrayed in a painting by Olivier Mersson, and also mentioned in Wilde's 'The Sphinx': set against Homer's world of 'sword and spear' is the image of the Virgin Mary and the Child resting between the monster's enormous paws during the flight to Egypt. In the divine light the disconcerting problem embodied in the sphinx is resolved:

Behold, the light
From out the Child,
The Child divine,
Shone up into the vast wide eyes,

And made the arching eyelids bright
Against the darkening midnight skies.[166]

Bell Scott's 'To the Sphinx', a poem in five parts introduced with an illustration, is of particular interest because it documents the transition from the sphinx motif found in Victorian paintings of ideas to its aestheticist representations. The symbolic sense remains unchanged ('answerless, / Yet questioning for life or death'),[167] but a number of features, the outlandish and exciting scene of the construction of the idol,[168] for example, anticipate Wilde and *fin de siècle* exoticism. Both the fascination with mysterious oriental cults[169] and the reminiscences of Cleopatra[170] as a *femme fatale* point in this direction. Since Bell Scott – like so many of his contemporaries – vacillates between different metaphysical positions, the solution to the riddle of the sphinx in his poem of 1875 is not found in the light of the idyllic Christian legend as in his poems mentioned above, but in the spirit of an anthropocentric mysticism:

> The question comes again
> Which nature cannot answer, but which thou,
> Watcher by temple-doors,
> Thou mightest have solved to entering worshippers,
> Making them turn away,
> Earthward, not starward, searching for their home.
> Inward and not down beyond the tomb
> Nor over Styx for fairer days than ours;
> For night is certain on the further shore.[171]

Like Bell Scott, Oscar Wilde conveys in his sphinx figure the experience of something colourfully but also disconcertingly foreign, of something remote[172] and timeless.[173] Where he differs is in the shift of interest from the metaphysical to the erotic and bizarre. The monstrous love affairs of Wilde's sphinx are of the sado-masochistic kind which Praz has identified as one of the features of the *femme fatale*:

> O smite him with your jasper claws! and bruise
>   him with your agate breasts![174]

The same element characterizes J. A. Symonds's poem 'Le Jeune Homme Caressant Sa Chimère (For an intaglio)', Moreau's painting *Oedipus and the Sphinx* (Pl. 24) and Franz von Stuck's *Der Kuss der Sphinx*.[175] On account of her ambivalence, the sphinx becomes a favourite image associated with the *femme fatale*:

> then like rubies smarted
> With smouldering flames of passion tiger-hearted;
> Then 'neath blue-veinèd lids swam soft and tender
> With pleadings and shy timorousness surrender.[176].

With its mixture of woman and animal, attraction and cruelty, the sphinx, like the hermaphrodite with its fascinating duality of beauty and sterility, reflects a peculiar 'transcendence', overstepping established physical and metaphysical borderlines. The hero in Gautier's *Mademoiselle de Maupin*, who compares himself with 'Salmacis, l'amoureuse du jeune Hermaphrodite' and is confronted with the doubtful sexuality of his counterpart, begins to wonder 'si je suis un homme ou une femme'. The beloved he encounters has the 'beauté ambiguë et terrible du sphinx'.[177] In 'Contralto' the sculpture of the hermaphrodite appears as a 'statue énigmatique / D'une inquiétante beauté . . . / Dans sa pose malicieuse . . .'[178] It is the mysterious ambiguity of the features[179] and the suggested transcendence of the bounds of possibility that connect the motif of the hermaphrodite with the sphinx. The famous *Hermaphrodite Endormi* of the Louvre inspired not only Gautier but Swinburne to express that 'terrible mystery of beauty'[180] also inherent in Solomon's androgynous figures: 'some utter sorrow of soul, some world-old hopelessness of heart, mixed with the strong sweet sense of power and beauty, has here been cast afresh into types'.[181] In 'Hermaphroditus' and 'Fragoletta' ambivalence appears in different variations.

> A strong desire begot on great despair,
> A great despair cast out by strong desire.[182]

Swinburne has recourse to numerous rhetorical tricks (chiasmus, oxymoron, parallels, series) and to imagery reminiscent of the poetic diction of the eighteenth century:

> The son of grief begot by joy
> Being sightless, wilt thou see?
> Being sexless, wilt thou be
> Maiden or boy?[183]

For Baudelaire, cats, with their dual nature ('Ils cherchent le silence et l'horreur des ténèbres'; 'puissants et doux . . . / Amis de la science et de la volupté[184]), awaken associations of sphinxes, heightening their mysteriousness.

> Ils prennent en songeant les nobles attitudes
> Des grands sphinx allongés au fond des solitudes . . .
>
> Leurs reins féconds sont pleins d'étincelles magiques,
> Et des parcelles d'or, ainsi qu'un sable fin,
> Étoilent vaguement leurs prunelles mystiques.

Characteristically, in *Music and Moonlight* the sphinx appears in conjunction with the central mystical experience:

> It was the mystic thing priest showed to priest,
> And pale memnonic sphinxes slow intoned.[185]

These examples from poems by Baudelaire and O'Shaughnessy reveal the late romantic implications of words like 'magic' or 'mystic' far better than abstract definitions.

Like the sphinx, the motif of the dance is one of the conceptions which seem to encapsulate various prevalent experiences of the period. O'Shaughnessy's 'The Daughter of Herodias' illustrates the inner affinity between the different aspects. While Salome's dance and song primarily function as a means of seduction (*femme fatale* motif), a religious element accompanies the erotic element[186] from the very outset ('A devil did support her head'). Salome explicitly rejects the heaven of the prophets who oppose her influence,[187] and in her apostasy, what we have called 'negative spirituality' converges with the 'transfiguration of the flesh':

> A certain measure that was like some spell
> Of winding magic, wherein heaven and hell
> Were joined to lull men's soul eternally
> In some mid ecstasy.[188]

The vivid description of her allurements ('The veils fell round her like thin coiling mists / Shot through by topaz suns, and amethysts') recalls Moreau's painting and leads to a sensual and spiritual ecstasy overcoming the polarity of stillness and motion in the beauty of art:

> And through the blazing of the numberless
> And whirling jewelled fires of her dress,
> Her perfect face no passion could disarm
> Of its reposeful charm.[189]

A fusion of the erotic, spiritual and aesthetic elements, the ultimate aim of symbolist mysticism, is the motivation behind many of the depictions of the dance in the period. Since the authors are not always clear about their goals and keep groping for them uncertainly, their emphasis tends to vary from work to work. In addition, there is a great variety in the treatment of the same motif arising from the diversity of the sources of inspiration as well as from the differences in style and technique. The model of the biblical figure of Salome leads to a different rendering of the dance motif in Moreau, Field or O'Shaughnessy from the music-hall experiences of Symons, Wratislaw or Degas. Yet as a poem like Symons's 'The Armenian Dancer' shows, the basic motif remains recognizable among the most diverging variants. The poem opens on a realistic level but this is ultimately transcended by a *fin de siècle* mysticism:

I strain, and would embrace
With ardours infinite
Some angel of delight
That turns his heavenly face
Ever into void space.[190]

The English poetesses united under the pseudonym Michael Field transform the subject, well known to them through French artists and poets from Moreau to Mallarmé, with epigonic ingenuity: Salome's dance on the ice becomes a 'Dance of Death'[191] when she falls through it and her head is sundered from her body. One may have doubts about the authors' taste, but the symbolist tendencies are undeniable. Characteristic features are already evident in the initial emphasis on 'mysterious' oppositions and earthly and heavenly correspondences.[192]

Symons, who surrounds Salome with sisters ('The Dance of the Daughters of Herodias') to make her the epitome of woman, similarly uses epigonic modes of expression ('each of them / carries a beautiful platter in her hand').[193] Like O'Shaughnessy and Moreau, he strives to render the effect of the jewels sparkling with Salome's movements; here again, the dance motif enhances the *femme fatale* aspects of the figure, whose 'mystical' aura emanates from images like 'invisible presences', 'eternal white unfaltering feet'.[194] The poem culminates with the *coincidentia oppositorum* of the dancer's innocent beauty and the dangerousness of her dance:

For beauty is still beauty, though it slay,
And love is love, although it love to death.[195]

Although most of Wratislaw's dance poems, like those by Symons,[196] hardly ever amount to more than music-hall impressionism, he clearly sought to give them a symbolist tone. With the ludicrous pathos of a minor poet, in 'To Salome at Saint James' he identifies the ballet dancer in whose company he is dining with the biblical heroine.[197]

Several English variants of the dance motif offer insights into the nature of the French 'influence' more frequently maintained or denied than actually analysed in literary criticism. O'Sullivan opens 'The Dancer at the Opera' with a fairly typical *femme fatale*:

The dancer at the opera
Had the calm eyes and mystic grace
Of gray-clad holy nuns, but ah!
Her soul reflected not her face.[198]

Normally the *femme fatale* observes with cold indifference the death of the youth who has succumbed to her charms; but this time she happens upon four men carrying a coffin and, instead of proceeding to the opera where she would have proven her seductiveness during the gala performance 'of Wagner's music dreams',[199] repentantly seeks out a church. Nevertheless, neither O'Sullivan's moral emphasis, Hake's idyllic ending to 'The Dancing Girl'[200] nor Le Gallienne's conscious break with the 'light-winged music out of France'[201] can conceal the Anglo-French parallels in the use of this motif.

In the title poem of his collection *The Lonely Dancer* Le Gallienne emphasizes from the beginning that the impressionistic rendering of the surface *à la* Degas or the refinement of *intérieur* scenes *à la* Moreau are not his intention. What he envisions is 'a shadow-dance of mystic pain' that takes place in his 'lonely brain' and that is simultaneously 'The wizard-dance of wind and tree, / The eddying dance of stream and star'. The human dance[202] is but another form of the same motion governing the whirling of the sun's atoms or the airy spirals of a butterfly, all of which, however, are subject to the same fatality:

> And what if all the meaning lies
> Just in the music, not in those
> Who dance thus with transfigured eyes,
> Holding in vain each other close;
> Only the music never dies,
> The dance goes on, – the dancer goes.[203]

Lines like Le Gallienne's 'The dance goes on, – the dancer goes' differ from Yeats's 'How can we know the dancer from the dance'[204] in their *fin de siècle* melancholy and their specific symbolism, yet there can be no doubt that the conception of the dance informing the conclusion of 'Among School Children', Eliot's 'Burnt Norton III' or Valéry's *L'Ame et la Danse* originates in the same movement that led Wilde to adopt the Platonic understanding of the dance,[205] Stuck to paint his art nouveau masterpiece and the dancer Loie Fuller to become one of the idols of her time.

Among the symbolist images sharing a mystical quality the dance is particularly close to the rose motif because of their pronounced artistic implications. The rose imagery with which Symons opens and closes 'The Dance of the Daughters of Herodias' – 'Your dancing fainter than the drift / Of the last petals falling from the rose'[206] – represents the refinement which made the motif so attractive to poets like Rilke ('Die Rosenschale'; 'Das Roseninnere'). Before exploring the literary sources or the symbolic content, a discussion of the special timbre of late romantic rose poems would seem to be in order:

> Your rose is *dead*,
> They said,
> *The Grand Mogul* – for so her splendour

Exceeded, masterful, it seemed her due
By dominant male titles to commend her:
But I, her lover, knew
That myriad-coloured blackness, wrought with fire,
Was woman to the rage of my desire.
My rose was dead? She lay
Against the sulphur, lemon and blush-gray
Of younger blooms, transformed, morose.[207]

Unlike most of the poems discussed here, the verses by Katherine Bradley and Edith Cooper are based on a real rose, but the extravagance of the depiction, particularly the striking anthropomorphisms, causes the reader to forget that a simple garden flower lies hidden underneath the symbolist veneer. As with so many late romantic symbols the contents of the rose motif cannot be precisely determined but a fundamental 'symbolist quality' is clearly recognizable. The following examples from works of various contemporaries, intended to illustrate the broader context for Yeats's poems,[208] seem to have been inspired by two sources: the *rosa mystica* of the Marian tradition, and the distantly related rose symbolism of the occult tradition. The Pre-Raphaelites are likely to have encountered the orthodox Christian version in the course of their Dante studies, while the poets of the nineties probably discovered the occult conception of the motif in authors like Péladan and Villiers de l'Isle-Adam. In both cases it would be difficult to ascertain the exact sources. Far more important, however, is the renewal of the motif and the restructuring of its contexts which the English late romantics felt was necessary to capture their spiritual experiences.

Swinburne's 'Dolores' with its transformation of the *rosa mystica* into a 'mystical rose of the mire'[209] and Symons's 'Stellae Anima Clamat' with its blasphemous description of a *femme fatale*'s relationship to her lovers ('. . . she to them had been / The *Rosa mystica* − rose passion-pale! / The poison 'neath the petals slept unseen')[210] are two representative cases in point. The title of Wilde's collection of fashionably catholicizing poems, 'Rosa Mystica', points in the same direction. In Lionel Johnson's 'Flos Florum', however, the origins of the motif are immediately identifiable:

Rose, o Rose of Gethsemani Garden!
Rose of the Paradise: Mystical Rose![211]

Here as in Yeats's secularized variation ('Lilies of death-pale hope, roses of passionate dream'),[212] the rose in the second stanza complements the lily in the first, illustrating together two aspects of a mystical experience. These poems by Yeats and Johnson differ in the symbolic meaning of the rose motif but not in its symbolist purpose.

The identification of the ideal beloved with an invisible rose links Le

Gallienne's 'Flos Aevorum' to Yeats's rose poems. In its perfect beauty the rose is 'flos aevorum', the work of all time, a sacral gift to eternity:

> You must mean more than just this hour,
> You perfect thing so subtly fair,
>   . . .
> All time hath travelled to this rose;
>   . . .
> Time brings Eternity a flower.[213]

To achieve their symbolist objectives Yeats and Le Gallienne sharply restrict the concreteness of the rose and the individual characteristics of the beloved. These tendencies culminate in John Davidson's 'The Last Rose' (1899). Here, too, the impulses surfacing in the figure of the madonna-like beloved live on, but the features of the woman merge with the mystical symbolism of the rose:

> At daybreak a vast rose,
> In darkness unfurled,
> O'er-petalled the world.[214]

Dowson's 'Flos Lunae', which appears to be a companion piece to Davidson's rose poem, is equally characteristic of symbolist development in English poetry. While in Davidson's poem the rose takes on cosmic dimensions and totally absorbs the idealized female figure, in Dowson's poem − despite its title − the cold eyes of the beloved predominate.[215] The title does, however, attest to the poet's endeavours to employ symbolist modes of expression and to transcend the theme of unhappy love through the association of the moonflower.

The rose poems written by Arthur Symons constitute an important intermediate stage in the tradition and also call attention to affinities between such different works as Yeats's *The Rose* and Remy de Gourmont's 'Litanie de la Rose'. Yeats's idealizing identification of woman and rose corresponds to Gourmont's association of specific kinds of roses with diverse representatives of the *femme fatale* type. Symons's 'Rosa Mundi' stands relatively close to Yeats's 'The Rose of the World'. Yeats emphasizes the tragedy inherent in the experience of beauty and love, and seeks to achieve the fulfilment impossible in this life through apotheosis; Symons sees love as 'a pain / Infinite as the soul':[216]

> Then I saw that the rose was fair,
> And the mystical rose afar
> A glimmering shadow of light,
> Pales to a star in the night;
> And the angel whispered Beware,
> Love is a wandering star.

The real affinity between the poems is not in the content, in Symons's case a rather obvious eroticism, but in the symbolist air by which he imitates Yeats. In 'Kisses' Symons calls the beloved 'rose of the world', in 'Wine of Circe' he chooses the metaphor 'the rose of fire descends'[217] in order to 'spiritualize the embrace', and in the sonnet 'In Carnival' he describes an *occasion manquée*:

> Life in her motley sheds in showers
> The rose of hours still delicate
> But you and I have come too late
> Into the Carnival of Flowers.[218]

If the symbolist use of the rose motif were restricted to Symons and Yeats, a biographical explanation would suffice; given the parallels in the works of other poets including Le Gallienne, Davidson and Swinburne, it seems probable that this is a more general phenomenon. Symons, who addresses the beloved as 'mystical Rose'[219] in 'Mauve, Black, and Rose', makes use of the same kind of symbolist epithet which Swinburne had applied to the hermaphrodites in 'Fragoletta': 'O mysterious flower, / O double rose of Love's'.[220] The similarities of the major stylistic impulses in these poets do not, of course, rule out considerable variety in their adaptation of the motif.[221] While Swinburne, driven by his exceptional rhetorical talents, seems to discover the stylizing effect of the rose motif by chance, Symons purposefully introduces it to endow his Bohemian experiences with the enigmatic flair that had intrigued him in the works of the French symbolists.

What unites these different authors is the striving to transcend the confines of an established poetic language and the limitations of a utilitarian world-view. The essay entitled 'The Autumn of the Body' written by the young Yeats during the nineties brings the basic elements of the movement to mind. Yeats's remarks do not arise from the self-indulgence visible in so many decadent contemporaries, but from the acute experience of a 'crowning crisis of the world'.[222] This crisis appears as an emotional and spiritual atrophy concomitant with the Victorian myth of economic success and technological progress, which in turn occasions the opposition of many artists to 'the "externality" which a time of scientific and political thought has brought into literature'.[223] Since religion, too, falls victim to the process of 'externalization', 'the arts are . . . about to take upon their shoulders the burdens that have fallen from the shoulders of priests'.[224]

Today the political and social commitment of the Victorians seems more understandable than the inwardness of the symbolists, but this does not absolve us from the responsibility of analysing the literary theory, prominent motifs and stylistic modes of the symbolist movement in the nineteenth century. Such studies will enable us to identify and interpret numerous features of early-twentieth-century modernism, as well as the literary and non-literary 'escapism' of our own time.

Postscript: A survey of critical works since 1971

The English version of the book gives me the opportunity to discuss recent works relevant to the topic it treats. In doing this, the intention is not to present an exhaustive bibliocritical study but to define some major research issues and to offer some suggestions for future work.

In the attempt to sketch the English symbolist tradition from 1848 to 1900 I was faced with terminological problems which apparently continue to trouble researchers in the area. While for bibliographical purposes W. E. Fredeman's 'tripartite schema' consisting of 'the Pre-Raphaelite Brotherhood, the Pre-Raphaelite Movement, Pre-Raphaelitism', and Dowling's use of the terms 'Aestheticism and Decadence as major artistic ideas' are wholly satisfactory,[1] difficulties arise in the study and comparison of the content and form of specific works. The unbiased critic finds himself in the embarrassing predicament that he would be equally justified in applying several of the established terms, 'Pre-Raphaelite', 'aestheticist', 'decadent', 'symbolist', to a particular text had he not already made up his mind what he is looking for. The problem seems only in part one of regrettable 'misuse and misapprehension' (R. Z. Temple's criticism).[2] It arises to a large extent from the heterogeneity of the historic phenomenon itself and the great variety of responses, contemporary and modern, which it has called forth.[3] Nevertheless, the total scepticism which prompts Wendell V. Harris to propose 'an alternative way of regarding the really very curious mixture of theories, events, influences and results which are gathered together under the rubric "aesthetic movement"', and to see the phenomenon in terms of only six formal tendencies: 'The medievalizing, the botanical, the ornamental, the omnibeautiful, the demand for the artist's sake and the dreamily melancholic', does not seem necessary.[4] Derek Stanford, taking an inclusive view ('Pre-Raphaelitism might be described as a postscript to the Romantic Movement, a final manifestation of that force inhabiting the domain of visual art') has shown that Pre-Raphaelitism remains a useful term after all, if we see it strictly in terms of particular authors and traditions: 'through D. G. Rossetti one wing of Pre-Raphaelitism merged with Aestheticism and, later still, even with the Symbolism and Decadence of the nineties'.[5] Bearing this in mind, we should perhaps not insist on 'truth' so much as on functionality in

247

literary 'labelling' and apply the terms only in conjunction with a concrete set of motifs, stylistic devices or Harris's six tendencies.

Just as important as a precise understanding of the historical meaning of the terms is the critical awareness that each of them elicits a different response from us and directs our attention to different aspects of the same phenomenon. Studying the period that saw perspectivism and multiple point of view evolve as a consequence of the 'relative spirit', one should perhaps consider each of the terms as valuable in offering a distinct approach to the subject.[6] We refer to the Pre-Raphaelite centrepiece 'The Blessed Damozel' as 'Victorian', where we mean to discuss specifically British features and, for instance, relate the poem to the ritualist tendencies in existence since the Oxford Movement; we speak of its 'symbolist' features when we envisage it in the international context and want to show its impact on the French symbolist poets or paintings such as Maurice Denis's *La Demoiselle Elue*. If we apply the term 'aestheticism' to 'The Blessed Damozel', then we will probably be prone to experience the religious imagery as 'spurious', whereas if we identify texts and paintings as 'symbolist' we are more likely to accept the inverted religious imagery as expressive of the new kind of spirituality. Despite the vagueness of these terms most users will feel at least with some of them that their reference is limited to a specific phase between 1848 and 1900. Since for most critics 'Pre-Raphaelite' seems to refer to an earlier, and 'decadent' to a later, phase of the 'aesthetic movement', they will not normally call 'The Blessed Damozel' 'decadent' nor Pater's 'Diaphaneité' 'Pre-Raphaelite', although the respective qualities in them could be pointed out easily enough. However, our attitude towards this whole range of terms should not be regulated by our historical sense alone but by considerations of expediency as well. Apart from the obvious disadvantage of negative biological and moral connotations, the term 'decadent' also has the advantage of bringing to light connections between the seemingly unrelated 'aesthetic movement' and the 'naturalism' of Zola.[7] For an appraisal of the spiritual dimension the term 'symbolist' is clearly preferable to 'decadent' in part no doubt because of that 'mellifluous diffuseness' on which Ulrich Horstmann has ironically commented.[8] This indeed seems to be one of the thoughts that brought Arthur Symons to change 'decadent' into 'symbolist movement'. The fact that the term 'symbolist' provides a focus for studying continuity and changes within the contents and the forms of the English contribution to a major international movement is certainly the reason why it appears in the title of this book. However, the study of the symbolist tradition in English literature promises to be rewarding only if we pay sufficient regard to the richness of its international affinities as well as to the diversity of its indigenous strands and origins. Carlyle's contribu-

tion to Victorian symbolism consists both in the rediscovery of
typological thinking (*Past and Present*) and the import of German
Idealism and Goethe's notion of the symbol (*Sartor Resartus*).
Typological thinking, in turn, derives its inspiration as much from the
study of the Church Fathers and medieval theology in the Oxford Movement as from the new pastoral fervour of evangelical preaching. The
Carlyle–Emerson correspondence reminds us of the affinities between
Carlyle's Goethean and Fichtean inspiration and the Transcendentalist
conception of the symbol. Hawthorne's use not only of one scarlet letter
but of the whole language of types clearly constitutes a parallel to the
typologically structured canvases of Holman Hunt; his typological and
emblematic structures and effects pose essentially the same kind of problems for the modern sensibility. On the level of themes and motifs,
Poe's disconcerting fusion of Eros and Thanatos appealed to Rossetti in
his melancholy search for a sensuous spirituality and to Baudelaire in his
new art of inversion. What unites these diverse symbolists, however, is
a basic conviction of, or yearning for, a 'correspondence', for a profound, if occult interrelationship within their disintegrating world. We
shall appreciate typological thinking and the search for correspondence
more fully in the knowledge that the Freudian or Jungian interpretation
of symbols, for all its scientism, proceeds from assumptions and thought
patterns resembling those of nineteenth-century symbolism: namely that
beneath an apparent or surface structure there is a hidden and more
powerful level of existence which acts upon it and, in turn, lends itself
to 'allegorization'. In deconstructivist terms, the mode in which both
typological and psychoanalytical readings contrive their different 'stories
of meaning' is remarkably similar.

The term 'symbolism' is used in literary history by John Lucas, who
describes it as a movement in opposition to and replacing naturalism,[9]
and by David Perkins who applies it to Yeats and Symons, though not
to Dowson and Lionel Johnson ('*L'Art Pour L'Art*'), nor to George
Moore and John Barlas ('The Decadence').[10] The use of the term is
much more widespread in art history, however, where Hans H. Hofstätter in his comprehensive study applies it to a wide range of theoretical
statements, motifs, and stylistic devices characteristic of a dominant
tradition in nineteenth-century European art,[11] while Philippe Jullian
limits it to French painters like Gustave Moreau, Puvis de Chavannes,
Odilon Redon, Carlos Schwabe, Paul Gauguin and Georges Rouault.[12]
The chronology in Alastair Mackintosh's *Symbolism and Art Nouveau*
opens in 1848–50 with *Ecce Ancilla Domini* and closes in 1904 with the
Willow Tea Room designed by Charles Rennie MacKintosh.[13] This introduction to the subject published as a Dolphin Art Book together with
the great success of major exhibitions of symbolist art in 1972 in Paris

and London and in 1975–6 in Rotterdam, Brussels and Baden-Baden attests to the amazing renewal of interest in an art tradition that had for a long time been considered dead and gone. Given our new recognition of the impact of critical response, a close study of the present fascination with symbolist art and literature promises new insights to supplement the historical assessment of nineteenth-century symbolism. Exhibitions like the one in Rotterdam which brought together Edward Burne-Jones and Arnold Böcklin, Dante Gabriel Rossetti and Giovanni Segantini, Aubrey Beardsley and Edvard Munch, have demonstrated the advantage of the wider perspective. It suggests to the literary historian the possibility of viewing the symbolist tendencies as a wide-ranging international and yet nevertheless coherent tradition linking the nineteenth and twentieth centuries.

This is confirmed by a number of comparative studies that have appeared since 1971. The papers presented at a series of interdisciplinary symposia sponsored by the Fritz Thyssen Foundation have been published in 1977 under the title *Fin de Siècle*.[14] What creates the special interest of this impressive document of international teamwork as regards our theme is the introductory section dedicated to 'Conceptions and Intentions' and the group of papers on Belgian, Dutch, Polish, Swiss and Scandinavian symbolism. These papers, together with those on the Christ-figure in painting and literature, on the occult, on the demonic and erotic, and on jewellery in poetry and arts and crafts make us aware how unsatisfactory it would be to study the Pre-Raphaelites in isolation or to identify symbolism with a shortlived school of French poetry. A potent antidote to any narrow view of the subject is a collection of essays by Hans Hinterhäuser.[15] Under the title *Fin de Siècle* he compares the treatment of a number of symbolist motifs, such as the Christ-figure, the dead city, the dandy, the centaur, in several Romance literatures. The study of the transformations which 'Pre-Raphaelite Women' undergo in D'Annuncio's *Il Piacere*, Valle-Inclán's *Sonant de Otoño* and *Sonata de Primavera* and in *De Sobremesa* by the Colombian Silva sheds a new light on the 'Victorian originals' from which they derive. With our present interest in the dynamics of response, the transfer of motifs and the assimilation of symbolist 'precursor figures' like Plato, Swedenborg, Blake, Poe, Wagner will probably receive more attention and this promises a more profound understanding of literary motifs. David Riede, for instance, throws new light on Swinburne by taking 'the mythmaker's' book on Blake and his affinities with Baudelaire and *l'art pour l'art* as a means of approaching the subject, and, like Francis J. Sypher who documents Swinburne's interest in Wagner, he helps us locate Swinburne in the international symbolist tradition.[16] Erwin Koppen's *Dekadenter Wagnerismus* is devoted to a major complex of symbolist motifs and makes an important contribution, although his definition of 'symbolism' as a complementary term to 'decadence', the former referring to questions of form, the latter to matters of content, has provoked a sceptical response from Sänger and others.[17]

Diametrically opposite Koppen we find John Goode, to whom 'symbolism' appears once again as a historical period term, designating the phase after the revolutionary power of the decadent movement has evaporated: 'By the time "Symbolism" has come to replace "Decadence" as the comprehensive word, this sense of a movement, the change in the relations of literary production signalled by the word "revolt", is dissolved in a vaguer assertion of continuity – all poetry is symbolic, symbolism is merely the self-consciousness of the symbol.'[18] The most recent attempt to present the several definitions of 'aestheticism', 'decadence', and 'symbolism' in a balanced relationship is by Monika Lindner who seeks to reconcile English roots and French influence.[19]

Of particular interest in connection with the attempt in this book to establish a 'poetics of English symbolism' is a view such as the one held by Gerald Monsman who perceives that Pater's 'concept of language as a vehicle for multiple meanings coincides so closely with the Symbolist conception of poetry that Pater's 1891–2 lectures seem almost verbally to echo Mallarmé's 1891 interview with Jules Huret'.[20] In a comparative study of Baudelaire, Ruskin, Proust, and Pater, Lee McKay Johnson examines the impact of 'the Symbolist interpretation of the metaphor of painting on the concept of language as a medium and the internal structure of literary composition'[21] and, through perspicacious poetological reflections, confirms the relevance of my study of respective poetic techniques in chapter 3 of this book. Among the various attempts at defining the concept of symbolism I particularly welcome McKay Johnson's because it is informed by the conviction that there *is* an English symbolist tradition and that it marks a relevant phase of English literary history between romanticism and modernism.

Hardly less significant than the final direction which the symbolist tendencies took in the era of Pater, Wilde, Symons, and Yeats was the transformation they underwent from the romantic through the Victorian era. In fact, it was the realization of the amazing metamorphosis of romantic symbolism into a Victorian 'language of types' that initially suggested the idea of continuous but changing symbolist tendencies, which in turn led to the first edition of this book. The idea of Victorian typology as one of several modes of symbolism evolving and disappearing in the course of nineteenth-century social and cultural history naturally produces a somewhat different picture from the one emerging in such studies in Victorianism as Herbert L. Sussman's *Fact into Figure* (1979) or George P. Landow's *Victorian Types* (1980) which have contributed so much to our historical understanding of the language of types. As Sussman's book and Landow's several studies have received the critical attention they so fully deserve, I shall confine myself to a few remarks on our different approaches and how we may proceed from here. Both Sussman and Landow are aware of the difficulties modern viewers and readers have with Victorian typological thinking. Sussman wants 'to reconstruct the artistic and literary paradigm of the Pre-Raphaelite Brotherhood' and, appealing to the reader's sympathy, pleads with him to take typological thinking as something *sui generis*, deserving historical and cultural appreciation: 'not as misguided groping toward modernism but as participation in a widespread effort in the 1830s and 1840s to revive sacramental forms of art and literature through the adaptation of figural methods'.[22] Landow, who has drawn a detailed picture of the role of typology in Victorian theological textbooks and sermons and the impact they made on the Victorian imagination, naturally insists that we 'exercise extreme caution' in our use of terms like 'figure' and 'type'.[23] However, what the vague, secularized use of the terms criticized by Landow brings home above all is that the Victorian language of types bespeaks not only religious fervour but also antiquarian eclecticism. Serving edifying and affirmative purposes, it at the same time fulfilled a desire for decorative patterning and thus should not be seen in isolation from the rediscovery of emblem books and the enormous popularity of the 'language of flowers'. Typologies had a high entertainment value which merits our future attention. Now that it has become clearer to us to what extent typological structures inform Carlyle's and Ruskin's thinking (Sussman), Victorian sermons, Pre-Raphaelite painting, contemporary novels (Landow), and how far Christina Rossetti's poetry and religious prose is indebted to the 'language of flowers' (Gisela Hönnighausen),[24] we might proceed to a critical as well as historical assessment of their status. In the assessment of the typological as a mode of thinking and as a structuring force in Victorian art, literature and social life, it would clearly be inappropriate to judge it by modernist standards, something of which Sussman is not unreasonably afraid.

Although it will not do to regard typological thinking as a regrettable anachronism, the fact remains that its resurgence in the nineteenth century did not possess the same authenticity it had enjoyed at its origins in the Middle Ages or, as Ursula Brumm has shown, later in Puritan theology and literature.[25] Victorian typology, in Schiller's terms, is not a 'naive' but a 'sentimental' force and clearly constitutes one of the many restorative and reconstructive efforts of the nineteenth century, manifesting themselves in the several 'neo-movements' from neo-gothic to neo-rococo.[26] Our task as literary critics would be to describe where and how the use of typological systems in the nineteenth century differs

from that informing medieval thinking and art.[27] This might help us to
get beyond the Victorian question of the 'appropriateness' of, for instance, the rainbow as 'an emblem of that grace which should always
show itself ready to return after wrath' (Patrick Fairbairn, *The Typology of Scripture*)[28], and to come to our own aesthetic appraisal of
the typological tradition: whether and in what sense Holman Hunt's
typological paintings and Hawthorne's emblematic imagery remain
artistically satisfactory solutions today. In the attempt to establish such
a 'typological aesthetics' we would have to supplement our historical
research with a critical assessment of the philosophical tensions and
aspirations underlying the rediscovery of medieval patterns of thinking.

One problem that springs to mind, for instance, is how to reconcile the
clash between 'reactionary' typological structures and the new 'Aesthetic
of Particularity' which Carol T. Christ has so successfully explored.[29]
Recent critics like David Riede present a discriminating picture of the
impact made by typological thinking on poetry: 'rather than functioning
fully as typological symbols, as they might if their materiality were
insisted upon, the objects remain only suggestive, half-defined adjuncts
of a dream vision'.[30] With our increased knowledge we can now proceed to examine just how the Victorian yearning for the reassurance of
comprehensive typological systems combines with the inescapable
impulse towards the isolated and clinically rendered detail to produce the
manneristic effect of a 'symbolic realism' (Sussman) that has attracted
the surrealist Dali.[31]

The 'rediscovery' of typologies which Sussman and Landow seem to
derive mainly from the tradition of Protestant exegesis was probably also
nourished by the new interest in the Church Fathers and scholastic
philosophy in the Oxford Movement. This seems all the more likely in
the light of G. B. Tennyson's study of Keble's nature imagery ('The
Sacramental Imagination') and D. M. R. Bentley's very important essay
on the concrete biographical impact of the Oxford Movement on the Pre-
Raphaelites.[32] Thus it should also be regarded as a feature of the wider
medievalizing tendencies of the time which are the subject of a recent
book-length study of Pre-Raphaelite art by Wolfgang Lottes.[33] K. J.
Höltgen, known for his work on sixteenth- and seventeenth-century
emblem books, sees the Victorian penchant for the 'language of types'
as closely related to the rediscovery of emblems (see chapter 2 of this
book). He points out that 'type, symbol and emblem are often used interchangeably by the Victorians'[34] and, drawing on examples like that of
the Revd George Spencer Cautley (1807–80), tutor at the home of the
Marquis of Northampton, he vividly depicts the social and cultural context from which the Victorian 'renaissance' of both typology and
emblem drew sustenance.

That the revival of emblem literature should coincide with that of typological art needing explanatory texts seems hardly surprising in a period fascinated by picture-poesy and sonnets for pictures. Thanks to Richard L. Stein we are now conscious that Rossetti's sonnets do not just explain the hidden symbolism of the picture in the way that the epigrams of sixteenth-century emblems did, but instigate a 'ritual of interpretation' during the course of which the poet and the reader share their communal epiphany. By envisaging the 'literature of art' of Ruskin, Rossetti and Pater as an ideal act of aesthetic communication and a celebration of a vision, Stein confirms the view put forth in chapter 3 of this book, that the painterly techniques in late romantic poetry do indeed emerge under the impact of symbolist tendencies: 'The literary treatment of other arts in the writing of all three [Ruskin, Rossetti, and Pater] moves toward the values and assumptions of the various symbolist movements at the end of the nineteenth century.'[35] The quality in the relationship between the art object outside the text and the text itself which Stein (p. 8), following G. Robert Stange, calls 'open-endedness', reflects the symbolists' problematic attitude to reality. This term, of which Derrida might say 'ce mot a de la chance', could also be applied to the ambiguous status of the frames of Pre-Raphaelite paintings, which use their function of de-fining to obscure the borderlines. The texts and ornaments on the frame or on the canvas of Rossetti's paintings anticipate Louis Welden Hawkins's *Portrait of Severine* (1895) in the Louvre (reproduced by Jullian) where the material presence of the name as an integral part of the portrait intensifies the sense of strangeness and disorientation.[36] In the study of painting and music as essential and distinctive features of nineteenth-century symbolist tendencies, we witness the transformation processes that produced a new understanding of verbal art and the 'poetic prose' of Joyce, Woolf and Faulkner.

The 'ritual of interpretation' may be regarded as a consequent development and refinement of those ecstatic moments which are central to late romantic poetry and art and which accordingly continue to exercise their fascination on critics.[37] To judge by the level of sophistication in the debate on the stylistic impact of the 'literature of art' and 'moment's monument' we shall probably soon see some systematic study of late romantic diction and imagery fill out the sketch I have attempted in chapter 3 of my book.[38] In these post-structuralist days, however, it seems unlikely that nineteenth-century imagery will ever become such a challenge to critical minds as sixteenth- and seventeenth-century imagery was to our predecessors.

Present-day interest seems to focus more on the content of themes and motifs, with a greater emphasis on psychological rather than social implications. Pauline Fletcher supplements the study of Pre-Raphaelite gardens in chapter 4 of this book by relating the Pre-Raphaelite bowers (Rossetti, Morris, Swinburne) to the landscapes in Tennyson, Arnold, Browning and Hardy, while Elizabeth G. Gitter extends the treatment of women's hair by including interesting material from Dickens and Hardy.[39] The next question to ask here, as in the case of the transfer of Pre-Raphaelite motifs into other national literatures (Hinterhäuser), would probably be how these 'poetic' motifs affect Dickens's and Hardy's novelistic context and how, in turn, they are affected by it. In view of the influence of the nineteenth-century tradition of 'allegorization' on the Freudian study of symbolic images, it seems quite appropriate that psychoanalytical interpretations should play an eminent role in present-day Pre-Raphaelite and *fin de siècle* scholarship. In Carole G. Silver's view 'literary Pre-Raphaelitism' is a 'movement to which dream is central, a movement which utilizes accounts of actual dream, dream language, dream symbol, and, most significantly, a movement with the characteristics of dream itself'.[40] She concludes her historical sketch of the dream as a poetic convention with a reference to Freud's *The Interpretation of Dreams* (1900), before discussing dream features in Pre-Raphaelite paintings (hyperclarity, proliferation of detail, 'unnatural' colour, p. 13) and in the poetry of Collinson, Rossetti, Morris and Swinburne. As regards the study of nineteenth-century symbolism it is of interest that in Silver's essay the psychoanalytical and literary aspects of the term 'symbolism' seem to merge quite naturally: 'In his [Swinburne's] work the gap between poem and dream is closed, the way to symbolism is further opened, and the Pre-Raphaelite dream bequest is finally completed' (p. 45). Frederick Kirchhoff in 'Heroic Disintegration: Morris' Medievalism and the Disappearance of the Self' sees Morris's colourful picture of the Middle Ages no longer as an escapist dream, but as 'the medium of Morris' libidinal projection' (p. 93).[41] Dianne Sadoff, starting from similar assumptions, uses the phenomenon of repetition (as studied by Kierkegaard, Barthes, Deleuze, Said and the Freud of *Beyond the Pleasure Principle*, 'the fort-da game') as a theoretical platform for a new approach to Morris's medievalism that would avoid the frustrating alternative 'escapism vs social criticism'.[42] Both Helene E. Roberts, who distinguishes between daydream and unconscious dream, and Barbara Charlesworth Gelpi, who addresses problems such as the 'motherliness of the Blessed Damozel', keep their sophisticated and convincing psychoanalytical approach well within the biographical context.[43] But what if Rossetti, the focus of their attention, is a reflection of more general patterns? The same problem confronts us in the case of Rossetti's guilt complex treated by Florence S. Boos under the heading 'Sex, Guilt, and Victorian Preoccupations'.[44] How are literary critics to distinguish between those aspects of 'the divided self' (Masao Miyoshi) which derive from social and cultural causes and those which stem from biographical sources?[45]

So far we all seem to have rather naively accepted the Pre-Raphaelite lack of interest in political and social matters as a fact not requiring further thought, although we are well aware that Holman Hunt and Millais together attended the great Chartist meeting on 10 April 1848[46] and that, like Wagner's Rienzi opera (1842), Hunt's Rienzi painting (1848–9) derives from the revolutionary spirit of the forties. Even in the softening light of reminiscence the social involvement of the young Holman Hunt is still recognizable: 'Like most young men, I was stirred by the spirit of freedom of the passing revolutionary time. The appeal to Heaven against the tyranny exercised over the poor and helpless seemed well fitted for pictorial treatment. "How long, O Lord!" many bleeding souls were crying at that time.'[47]

If the Pre-Raphaelites were indeed moved by the social situation, why did they not artistically express their concern? Should we not look in their works, letters and commentaries for signs why and how they repressed their social experience? What were the psychological consequences of this repression? It seems likely that the unadmitted pressure of the social situation, as instanced by the melodramatic and sentimental quality in Rossetti's 'Jenny' and 'Found', influenced the choice of literary motifs as well as the style in which they were rendered. The questions are, however, complicated by the fact that established motifs such as the *Doppelgänger*, which Riede considers central to Rossetti's images of the double,[48] tend, on account of their historical weight, to develop their own momentum and make the individual impulses that occasioned them difficult to recognize. In future research we should perhaps take greater care to distinguish between the social and psychoanalytical content and the specific artistic and literary treatment of traditional motifs. The *Doppelgänger* motif, for example, represents a general psychoanalytical phenomenon that is realized in a particular historical and biographical situation, as in Chamisso's German *Peter Schlemihl* of 1814 or in Rossetti's *How They Met Themselves* of 1851–60. Then, however, through its literary use as a motif, it becomes part of an artistic tradition. As such it offers later authors an opportunity of structuring and stylizing their own personal experience of a 'split personality'.

The urge to transform the real into the visionary is particularly striking in the landscape of Holman Hunt's *The Scapegoat*, painted from nature on the shores of the Dead Sea in the early autumn of 1854, and Allen Staley has drawn attention to the 'fantastic' quality of this 'realistic' landscape:

Hunt may have painted what he saw, but by choice he saw strange things, and he saw them at their most vivid pitch. He chose to paint at sunset, and he waited for months in Jerusalem before finishing the picture so he could paint pink clouds into the normally empty sky. The colours are seen with an intensity and expressive power which go beyond naturalistic observation. Behind the goat, the landscape screams out in oppressive, strident chords which underscore the message of the impersonal and implacable doom.[49]

The question that remains to be answered, of course, is whether it was the typological intention of the painting which subconsciously led the painter to a distorted vision of reality or whether we should think of them as two separate factors contributing independently to the manneristic total effect.

Martin Meisel in his subtle study of such motifs as mirror, enclosure and picture has shown how the Pre-Raphaelites used them to dramatize their epistemological and aesthetic view of the relationship between nature and art.[50] With our Derridean interests in 'enclosure, marginality and parerga' we should perhaps also pay attention to an aspect of the relationship between nature and art that is implied by the mutual 'framing' of Pre-Raphaelite poem and painting. Each of them functioning as 'parergon' to the other, they create in the experience of the viewer–reader a multivalent tension which contributes to the 'relative spirit' and puts in doubt the ontological status of reality.

Given the relationship between canvas and surrounding space later to develop in art nouveau, the full implications of the Pre-Raphaelite use of the actual picture-frames also deserve further study. With their inscribed poetry, their symbolic decorations and ornamental shapes, the frames both separate and relate the painting and the surrounding world. Just as the dominance of literary, historical and biblical subjects gives an artificial air to the natural details introduced into them, the ornamental frames fend off any disturbing encroachment of reality.

One of the central issues in any discussion of symbolism is its religious or spiritual preoccupation, as illustrated by a favourite theme, Rossetti's 'The Blessed Damozel', and 'the problem of meaning in relationship to the reality or unreality of the supernatural' (Weatherby).[51] Riede describes Rossetti's 'Art-Catholicism' well enough, but, feeling as uncomfortable with it as most previous critics have done, he is obviously relieved that the poet discarded it and 'accepted the burden of speaking honestly and for himself'.[52] Ronnalie Roper Howard seems more willing to accept Rossetti's religious imagery on its own terms. She points at the frustration of the reader's orthodox Christian expectations as the root cause for the unfavourable reception of the poem:

The difficulty of willing suspension of disbelief in 'The Blessed Damozel' is that so many readers have a metaphysical stake in a Christian cosmology. Once go beyond that and concede the heaven 'real' so far as the poem goes, and the heaven becomes not mere decoration but an integral part of the meaning of the poem.[53]

John P. McGowan in his recent essay has elaborated on this point and shown that we have to appreciate Rossetti's special kind of non-orthodox elevation if we want to do justice to his poetry.[54] Similarly, rereading Christina Rossetti and allowing ourselves to be guided more by her unique tone than by abstracted themes, we may come to the realization that there is a new kind of spirituality linking her secular and her religious poetry. In D. G. Rossetti's Art-Catholicism, as in that of the *fin de siècle* poets, which was so convincingly presented by Karl Beckson, it is not simply that religious motifs have been emptied of their original meaning and filled with a new aestheticist content.[55] The distinctive feature is the additional element of inversion which the aestheticist use of religious imagery entails. This new 'metaphysics of provocation' which is treated in chapter 6 of this book, has been designated by C. Snodgrass — with regard to Swinburne — as the 'dynamics of transgression' and by Linda Dowling as 'the antinomianism, the *renversement* we expect to find in Decadent literature'.[56] It is the same kind of 'black' spirituality which is manifest in the replacement of religious orthodoxy by mysticism and the occult,[57] as well as in the demonic dimension of the new eroticism embodied in the Salomes of Wilde, Beardsley and Strauss.[58]

Having studied the contents of motifs and the iconography of the time, it would probably be worth paying more attention to the forms and processes of stylization to which they are subjected. As Mary Wayne Fritzsche has shown, the conflict of mimesis and symbolism is more conspicuous in the painted portraits than in their abstract verbal counterparts (e.g. Rossetti's paintings and sonnets *Lilith*, 'Body's Beauty' and *Sibylla Palmifera*, 'Soul's Beauty'), because of the more direct impact of the models, Fanny Cornforth and Alexa Wilding.[59] Douglas C. Fricke quotes Burne-Jones's famous dictum 'Of course my faces have no expression . . . ',[60] which also covers Rossetti's symbolic portraits and their verbal equivalents (see chapter 2 of this book). With Burne-Jones's disavowal of any psychological interest in the individual, Fricke's theme, the problem of stylization and the question of comparable artistic and poetic techniques, gains significantly in importance. The social and psychological realities as well as the transformations they undergo before emerging as literary motifs are forcefully brought home in two quotations in Peter Stansky's book on Morris. The letter in which Morris, urging a reform of the Victorian marriage system, speaks of 'the grotesquery of the act of copulation', casts a new light on the complementary portraits of the *femme fatale* and the ideal beloved.[61] An equally compelling text is Henry James's letter to his sister describing a visit to the Morris's. Depicting Jane, the original of so much stylized portrayal, as suffering from toothache, James is careful not to let his irony impair the fascinating force of the art image on his and the reader's experience. In view of this 'ritual of interpretation' to which James invites his sister and us, response criticism would seem to offer an appropriate means of adequately coping with the clash of fact and figure in symbolist art:

She haunts me still. A figure cut out of a missal – out of one of Rossetti's or Hunt's pictures – to say this gives but a faint idea of her, because when such an image puts on flesh and blood, it is an apparition of fearful and wonderful intensity. It's hard to say [whether] she's a grand synthesis of all the Pre-Raphaelite pictures ever made – or they a 'keen analysis' of her – whether she's an original or a copy. In either case she is a wonder. Imagine a tall lean woman in a long dress of some dead purple stuff, guiltless of hoops (or of anything else, I should say), with a mass of crisp black hair heaped into great wavy projections on each of her temples, a thin pale face, a pair of strange sad, deep, dark Swinburnish eyes . . . After dinner . . . Morris read us one of his unpublished poems . . . and his wife having a bad toothache, lay on the sofa, with her handkerchief to her face . . . this dark silent medieval woman with her medieval toothache. Morris himself is extremely pleasant and quite different from his wife.[62]

Like Henry James we know Jane, the art figure, only as Morris's and Rossetti's Pre-Raphaelite projection.

It seems that we are beginning to relate differently to the symbolist tradition in English literature since we now have our doubts about Eliot's hasty dismissal of Swinburne and Pater, and, with Pound's 'Mauberley', we have again come to feel the force of 'Yeux Glauques'. Critics have become increasingly aware of the complex relationship between modernism and late romanticism. Pound's little poem 'Shop Girl' illustrates clearly the impact of the 'discarded tradition' on the new artistic sensitivity. The focus of the poem is undoubtedly the chance encounter, rendered with imagistic poignancy, but the scornful dismissal of the great tradition is in actual fact an ironic means of bringing it to the attention of the reader. It helps Pound to endow his modernist Shop Girl with the profundity of symbolist portrayal.

> For a moment she rested against me
> Like a swallow half blown to the wall,
> And they talk of Swinburne's women,
> And the shepherdess meeting with Guido,
> And the harlots of Baudelaire.[63]

Notes

Abbreviations

'CDN'   'City of Dreadful Night', James Thomson B.V.
EI   *Essays and Introductions*, William Butler Yeats.
PB   *Poems and Ballads*, Algernon Charles Swinburne.
Wilde   *The Works of Oscar Wilde.*

Introduction

1 M. Praz, *The Romantic Agony*. Compare Praz's equally pragmatic attitude toward the term 'romantic', pp. 1–16. See also H. Mainusch, *Romantische Ästhetik*.

2 For examples of the different approaches, see A. E. Carter, *The Idea of Decadence in French Literature 1830–1900*; W. Harris, 'Innocent Decadence: The Poetry of the Savoy'; B. Charlesworth, *Dark Passages*; E. Koppen, *Dekadenter Wagnerismus*. On poetological questions in aestheticism, see L. Rosenblatt, *L'Idée de l'Art pour l'Art dans la Littérature Anglaise*; D. Cecil, 'Fin de Siècle'; J. Wilcox, 'The Beginnings of l'Art pour l'Art'; and I. Singer, 'The Aesthetics of "Art for Art's Sake" '. On the literary–historical context see, in addition to W. Gaunt's *The Aesthetic Adventure*, A. J. Farmer, *Le Mouvement Esthétique et Décadent en Angleterre (1873–1900)* as well as the more recent studies on major literary figures of the times by A. Lombardo, *La Poesia Inglese dall'Estetismo al Simbolismo*. For a discussion of the terminological problems, see L. Hönnighausen, *Grundprobleme der englischen Literaturtheorie des neunzehnten Jahrhunderts*.

3 On the use of the concept, see W. E. Fredeman, *Pre-Raphaelitism*, pp. 1ff, as well as his elaborations in *The Victorian Poets*, pp. 252ff. For a general survey of the movement, see W. Gaunt, *The Pre-Raphaelite Tragedy* (1942), reissued under the title *The Pre-Raphaelite Dream* (1966). G. H. Fleming (*Rossetti and the Pre-Raphaelite Brotherhood*) limits his study to an historical investigation from Rossetti's childhood until 1853, the year when the first, genuine 'Brotherhood' was dissolved; the Oxford group and the wider Pre-Raphaelite movement, which continued well into the nineties, are not discussed. J. D. Hunt (*The Pre-Raphaelite Imagination 1848–1900*) documents the continuity from Pre-Raphaelite literature to that of the nineties, and, in contrast to many earlier English scholars, recognizes the Anglo-French parallels.

4 J. H. Buckley, *The Victorian Temper* (p. 171) sees Rossetti primarily as a

Victorian, while for G. Hough (*The Last Romantics*, p. 53), 'Rossetti is an-
nouncing a new phase, in which the emotions that had before exclusively
belonged to religion are transferred bodily to art'. Rossetti is, of course, not
only the author of lines such as 'Thy soul I know not from thy body nor /
Thee from myself, neither our love from God' ('Heart's Hope'), which
helped to provoke Buchanan's attack and the 'fleshly controversy', but also
the poet of the Victorian sonnet and painting *Found*, which have much in
common with Hunt's *Awakened Conscience*.

5 W. Iser, *Walter Pater*, pp. 19ff and 49ff; P. Pütz, *Kunst und Künstlerexistenz bei Nietzsche und Thomas Mann*, pp. 1ff and my essay ' "Point of
View" and its Background in Intellectual History'. Evidently it is an international phenomenon which calls for a comprehensive poetological survey taking both national and individual nuances into account.

6 See U. Christoffel, *Malerei und Poesie*, and H. Hofstätter, *Symbolismus
und die Kunst der Jahrhundertwende*.

7 See also C. M. Bowra, *The Heritage of Symbolism*; W. Kayser, 'Der
europäische Symbolismus'; W. Sypher, *Rococo to Cubism in Art and
Literature*, pp. 169ff; R. Wellek, *A History of Modern Criticism 1750–1950*,
The Later Nineteenth Century, pp. 433ff.

8 On French symbolism, see G. Michaud, *Message Poétique du Symbolisme*.
Although his authoritative study covers the entire symbolist tradition from
Baudelaire to Valéry and Claudel, other scholars limit the term 'symbolism'
to the final phase: A. C. Lehmann, *The Symbolist Aesthetic in France:
1885–1895*; K. Cornell, *The Symbolist Movement*; A. Schmidt, *La Littérature Symboliste 1870–90*. Since the present study also explores 'symbolist' forms and motifs in the works of E. A. Poe, mention should be made
of his significance for the French symbolists. J. Chiari (*Symbolism from Poe
to Mallarmé*) denies such an influence, though not convincingly. T. S. Eliot
('From Poe to Valéry' [1948], esp. 28ff) faces the problem with due
discrimination.

9 On the Anglo-French literary relationships of the time, see R. Z. Temple,
The Critic's Alchemy; H. Dale, *La Poésie Francaise en Angleterre:
1850–1890*; E. Starkie, *From Gautier to Eliot*.

10 Hough, p. 210.

11 These two writers were the most frequently translated into English at the
time, as documented by the following representative volumes of poetry: *The
Collected Poems of Lord Alfred Douglas*; Dowson, *Decorations*; Michael
Field, *Underneath the Bough*; John Gray, *Silverpoints*; O'Shaughnessy,
Songs of a Worker; Vincent O'Sullivan, *Poems*; Theodore Wratislaw,
Love's Memorial, Some Verses.

12 In his essay 'La Poésie Nouvelle: A Propos des Décadents et Symbolistes'
(1891) the symbolist G. Rodenbach summarizes the essential features of the
movement – significantly emphasizing the same aspects as Michaud does
in his comprehensive study (II, 402–19) – and explicitly, if somewhat inexpertly, ascertains a connection with English poetry: '. . . une œuvre d'âme,
avant tout, sobre, sans plus de déclamation surtout ni grands gestes ni
délayage; mais mystique, ingéniée à ne peindre que des visions, des rêves,
des synthèses – les choses non plus comme un point dans l'espace et une
heure dans le temps, mais dans leur fixité hiératique et avec déjà leur part

d'éternité . . . La poésie anglaise a entretenu un tel idéal dont le germe existe dans Rosetti [sic], la Maison de vie, et dans Shelley – ces préraphaélites littéraires.' (*Revue Bleue*, 47 (1891), 430).

13 The impact of the Pre-Raphaelites, who were of considerable interest not only to Maeterlinck, but also to Stefan George and Hugo von Hofmannsthal as well as the artists Lechter and Vogeler, requires a specialized study. The fact that the same authors who were attracted to the French symbolists often showed a marked interest in the Pre-Raphaelites as well clearly demonstrates the interconnections within European symbolism. In the present study the relationship of the German late romantics to the Pre-Raphaelites is only mentioned insofar as it sheds light on the Anglo-French relationship (as in Hofmannsthal's essays, for instance). On the significance of the Pre-Raphaelites for European *Jugendstil*, see R. Schmutzler, *Art Nouveau – Jugendstil*.

14 For the way Blake was received by Symons and other late romantics important to the development of symbolist tendencies in England, see my article, 'Aspekte des Blake-Verständnisses in der Ästhetik des 19. Jahrhunderts'.

15 A. Symons, 'The Decadent Movement in Literature', 859.

16 On the relationship of impressionism in the visual arts and literature on the one hand to naturalism and on the other hand to symbolism, see W. Sypher, pp. 169ff and A. Hauser, *Sozialgeschichte der Kunst und Literatur*, II, pp. 415–60.

17 'The Moods' (1895); 'William Blake and his Illustrations to the Divine Comedy' (1897); 'William Blake and the Imagination' (1897); 'Symbolism in Painting' (1898); 'The Symbolism of Poetry' (1900); 'Magic' (1901).

18 If we think of the symbolist tendencies in such markedly different authors as Alexander Blok (see Bowra, *The Heritage of Symbolism*, 144ff) and Hawthorne, then the boundaries must be extended considerably. C. Feidelson (*Symbolism and American Literature*) has particularly stressed the specifically American situation.

19 W. B. Yeats, *EI*, p. 149, 'Symbolism in Painting'.

20 A. Symons, *The Symbolist Movement in Literature*, p. 3.

21 Symons, *The Symbolist Movement*, p. 1. On Carlyle's significance for the French symbolists, see Michaud, I, pp. 200ff.

22 *The Works of Thomas Carlyle*, I, p. 175, *Sartor Resartus*, book III, chap. 3.

23 Symons, *The Symbolist Movement*, pp. 2ff.

24 Ibid., p. vi.

25 *The Complete Plays of Gilbert and Sullivan*, p. 199, *Patience*.

26 Symons, *The Symbolist Movement*, pp. 1ff.

27 Ibid., p. 8.

28 Ibid., p. vi.

29 Ibid., p. 174. On Shelley see J. A. Notopoulos, *The Platonism of Shelley*; M. H. Abrams, *The Mirror and the Lamp*, pp. 126ff, and C. M. Bowra, *The Romantic Imagination*, pp. 20ff. On Pater's Platonism see Iser, esp. pp. 113ff. A systematic comparative investigation of Platonism in the nineteenth century remains a desideratum. Schopenhauer, for example, evidently influenced not only the decadent movement through his pessimism, but also the symbolist tendencies of late romanticism through his Platonism.

30 Symons, *The Symbolist Movement*, p. 174.

31 Plato, *The Republic*, trans. T. Taylor, ed. Theodore Wratislaw, 1894.
32   Then a sentimental passion of a vegetable fashion must
            excite your languid spleen,
        An attachment *à la* Plato for a bashful young potato, or
            a not-too-French French bean!
    (*The Complete Plays of Gilbert and Sullivan*, p. 200). The phrase 'attach-
    ment à la Plato' alludes only indirectly to the Platonic trends in contem-
    porary theory. The real targets of the attack are most likely the cultivation
    of an ethereal female beauty in the style of Burne-Jones and the related
    preference for the Antinous type and the hermaphrodite. See also Beards-
    ley's drawing *A Platonic Lament* in this context.
33 *The Works of Oscar Wilde*, p. 911, 'The Decay of Lying'.
34 Ibid., p. 957, 'The Critic as Artist'.
35 Ibid., p. 979; see also *The Works of Walter Pater*, V, *Appreciations*, p. 68,
    'Coleridge'.
36 Wilde, p. 981, 'The Critic as Artist'.
37 Ibid., p. 980.
38 Symons, *The Symbolist Movement*, p. 174: 'as we realize the infinite in-
    significance of action, its immense distance from the current of life'. For
    Symons, too, the artist is unable and unwilling to act; he tries to resist the
    'terrifying eternity of things about us' and to transform them into shadows
    by recourse to the Platonic–Plotinian viewpoint.
39 On the difference between the 'traditional' and the 'new' symbolism see also
    H. Bahr ('Studien zur Kritik der Moderne' [1894] in *Zur Überwindung des
    Naturalismus*, pp. 111–15, esp. p. 112): 'The new Symbolism makes a quite
    different use of the symbol. It too aspires to the spiritual, but it does so by
    a different means . . . It attempts to work the nerves into such a condition
    that they reach for the spiritual of their own accord, and it attempts this by
    sensuous means . . . The symbol is of great significance to the new Sym-
    bolism, but its significance is solely as an enrichment of the craft. In it, Sym-
    bolism has acquired a new technique, a previously unknown poetic strategy,
    a special lyrical method' (my translation).

1 Changing conceptions of the symbol in the nineteenth century

1 Since the romantic conception of the symbol (Wordsworth and Coleridge)
   has been exhaustively dealt with, it seems sufficient to summarize some of
   the main aspects. For a detailed analysis see M. H. Abrams, *The Mirror and
   the Lamp*.
2 '. . . who rejoices more than other men in the spirit of life that is in him;
   delighting to contemplate similar volitions and passions as manifested in the
   goings-on of the Universe . . .', Wordsworth and Coleridge, *Lyrical Ballads*,
   p. 250.
3 Pater, *Appreciations*, p. 85, 'Coleridge'.
4 Wordsworth and Coleridge, *Lyrical Ballads*, p. 113, 'Tintern Abbey', line
   49.
5 *The Poetical Works of Wordsworth*, p. 148, 'The Simplon Pass'.
6 Coleridge, *Biographia Literaria*, II, p. 258: 'to make the external internal,

the internal external, to make nature thought, and thought nature, – this is the mystery of genius in the Fine Arts'.

7 See Abrams, p. 258. For 'overflowing mind' see Wordsworth's 'spontaneous overflow of powerful feelings', *Lyrical Ballads*, p. 240.

8 'And now the Genius of Mechanism smothers him worse than any Nightmare did; till the soul is nigh choked out of him, and only a kind of Digestive, Mechanic life remains. In Earth and Heaven he can see nothing but Mechanism . . .', *The Works of Thomas Carlyle*, I, p. 176, *Sartor Resartus*, III.

9 See the short but very instructive essay by I. Fletcher, 'Some Types and Emblems in Victorian Poetry'.

10 'The invisible things of Him from the creation of the world are clearly seen, being understood by the things which are made', Romans 1.20, in John Keble, *The Christian Year. Thoughts in Verse for the Sundays and Holydays throughout the Year*, 1887, p. 65. The great number of new editions and reprints that appeared as early as 1827, the year Keble's book was first published, must strike a modern reader as particularly surprising and brings to light how foreign the Victorians are to us nowadays.

11 For the widespread use of the image see e.g. Christina Rossetti's poem 'Books in the Running Brooks', 1852, and Carlyle (*Sartor Resartus*, pp. 250–1): 'We speak of the Volume of Nature: and truly a Volume it is, – whose Author and Writer is God.' See also the following formulation by James Thomson, generally known as an atheist: 'And the whole universe being the volume of the Scriptures of the living word of God' ('Shelley, a Poem', p. 121, *The Poems of William Blake*, 1884, privately printed, BL).

12 'For our God is a consuming fire' and 'The wind bloweth where it listeth, and thou hearest the sound thereof, but canst not tell whence it cometh, and whither it goeth: so is every one that is born of the spirit'.

13 For the interest in the Metaphysicals see J. E. Duncan, *The Revival of Metaphysical Poetry*.

14 'Two worlds are ours: 'tis only Sin / Forbids us to descry the mystic heaven and earth within, / Plain as the sea and sky. – Thou who dost give me eyes to see / And love this sight so fair, / Give me a heart to find out Thee, / And Read Thee everywhere.'

15 Keble's *Lectures on Poetry 1832–41*, II, p. 480.

16 In view of the numerous parallels between the later Wordsworth and Keble, Ruskin and others it no longer seems appropriate to explain the changes in the works of Wordsworth as an indication of his diminishing poetical faculties. The ageing Wordsworth appears in a new light if considered as an 'early Victorian'.

17 Keble, *Lectures*, II, p. 400.

18 *The Works of Francis Thompson*, III, pp. 29 and 82, 'Shelley' and 'Nature's Immortality'.

19 *The Works of John Ruskin*, XI, p. 41.

20 Carlyle, *Works*, I, p. 175. For Carlyle's concept of the symbol see the formulation: 'In the Symbol proper, what we can call a symbol, there is ever more or less distinctly and directly, some embodiment and revelation of the Infinite; the Infinite is made to blend itself with the Finite, to stand visible, and as it were, attainable there', ibid.

21 Ibid., p. 57.
22 Ibid., p. 176.
23 Although Ruskin and Darwin were on good terms personally there can be no doubt as to the irreconcilability of their philosophical positions: 'Ruskin himself was even more sceptical of Darwin's theories than Darwin was of the genius of Turner, and often ridiculed them mercilessly in print, as in *Love's Mimic*', D. Leon, *Ruskin the Great Victorian*, p. 547.
24 William Holman Hunt, *Pre-Raphaelitism and the Pre-Raphaelite Brotherhood*, I, p. 350.
25 Ruskin, *Works*, XV, p. 117.
26 Ibid., p. 118.
27 It would, however, be unjust to blame Ruskin for not realizing this anachronism; for even a modern critic as astute as Wellek declares: 'he held a theory of art (and literature) which is far from incoherent or even old-fashioned, but it is an impressive restatement of romantic organicism', Wellek, *A History . . ., The Age of Transition*, p. 138.
28 'there is a message to be received from all things', Ruskin, *Works*, XXXVI, p. 123.
29 *The Poetical Works of Matthew Arnold*, p. 231.
30 Ibid., p. 233, 'The Youth of Man', lines 27–37.
31 'Bounded by themselves and unregardful / In what state God's other works may be', ibid., p. 240, 'Self Dependence', lines 25–6.
32 *Poems and Some Letters of James Thomson*, p. 139, 'CDN', canto XVII, lines 19–20, further quoted as James Thomson, *Poems*. By contrast see Keble, *Lectures*, I, p. 480: 'they guide us by *gentle hints* and no uncertain signs, to the very utterances of Nature, or we may more truly say, of the author of Nature', my italics.
33 James Thomson, *Poems*, p. 196, 'CDN', canto XIV, lines 73–5, my italics.
34 *The Collected Poems of W. B. Yeats*, p. 9.
35   How the moon triumphs through the endless nights!
          How the stars throb and glitter as they wheel
          Their thick processions of supernal lights
          Around the vault obdurate as steel!
          And men regard with passionate awe and yearning
          The mighty marching and the golden burning,
          And think the heavens respond to what they feel.
                  James Thomson, *Poems*, p. 198, 'CDN', canto XVII, lines 1–7.
36 Wilde, pp. 909–10, 'The Decay of Lying'.
37 The interesting role of the 'scientific principle of Heredity' as a 'warrant of the contemplative life' (Wilde, p. 970, 'The Critic as Artist') and the aestheticist 'escape' as a reaction against post-Darwinian scepticism would deserve a thorough study.
38 Wilde, p. 997, 'The Critic as Artist'.
39 For Pater's conception of the symbol see Iser, p. 82.
40 Pater, *Works*, I, p. 233, *The Renaissance*.
41 Ibid., p. 236.
42 Pater, *Works*, II, *Marius*, I, p. 116.
43 Ibid., p. 173.
44 Ibid., *Marius*, II, p. 20.

45 Pater, *Works*, VI, *Plato and Platonism*.
46 Ibid., p. 27.
47 Pater, *Appreciations*, p. 103, 'Coleridge'.
48 We are concerned here only with the aspect directly related to the problem of the symbol; for a systematic study of epistemological and aesthetic questions see Iser, pp. 113–14.
49 *Plato and Platonism*, p. 168.
50 Pater, *Appreciations*, pp. 46–7.
51 Pater, *Works*, VIII, *Miscellaneous Studies*, pp. 193–4, 'The Child in the House'.
52 Pater, *Marius*, II, p. 185.
53 The 'red hawthorn' is a particularly impressive example; see *Miscellaneous Studies*, pp. 185–6, 'The Child in the House'.
54 Ibid., p. 178.
55 Pater, *Appreciations*, p. 34, 'Style'.
56 Ibid., p. 31.
57 *Miscellaneous Studies*, 'Home . . . our ideal or typical conception of rest and security' (p. 179); 'a constant substitution of the typical for the actual' (p. 194), 'The Child in the House'.
58 Pater, *Appreciations*, p. 206, 'Rossetti'.
59 Pater, *Marius*, II, p. 71.
60 'after the world has starved its soul long enough in the contemplation and the re-arrangement of material things, comes the turn of the soul', Symons, *The Symbolist Movement*, p. 4.
61 Pater, *Marius*, II, p. 94.
62 Ibid.
63 Wilde, p. 857, 'De Profundis'.
64 Carlyle, *Works*, I, p. 178, *Sartor Resartus*. See also Wilde's distinction between Byron and himself as symbolic figures: 'Byron was a symbolic figure, but his relations were to the passion of his age and its weariness of passion. Mine were to something more noble, more permanent, of more vital issue, of larger scope', Wilde, p. 857, 'De Profundis'.
65 Carlyle, *Works*, I, pp. 178–9, *Sartor Resartus*.
66 Wilde, p. 867, 'De Profundis'.
67 Carlyle, *Works*, I, p. 179, *Sartor Resartus*.
68 See Wilde, p. 870: 'Renan in his *Vie de Jésus* – that gracious fifth gospel, the gospel according to St Thomas, one might call it – . . .'
69 Wilde, p. 872, 'De Profundis'.
70 Ibid.
71 Ibid., p. 869; compare 'Nay the highest ensign that men ever met and embraced under, the Cross itself . . .', Carlyle, *Works*, I, p. 178, *Sartor Resartus*.
72 Wilde, p. 868, 'De Profundis'.
73 Ibid., p. 869.
74 Ibid., p. 873: 'out of his own imagination entirely did Jesus of Nazareth create himself'.
75 It is for this reason that Wilde claims with regard to his companion prisoners in Reading Prison: 'There is not a single wretched man in this wretched place along with me who does not stand in symbolic relation to the very secret of

life. For the secret of life is suffering', ibid., p. 865.

76 Ibid., p. 871.
77 Ibid., p. 870.
78 Ibid., p. 871.
79 Ibid., p. 868.
80 Ibid., p. 864.
81 Ibid., p. 859: 'But whether it be faith or agnosticism it must be nothing external to me. Its symbols must be of my own creating. Only that is spiritual
   which makes its own form.'
82 Symptomatic of this approach is A. N. Jeffares, *W. B. Yeats*. The author
   is solely concerned with the difference between Yeats and the Pre-
   Raphaelites, ignoring all those features by which they seem related. The
   studies of F. Reid (*W. B. Yeats*, 1915) and P. Gurd ('The Early Poetry of
   W. B. Yeats', 1916/17) lack the historic distance to see Yeats within an
   English symbolist tradition. F. Kermode is the first to outline and prove the
   connection – following the example of Hough and Adams (*Blake and
   Yeats*) – by tracing the continuity of the central imagery. For W. G. Tindall
   ('The Symbolism of W. B. Yeats'), N. Frye ('Yeats and the Language of
   Symbolism'), and D. A. Stauffer ('W. B. Yeats and the Medium of Poetry')
   the early works only mark a preparatory stage for the symbolism of Yeats's
   later work.
83 Edwin John Ellis and William Butler Yeats, *The Works of William Blake*,
   I, p. 237.
84 See C. M. Bowra, *The Romantic Imagination*.
85 *Plato and Platonism*, p. 19. Compare Pater's striking interest in Hegel. See
   B. Fehr, 'Walter Pater and Hegel' and Iser, pp. 95–6.
86 N. Frye, *Fearful Symmetry*.
87 Yeats and Ellis, p. 239. See also: 'needing an always less delicate body, or
   symbol', *EI*, p. 158, 'The Symbolism of Poetry'.
88 Pater, *Marius*, II, pp. 93–4.
89 See J. Senior, *The Way Down and Out*.
90 *EI*, p. 150, 'Symbolism in Painting'.
91 Ibid., p. 160, 'The Symbolism of Poetry'.
92 Ibid., p. 161, my italics: *allegorist* as opposed to *symbolist*.
93 In 'Symbolism in Painting' (p. 149) Yeats sees 'The Poetry of Verlaine' as
   part of an international symbolist movement.
94 See his discussion of Pre-Raphaelite emblems in 'Symbolism in Painting',
   p. 147. See also Rossetti's paintings *Ecce Ancilla Domini* and *The Girlhood
   of Mary Virgin* (Pl. 17).
95 Maeterlinck's affinity with the Pre-Raphaelites constitutes a special case.
   Individual relationships which sometimes surprise the modern reader occur,
   however, with considerable frequency, e.g. Rimbaud's verses for Millais's
   painting of Ophelia or Debussy's music for Rossetti's *The Blessed Damozel*.
96 Yeats, *Collected Poems*, p. 47.
97 Frye, 'Yeats and the Language of Symbolism', 4.
98 'He [Blake] was a symbolist who had to invent his symbols; and his coun-
   ties of England, with their correspondence to tribes of Israel . . . are arbitrary as some of the symbolism in the *Axël* of the symbolist Villiers de
   l'Isle-Adam is arbitrary . . .', 'Symbolism in Painting', p. 114.

99 *EI*, p. 140, 'Blake's Illustrations to Dante'.
100 Ibid., p. 155, 'The Symbolism of Poetry'.
101 Ibid., p. 156.
102 Ibid., p. 157.
103 Ibid., p. 163.
104 Ibid., p. 159.
105 Ibid., p. 162.
106 Compare Symons, *The Symbolist Movement*, p. 174: 'as we realize the infinite insignificance of action'.
107 *EI*, 'The Symbolism of Poetry', p. 162.
108 See Yeats's commentary on 'The Caps and Bells' in *Collected Poems*, p. 526.
109 See Yeats's description in 'Symbolism in Painting', *EI*, p. 151: 'I closed my eyes a moment ago and a company of people in blue robes swept by me in a blinding light.'
110 *EI*, p. 28, 'Magic'.
111 Of the great number of studies on Yeats's occultism the concern here is restricted to those that deal with the special relationship of occultism and symbolism: see Senior, *The Way Down and Out*; Tindall, 'The Symbolism of W. B. Yeats'; M. Rudd, *Divided Image*. Occultism is not only a characteristic element in Yeats, but of nineteenth-century symbolism in general.
112 *EI*, pp. 156–7, 'The Symbolism of Poetry'. Compare the quotations from Pater's 'Style', *Appreciations*, pp. 34 and 31 (nn. 17 and 18).
113 *EI*, p. 148, 'Symbolism in Painting'.
114 See Hofstätter, *Symbolismus und die Kunst der Jahrhundertwende*.
115 Stylistic imitations are frequent in both poetry and painting; Swinburne's *Poems and Ballads* (1866) are a notorious example.
116 Charles Baudelaire, *Œuvres Complètes*, p. 705, 'Victor Hugo'.
117 Ibid., p. 1044, 'Salon de 1859'.
118 'La Nature est un temple où de vivants piliers / Laissent parfois sortir de confuses paroles; / L'homme y passe à travers de forêts de symboles / Qui l'observent avec des regards familiers', Baudelaire, *Les Fleurs du Mal*, p. 13, 'Correspondances'.
119 Ibid., line 8.
120 Théophile Gautier, *Emaux et Camées*, p. 5, 'Affinités Secrètes', stanza 5.
121 Ibid., stanzas 6 and 7.
122 Symons, *The Symbolist Movement*, p. 3.
123 For the special idea of correspondence in the Metaphysicals see Duncan, p. 32; Duncan also analyses the different ideas of analogy in the Metaphysicals and the nineteenth-century symbolists.
124 See Duncan, pp. 54–5.
125 In 'Symbolism in Painting' (*EI*, p. 146) Yeats establishes the relationship between the modern conception of the symbol and the correspondences of the occult tradition: 'The things below are as the things above "of the Emerald Tablet of Hermes".'
126 Compare e.g. Balzac's novel *Séraphita*, 1846 (published in vol. 16 of the *Comédie Humaine*, vol. 3 of the 5th edn of *Etudes Philosophiques*. The first parts appear in the *Revue de Paris*, June and July, 1834). For the influence

of Swedenborg see K. E. Sjöden, 'Balzac et Swedenborg'.

2 Typology and allegory in late romantic literature

1 Charlotte M. Yonge, *Heartsease, or The Brother's Wife*, 1853, pp. 231–2.
2 William Bell Scott, *Poems by a Painter*, 1854, p. 70.
3 'the light and the appearances of the declining and the setting sun are much more fitted to be types and characters of the infinite', *The Collected Writings of Thomas De Quincey*, III, p. 444, *Confessions*; (hereafter De Quincey, III, *Confessions*).
4 Revd. Richard Glover, *'The Light of the World' or Holman Hunt's Great Allegorical Picture, Translated into Words*, 1862, p. 3; see also Hunt's own commentary on his painting (p. 13 of the present book).
5 Revd. Hugh C. Chapman, *Sermons in Symbols*, 1888, pp. 8–9: 'An alternative is offered underneath in the shape of a yoke, at the extremities of which are two circular cords, to be occupied presumably by the Christian and his Master, so that they become yoke-fellows, and associated in their work of ploughing for the glory of God. In the centre of the yoke is a cross, without which principle no perseverance is possible, and which reminds us that it is a labour of love, thereby abstracting any unwillingness which we might feel in undertaking the same. Wreathed round the yoke is a trail of heartsease, teaching that it is an easy one, and that it brings rest to the soul which accepts it'. On Victorian typology see G. P. Landow, *Victorian Types, Victorian Shadows: Biblical Typology in Victorian Literature, Art, and Thought* and *William Holman Hunt and Typological Symbolism*; and H. Sussman, *Fact into Figure: Typology in Carlyle, Ruskin, and the Pre-Raphaelite Brotherhood*.
6 E. Mills, *The Life and Letters of Frederic Shields*, p. 309. See also the report of the work in progress in The Chapel of the Ascension in Bayswater, Mills, p. 313, letter to Watts 13 November 1891. Rossetti's *Sonnets for Pictures* have to be seen in connection with the same tendencies.
7 For the Victorian taste in decoration and Victorian theories of design see A. Boe, *From Gothic Revival to Functional Form*. For emblematic decoration see Buckley, *The Victorian Temper*, p. 139. For the increasing aestheticist tendencies which resulted from the Industrial Revolution see also Q. Bell, *Victorian Artists*, pp. 5–6.
8 *Rossetti's Poems*, p. 25 (hereafter cited as Rossetti, *Poems*).
9 Mills, pp. 269–70; for the motif of the scapegoat see also Hunt's painting and his comment on *The Scapegoat* (Azazael) in *Pre-Raphaelitism and the Pre-Raphaelite Brotherhood*, II, pp. 108–9.
10 Mills, p. 268.
11 Rossetti, *Poems*, pp. 25–6, 'Ave'.
12 Ibid., p. 140, 'The Passover in the Holy Family'.
13 Ibid., p. 141, 'Mary Magdalene at the Door of Simon the Pharisee' (For a Drawing).
14 Ibid., p. 137, 'For Our Lady of the Rocks by Leonardo Da Vinci'.
15 *Letters of Dante Gabriel Rossetti*, I, p. 44.
16 *The Germ. Thoughts towards Nature in Poetry, Literature, and Art*, with an introduction by W. M. Rossetti, p. 20 (introduction).

17 I. Full of anguish and terror the Child Jesus watches a falcon slay his dove ('The Agony in the Garden'). II. He witnesses two young men maltreating an ass ('The Scourging'). III. His playmates crown him with a wreath of hawthorn blossoms ('The Crowning with Thorns'). IV. He wants to help Joseph to carry some wood ('Jesus Carrying the Cross'). V. Mary tells him her dream: she saw His little lamb falling into a hole and dying ('The Crucifixion'). *The Germ*, 2 (February 1850), pp. 49–57.

18 *The Germ*, p. 55:

> And Jesus, kneeling by it, fondled with
> The little creature, that could scarce find how
> To show its love enough; licking his hands,
> Then starting from him, gambolled back again,
> And, with its white feet upon Jesus' knees,
> Nestled his head by his.

19 Ibid., p. 51.

20 Ibid., p. 57, 'Which tells us about the patient suffering lamb.'

21 George William Russell (AE), *Collected Poems*, 1913, pp. 15 and 48, 'Symbolism': 'We rise, but by the symbol charioted, / Through loved things rising up to Love's own ways' (hereafter AE, *Collected Poems*).

22 'Le *macrocosme*, ou grand monde, a été construit par art cabalistic; le *microcosme*, ou petit monde, est son image réflechi dans tous les cœurs', Nerval, *Œuvres*, I, p. 415, *Aurélia* and: 'Fourier et Swedenborg, l'un avec ses analogies, l'autre avec ses correspondances', Baudelaire, *Œuvres*, p. 376, *Les Paradis Artificiels*.

23 *The Works of Francis Thompson*, III, p. 25, 'Shelley', and I, p. 125.

24 Ibid., I, p. 118.

25 Ibid., pp. 126–7.

26 Compare e.g. Michael Field's 'A Dance of Death', *An Anthology of 'Nineties' Verse*, pp. 57ff: While Salome is dancing on the ice, the ice breaks and her head is severed 'by the ice-brook sword' and goes on dancing on the 'bright and silver ice'.

27 Michael Field, *Wild Honey from Various Thyme*, 1908, p. 8:

> To give me its bright plumes, they shot a jay:
> On the fresh jewels, blood! Oh, sharp remorse!
> The glittering symbols of the little corse
> I buried where the wood was noisome, blind,
> Praying that I might nevermore betray
> The universe, so whole within my mind.

28 *The Works of Francis Thompson*, II, p. 181.

29 Wilde, p. 969, 'The Critic as Artist'.

30 Wilde, p. 912, 'The Decay of Lying'; see also p. 918: 'As a method realism is a complete failure.'

31 Tupper, 'The Subject in Art', *The Germ*, p. 11.

32 Hunt, *Pre-Raphaelitism and the Pre-Raphaelite Brotherhood*, I, p. 132; for the influence of the Nazarenes, see K. Andrews, *The Nazarenes*; on the Pre-Raphaelite tendencies towards medievalism see J. D. Hunt, 'Embroideries of Myth: Mediaevalism' in *Pre-Raphaelite Imagination*, pp. 33–72; and W. Lottes, *Wie ein goldener Traum – Die Rezeption des Mittelalters in der Kunst der Präraffaeliten*.

33 *The Collected Works of William Morris*, I, p. 124, 'The Haystack in the Floods'.
34 Ford Madox Brown, 'On the Mechanism of a Historical Picture', *The Germ*, p. 70.
35 Tupper, 'The Subject in Art, No. II', *The Germ*, p. 121.
36 Stephens, 'Modern Giants', *The Germ*, p. 171.
37 Tupper, 'The Subject in Art, No. II', *The Germ*, p. 125.
38 Rossetti, *Poems*, p. 64.
39 For melodramatic features see Bell Scott, *Poems*, 1854, p. 33, 'Maryanne'; for sentimental features, Vincent O'Sullivan, *The Houses of Sin*, 1897, p. 56, 'A Slave of the Street'; for moralism, Philip Bourke Marston, *The Collected Poems*, 1892, pp. 44–5.
40 Stephens, 'The Purpose and Tendency of Early Italian Art', *The Germ*, p. 59.
41 Ibid., p. 58.
42 Ibid., p. 61.
43 Ibid., pp. 58 and 64.
44 For a general survey see Fleming, *Rossetti and the Pre-Raphaelite Brotherhood*.
45 Stephens, 'The Purpose and Tendency of Early Italian Art', p. 63.
46 Compare e.g. Laurence Housman, 'Pre-Raphaelitism in Art and Poetry', esp. pp. 7–8 and H. House, *All in Due Time*, for the Victorian preference 'for facts', pp. 141–2.
47 *Letters of James Smetham*, p. 308. For the importance attached to models as an immediate consequence of Pre-Raphaelite realism compare the well-known anecdote about Lizzie Siddal falling ill after lying for hours in a bathtub as a model for Millais's drowning *Ophelia*. Smetham's remarks, too, must appear rather strange to a modern reader: 'I want a dead lamb for my "First Passover" and I must have a model. I want it soon. I send to our butcher. He "does not kill lamb yet; it is too expensive; in a week or two, he may and will let me know". This morning his man says, he can't when they kill, bring the lamb here, for "unless the skin is taken off while it is warm they can't take it off". So I have to go to it, and be quick about it.' For the rendering of detail see C. Christ, *The Finer Optic*.
48 According to Ruskin every painter should ask himself the following questions (*Works*, III, pp. 662–3): '(1) Is my whole right? (2) Can my detail be added to it? Is there a single space in the picture where I can crowd in another thought? . . . Is there a single spot which the eye, by any peering or prying, can further exhaust?'
49 Hunt, I, p. 276; for the technique of the Pre-Raphaelites, see Bell, pp. 33–4.
50 For the seemingly heterogeneous elements in Pre-Raphaelite art, see Bowra (*The Romantic Imagination*, p. 199) and H. M. Jones (in *The Victorian Poets*, ed. F. E. Faverty, p. 174); and esp. Fredeman (*Pre-Raphaelitism*, pp. 7–38).
51 T. Woolner, *My Beautiful Lady*, 1836, p. 125.
52 Woolner, *My Beautiful Lady*, *The Germ*, p. 2.
53 See, for example, the effect of the numerous bird metaphors.
54 Woolner, 'Of My Lady in Death', *The Germ*, p. 5.
55 Woolner, *My Beautiful Lady*, *The Germ*, p. 2.

56 C. K. D. Patmore, 'The Seasons', *The Germ*, p. 19, and *The Poetical Works of John Payne*, 1902, II, p. 100, 'Madonna Dei Sogni'.

57 J. Collinson, 'The Child Jesus', *The Germ*, p. 52.

58 Bell Scott's book on Dürer (*Albrecht Durer* [*sic*]: *His Life and Works*, 1869) is an illuminating example of this aspect of Pre-Raphaelitism.

59 Tupper, 'A Sketch from Nature', *The Germ*, p. 47.

60 See A. Benson, *Dante Gabriel Rossetti*, p. 95, 'There is no English poet of the nineteenth century who has so little of the instinctive love of nature as Rossetti.'

61 Rossetti, *Poems*, p. 216.

62 Tupper, 'A Sketch from Nature', *The Germ*, p. 47.

63 Rossetti, *Poems*, p. 215.

64 Ibid., p. 216.

65 As examples of stylized nature description see Wilde's 'Le Jardin' and the first six stanzas of 'The Burden of Itys'.

66 See e.g. 'Fantaisies d'Hiver' or 'Premier Sourire du Printemps'.

67 Wilde, p. 941, 'Pen, Pencil and Poison'.

68 Hunt, II, pp. 110–11 – for the tension between realism and the intended symbolic interpretation see H. L. Weatherby, 'Problems of Form and Content in the Poetry of Dante Gabriel Rossetti'.

69 Rossetti, *Poems*, p. 258: 'Ah! gave not these two hearts their mutual pledge / Under one mantle sheltered 'neath the hedge'.

70 Bell Scott, *William Blake, Etchings from his Works*, 1878: 'photography showed them the miracles of unselected detail' (p. 4) and 'We have mentioned photography as an influence in the external development of modern painting. It gave the suggestion of indiscriminate detail, distinguishing the movement called Pre-Raphaelite, and made realism absolutely necessary to the canvas of the painter' (p. 5).

71 Yeats, *EI*, p. 140, 'William Blake and his Illustrations to the Divine Comedy': 'True art is expressive and symbolic, and makes every form, every sound, every colour, every gesture, a signature of some unanalysable imaginative essence. False art is not expressive, but mimetic, not from experience but from observation.'

72 *The Works of Francis Thompson*, III, p. 83, 'Nature's Immortality': 'Not the so-called Art which aims at the mere photographic representation of external objects, for that can only reproduce'.

73 Wilde, p. 970, 'The Critic as Artist'. Anglo-French parallels are obvious. As early as his 'Salon de 1859' Baudelaire had expressed the same idea under the title 'Le Public Moderne et la Photographie': 'Où il ne faudrait voir que le Beau, notre public ne cherche que le Vrai . . .' – 'je suis convaincu que le progrès de la photographie, comme d'ailleurs, tous les progrès purement matériels ont beaucoup contribué à l'appauvrissement du génie artistique français déjà si rare' (*Œuvres*, p. 1033).

74 Wilde, p. 970, 'The Critic as Artist'.

75 Gisela Hönnighausen, *Christina Rossetti als viktorianische Dichterin*, pp. 137ff and 189ff and 'Emblematic Tendencies in the Works of Christina Rossetti'. Here and in following paragraphs I am indebted to my wife's study of Victorian flower emblems.

76 Keble, *The Christian Year*, pp. 82–5.

77 Wordsworth, *Poetical Works*, p. 134.
78 *The Flower Book* by Edward Burne-Jones, 1905, Preface by Georgina Burne-Jones, pp. 1–2.
79 'He wished them not to be separated' – see, for example, the following description: 'I. Love in a Mist. A mist which does not arise from the earth but is made of heaven's blue, swirls round and round the struggling figure of a winged-man, who is Love himself, baffled and blinded by its folds.' For the practice of developing entire scenes from the names of flowers see Walter Crane, *A Floral Fantasy in an Old English Garden*, 1898.
80 William Allingham, *Flower Pieces and Other Poems*, 1888, e.g. pp. 17 or 24.
81 Ibid., p. 16: 'Thus each modal element / A faculty doth represent . . .'.
82 Texts which belong to this tradition are of particular interest (e.g. C. Rossetti, *Called to be Saints*, or *Time Flies*): botanical descriptions are most ingeniously interpreted in an emblematic way; see G. Hönnighausen, 'Emblematic Tendencies in the Works of Christina Rossetti'.
83 Compare the select bibliography of Victorian flower books in G. Hönnighausen, *Christina Rossetti*, pp. 189ff.
84 Algernon Charles Swinburne, *Poems and Ballads*, 1866, p. 214.
85 Ibid., p. 215.
86 Rossetti, *Poems*, p. 134.
87 For a modern interpretation see H. Talon, *D. G. Rossetti: The House of Life*, pp. 33–45.
88 Richard Le Gallienne, *English Poems*, 1892, p. 37; see also *The Collected Works of Arthur Symons, Poems*, vols. I–III, I, p. 175 (hereafter Symons, *Poems*).
89 Michael Field, *Underneath the Bough*, 1893, p. 108.
90 Woolner, *My Beautiful Lady*, p. 49, Section VIII, 'Her Garden'.
91 Ibid., p. 50.
92 See Hunt, I, p. 350 on *The Light of the World*: 'The closed door was the obstinately shut mind, the weeds the cumber of daily neglect.' See Landow, *William Holman Hunt and Typological Symbolism*.
93 Compare stylized Pre-Raphaelite variants such as Morris's 'A Garden by the Sea' (*Works*, IX, p. 149) or Dowson's 'The Garden of Shadow' (*The Poems of Ernest Dowson*, p. 79).
94 *The Poems of A. C. Swinburne*, 1905, III, pp. 22ff, 'A Forsaken Garden'.
95 Nerval, *Œuvres*, I, p. 377, *Aurélia*: 'La culture était négligée depuis de longues années, et des plants épars de clématites, de houblon, de chèvre-feuille, de jasmin, de lierre, d'aristoloche, étendaient entre des arbres d'une croissance vigoureuse leurs longues traînées de lianes. Des branches pliaient jusqu'à terre chargées de fruits, et parmi des touffes d'herbes parasites s'épanouissaient quelques fleurs de jardin revenues à l'état sauvage.'
96 Ibid., p. 378: 'entoura gracieusement de son bras nu une longue tige de rose trémière, puis elle se mit à grandir sous un clair rayon de lumière, de telle sorte que peu à peu le jardin prenait sa forme, et les parterres et les arbres devenaient les rosaces et les festons de ses vêtements'.
97 Ibid.
98 Woolner, *The Germ*, p. 127.
99 Rossetti, *Poems*, p. 141.
100 Ibid., p. 120: 'The gloom that breathes upon me these airs / Is like the drops

which strike the traveller's brow.'

101 Ibid., p. 113.
102 Ibid., p. 121.
103 Nerval, *Œuvres*, I, p. 367, *Aurélia*.
104 See Rossetti, *Poems*, p. 214, 'The Lover's Walk'; for a detailed analysis of the corresponding inner and outer elements, see the German edition of this book, p. 75.
105 Ibid., p. 112: 'Sees through the untuneful bough the wingless skies.'
106 On Hopkins's relationship with the Pre-Raphaelites see E. Rothenstein, 'The Pre-Raphaelites and Ourselves', esp. p. 188: 'Hopkins was able to take the rather scientifically-literal examination of nature peculiar to the Pre-Raphaelites and to illumine and expand it with insights gained from his philosophy and his theology.'
107 Quoted in Rothenstein, p. 190. For the Victorianism of Hopkins see also Landow, *Victorian Types*, pp. 177–87.
108 Rossetti, *Letters*, I, p. 239.
109 Ibid.
110 *The Works of E. A. Poe, Literary Criticism*, VI, p. 148, 'Nathaniel Hawthorne'.
111 Ibid.
112 Baudelaire, *Œuvres*, p. 376, *Les Paradis Artificiels*.
113 For the influence of the personifications of the Early Italians on Rossetti see R. L. Mégroz, *Dante Gabriel Rossetti*, pp. 160–1; for their impact on similar tendencies in Swinburne see P. de Reul, *L'Œuvre de Swinburne*, pp. 76–7. Another source of inspiration for the late romantic use of allegory can be recognized in medieval moralities; see e.g. Swinburne's 'The Masque of Queen Bersabe' or A. Symons's 'The Dance of the Seven Sins'.
114 See Bell Scott, *Poems*, 1854, pp. 151–4, 'Lines sent with Spenser's "Faery Queen" ' [*sic*] and J. Payne, *Poetical Works*, II, p. 150, 'The Garden of Adonis', or Allingham, *Flower Pieces*, p. 17.
115 See *The Works of Francis Thompson*, III, p. 142, 'The Poet's Poet'.
116 Yeats, *EI*, p. 368, 'Edmund Spenser'.
117 Mills, p. 268.
118 Edmund Spenser, *Faerie Queene*, portrayed in a series of designs by Walter Crane, 1894.
119 James Thomson, *Essay and Phantasies*, p. 178, 'An Evening with Spenser'.
120 See Mills, p. 91, Rossetti's commentary on Shields's illustration *Christian Reading*.
121 See *Lyrical Ballads*, p. 244. Also Bronson, 'Personification Reconsidered', p. 166.
122 *The Works of Francis Thompson*, III, p. 24, 'Shelley'.
123 Ibid., p. 25.
124 James Thomson, *Poems*, p. 61: 'Sweating mere blood flowers gloomed the heather / Like a festering gash left gaping wide / That foul canal, long swooned from tide.'
125 Ibid., p. 65.
126 Ibid., p. 70.
127 Ibid., p. 227, 'Insomnia'.
128 Ibid., p. 199. For James Thomson's allegories see W. D. Schaefer, 'The Two

Cities of Dreadful Night'; W. D. Schaefer, *James Thomson (B.V.): Beyond 'The City'*; I. B. Walker, *James Thomson (B.V.)*; R. Langbaum, *The Poetry of Experience*. On Thomson's pessimism, see H. Peyre, 'Les Sources du Pessimisme de Thomson'; K. H. Byron, *The Pessimism of James Thomson, B.V. in Relation to his Time*.

129 A. C. Swinburne, 'Simeon Solomon: Notes on his "Vision of Love" and other Studies', p. 295.

130 *The Collected Works of Dante Gabriel Rossetti*, ed. W. M. Rossetti, I, p. 506.

131 Simeon Solomon, *A Vision of Love Revealed in Sleep*, 1871 (BL 12352. h. 28).

132 Swinburne, 'Simeon Solomon', p. 299.

133 See e.g. Solomon, p. 3: 'on its grey sands sat one whom I knew for Memory', or p. 4, 'Pleasure which is past', or p. 29, 'Two Holy Ones'. For a complete list of these 'titles' see the German edition of this book, p. 84. All these allegorical figures give a strange impression of holding a pose as if they had been suddenly arrested in their motion. This conspicuous attitudinizing also links paintings otherwise as different as Watts's *Hope*, Rossetti's *Mary Magdalene at the Door of Simon the Pharisee*, and Hunt's *Awakened Conscience*.

134 See I. Jack, *Keats and the Mirror of Art*.

135 A. Livermore, 'J. M. W. Turner's Unknown Verse-Book', p. 78.

136 Rossetti's 'Sonnets for Pictures' is one of the best-known examples, see also Ford Madox Brown's sonnets for *Work* and *The Last of England* or Crane's poems 'For the Picture *The Bridge of Life*' and 'For the Picture *The Earth and Spring*'.

137 The first of Rossetti's sonnets for his painting *The Girlhood of Mary Virgin* was published in the catalogue of the *Free Exhibition, Hyde Park Corner 1849*, the second is inscribed in the frame; the sonnet for *Venus Verticordia* is in the top right-hand corner of the canvas itself.

138 See also Laurence Housman, 'The School of Pan' (Signorelli); Arthur Symons, 'The Wood-Nymph' (after a picture by Burne-Jones); Walter Crane, 'The Soul's Prism' (Sonnet to a picture by G. F. Watts). H. W. Shrewsbury's volume of poems on paintings by Millais and Hunt (*Brothers in Art*, 1920) is a revealing example of this type of interpretative poetry, but some of Baudelaire's poems already betray a similar tendency, as Adam points out in his comment on Baudelaire's 'Don Juan aux Enfers', a poem inspired by Delacroix: '*Don Juan aux Enfers* n'est pas une *transposition d'art* à la façon de Gautier, C'est l'interprétation morale d'un mythe', *Les Fleurs du Mal*, p. 292. But even in Gautier's *Emaux et Camées*, although less frequently than in Baudelaire, it is possible to trace examples of the same type. In 'Sur le Prométhée du Musée de Madrid', and even in 'Contralto', which follows its model, the Hermaphrodite in the Louvre, much more closely than Swinburne's lines on the same sculpture ('Hermaphroditus'), interpretative elements are prevalent.

139 See e.g. J. A. Symonds, 'Dic mihi quid feci, nisi non sapienter amavi' (a picture by Burne-Jones), 'The Genius of the Vatican'; Christina Rossetti, 'Books in the Running Brooks' (For a picture in the Portland Gallery); J. Payne, 'Jacob and the Angel' (For a design by Nettleship); Ford Madox

Hueffer, 'St. Aethelburga'.

140 E. Lee-Hamilton, *Sonnets of the Wingless Hours*, 1894, p. 39.

141 Ibid., p. 41.

142 *Poems by William Bell Scott*, illustrated by 17 etchings by the author and L. Alma Tadema, 1875, p. ix, Preface.

143 Shrewsbury, *Brothers in Art*, p. 77, 'Ophelia' (Millais); John Gray, *Silverpoints*, 1893, p. xxi, 'On a Picture' (the octave of this sonnet together with the first two stanzas of the first part of Rimbaud's 'Ophélie' are reproduced in connection with Millais's painting), (Pl. 4) – Arthur Rimbaud, *Œuvres Complètes*, pp. 51–2, 'Ophélie'.

144 *Picture Poesies, Poems chiefly by Living Authors*, 1874. *The Painter-Poets*, ed. Kineton Parkes [1890]; Joseph Noel Paton, *Poems by a Painter*, 1861; William Bell Scott, *Poems by a Painter*, 1854; Ford Madox Hueffer, *Poems for Pictures and Notes for Music*, 1900. Oscar Wilde has commented in a most interesting way on the predilection for illustration so typical of the period as a whole: 'Since . . . the fatal development of the habit of reading amongst the middle and lower classes of this country there has been a tendency in literature to appeal more and more to the eye', Wilde, p. 955, 'The Critic as Artist'.

145 Rossetti, *Works*, I, p. 499.

146 Ibid., p. 506.

147 On the Victorian emblematic revival see K. J. Höltgen, *Aspects of the Emblem*, esp. chap. 4.

148 *Sacred Emblems with Miscellaneous Pieces Moral, Religious, and Devotional in Verse*, 1828, p. 83, 'To Francis Quarles', written on a blank leaf of his *Emblems*.

149 In *Flower-Lore, The Teachings of Flowers, Historical, Legendary, Poetical, and Symbolical*, 1879, the following lines by Quarles are reprinted: 'Virgins, tuck up your silken laps and fill Ye / With the fair wealth of Flora's magazine; / The purple violet and the pale-faced lily, / The pansy . . .'.

150 R. Freeman, *English Emblem Books*, p. 228. On the question of the Victorian emblem book and the emblematic tradition see Freeman, pp. 205ff and M. Praz, *Seventeenth Century Imagery*, pp. 230–1; see also *Emblemata*, ed. A. Henkel and A. Schöne.

151 Henry Green, *Shakespeare and the Emblem Writers. An Exposition of their Similarities of Thought and Expression*, 1869, p. 30.

152 Rossetti, *Letters*, IV, letter to his mother (27 April 1880) to whom the design is dedicated: 'I have no doubt that your discerning eyes plucked out the heart of the mystery in the little design. In it the Soul is instituting the "memorial to one dead deathless hour", a ceremony easily effected by placing a winged hour-glass in a rose-bush, at the same time that she touches the fourteen-stringed harp of the Sonnet, hanging round her neck. On the rose-branches trailing over in the opposite corner is seen hanging the Coin, which is the second symbol used for the Sonnet. Its "face" bears the soul, expressed in the butterfly; its "converse" the Serpent of Eternity enclosing the Alpha and Omega.'

153 Baudelaire, *Les Fleurs du Mal*, p. 138.

154 For the material used in the following passage see Claude Pichois and François Ruchon, *Iconographie de Charles Baudelaire*, pp. 100–21, Plates

108–12 and 115–17; page numbers following the quotations refer to the page numbers of this edition.

155 Green, p. vii.
156 Solomon, p. 18.
157 Ibid., p. 26.
158 Wilde, 'The Artist', p. 843.
159 J. A. Symonds, *New and Old*, 1880, pp. 12–13; see also 'Dic mihi quid feci, nisi non sapienter amavi' (A picture by Burne-Jones) or John Payne's 'A Song Before the Gates of Death' (suggested by Mr Burne-Jones' picture).
160 Harrold Johnson, *The House of Life. Interpretations of the Symbolical Pictures of the Late G. F. Watts*, 1911. The title of this book obviously modelled on Rossetti's reveals the affinity between Pre-Raphaelite allegory and nineteenth-century paintings of ideas.
161 Compare Bell Scott's poem for Watts's painting *Love and Death* (*A Poet's Harvest Home*, p. 61); in the works of the Scottish painter-poet we find several descriptions of paintings directly connected with symbolist motifs: 'Self-Accusation' (divided self), 'The Madonna Di San Sisto' (madonna cult), 'I go to be cured at Avilon' (Arthurian myth, escapism), 'The Norns Watering Yggdrasil' (mythological interest).
162 Johnson, Preface, letter by Watts.
163 Ibid., p. 26. For the specific late romantic understanding of hope see also 'CDN', canto IV: the refrain 'No hope could have no fear' is changed into 'Hope travailed with such fear', James Thomson, *Poems*, p. 182.
164 See also Crane's lines on his allegorical painting *The Bridge of Life* in the anthology *Painter-Poets*, ed. Kineton Parkes. This anthology, which provides such an important insight into the tastes of the period, combines verses by Rossetti and Ford Madox Brown with Turner's poems for his catalogues and works by entirely unknown authors like Washington Allston. Shrewsbury's collection of poems for paintings by Hunt and Millais, published as late as 1920 (*Brothers in Art*) shows how important this tradition was. See also *Pictures and Poems by Dante Gabriel Rossetti*, 1899: 'Beautiful in themselves as are Rossetti's paintings, their inspiration is so often literary, that their full significance can only be properly understood and appreciated when they are studied with the aid of the enlightening text', Preface.
165 Johnson, pp. i–ii, Preface.
166 Thirteen of the thirty-two poems in Michael Field's *Sight and Song* describe mythological paintings, nine describe paintings of saints. Among the remaining poems we find lines on such famous works of art as Leonardo Da Vinci's *Mona Lisa* and Bartolommeo Veneto's well-known portrait from the Städel museum in Frankfurt.
167 Swinburne, 'Notes on Some Designs of the Old Masters at Florence' (1864), *Essays and Studies*, 1875, pp. 319–20, Botticelli, p. 327, Giorgione, p. 343; apart from Titian and Veronese, Swinburne's selection corresponds exactly to the taste of his time.
168 Rossetti, *Poems*, p. 251: 'what masque of what old wind-withered New Year/ Honours this Lady'.
169 Field, *Sight and Song*, p. 22.
170 Rossetti, *Poems*, p. 251.

171 Field, *Sight and Song*, p. 26.
172 Baudelaire, *Les Fleurs du Mal*, p. 139, 'L'Amour et le Crâne: Vieux Cul-de-Lampe'.
173 Geoffrey Whitney, *A Choice of Emblems*, 1586.
174 Baudelaire, *Les Fleurs du Mal*, p. 194.
175 On the *Sonnets for Pictures* in general, see Kermode, *Romantic Image*, p. 62: 'Rossetti here revives those extravagant glosses, ut pictura poesis, on paintings, which Marino had made fashionable two hundred and fifty years earlier.'
176 Rossetti, *Poems*, p. 138.
177 Gautier, *Emaux et Camées*, p. 216: 'O symbole muet de l'humaine misère'.
178 Swinburne, 'Cleopatra', quoted in T. E. Welby, *A Study of Swinburne*, pp. 222–3: 'She sees the hand of death made bare'.
179 Rossetti, *Poems*, p. 259, 'Fiammetta'.
180 Ibid., p. 262.
181 Ibid., p. 261: 'Afar the flowers of Enna from this drear / Dire fruit . . . Afar those skies from the Tartarean grey'. The Italian version is inscribed on the painting.
182 Ibid., p. 260. More recently R. L. Stein (*The Ritual of Interpretation. The Fine Arts as Literature in Ruskin, Rossetti, and Pater*) has made this 'ritual' of depiction and interpretation the subject of a subtle and innovative study.
183 Ibid., p. 261.
184 Ibid., p. 260.
185 Pater, *The Renaissance*, p. 125.
186 Gautier, p. 216.
187 Praz, *The Romantic Agony*, p. 399.
188 *An Anthology of 'Nineties' Verse*, p. 64.
189 On green eyes as a mark of perversity see Praz, *Romantic Agony*, p. 313. In Joyce's 'An Encounter' green eyes appear as a symbol of the enigmatic and perverse: 'I came back and examined the foreign sailors to see had any of them green eyes . . .' (*Dubliners*, p. 21); 'I met the gaze of a pair of bottle-green eyes peering at me from under a twilight forehead' (*Dubliners*, p. 25).
190 *An Anthology of 'Nineties' Verse*, p. 65.
191 Pater, *The Renaissance*, p. 123.
192 Yeats's remarks (*EI*, p. 150) on the symbolic portrait with its wide spectrum of ambiguous implications are particularly revealing: 'If you paint a beautiful woman and fill her face, as Rossetti filled so many faces, with an infinite love, one's eyes meet no mortal thing when they meet the light of her peaceful eyes, as Michelangelo said of Vittoria Colonna; but one's thoughts stray to mortal things, and ask, maybe, "Has her lover gone from her, or is he coming?" . . . If you paint the same face, and set a winged rose or a rose of gold somewhere about her, one's thoughts are of her immortal sisters, Piety and Jealousy, and of her mother, Ancestral Beauty, and of her high kinsmen, the Holy Orders, whose swords make a continual music before her face.'
193 Nerval, *Œuvres*, I, p. 33, 'Les Chimères', 'El Desdichado'.
194 Spring: a branch of blossoms, sturdy but collarless gown; Summer: roses, veil; Autumn: water lilies, apple, dark dress with rich cast of folds; Winter: leafless trees, fire, Psalter, habitlike cloak.

195 *The Collected Poems of Lord Alfred Douglas*, 1919, p. 69, 'Ode to Autumn'.
196 Olive Custance, *Rainbows*, 1902, pp. 74–5, 'A Rainy Day'.
197 Dowson, *Poems*, p. 45, 'My Lady April.'
198 *The Poetical Works of Christina Georgina Rossetti*, ed. W. M. Rossetti, p. 311, 'A Soul'; all quotations from this edition.
199 Rossetti, 'Hand and Soul', *The Germ*, p. 30.
200 See also Thompson's poem 'Manus Animam Pinxit', *The Works of Francis Thompson*, I, pp. 82–3.
201 *The Germ*, p. 32.
202 Pater, *The Renaissance*, p. 194, 'Conclusion', and *Marius*, I, p. 127.
203 Olive Custance, *The Blue Bird*, p. 9. The title poem takes a passage from Wilde's 'The Decay of Lying' as its motto: 'And over our heads will float the Blue bird singing of beautiful and impossible things . . .'. The bird motif, well known in connection with Yeats's poetry (see e.g. 'The White Birds') as an expression of late romantic sensitivity, deserves a special study.
204 James Thomson, *Poems*, pp. 183–4.
205 Rossetti, *Poems*, p. 127.
206 Nerval, *Œuvres*, I, pp. 368–9, 'Aurélia'.
207 For the motif of the wraith, or *Doppelgänger*, in English late romantic poetry: Poe, 'Dream Land', 'Ulalume'; Rossetti, 'The Morrow's Message', 'Willowwood', 'Lost Days', 'A Superscription', 'Love's Nocturn', 'The Portrait' (This is her picture as she was), 'Love's Fatality'; Bell Scott, 'Self-Accusation, Seeking Forgetfulness'; Bourke Marston, 'Love's Lost Days'; Payne, 'Haunted Life', 'Light O'Love', 'Life Unlived'; O'Shaughnessy, 'Death, The Spectre of the Past'; Lee-Hamilton, 'Meeting the Ghost', 'Ipsissimus', 'The Silent Fellow'; O'Sullivan, 'Nights of Dreaming', 'Brain Fever'; Sidney R. Thompson, 'The Land of Might Have Been', 'In the Resurrection'.
208 Custance, 'Ritornello'; Payne, 'Sovran Sorrow'; James Thomson, 'A Lady of Sorrow'; L. Johnson, 'Before the Cloister'; Yeats, 'The Sad Shepherd'.
209 Yeats, 'He Remembers Forgotten Beauty' and 'Maid Quiet'.
210 Payne, 'Hesperia', 'Flitting Hope'; Bourke Marston, 'Hope' and 'In Extremis', 'At Hope's Grave'; J. A. Symonds, 'Anticyra'; Bourke Marston, 'Love's Ghost'.
211 O'Shaughnessy, 'A Whisper from the Grave'.
212 Payne, *Poetical Works*, II, p. 145, 'Hesperia': 'musingly slow'; Christina Rossetti, *Poetical Works*, p. 311, 'A Soul': 'pale she stands'; Rossetti, *Poems*, p. 126, 'The Vase of Life': 'A youth stands somewhere crowned, with silent face'; Douglas, *Collected Poems*, p. 26, 'Night Coming out of a Garden'; ibid., p. 69, 'Ode to Autumn'; ibid., p. 95, 'The Green River'; James Thomson, *Poems*, p. 71, 'To our Ladies of Death'.
213 Bourke Marston, *Collected Poems*, p. 311, 'My Life', 'half-veiled'; Payne, *New Poems*, p. 113, 'Faded Love', 'white-robed'; Allingham, *Poems*, 1850, p. 181, 'The Lullaby', 'hooded eyes'; *The Complete Poetical Works of Austin Dobson*, 1923, p. 131, 'A Song of Angiola in Heaven', 'shrouded shapes'; Yeats, *Collected Poems*, p. 78, 'Maid Quiet', 'russet hood'; James Thomson, *Poems*, p. 71, 'To our Ladies of Death', 'shrouded in a gauzy veil'.

214 Allingham, *Poems*, p. 154, 'Wakening'; Custance, *Rainbows*, p. 40, 'Ritornello'; Douglas, *Collected Poems*, p. 26, 'Night Coming Out of a Garden'; Bourke Marston, *Collected Poems*, p. 81, 'At Dawn'; Payne, *New Poems*, 1880, p. 133, 'Faded Love'. The following lines from Payne, *Poetical Works*, II, p. 164, 'Siren': 'Upon that vision of a dead delight / I saw therein a white sad face arise' could serve at a motto for most of the poems quoted here.

215 See Christoffel, p. 80; Hofstätter, *Symbolismus und die Kunst der Jahrhundertwende*, pp. 110 and 121, and Schmutzler, pp. 110 and 240. See also Hunt's (II, p. 104) striking interest in two pendant pieces by Burkner, *Death as a Friend* and *Death as an Enemy*.

216 Rossetti, *Poems*, pp. 108–9, 'Passion and Worship'.

217 Yeats, *Collected Poems*, pp. 71–2, 'The Cap and Bells'.

218 Compare the positions of the symbolic flowers rose and lily in poems by Yeats and Ellis: Yeats, *Collected Poems*, p. 79, 'The Travail of Passion': 'Lilies of deathpale hope, roses of passionate dream' or ibid., p. 47: 'dewdabbled the lily and rose . . . Soon far from the rose and the lily and fret of the flames would be'. *The Book of the Rhymers' Club*, 1892, p. 22; Edwin J. Ellis, 'New Words and Old', III: 'The Rose and Lily gently, without hate, / Disputed which should be the flower of choice . . .'. The relationship with Rossetti's 'Passion and Worship' is immediately evident.

219 *An Anthology of 'Nineties' Verse*, p. 32, John Davidson, 'Insomnia'.

220 Compare the symmetry in Burne-Jones's *The Resurrection*.

221 Baudelaire, *Les Fleurs du Mal*, p. 132, 'Les Deux Bonnes Soeurs'.

222 Swinburne, *PB*, p. 2, 'A Ballad of Life'.

223 Ibid., p. 337, 'The Year of Love'. The tradition still persists in Yeats's 'The Cloak, the Boat, and the Shoes', *Collected Poems*, p. 10.

224 Yeats, *Collected Poems*, p. 55; Bourke Marston, *Collected Poems*, p. 31: 'The days whereof my heart is still so fain, / Passed by my soul in strange and sad procession'.

225 Olive Custance, *Opals*, 1897, p. 33, 'Fantasy': 'Dusk and the darkness, sisters twain, / Kiss through a silver veil of rain'; Laurence Housman, *The Green Arras*, 1896, p. 52: 'O, sad-eyed, will ye never cease entreating / Each other's gaze, whether known, whether strange?' The allegorical scenes in Bell Scott's cycle 'Outside the Temple, Birth, Death, Life' (*Poems*, 1875, pp. 73–5) seem related to the paintings of Watts, whilst Symonds's sonnet 'Friendship, Love and Death' (*New and Old*, 1880, p. 121) shows a greater affinity to Burne-Jones's *Fortune, Fame, Oblivion, Love*, which he also translated into verse.

226 Rossetti, *Poems*, pp. 127–8:

> To-day Death seems to me an infant child
> Which her worn mother Life upon my knee
> Has set to grow my friend and play with me,
>
> . . .
>
> II.
>
> Lo! Love, the child once ours; and Song, whose hair
> Blew like a flame and blossomed like a wreath;
> And Art, whose eyes were worlds by God found fair;

227 As this example illustrates, the Pre-Raphaelite medievalism still lingers on in the nineties.
228 Evelyn Douglas, *Selections from Songs of a Bayadere and Songs of a Troubadour*, 1893, p. 56.
229 Ibid., p. 57: 'In black hearse-feathers and pall from the tomb / Sings Death the Troubadour'.
230 *The Book of the Rhymers' Club*, p. 42:

> Time came down from the far-off stars
> And warmed his feet before the glow.
>
> Then Love drew near the further side, –
> Between the two, my bride and I, –
> . . .
> But Pity crept into the room . . .

231 Yeats, *Collected Poems*, p. 46.
232 Cornell, p. 71; Bowra, *The Heritage of Symbolism*, p. 88; E. A. Bloom, 'The Allegorical Principle'.
233 Pater, *Appreciations*, p. 208, 'Rossetti'.
234 Rossetti, *Poems*, p. 117: 'I and this Love are one, and I am Death'; ibid., p. 113, 'The Morrow's Message': ' "Thou Ghost", I said, "and is thy name To-day?" '; ibid., p. 213, 'Love Enthroned': 'Though Truth foreknew Love's heart, and Hope foretell, / And Fame be for Love's sake desirable, / And Youth be dear, and Life be sweet to Love'.
235 Wilde, p. 774, 'Apologia'.
236 Rossetti, *Poems*, p. 123.
237 Ibid., p. 218, 'Pride of Youth'.
238 Ibid., p. 119, 'Known in Vain': 'As two whose love, first foolish scope, . . . So it happeneth / When Work and Will awake too late . . .'; ibid., p. 125, 'Lost on Both Sides': 'As when two men have loved a woman well, . . . So separate hopes . . .'; ibid., p. 234, 'The Sun's Shame II': 'As some true chief of men bowed down with stress . . . Even so the World's grey Soul to the green World . . .'.
239 Bourke Marston, *Collected Poems*, p. 366, 'Love Asleep'.
240 Theodore Wratislaw, *Love's Memorial*, 1892, p. 35.
241 Christina Rossetti, *Poetical Works*, p. 292.
242 Richard Le Gallienne, *The Lonely Dancer and Other Poems*, 1914, 'Green Silence'.
243 Christina Rossetti, p. 292.
244 Baudelaire, *Les Fleurs du Mal*, p. 6, 'Au Lecteur'; p. 134, 'Allégorie'; p. 77, 'Le Tonneau de la Haine'.
245 Ibid., pp. 80–1, 'Spleen', 'Quand le ciel bas et lourd pèse comme un couvercle'; p. 87, 'L'Horloge'; p. 178, 'L'Examen de Minuit'.

3 The impact of symbolist tendencies on late romantic poetry

1 Pater, *Appreciations*, p. 31, 'Style'.
2 Douglas, *Collected Poems*, p. 84, 'A Triad of the Moon'.
3 *The Poetical Works of Sydney Dobell*, 1875, I, p. 215, 'The Snowdrop in

the Snow'; see also Le Gallienne, *English Poems*, pp. 85–6, 'Autumn', and *The Works of Francis Thompson*, II, p. 48, 'Any Saint'.

4 Douglas, *Collected Poems*, p. 81, 'The City of the Soul'.
5 Ibid., p. 88, 'The Dead Poet'.
6 Ibid., p. 90, 'To a Silent Poet'.
7 Baudelaire, *Les Fleurs du Mal*, p. 12.
8 Payne, *Poetical Works*, II, p. 152.
9 O'Shaughnessy, *Songs of a Worker*, 1881, p. 93, 'Her Beauty'.
10 Housman, *Green Arras*, p. 26, 'Inspiration'.
11 Wilde, p. 969, 'The Critic as Artist'.
12 Baudelaire, *Les Fleurs du Mal*, p. 24, 'La Beauté'; see also Douglas, *Collected Poems*, p. 96, 'La Beauté' (From the French of Baudelaire).
13 Together with 'La Beauté' see also 'La Muse Malade' or 'Le Gouffre'.
14 O'Shaughnessy, *Music and Moonlight*, 1874, p. 93, 'The Disease of the Soul'.
15 Ibid., p. 155, 'Nostalgie des Cieux'.
16 Baudelaire, *Les Fleurs du Mal*, p. 12, 'L'Albatros'; see also Gautier's poems 'Consolation' and 'Le Poète et la Foule', *Emaux et Camées*, pp. 280 and 282 respectively.
17 In *An Anthology of 'Nineties' Verse*, p. 62.
18 Gautier, *Emaux et Camées*, p. 232, 'Terza Rima'.
19 *The Complete Poems of Lionel Johnson*, pp. 38–9.
20 Wilde, p. 987, 'The Critic as Artist'.
21 L. Johnson, *Complete Poems*, p. 38, 'Upon a Drawing'. For the poet's isolation in a hostile world see also a poem such as O'Sullivan's 'Papillon du Pavé' in *An Anthology of 'Nineties' Verse*, p. 109.
22 *The Works of Francis Thompson*, III, p. 119, 'Finis Coronat Opus'.
23 *The Complete Plays of Gilbert and Sullivan*, p. 199.
24 Ibid., p. 219.
25 Ibid., p. 225.
26 Douglas, *Collected Poems*, pp. 63–4.
27 Harry Quilter, 'The New Renaissance; or the Gospel of Intensity', p. 400.
28 Symons, *Poems*, I, p. 3, 'Prologue'.
29 Ibid., III, p. 8, 'The Brother of a Weed', section II.
30 Custance, *Opals*, pp. 3–4, 'The Song Spinner'.
31 Symons, *Poems*, II, p. 123.
32 Arthur Symons, *William Blake*, 1924, pp. 75–6; see also my essay on Blake. Compare the striking interest of the *fin de siècle* in Schopenhauer.
33 Yeats, *EI*, p. 159, 'The Symbolism of Poetry'.
34 Ibid; *The Works of Francis Thompson*, II, p. 189.
35 Yeats, *Collected Poems*, p. 7.
36 *The Works of Francis Thompson*, II, p. 189, 'The Hollow Wood'.
37 Olive Custance, *The Inn of Dreams*, 1911, p. 43, 'Black Butterflies'.
38 A. W. E. O'Shaughnessy, *Epic of Women*, 1870, p. 78.
39 Yeats, *EI*, 'The Symbolism of Poetry', p. 164.
40 Lee-Hamilton, *Sonnets of the Wingless Hours*, p. 101, 'Gold of Midas'.
41 *The Works of Francis Thompson*, III, p. 4, 'Shelley'.
42 Wilde, p. 959, 'The Critic as Artist'.
43 Yeats, *EI*, p. 378, 'Edmund Spenser'.

44 Pater, *Appreciations*, p. 23, 'Style'.

45 See e.g. Payne, *Poetical Works*, II, p. 152, 'Evocation'; ibid., p. 55, 'Jacob and the Angel' (For a design by Nettleship); Douglas, *Collected Poems*, p. 83, 'Sonnet on the Sonnet'. Rossetti's 'A Sonnet is a Moment's Monument' is the *locus classicus*.

46 Baudelaire, *Œuvres*, p. 1222, 'Richard Wagner et *Tannhäuser* à Paris'.

47 *Letters of Dante Gabriel Rossetti*, ed. George Birbeck Hill, 1897, p. 184 (10 May 1857).

48 The letter belongs to a group of handwritten letters by Rossetti to O'Shaughnessy included in a copy of *Epic of Women* (BL C. 117. a. a. 15).

49 Quoted from the appendix of O'Shaughnessy's *Music and Moonlight*.

50 See e.g. Douglas, *Collected Poems*, p. 81, 'The City of the Soul III'; Gray, *Silverpoints*, p. xxxiii, 'A une Madone' (Imitated from the French of Charles Baudelaire).

51 Rossetti, *Poems*, p. 212, 'A Sonnet is a Moment's Monument' (Pl. 5).

52 Pater, *Appreciations*, p. 260, 'Postscript'.

53 O'Shaughnessy, *Songs of a Worker*, p. 106, 'The Line of Beauty'; see also Douglas, *Collected Poems*, p. 82, 'The City of the Soul, IV'.

54 Pater, *Appreciations*, p. 12, 'Style'.

55 W. B. Yeats, *Autobiographies*, esp. pp. 303–5.

56 Wilde, p. 917, 'The Decay of Lying'.

57 Pater, *Appreciations*, p. 211, 'Rossetti'.

58 Ibid., pp. 80–1, 'Coleridge': 'instead of the most luminous and self-possessed phase of consciousness, the associative act in art or poetry is made to look like some blindly organic process of assimilation. The work of art is likened to a living organism . . . it hardly figures the process by which such work was produced.'

59 As regards the predilection for complicated and ancient forms see also Bell Scott's satirical poem 'Ancient Forms' (*A Poet's Harvest Home*, p. 110). See also the parody in *Patience* (*The Complete Plays of Gilbert and Sullivan*, p. 197): 'Florentine fourteenth century, trimmed with Venetian leather and Spanish altar lace, and surmounted with something Japanese – it matters not what – would at least be Early English'.

60 Compare e.g. the following titles from Payne's *New Poems* (1880): 'Chant Royal of the God of Love' (p. 10), 'The Ballad of the King's Orchard' (From Theodore de Banville) (p. 14), 'Virelay' (p. 91), 'Double Ballad' (p. 127), 'Madrigal Gai' (p. 130), 'Villanelle' (p. 134), 'Ritournel' (p. 136), 'Rondel' (p. 140), 'Rondel' (From Charles d'Orléans).

61 Austin Dobson, *Proverbs in Porcelain and Other Verses*, 1877.

62 Wilde, p. 935.

63 Yeats, *EI*, p. 189, 'The Autumn of the Body': 'against that "externality" which a time of scientific and political thought has brought into literature'.

64 Ibid., pp. 190–1.

65 James Joyce, *A Portrait of the Artist as a Young Man*, 1916, pp. 217ff.

66 Charles Baudelaire, *Petits Poèmes en Prose*, p. 7.

67 Pater, *Appreciations*, p. 11, 'Style'.

68 Compare the version in Pater, *The Renaissance*, p. 125, with the version in Yeats's anthology *The Oxford Book of Modern Verse 1892–1935*, 1936, p. 1.

69 Yeats, *EI*, p. 189, 'The Autumn of the Body'.
70 Baudelaire, *Petits Poèmes en Prose*, p. 16, 'Le "Confitéor" de l'Artiste'.
71 See his remarks: 'I am always struggling after purity of contour, elevation of individual character, and intensity of expression', Mills, p. 229.
72 A. C. Swinburne, *Essays and Studies*, 1875, p. 63, 'The Poems of Dante Gabriel Rossetti'.
73 Rossetti, *Poems*, p. 213.
74 Swinburne, *PB*, p. 296:
    All things felt sweet were felt sweet overmuch;
            . . .
    Too keen the breathèd honey of the rose,
    Its red too harsh a weight on feasted eyes.
75 *The Complete Plays of Gilbert and Sullivan*, p. 194. The title of Harry Quilter's critical essay is also relevant in this context: 'The New Renaissance; or, The Gospel of Intensity'.
76 Dobson, *Poetical Works*, p. 191, 'Household Art'.
77 Wilde, p. 880, 'De Profundis'.
78 Poe, *Works*, XIV, p. 266, 'The Poetic Principle'.
79 Ibid., XIV, p. 271.
80 Ibid., XIV, pp. 274–5.
81 Wilde, p. 932, 'Pen, Pencil, and Poison'.
82 For the late romantic reappraisal of the sonnet see Wilde, p. 991, 'The Critic as Artist': 'For the real artist is he who proceeds, not from feeling to form, but from form to thought and passion. He does not first conceive an idea, and then, say to himself, "I will put my idea into a complex metre of four-teen lines", but realizing the beauty of the sonnet-scheme, he conceives cer-tain modes of music and methods of rhyme, and the mere form suggests what is to fill and make it intellectually and emotionally complete.'
83 For the text of Rossetti's 'A Sonnet is a Moment's Monument' see Pl. 5. For the continuation of this tradition see Douglas, *Collected Poems*, p. 83, 'Son-net on the Sonnet':
    To see the moment holds a madrigal,
    To find some cloistered place, some hermitage
    For free devices, some deliberate cage
    Wherein to keep wild thoughts like birds in thrall . . .
84 Lee-Hamilton, *Sonnets of the Wingless Hours*, p. 87, 'What the Sonnet is'.
85 Wilde, p. 986, 'The Critic as Artist'. For the widespread use of the 'mood' concept see also Derek Stanford in *Poets of the Nineties. A Biographical Anthology*, p. 34.
86 Pater, *Marius*, I, p. 135.
87 Wilde, p. 986.
88 Pater, *Marius*, I, p. 159.
89 Symons, *Poems*, I, pp. 166–7.
90 Wilde, p. 966, 'The Critic as Artist'. See also p. 981: 'For action of every kind belongs to the sphere of ethics. The aim of art is simply to create a mood.'
91 Ibid., p. 951.
92 Pater, *Marius*, II, p. 73.
93 AE, *Collected Poems*, p. 47, 'Symbolism'.

94 Symons, 'William Blake', p. 116.
95 *The Works of William Blake, Poetic, Symbolic, and Critical*, ed. W. B. Yeats and Edwin J. Ellis, 1893, I, p. 239.
96 Ibid., I, p. 241.
97 *The Works of Francis Thompson*, II, p. 181, 'The Heart II'.
98 O'Shaughnessy, *Music and Moonlight*, p. 1, 'Ode' (We are the music makers).
99 Yeats, *EI*, p. 195, 'The Moods'.
100 Rossetti, *Poems*, p. 131.
101 Dowson, *Poems*, p. 95.
102 Custance, *The Inn of Dreams*, pp. 56–7, 'Peacocks, A Mood'.
103 For Pound's misleading comparison Imagism–Symbolism: 'Imagisme is not Symbolism. The symbolists dealt in "association", that is, in a sort of allusion, almost of allegory. They degraded the symbol to the status of a word. They made it a form of metonymy. . . The symbolists' symbols have a fixed value, like the numbers in arithmetic, like 1, 2, and 7. The imagists' images have a variable significance, like the signs a, b, and x in algebra', Ezra Pound, *Gaudier-Brzeska, A Memoir*, p. 85.
104 Custance, *Opals*, p. 56.
105 O'Sullivan, *The Houses of Sin*, p. 14.
106 Yeats, *Collected Poems*, p. 62.
107 Rossetti, *Poems*, p. 212, 'A Sonnet is a Moment's Monument'.
108 For a discussion of respective stylistic features see F. S. Boos, *The Poetry of D. G. Rossetti. A Critical Reading and Source Study*; L. Gallasch, *The Use of Compounds and Archaic Diction in the Works of William Morris*; A. H. Harrison, 'Swinburne's Craft of Pure Expression'; F. B. Tolles, 'The Praetorian Cohorts: A Study of the Language of Francis Thompson's Poetry'.
109 Swinburne, *PB*, pp. 1–2, 'A Ballad of Life', 'Laus Veneris'.
110 Dobson *Poetical Works*, p. 136, 'The Dying of Tanneguy Du Bois'.
111 Swinburne, *PB*, p. 277, 'St Dorothy'.
112 Morris, *Works*, I, p. 122. 'Jacqueline . . . Berthe . . . Sainte-Margotwise . . . Ysabeau'; Gray, *Silverpoints*, p. v.
113 Rossetti, *Poems*, p. 6.
114 Ibid., p. 111, 'Love's Baubles'; ibid., p. 113, 'The Morrow's Message'; ibid., p. 215, 'Youth's Spring-tribute'; ibid., p. 110, 'A Day of Love'; ibid., p. 111, 'Love-Sweetness'.
115 Lionel Johnson, *Complete Poems*, p. 67, 'The Dark Angel': 'dead-comforted'; *The Works of Francis Thompson*, I, p. 89, 'Scala Jacobi Portaque Eburnea': 'hers-traffickers; wist-amethyst'.
116 Swinburne, *PB*, p. 5, 'A Ballad of Death'; ibid., p. 21, 'Laus Veneris'; ibid., p. 78, 'Hymn to Proserpine'. See also p. 105, 'A Litany': 'In that hour thou shalt say to the night, / Come down and cover us; / To the cloud on thy left and thy right, / Be thou spread over us.'
117 Swinburne, *PB*, p. 14, 'Laus Veneris'.
118 Ibid., p. 21.
119 T. S. Eliot, *Selected Essays*, p. 327, 'Swinburne as Poet'.
120 *The Works of Francis Thompson*, III, p. 5, 'Shelley'.
121 Ibid., I, p. 93, 'Her Portrait'; I, pp. 121 and 123, 'Ode to the Setting Sun';

ibid., I, p. 98, 'Epilogue to the Poet's Sitter'.

122 Wilde, pp. 815 and 820, 'The Sphinx'.

123 Swinburne, *PB*, pp. 261–2.

124 Pater, *Marius*, I, p. 97; ibid., I, p. 59.

125 Pater, *Appreciations*, p. 12, 'Style'.

126 Johnson, *Complete Poems*, p. 65, 'The Dark Angel'; ibid., p. 66.

127 De Quincey, III, pp. 437 and 438, *Confessions*.

128 Baudelaire, *Œuvres*, p. 376, *Les Paradis Artificiels*.

129 Joyce, *A Portrait of the Artist as a Young Man*, pp. 178–9.

130 Rossetti, *Poems*, p. 215, 'Beauty's Pageant'; p. 219, 'Heart's Compass'. See also phrases like: 'This harp still makes my name its voluntary' (p. 109, 'Passion and Worship'); 'her soul sought / My soul, and from the sudden confluence caught' (p. 110, 'The Love-Letter'); 'a single simple door, / By some new Power reduplicate, must be / Even yet my life-porch in eternity' (p. 233, 'Memorial Threshold'); 'My lady's lips did play / With these my lips, such consonant interlude' (pp. 106–7, 'The Kiss').

131 Ibid., p. 105, 'Bridal Birth'; p. 219, 'Soul-light'; p. 215, 'Spring-tribute'.

132 Ibid., p. 112, 'Winged Hours': '. . . the sweet strain suffers wrong'. Bourke Marston, p. 327, 'The Soul's Pregnancy': '. . . the pain-wed soul is conscious of / Some in-wombed child of spiritual good'.

133 Rossetti, *Poems*, p. 112, 'Winged Hours': 'Each hour until we meet is as a bird / That wings from far his gradual way along / The rustling covert of my soul, – his song / Still loudlier trilled through leaves more deeply stirred'.

134 Numerous other titles could be added: 'Moesta et Errabunda', 'Semper eadem', 'Amoenitates Belgiae' (Baudelaire); 'Ilicet', 'Laus Veneris' (Swinburne); 'Ad Manus Puellae', 'Amor Profanus' (Dowson); 'Ad Patronem', 'Flos Florum', 'Sancta Silvarum' (L. Johnson); 'Quia Multum Amavi', 'Silentium Amoris', 'Taedium Vitae' (Wilde); 'Amoris Exsul', 'Amor Triumphans', 'Munda Victima' (Symons). See also Baudelaire, *Les Fleurs du Mal*, pp. 66–7, note.

135 See Dowson, *Poems*, p. 208, note: 'The title comes from the first ode of the Fourth Book of Horace. "Horace suggested, but Propertius inspired".'

136 Rossetti, *Poems*, p. 108, 'Supreme Surrender'; Johnson, *Complete Poems*, p. 66, 'The Dark Angel'.

137 Rossetti, *Poems*, p. 107, 'The Kiss'; Johnson, *Complete Poems*, p. 67, 'The Dark Angel'.

138 Johnson, *Complete Poems*, p. 194, 'Vinum Daemonum'.

139 Swinburne, *PB*, p. 17, 'Laus Veneris'.

140 Rossetti, *Poems*, p. 117, 'Willowwood III'.

141 Ibid., p. 107, 'Nuptial Sleep'.

142 Ibid., p. 111, 'Love's Baubles'; p. 115, 'Parted Love'.

143 *The Complete Plays of Gilbert and Sullivan*, pp. 201 and 219.

144 Rossetti, *Poems*, p. 114, 'Secret Parting'; p. 116, 'Death-in-Love'. Yeats, *Collected Poems*, p. 71, 'He Gives His Beloved Certain Rhymes'. Poe, *Works*, VII, pp. 107–8, 'To Helen'. Payne, *Complete Poems*, II, p. 145, 'Winter Roses'; II, p. 172, 'Buried Cities'.

145 Rossetti, *Poems*, p. 110, 'A Day of Love'.

146 Payne, *Complete Poems*, II, p. 148, 'Winter Roses'.

147 Yeats, *Collected Poems*, p. 49, 'The Man Who Dreamed of Faeryland'.
148 Bourke Marston, *Collected Poems*, p. 327, 'The Soul's Pregnancy'.
149 Rossetti, *Poems*, p. 111, 'Love-sweetness'.
150 Payne, *New Poems*, p. 159, 'Light O'Love'; Rossetti, *Poems*, p. 230, 'The Soul's Sphere'; Bourke Marston, *Collected Poems*, p. 303, 'A June Day'; Yeats, *Collected Poems*, p. 71, 'Caps and Bells'.
151 Rossetti, *Poems*, p. 148, 'Monochord'; p. 214, 'The Lovers' Walk'.
152 Poe, *Works*, VII, p. 107, 'To Helen'. *The Works of Francis Thompson*, I, p. 110, 'The Hound of Heaven'.
153 For moods see also Ford Madox Brown, 'The Love of Beauty', in *The Germ*, p. 10; Yeats, *Collected Poems*, p. 70, 'He Remembers Forgotten Beauty'; Payne, *New Poems*, p. 148, 'The Light O'Love'; Rossetti, *Poems*, p. 214, 'The Lovers' Walk'; for dream states see Yeats, *Collected Poems*, p. 74, 'He Tells of a Valley Full of Lovers'; p. 70, 'He Remembers Forgotten Beauty'; Payne, *Poetical Works*, II, p. 151, 'Evocation'. For the wavering between eroticism and spirituality, see Poe, *Works*, VII, pp. 107–9, 'To Helen'; Bourke Marston, *Collected Poems*, p. 13, 'A Poem'.
154 Poe, *Works*, VII, p. 107, 'To Helen'; Rossetti, *Poems*, p. 132, 'The Song of the Bower'; p. 116, 'Willowwood II'; Dowson, *Poems*, p. 94, 'Quid non speremus, amantes'.
155 Rossetti, *Poems*, p. 116, 'Death-in-Love' and p. 94, 'The Stream's Secret'; p. 222, 'Venus Victrix'.
156 Rossetti, *Poems*, p. 218.
157 Ibid., p. 219; see also 'Love-moon', ibid., p. 113.
158 Payne, *Poetical Works*, II, pp. 167–8, 'Silentia Lunae'.
159 Swinburne, *PB*, 17, 'Laus Veneris'.
160 Rossetti, *Poems*, pp. 109–110.
161 Swinburne, *PB*, p. 94, 'Fragoletta'.
162 Symons, *Poems*, I, p. 262, 'Bianca', no. VII, 'Presages'.
163 T. S. Eliot, *Selected Essays*, pp. 287–8, 'The Metaphysical Poets'.
164 Housman, *Green Arras*, p. 60, 'The Dead Mistress'.
165 Johnson, *Complete Poems*, p. 66, 'The Dark Angel'.
166 Compare e.g. 'The crystal flame, the ruby flame, / Alluring, dancing, revelling', ibid., p. 194, 'Vinum Daemonum'.
167 Rossetti, *Poems*, p. 110, 'The Birth-bond': 'Have you not noted in some family . . . Even so'; p. 119, 'Known in Vain': 'As two whose love, first foolish . . . So it happeneth / When Work and Will awake too late'.
168 'Sensitivity of a cultivated intellectual type' is a variation on Harry Quilter's formulation 'sensuality of a cultivated intellectual type', a quality he criticizes in Rossetti's *House of Life*, Quilter, 'The New Renaissance; or the Gospel of Intensity', 396.
169 Douglas, *Collected Poems*, pp. 84–5, 'A Triad of the Moon'.
170 On the question of synaesthesia, see A. Schinz, 'Literary Symbolism in France'; E. von Siebold, 'Synästhesien in der englischen Dichtung des 19. Jahrhunderts'; St von Ullmann, 'Synästhesien in den dichterischen Werken von Oscar Wilde'; St von Ullmann, 'Romanticism and Synaesthesia'.
171 'Comme de longs échos qui de loin se confondent / . . . Les parfums, les couleurs et les sons se répondent', Baudelaire, *Les Fleurs du Mal*, p. 13.
172 Swinburne, *PB*, p. 201, 'Hesperia'.

173 Ibid., p. 200.
174 Rossetti, *Poems*, p. 218.
175 Ibid., p. 216.
176 Payne, *Poetical Works*, II, p. 97, 'Madonna Dei Sogni'.
177 *The Works of Francis Thompson*, I, p. 94, 'Her Portrait'.
178 Rossetti, *Poems*, p. 219.
179 Theodore Wratislaw, *Orchids*, 1896, p. vii, title poem.
180 John Davidson, *A Collection from his Poems*, preface by T. S. Eliot, p. 140.
181 For the same procedure see also Thomson's B.V. poem 'He Heard Her Sing' (1882).
182 Davidson, *A Selection*, pp. 141–2, 'A Threnody Celebrating the Fall of the Leaf' (from *Bartlemas*).
183 Rossetti, *Poems*, p. 213, 'Heart's Hope'. Compare also the *Orpheus* metaphor in 'The Kiss' (p. 107) and the Hyacinthus image in 'The One Hope' (p. 128); see also 'Sleepless Dreams' (p. 114).
184 Ibid., p. 216, 'Genius in Beauty'.
185 Ibid., p. 227, 'True Woman' II, 'Her Love': 'She loves him; for her infinite soul's Love, / And he her lodestar', p. 217, 'Gracious Moonlight'; Michael Field, 'A Dying Viper', in *An Anthology of 'Nineties' Verse*, p. 70: 'She like a star has central gravity / That draws and fascinates the soul to death'.
186 Duncan, *The Revival of Metaphysical Poetry*; G. and K. Tillotson, *Mid-Victorian Studies*, 'Donne's Poetry in the Nineteenth Century'.
187 T. S. Eliot, *Selected Essays*, p. 290, 'The Metaphysical Poets'.
188 Richard Le Gallienne, *Retrospective Reviews*, 1896, II, p. 25: '[Thompson] must simply be Crashaw born again'.
189 Ibid., I, p. 232: 'Though frankly a disciple of modern French poets, Mr Gray's verses remind one more, in their quaint deliciousness, of certain old English poets, of Crashaw especially.'
190 Swinburne, 'Simeon Solomon . . .', pp. 313–14.
191 *The Works of Francis Thompson*, III, p. 21, 'Shelley'.
192 Ibid.; see also his essay 'Crashaw', ibid., p. 177.
193 Arthur Symons, *Dramatis Personae*, p. 181, 'Francis Thompson'.
194 Ibid., p. 168.
195 Ibid., p. 167: 'A profound thought, a profound emotion speaks as if it were unconscious of words'; ibid., p. 166: 'He thinks in words, he receives his emotions and sensations from words . . .'; ibid., p. 160.
196 *The Works of Francis Thompson*, III, p. 177, 'Crashaw'. Formulations like 'extraordinary verbal achievement' betray the new poetic ideal.
197 Rossetti, *Poems*, p. 128.
198 Swinburne, *PB*, p. 318, 'Madonna Mia'; Rossetti, *Poems*, p. 111, 'Love-sweetness'.
199 Custance, *Opals*, p. 42, 'An Impression'.
200 Rossetti, *Poems*, p. 132, 'The Song of the Bower'.
201 Douglas, *Collected Poems*, p. 23, 'Impression de Nuit'; see also Gray, *Silverpoints*, p. vi, 'Heart's Demesne'; see also the quotations from 'The Song of Solomon' in Simeon Solomon's *A Vision of Love Revealed in Sleep*.
202 Wilde, p. 720, 'The Burden of Itys'; see also Gray, *Silverpoints*, p. ix, 'Complaint' and Theodore Wratislaw, *Some Verses*, 1892, p. 5, 'Envy'.
203 Rossetti, *Poems*, p. 3; Davidson, *A Selection*, p. 97.

204 See e.g. Davidson, p. 140.
205 Ibid., p. 139.
206 Ibid., 'Preface', T. S. Eliot.
207 Ibid., pp. 139–40.
208 Baudelaire, *Les Fleurs du Mal*, p. 191.
209 Thomson, *Poems*, p. 183.
210 Rossetti, *Poems*, p. 4. This tradition lives on in Le Gallienne's 'The Day of the Two Daffodils'.
211 *An Anthology of 'Nineties' Verse*, p. 115, O'Sullivan, 'The Veil of Light'. For distorting effects in imagery see V. O'Sullivan, *Poems*, 1896, p. 13, 'White Dreaming' and p. 21, 'Brain Fever'.
212 Baudelaire, *Œuvres*, p. 373, *Les Paradis Artificiels*.
213 Gray, *Silverpoints*, p. xx, *Poems*; T. S. Eliot, *Collected Poems 1909–1935*, p. 24, 'Rhapsody on a Windy Night'.
214 Sydney Dobell, *Poetical Works*, 1875, I, p. 407.
215 Ibid., pp. 409–10.
216 Ibid., p. 405.
217 On the problem of the interrelationship of the arts in general see *Actes du Cinquième Congrès International de la Littérature Comparée* (1951); C. S. Brown, *Music and Literature*; Northrop Frye, 'Lexis and Melos', *Sound and Poetry*; R. L. Stein, *The Ritual of Interpretation*.
218 Allingham, *Poems*, 1850, p. 41.
219 Baudelaire, *Œuvres*, p. 877, 'Salon de 1846'.
220 Baudelaire, *Œuvres*, p. 1213, 'Richard Wagner et *Tannhäuser* à Paris'.
221 The enthusiasm for Wagner in England going back to Swinburne is reflected in such poems as Wratislaw's 'Tannhauser', 'Songs to Elizabeth', 'Brynhildr', 'Siegfried' as well as in the drawings of Beardsley. On the influence of Wagner see the study by E. Koppen.
222 John Davidson, *Holiday and Other Poems*, 'On Poetry', quoted from Davidson, *A Selection*, p. 27.
223 Baudelaire, *Œuvres*, p. 1037, 'Salon de 1859'.
224 *The Works of Francis Thompson*, III, p. 83, 'Nature's Immortality'. See also Yeats's use of Blake's formulation: 'painting, poetry, and music, the three powers in man of conversing with Paradise which the flood "of time and space" did not sweep away', *EI*, p. 117, 'William Blake and his Illustrations to the Divine Comedy'.
225 Allingham, *Poems*, p. 41.
226 Baudelaire, *Œuvres*, p. 1213, 'Richard Wagner et *Tannhäuser* à Paris'.
227 Liszt did not only write music for Raphael's painting *Sposalizio* and Michelangelo's sculpture *La Notte* or orchestra pieces like *Mazeppa* or *Die Ideale* (after Schiller) but also such compositions as the *Totentanz* inspired by the Campo Santo frescoes or the oratorio *Die Legende der heiligen Elisabeth* after Schwind's frescoes in the Wartburg. According to Ludwig Kusche (*Franz Liszt*, pp. 35–46) Liszt, under the impression of paintings by Kaulbach, intended to write a whole cycle of symphonic poems, *Die Weltgeschichte*, and even planned to translate into music the entire *Divina Commedia* for which the painter Bonaventura Genelli was supposed to provide the illustrations. It was intended that in the concert hall these pictures should be presented to the view of the public in the form of dioramas during

the course of Liszt's music.
228 Yeats, *EI*, p. 162.
229 Pater, *Renaissance*, p. 130, 'The School of Giorgione'.
230 Ibid., p. 135.
231 Ibid., p. 131: 'To such a philosophy of the variations of the beautiful, Lessing's analysis of the spheres of sculpture and poetry, in the *Laocoon* [*sic*], was a very important contribution.'
232 Ibid., pp. 133–4; see also: 'je reconnus, en effet, que précisément là où l'un de ces arts atteignait à des limites infranchissables, commençait aussitôt, avec la plus rigoureuse exactitude, la sphère d'action de l'autre', quoted from Baudelaire, *Œuvres*, p. 1218, 'Richard Wagner et *Tannhäuser* à Paris'.
233 Wilde, p. 971, 'The Critic as Artist'.
234 Ibid., p. 970.
235 Swinburne, 'Simeon Solomon . . .', p. 292.
236 Pater, *Appreciations*, p. 22, 'Style'.
237 *Memorials of Edward Burne-Jone*, I, p. 145.
238 Yeats, *EI*, p. 156, 'The Symbolism of Poetry'.
239 Ibid., p. 157.
240 Pater, *Marius*, I, p. 59: 'conveying with a single touch, the sense of textures, colours . . .'.
241 Le Gallienne, *Retrospective Reviews*, I, pp. 229–30.
242 Wilde, p. 926, 'The Decay of Lying'.
243 Yeats, *Autobiographies*, p. 279.
244 Wilde, p. 940, 'Pen, Pencil, and Poison'.
245 Of course, the influence of the impressionists on Wilde should not be overlooked. See O. Roditi, *Oscar Wilde*.
246 As a fashionable variant of this tendency compare also the subtitle 'A Study in Green' of Wilde's essay on Wainewright ('Pen, Pencil, and Poison').
247 Payne, *Poetical Works*, I, p. 289, 'The Masque of Shadows'.
248 See Wilde, p. 817, 'The Sphinx'.
249 Baudelaire, *Les Fleurs du Mal*, p. 163.
250 Ibid., p. 33, 'Avec ses vêtements ondoyants et nacrés'. J. A. Symonds, *Many Moods*, 1878, p. 37: 'Then turned to topaz: then like rubies smarted / With smouldering flames of passion tiger-hearted'.
251 Victor Plarr, *In the Dorian Mood*, 1896, p. 75.
252 See e.g. poems like Baudelaire, 'Le Chat', 'Dans ma cervelle . . .', 'Tristesse de la Lune'; Olive Custance, 'Opals'; AE, 'Alien', 'The Fountain of Shadowy Beauty', 'Weariness'; see also Nerval, *Œuvres*, I, p. 378, *Aurélia*.
253 Symons, *Poems*, II, p. 89.
254 C. W. King, *The Natural History, Ancient and Modern, of Precious Stones and Gems*, 1865; H. Emanuel, *Diamonds and Precious Stones; their History, Value, and Distinguishing Characteristics, with Simple Tests for their Identification*, 1865. For the combination of scientific and emblematic features in the late romantic use of precious stones see G. Hönnighausen, *Christina Rossetti*, pp. 151ff.
255 Wilde, pp. 952–3, 'The Critic as Artist'.
256 Pater, *Marius*, I, p. 160.
257 Gautier, *Mademoiselle de Maupin*, p. 190.
258 Pater, *Marius*, I, pp. 59–60.

259 Yeats, *Collected Poems*, p. 218, 'Sailing to Byzantium' and p. 281, 'Byzantium'.
260 See the handwritten letter in O'Shaughnessy, *Epic of Women* (BL C. 117 a. a. 15). The title *Songs of a Worker* is meant to express the combination of musical qualities and the craftsmanship of the sculptor's art.
261 O'Shaughnessy, *Songs of a Worker*, pp. vii–viii, Preface.
262 Ibid., p. 105. For the exotic aspect see Baudelaire's 'A une Dame Créole' and 'A une Malabraise'.
263 O'Shaughnessy, *Songs of a Worker*, p. 106.
264 Ibid., p. 111.
265 Gautier, *Mademoiselle de Maupin*, p. 200.
266 Baudelaire, 'Un Fantôme' III, 'Le Cadre', 'A une Madone'; Gautier, 'Le Poème de la Femme' (Marbre de Paros).
267 Gautier, *Mademoiselle de Maupin*, p. 243.
268 *The Germ*, p. 2.
269 Swinburne, 'Madonna Mia', 'A Christmas Carol', 'The Two Dreams', 'The King's Daughter', 'August'; Douglas, 'Jonquil and Fleurs-de-lys', 'The Ballad of Saint Vitus'; Wilde, 'Ballade de Marguerite', 'The Dole of the King's Daughter'; O'Shaughnessy, 'May'; Wratislaw, 'A Summer's Love'; Davidson, 'A Ballad of Lancelot', 'The Last Ordeal'; Yeats, 'The Cap and Bells'.
270 Morris, *Collected Works*, I, pp. 111 and 112, 'The Blue Closet'.
271 Wilde, p. 730, 'Impression de Nuit'.
272 See Wilde, 'Impression du Matin', 'Impression du Voyage', 'Symphony in Yellow', 'Fantaisies Decoratives'; Douglas, 'Ode to Autumn'; Symons, 'Maquillage', 'Morbidezza'; Symonds, 'In the Key of Blue'; Swinburne, 'Before the Mirror'.
273 J. Drinkwater, *William Morris*, p. 65.
274 Baudelaire, *Œuvres*, p. 881, 'Salon de 1846'.
275 Ibid., pp. 883–4.
276 Swinburne, 'Tebaldeo Tebaldei's Treatise of Noble Morals', in Lafourcade, *La Jeunesse de Swinburne*, I, p. 226.
277 Morris, *Works*, I, pp. 9, 7, 2, 'The Defence of Guenevere'.
278 Ibid., pp. 116–23.
279 Swinburne, 'Tebaldeo . . .', Lafourcade, I, p. 226.
280 Morris, *Works*, I, p. 117.
281 Ibid., p. 123. Swinburne's 'August' is a less extreme and much more convincing example of colour patterning.
282 J. A. Symonds, 'In the Key of Blue', 1893, p. 15: 'An artist in language must feel the mockery of wordpainting . . . Wordpaintings are a kind of hybrid, and purists in art criticism not irrationally look askance at the mixed species.' Cf. Le Gallienne's criticism: Le Gallienne, *Retrospective Reviews*, p. 241 (review of 'In the Key of Blue').
283 J. A. Symonds, 'In the Key of Blue', p. 13.
284 Ibid., pp. 5–6.
285 Ibid., p. 16.
286 Wilde, p. 917, 'The Decay of Lying'. See also p. 990, 'The Critic as Artist': 'Mere colour, unspoiled by meaning, and unallied with definite form, can speak to the soul in a thousand different ways'.

287 Gautier, *Emaux et Camées*, p. 21.

288 Ibid., pp. 22 and 23.

289 Swinburne, *PB*, p. 150.

290 *A Comprehensive Anthology of American Poetry*, John Gould Fletcher, 'White Symphony', pp. 332–8.

291 *The Faber Book of Modern Verse*, Vernon Watkins, 'Music of Colours – White Blossom', p. 366.

292 See also Ciurlioni's painting *Fugue*, reproduced and analysed by Hofstätter, *Symbolismus*, p. 95.

293 See C. Murciaux, 'Christina Rossetti, La Vierge Sage des Préraphaélites', p. 71.

294 See Wratislaw's Wagner poems and Beardsley's drawings, Payne's poem 'Bride-Night' (Wagner's *Tristan and Isolde*, Act II, scene 2), John Todhunter, *Selected Poems*, pp. 126–7, 'Beethoven's "Sonata Appassionata" ', and p. 134, 'Schumann's "Forest Scenes" '; Wratislaw, *Orchids*, p. 50, 'To a Pianist: "This song of Schumann's" '; Custance, *Opals*, p. 73, 'The Music of Dvořák'. See also Wilde, p. 949, 'The Critic as Artist'; 'Shall I play you a fantasy by Dvořák? He writes passionate, curiously-coloured things'; see also *The Works of Francis Thompson*, III, p. 30, 'Shelley': 'In some respect, is not Brahms the Browning of music?'.

295 Wilde, p. 950, 'The Critic as Artist'.

296 *The Works of Francis Thompson*, III, p. 30, 'Shelley'.

297 Bourke Marston, 'The River' (Suggested by the Fifteenth Prelude of Chopin); O'Shaughnessy, 'The Heart's Question' (Chopin's Nocturne Op. 15, no. 3), 'Charmed Moments' (Chopin's Nocture Op. 37, no. 1); Symons, 'The Chopin Player'; 'Chopin'.

298 Eliot, *Collected Poems*, p. 16.

299 Johnson, *Complete Poems*, p. 253.

300 Symons, *Poems*, I, p. 134.

301 Yeats, *EI*, p. 156, 'The Symbolism of Poetry'.

302 Gautier, *Emaux et Camées*, p. 133: 'Sculpte, lime, cisèle'.

303 Verlaine, *Œuvres poétiques*, p. 206: 'De la musique avant toute chose'.

304 Wilde, p. 855, 'De Profundis'.

305 Ibid., p. 970, 'The Critic as Artist'.

306 Swinburne, *PB*, pp. 248–50.

307 Bowra, *The Heritage of Symbolism*, p. 9.

308 Wilde, p. 951, 'The Critic as Artist'.

309 Yeats, *EI*, p. 159, 'The Symbolism of Poetry'.

310 Compare e.g. Payne's 'In Armida's Garden' (Gluck's *Armide*, Act II, Scene 3).

311 Symons, *Poems*, II, p. 79.

312 Swinburne, 'A Cameo'; Dobson, 'Love's Quest'; Sidney R. Thompson, 'A Fresco'. It should, however, be pointed out that the descriptions of imaginary or real paintings are much more frequent than those of pieces of music.

313 Todhunter, *Selected Poems*, p. 112.

314 O'Shaughnessy, *Epic of Women*, p. 217.

315 Bourke Marston, *Collected Poems*, pp. 345–6.

316 Todhunter, *Selected Poems*, pp. 126ff, 'Beethoven's "Sonata Appas-

sionata" ' (Inscribed to the Memory of Anton Rubinstein).
317 O'Shaughnessy, *Songs of a Worker*, p. 86.
318 Symonds, *Many Moods*, p. 176.

4 The imaginary landscape

1 Christina Rossetti, *Poetical Works*, pp. 317–18.
2 Gautier, *Emaux et Camées*, p. 170.
3 W. Sypher, p. 91.
4 Bowra, *Romantic Imagination*, esp. pp. 13, 180, 182, 198.
5 See e.g. Anne Ridler's comment (Preface to *Poems and Some Letters of James Thomson (B.V.)*, p. xliii): 'Before I read Mr T. S. Eliot's preface to a recent selection of John Davidson's poems, it had struck me that the "unreal city" of the *Waste Land* owed something to Thomson as well as to Baudelaire'. On the city in Yeats's 'Byzantium' poems see Hough, p. 254. The detailed and subtle analysis of Baudelaire's landscapes by G. Hess (*Die Landschaft in Baudelaires 'Fleurs du Mal'*) remains one of the most convincing studies of the late romantic landscape.
6 On the late romantic experience of time see J. H. Buckley, *The Triumph of Time*. Compare also Senior (p. 170) who considers time 'a major theme in symbolist literature'. On the experience of time and the decadent consciousness see Charlesworth, *Dark Passages*.
7 Charlesworth, p. 11.
8 Ibid., pp. 12, 14, 15.
9 Rossetti, *Poems*, p. 4.
10 Dobson, *Poetical Works*, p. 131.
11 See e.g. Rossetti, *Poems*, p. 118, 'Stillborn Love': 'The hour which might have been yet might not be, / . . . on what shore / Bides it the breaking of Time's instantaneous pause; / An instant, on my eye / Flashed all Eternity'.
12 Yeats, *Collected Poems*, p. 7, 'The Song of the Happy Shepherd'.
13 Rossetti, *Poems*, p. 126.
14 Ibid., p. 230.
15 Swinburne, *PB*, p. 250.
16 Poe, *Works*, VII, *Poems*, p. 90; Rossetti, *Poems*, p. 117; Dobson, *Poetical Works*, p. 130.
17 Allingham, *Poems*, p. 107.
18 Bourke Marston, *Collected Poems*, p. 321.
19 Bell Scott, *A Poet's Harvest Home*, p. 143: 'all alien, long-abandoned masks, / That in some witches' sabbath long since past / Did dance awhile in my life's panoply'.
20 O'Shaughnessy, *Music and Moonlight*, p. 168; see also *Epic of Women and Other Poems*, pp. 192–3, 'The Spectre of the Past'.
21 Payne, *Poetical Works*, II, p. 167.
22 Baudelaire, *Œuvres*, p. 375, *Les Paradis Artificiels*. See also the experience of time as described in the following poems by Baudelaire: 'Un Fantôme', pt IV; 'Le Portrait'; 'Le Goût du Néant'; 'Le Voyage', pt VII; 'L'Horloge'.
23 In *A Sextet of Singers or Songs of Six*, p. 93.
24 J. A. Symonds, *Many Moods*, p. 113.

25 Payne, *Poetical Works*, II, p. 172.
26 Symons, *Poems*, III, p. 205.
27 Douglas, *Collected Poems*, p. 98.
28 Baudelaire, *Les Fleurs du Mal*, p. 189.
29 Douglas, *Collected Poems*, p. 97.
30 Published in *The Germ*, 1, p. 20: 'Rest, rest that shall endure, / Till time shall cease'.
31 'Where Time would surely forget us, and Sorrow come near us no more', *Collected Poems*, p. 47, 'The Rose' (1893).
32 Dowson, *Poems*, p. 91.
33 Ibid., p. 143.
34 Baudelaire, *Les Fleurs du Mal*, p. 79, 'Spleen' and p. 13, 'J'aime le souvenir de ces époques nues'. As an example of this fashionable pose: 'But we who are born at the close of this wonderful age are at once too cultured and too critical, too intellectually subtle and too curious of exquisite pleasures . . . And so it is not our own life that we live, but the lives of the dead. . .', Wilde, pp. 978–9, 'The Critic as Artist'.
35 O'Shaughnessy, *Epic of Women*, p. 187.
36 Gautier, *Emaux et Camées*, p. 214.
37 Wilde, p. 997, 'The Critic as Artist'; the concept 'relative spirit' is mainly known from Pater's use of it; see e.g. *Appreciations*, p. 66, 'Coleridge': 'Modern thought is distinguished by its cultivation of the "relative spirit" in place of the "absolute".'
38 Morris, *Works*, I, p. 11, 'King Arthur's Tomb'.
39 Ibid., I, p. 4, 'The Defence of Guenevere'.
40 Rossetti, *Poems*, p. 6.
41 J. A. Symonds, *New and Old*, 1880, pp. 30–1.
42 Dobson, *Poetical Works*, p. 130.
43 *The Works of Francis Thompson*, II, pp. 3ff; 'The Mistress of Vision', pp. 6ff.
44 O'Shaughnessy, *Music and Moonlight*, p. 16.
45 T. S. Eliot, *Four Quartets*, pp. 14, 35–6.
46 *PB*, p. 317. The idiosyncratic use of the Pre-Raphaelite orchard scenery as an expression of masochistic impulses in Swinburne's 'In the Orchard' (Provençal Burden) attests to the widespread use of the motif, *PB*, pp. 116 and 117.
47 Ibid., p. 250.
48 *Art and Poetry* (*The Germ*), 4 (May 1850), pp. 167–8.
49 J. A. Symonds, *New and Old*, p. 30.
50 *Art and Poetry* (*The Germ*), 4 (May 1850), p. 168, 'On a Whit-Sunday Morn in the Month of May'.
51 O'Sullivan, *Poems*, p. 19, stanzas 1, 4, and 5.
52 Rossetti, *Poems*, p. 307.
53 Wratislaw, *Love's Memorial*, p. 35.
54 Ibid., pp. 42–3.
55 Gray, *Silverpoints*, p. v.
56 Dowson, *Poems*, p. 52.
57 Quite often the images of the grove or the bower are replaced by that of the nest with similar implications; see e.g. 'Silent Noon', Rossetti, *Poems*, p.

216; see also: 'My nest is all untrod' and 'From visionary groves / Imagined lutes make voiceless harmonies', Douglas, *Collected Poems*, p. 65, 'Wine of Summer'.

58 Rossetti, *Poems*, p. 114, 'Sleepless Dreams'.
59 Ibid., p. 214, 'Youth's Antiphony'.
60 Payne, *New Poems*, pp. 146 and 147.
61 Payne, *Poetical Works*, II, p. 110, 'Madonna Dei Sogni'.
62 In *A Sextet of Singers*, p. 51.
63 Rossetti, *Poems*, p. 108; see also his story 'Hand and Soul' (*The Germ*, p. 31): 'And Chiaro held silence and wept into her hair which covered her face'.
64 Dowson, *Poems*, p. 90, 'Cease Smiling, Dear!'; see also p. 87, 'Impenitentia Ultima' and Rossetti, *Poems*, p. 3, 'The Blessed Damozel'.
65 Yeats, *Collected Poems*, pp. 78–9 (scourge, thorns, wounds in the palm and side).
66 Ibid., p. 74, 'He Tells of a Valley Full of Lovers'.
67 Ibid., p. 69, 'He Reproves the Curlew': 'passion-dimmed eyes and long heavy hair / That was shaken out over my breast'.
68 Ibid., p. 67.
69 Ibid., p. 69:

> The Horses of Disaster plunge in the heavy clay:
> Beloved, let your eyes half close, and your heart beat
> Over my heart, and your hair fall over my breast,
> Drowning love's lonely hour in deep twilight of rest,
> And hiding their tossing manes and their tumultuous feet.

Similar experiences are described in *The Shadowy Waters* and other dramas by Yeats.
70 Yeats, *Collected Poems*, p. 47, 'The White Birds'.
71 *PB*, p. 205.
72 Christina Rossetti, *Poetical Works*, p. 371, 'If I Had Words'.
73 Yeats, *Collected Poems*, p. 20, 'The Stolen Child'.
74 Christina Rossetti, *Poetical Works*, p. 295, 'How One Chose'.
75 Ibid., p. 321, 'By the Water'.
76 Dowson, *Poems*, p. 111, 'Villanelle of Acheron'.
77 Christina Rossetti, *Poetical Works*, p. 292, 'Dream Land'; compare also the following lines from the same poem: 'Rest, rest a perfect rest / Shed over brow and breast; / Her face is toward the west, / The purple land'.
78 Ibid., p. 311.
79 Dowson, *Poems*, p. 138, 'A Last Word'.
80 Douglas, *Collected Poems*, p. 51. For this type see Housman, 'The Garden of Life'; Wilde, 'The Garden of Eros'; Payne, 'The Garden of Adonis'. (In Payne's poem the literary sources are easily traceable, as the poem bears the reference 'Spenser's Faery [*sic*] Queene. The Legend of Britomart', pt VI, p. 29.)
81 'No natural sweet they lack, a chrysolite / Of perfect beauty each. No wisdom comes / To mar their early folly, no false laws / Man-made for man . . .'.
82 Payne, *New Poems*, pp. 122–3.
83 Payne, *Poetical Works*, II, p. 145: 'My dream is of a city in the West / Built with fair colours, still and sad as flowers'.

84 Poe, *Works*, VII, p. 49.
85 'The Doom of a City' and 'CDN'.
86 Payne, *Poetical Works*, II, p. 164, 'Nirwana'.
87 Bourke Marston, *Collected Poems*, p. 89, 'Sleepland Forsaken'; p. 310, 'In Praise of Sleep'.
88 Dowson, *Poems*, p. 70.
89 O'Shaughnessy, *Epic of Women*, p. 23.
90 Custance, *Opals*, pp. 62–3.
91 J. A. Symonds, *Many Moods*, p. 113, 'Oblivion'; see also p. 190, 'Anticyra'.
92 *PB*, p. 196, 'The Garden of Proserpine'.
93 Dowson, *Poems*, p. 71, 'Beata Solitudo'.
94 James Thomson, *Poems*, p. 72.
95 Nerval, *Œuvres*, I, p. 366, *Aurélia*.
96 Gautier, *Mademoiselle de Maupin*, p. 360.
97 For reference see the titles quoted in Adam's commentary on *Les Fleurs du Mal* and the works of G. F. Renier, *Oscar Wilde,* and K. Hartley, *Oscar Wilde: L'Influence Française dans son Œuvre*.
98 Rossetti, *Poems*, pp. 14ff.
99 In 1849 Layard published his *Niniveh and its Remains*; in 1853 *Discoveries at Niniveh and Researches at Babylon*. Compare also Evelyn Douglas's poem 'The Ruins of Niniveh' in *Selections from Songs of a Bayadere and Songs of a Troubadour*.
100 Gautier, *Emaux et Camées*, p. 41.
101 Wratislaw, *Orchids*, p. vii, 'Orchids'.
102 Ibid., p. 23. The influence of Huysmans's *A Rebours* is just as obvious as that of *Les Fleurs du Mal*.
103 Payne, *New Poems*, p. 152.
104 'Its depths are strewn with all that youth misspends; / With all the wasted chances that life has; / And there all Ophir, all Golconda lies', Lee-Hamilton, *Sonnets of the Wingless Hours*, p. 68. Numerous examples prove the relationship with the poetry of the Pre-Raphaelites. See also the poem on Rossetti in the same volume (p. 93), 'In Memoriam': 'Marston, mourn not; Rossetti is not dead'.
105 *The Works of Francis Thompson*, II, p. 6. The fact that for Gautier, too, the memory of his 'Mistress of Vision' recalls the image of Cathay illustrates the Anglo-French parallels (*Mademoiselle de Maupin*, p. 57).
106 These elements constitute one of the essential differences between the poetry of the Pre-Raphaelites and their realistic paintings which has remained unnoticed so far.
107 In *An Anthology of 'Nineties' Verse*, p. 44.
108 Dobson, *Poetical Works*, p. 191, 'Household Art'.
109 Wilde, p. 816.
110 See also 'The Memphian Temple' by Evelyn Douglas in *An Anthology of 'Nineties' Verse*, pp. 46–7.
111 O'Shaughnessy, *Music and Moonlight*, pp. 93–4.
112 De Quincey, *Collected Writings*, III, p. 442, *Confessions*.
113 Wilde, p. 812.
114 De Quincey, *Collected Writings*, III, p. 442, *Confessions*.

115 Evelyn Douglas, 'The Palace of Pleasure', in *An Anthology of 'Nineties' Verse*, pp. 47–8.
116 Wilde, *Works*, XI, p. 119, *The English Renaissance of Art*.
117 Wilde, p. 887, 'De Profundis'.
118 O'Shaughnessy, *Music and Moonlight*, pp. 14–15. Compare also Rossetti's 'Love's Last Gift', *Poems*, p. 228. On the symbolist motif of the deep-sea landscape see: W. Vortriede, *Novalis und die französischen Symbolisten*, pp. 72–3; on the motif of the dead and sunken cities see H. Hinterhäuser, 'Tote Städte in der Literatur des Fin de Siècle', esp. p. 341.
119 See also James Thomson, 'A Lady of Sorrow', II, 'The Siren', *Essays and Phantasies*, 1881, p. 13: 'Then she would lead me into labyrinthic caverns, shut in from the waters with marble doors, tapestried with mossy growths and long slender sea-blooms purple and crimson and amber; floored with golden sand and iridescent shells, walled with emerald, roofed with crystal, lit with gleaming pearls and flashing precious stones . . .'. Compare also Eugene Lee-Hamilton, *Apollo and Marsyas and Other Poems*, 1884, p. 131. See also De Quincey's 'Savannah-La-Mar' (*Collected Writings*, XIII, *Tales and Prose Phantasies*, pp. 359–61) and Poe's poem 'The City in the Sea', *Works*, VII, pp. 49–50.
120 Wilde, p. 817.
121 J. A. Symonds, *Many Moods*, p. 121.
122 *Les Fleurs du Mal*, p. 115, 'Rêve Parisien'.
123 Ibid., p. 29.
124 O'Shaughnessy, *Epic of Women*, pp. 71–2.
125 Wratislaw, *Caprices*, p. 35.
126 This escapist feature distinguishes O'Shaughnessy from De Quincey for whom the exotic landscape is most of the time associated with nightmare sceneries. The protagonist in Gautier's *Mademoiselle de Maupin* wishes he had wings which would allow him to escape into a world 'où je puisse oublier que je suis moi, et vivre une vie étrange et nouvelle, plus loin que l'Amérique, plus loin que l'Afrique, plus loin que l'Asie' (p. 57).
127 See De Quincey, *Collected Writings*, III, p. 395, *Confessions*.
128 *Les Fleurs du Mal*, p. 53.
129 *The Poems of Samuel Taylor Coleridge*, p. 295.
130 Dowson, *Poems*, p. 143.
131 J. L. Lowes, *Road to Xanadu* and A. Hayter, *Opium and the Romantic Imagination*.
132 Baudelaire, *Œuvres*, p. 385, *Les Paradis Artificiels*.
133 Since Talon has given a convincing interpretation of Rossetti's 'Willowwood' sonnets (*D. G. Rossetti*, pp. 33–45) the present analysis can focus on the specific question of the symbolic landscape.
134 *The Complete Works of Lewis Carroll*, p. 966.
135 Christina Rossetti, *Poetical Works*, p. 406, 'In the Willow Shade'.
136 Ibid., p. 368, 'Under Willows'.
137 Rossetti, *Poems*, p. 117.
138 Ibid.
139 Ibid., p. 73.
140 See the painting *How They Met Themselves* (Pl. 12).
141 Rossetti, *Poems*, p. 75.

142 Johnson, *Complete Poems*, p. 141.
143 Ibid., p. 142.
144 Lee-Hamilton, *Sonnets of the Wingless Hours*, p. 68.
145 Baudelaire, *Œuvres*, p. 1063, 'Salon de 1859'. See also *Les Fleurs du Mal*, p. 20, 'La Vie Antérieure': 'J'ai longtemps habité sous de vastes portiques' and Evelyn Douglas, 'Dreamland', in *An Anthology of 'Nineties' Verse*, p. 44: 'Close by porches vast and plinths Titanic'.
146 De Quincey, *Collected Writings*, III, p. 438, *Confessions*.
147 Nerval, *Œuvres*, I, p. 366, *Aurélia*; see also I, p. 386.
148 De Quincey, *Collected Writings*, XIII, pp. 323–4, 'The English Mail-Coach'.
149 Ibid., III, p. 435, *Confessions*.
150 Poe, *Works*, VII, p. 89.
151 Ibid., VIII, p. 102.
152 James Thomson, *Poems*, p. 183, 'CDN', canto IV, lines 46–9 and 53–6.
153 James Thomson, *Essays and Phantasies*, p. 20, 'A Lady of Sorrow', III, 'The Shadow'.
154 Payne, *Poetical Works*, I, p. 286.
155 James Thomson, *Poems*, p. 178; 'CDN', canto I, line 25.
156 *Les Fleurs du Mal*, p. 26.
157 Gautier, *Emaux et Camées*.
158 Ibid., p. 212, *Melancholia*.
159 Nerval, *Œuvres*, I, p. 366, *Aurélia*.
160 See the notes in Ridler's edition of Thomson, *Poems*, p. 263.
161 Ibid., p. 66, *The 'Melencolia' of Albrecht Dürer*.
162 Ibid., p. 203, 'CDN', canto XXI, lines 1–3; see also James Thomson, 'A Lady of Sorrow', 20–1: 'A colossal image of black marble, the Image and the concentration of the whole blackness of Night, as of a Woman seated, veiled from head to foot.'
163 Ibid., p. 304, lines 46–7.
164 *Mademoiselle de Maupin*, p. 57.
165 Ibid., p. 66.
166 Christina Rossetti, *Poetical Works*, pp. 99ff. According to William Michael Rossetti (p. 466) the original title 'The City of Statues' goes back to the story from the *Arabian Nights*. See also Ridler's commentary on 'The Doom of a City', James Thomson, *Poems*, p. xxxix.
167 Lee-Hamilton, *Sonnets of the Wingless Hours*, p. 83.
168 Bourke Marston, *A Last Harvest*, p. 337.
169 James Thomson, *Poems*, p. 25, lines 209ff.
170 Ibid., p. 21, 17–20.
171 Ibid., p. 26, lines 248–52.
172 Poe, *Works*, VII, p. 49 (. . . bowers / Of sculptured ivy and stone flowers . . . wreathed friezes . . . riches there that lie / In each idol's diamond eye – Not the gaily-jewelled dead . . . wilderness of glass).
173 Ibid., p. 102.
174 James Thomson, *Poems*, p. 189, 'CDN', canto IX, line 5.
175 Ibid., p. 178, 'CDN', canto I, line 24.
176 Ibid., p. 201, 'CDN', canto XIX, line 4.
177 Ibid., p. 178, canto I, lines 1–2.

178 '. . . for never there / Can come the lucid morning's fragrant breath . . .' (ibid., p. 178, canto I, lines 2–3); 'the sun has never visited that city' (ibid., p. 178, canto I, line 6).
179 Ibid., p. 178, canto I, line 13: '. . . can any / Discern that dream from real life in aught?'
180 See e.g. the section 'Tableaux Parisiens' in *Les Fleurs du Mal*.
181 *The Prophetic Writings of William Blake*, I, p. 491, *Jerusalem*.
182 AE, *Collected Poems*, pp. 30–1, 'The City'.
183 Le Gallienne, *Nightingales*, pp. 6–7.
184 Symons, *Poems*, III, p. 44, 'Venice'.
185 Ibid., II, p. 199, 'London'.
186 Douglas, *Collected Poems*, p. 23.
187 Payne, *Poetical Works*, II, p. 150.
188 *The Works of Francis Thompson*, I, p. 107.
189 *Les Fleurs du Mal*, p. 129.
190 J. A. Symonds, *New and Old*, p. 248, 'Notes'.
191 'CDN', canto II, lines 7–18.
192 Ibid., lines 13, 19, 37.
193 O'Sullivan, *The Houses of Sin*, p. 12, title poem.
194 E.g.: 'the golden house of Love' – 'the dark house of Death'.
195 Custance, *The Inn of Dreams*, pp. 18–19.
196 Dowson, *Poems*, p. 61.
197 Ibid., p. 67, 'April Love': 'We have walked in Love's land a little while'. See e.g. Rossetti, *Poems*, p. 114, 'Secret Parting': 'roof of Love'; p. 106, 'Lovesight': 'Life's darkening slope'.
198 J. A. Symonds, *Many Moods*, p. 190.
199 Verlaine, *Œuvres poétiques*, pp. 57–8: 'Comme un vol criard d'oiseaux en émoi / Tous mes souvenirs s'abattent sur moi . . .'.
200 Rossetti, *Poems*, p. 112: 'Each hour until we meet is as a bird / That wings from far his gradual way along / The rustling covert of my soul'. The image of the song-bird is a very common metaphor in the works of Rossetti and his epigones; together with other elements of their mannered imagery, it therefore deserves special attention; see also Custance, *Opals*, pp. 62–3, 'The Song Bird': 'There is a garden in my soul, / A garden full of singing birds'.
201 *Les Fleurs du Mal*, p. 61.
202 Custance, *The Inn of Dreams*, title poem.
203 Payne, *Poetical Works*, II, p. 166, 'Lonely Thought'.
204 Sidney R. Thompson, in *A Sextet of Singers*, p. 77, 'In the Resurrection'.
205 Bourke Marston, *Collected Poems*, p. 307, 'Parables', no. IV.
206 Rossetti, *Poems*, p. 107.
207 Bourke Marston, *Collected Poems*, p. 8.
208 Custance, *Opals*, p. 62, 'The Song Bird'.
209 *Les Fleurs du Mal*, pp. 18–19, 'L'Ennemi'.
210 Douglas, *Collected Poems*, p. 80, 'The City of the Soul'.
211 Ibid., p. 54, 'Ode to My Soul'.
212 Christina Rossetti, *Poetical Works*, p. 288, 'Three Stages'.
213 See e.g. Housman, *The Green Arras*, p. 30, 'The Garden of Life'.
214 *Les Fleurs du Mal*, p. 58.

215 Ibid., p. 54, 'Ciel Brouillé'; p. 61, 'Causerie': 'Vous êtes un beau ciel d'autumne, clair et rose'; p. 186, 'Les Yeux de Berthe': 'Vous ressemblez beaucoup à ces grottes magiques'.
216 Symons, *Poems*, III, p. 203, 'Laus Stellae': 'Thy beauty is a garden planted / With tropic flowers'.
217 Housman, *The Green Arras*, p. 60, 'The Dead Mistress'.
218 Gray, *Silverpoints*, p. xviii, 'Lean Back and Press the Pillow Deep'; see also ibid., p. vi, 'Heart's Demesne'.
219 Verlaine, *Œuvres poétiques*, p. 83.
220 O'Shaughnessy, *Songs of a Worker*, p. 187; Gray, *Silverpoints*, p. xxvi.

5 The ideal beloved

1 See Bowra, *The Heritage of Symbolism*, pp. 144–5 and O. A. Maslenikow, *The Frenzied Poets*, p. 157, with its description of Blok's endeavour to stylize his fiancée as Lady Beautiful in such a way that 'the love that she aroused in him was akin to a lofty, devout adoration'.
2 See my essay 'Dowsons *Seraphita*-Gedichte'.
3 T. Gautier, *Souvenirs Romantiques*, p. 307.
4 Hugo von Hofmannsthal, *Gesammelte Werke*, pp. 99–105, 'Algernon Charles Swinburne' (1893); pp. 194–201, 'Über moderne englische Malerei' (1894); pp. 202–6, 'Walter Pater' (1894).
5 Ibid., pp. 251–9, 'Englischer Stil' (1896).
6 Ibid., p. 103 (My translation.)
7 Praz, *Romantic Agony*, p. 318.
8 James Thomson, *Essays and Phantasies*, p. 5, 'A Lady of Sorrow'. For the transformations these symbolic dream figures very often undergo, see also Nerval, *Œuvres*, I, p. 408, *Aurélia*: 'Je reportai ma pensée à l'éternelle Isis, la mère et l'épouse sacrée . . . et parfois elle m'apparaissait sous la figure de la Vénus antique, parfois aussi sous les traits de la Vierge des chrétiens.'
9 Thomson, 'A Lady of Sorrow', p. 7: 'For she was simply the image in beatitude of her who died so young. The pure girl was become the angel.'
10 Ibid., p. 11.
11 Ibid., p. 13.
12 O'Shaughnessy, *An Epic of Women*, p. 147.
13 On the biographical background see O. Brönner, *Das Leben Arthur O'Shaughnessys*.
14 'Creation', pp. 79–80; 'The Wife of Hephaestus', p. 86; 'Cleopatra', p. 93.
15 Quoted from *The Oxford Book of Modern Verse 1892–1935*, p. 1.
16 *PB*, p. 4: 'Come thou before my lady and say this; / Borgia, thy gold hair's colour burns in me'.
17 Rossetti, *Poems*, p. 307.
18 *Les Fleurs du Mal*, p. 63, 'A Une Madone' and 'Tu Mettrais l'Univers Entier dans ta Ruelle', p. 31; see also the formulation: 'o femme, o reine des péchés'.
19 In addition to this illustrative combination of opposites in 'Hesperia', *PB*, pp. 204–5, see also the subtitle of 'Dolores', ibid., pp. 178–9; 'Notre-Dame des sept douleurs' and the refrain-like use of the address 'Our Lady of Pain'.

20 'She passes, the Destroying Angel of Love's host', Symons, *Poems*, I, p. 311.

21 Wratislaw, *Caprices*, p. 32. In most of the copies of this edition 'L'Eternel Féminin' is replaced by 'At Midnight', a poem dedicated to Beardsley.

22 O'Shaughnessy, *Epic of Women*, pp. 79–80; see also the apotheosis in Le Gallienne, *English Poems*, p. 95, 'Beauty Accursed'.

23 Victor Plarr, *In the Dorian Mood*, pp. 73–4, 'The Goddess of the Islanders.' Echoes of Swinburne are all too obvious.

24 Ibid., p. 75.

25 'Will you not slay me? Stab me; Yea, somehow, / Deep in the heart . . . / And fall down there and writhe about my feet / The crooked loathly viper I shall bruise / Through all eternity', *Epic of Women*, p. 167.

26 Ibid., p. 166.

27 Gautier, *Emaux et Camées*, p. 34, 'Caerulei Occuli': 'Et leurs cils, comme des mouettes / Qui rasent le flot aplani / Palpitant, ailes inquiètes, / Sur leur azure indéfini'; and ibid., p. 35 ('La coupe du roi de Thulé', 'Cléopâtre', 'Salomon', 'La ballade de Schiller', 'Harald Harfagar').

28 Praz, *Romantic Agony*, p. 206.

29 In *Poems* (1870) Rossetti makes a reference to his source: 'Herodotus says that Helen offered in the temple of Venus a cup made in the likeness of her own bosom'. It is symptomatic that Rossetti should choose this particular scene as the subject of his poem.

30 Rossetti, *Poems*, p. 12.

31 See Marillier, *Dante Gabriel Rossetti*, pp. 129–30.

32 Rossetti, *Poems*, p. 19 and ibid., p. 142.

33 O'Shaughnessy, *Epic of Women*, p. 139.

34 Wilde, p. 733.

35 Symons, *Poems*, III, p. 222.

36 Wilde, pp. 717–18: 'Like a star / Hung in the silver silence of the night'; 'Sidon, that enchanted land . . . forlorn Calypso knew'.

37 Yeats, *Collected Poems*, p. 41.

38 Ibid., pp. 45–6; see p. 46 and also p. 41: 'For these red lips with all their mournful pride'.

39 Hough, p. 76. On Rossetti's transformation of figures from real life into imaginary and symbolic figures, see also Dixon Hunt, pp. 179ff. On the relation of biographical elements and their literary transformation see K. L. Knickerbocker, 'Rossetti's "The Blessed Damozel" '.

40 As Thomson points out in the Ms. (p. 18) he used the 5th edn of Tieck's edition of Novalis (1837), whereas Carlyle used the 4th edn (1826).

41 *The Works of Thomas Carlyle*, XXVII, *Critical and Miscellaneous Essays*, II, p. 44.

42 Ibid., p. 15. See also Schaefer, *James Thomson: Beyond 'The City'*, p. 19.

43 Bodleian Ms. Don. e. 48, pp. 146–69, pp. 1–22, respectively.

44 See e.g. Walker, who interprets Thomson's relationship to Novalis as mere biographical coincidence.

45 *Novalis' Schriften*, 1: *Das dichterische Werk, Hymnen an die Nacht*, pp. 119–20 and 188. For the cult of the dead beloved, Novalis's *Tagebücher nach Sophies Tod* are of special interest.

46 James Thomson, *Poems*, p. 1, 'Four Points in a Life', no. I, 'Love's Dawn'.

47 For Thomson the dead beloved has the same moralizing effect as that described by Novalis in *Tagebücher nach Sophies Tod*.
48 James Thomson, *Poems*, p. 65, 'Mater Tenebrarum', lines 15–16.
49 Poe, *Works*, VII, p. 99, 'The Raven':
    Tell this soul with sorrow laden if, within the distant Aidenn
    It shall clasp a sainted maiden whom the Angels name Lenore –
    Quoth the raven 'Nevermore'.
    In the works of Poe the motif often recurs both in his stories (e.g. 'Berenice', 'Ligeia', 'Morella' and 'Eleonora') and in his poetry ('To One in Paradise', 'Ulalume' or 'Annabel Lee').
50 Thomson translated Goethe, Heine and Leopardi and was well versed in French literature.
51 James Thomson, *Poems*, p. 96, 'Vane's Story', line 271.
52 'Vane's Story', lines 383–4.
53 With Matilda's death, the Fountain of life 'ceased to wave' and 'the stream fell stagnant' for Thomson (Vane), but when the beloved returns at night from the realm of death she rolls away the stone that had 'sealed the gloom' and brought about the change in Vane's character so disconcerting to his friend Jones. The Fountain 'ever ready now as then / To leap into the air again' immediately begins to sing 'its old unwearied tune' (pp. 962ff).
54 James Thomson, *Poems*, p. 183, 'CDN', canto IV, line 69.
55 Walker, p. 100.
56 Quoted from Leon, p. 510.
57 Ruskin, *Works*, XXXIII, p. 507.
58 Johnson, *Complete Poems*, p. 52.
59 Quoted in M. Longaker, *Ernest Dowson*, pp. 202 and 155.
60 Yeats, *Autobiographies*, p. 311.
61 Apart from Sophie von Kühn, Matilda Weller, Rose La Touche and Adelaide Foltinowicz, Verlaine's 'girl-wife' (see A. Symons, *The Symbolist Movement*, p. 83) and Poe's 'child-wife', Virginia Clemm, should also be mentioned here; see Bowra, *Romantic Imagination*, p. 185.
62 Longaker (p. 27) talks about a 'cult of little girls at Oxford during the eighties'.
63 Wilde, p. 875, 'De Profundis'.
64 Wordsworth, *Poetical Works*, p. 461.
65 *The Works of Francis Thompson*, III, pp. 7–8, 'Shelley'.
66 Ibid., I, p. 3. See also: '*I* was a child and *she* was a child, / In this kingdom by the sea: / But we loved with a love that was more than love . . .', Poe, *Works*, VII, p. 117, 'Annabel Lee'.
67 Thompson, I, p. 4: 'Tokens three: – / A look, a word of her winsome mouth, / And a wild raspberry'.
68 Ibid., p. 6.
69 Ibid., p. 8.
70 Ibid., p. 13.
71 Ibid., p. 11. The speaker visualizes death absurdly repeating lines which the child had sung while alive: 'A cup of chocolate, / One farthing is the rate'.
72 Ibid., p. 20.
73 Ibid., p. 40.
74 Ibid., p. 43.

75 Ibid.
76 See Rossetti's poem 'Aspecta Medusa' (*Poems*, p. 100) together with the painting of the same title.
77 Yeats, *Autobiographies*, p. 311.
78 See also Swinburne's strange love of children.
79 Dowson, *Poems*, p. 55; see also: 'Do I want to keep her from growing up? Of course I do!', quoted from J. Evans, *John Ruskin*, p. 265.
80 Dowson, *Poems*, p. 47, 'Ad Domnulam Suam'.
81 In *An Anthology of 'Nineties' Verse*, p. 29: 'A simple child-like creature fair, / Yet shadowed by a haunting mystery'.
82 Johnson, *Complete Poems*, p. 45.
83 Ibid., p. 44: 'At us, whose disenchanted eyes / Imagination dares despise'.
84 Yeats, *Autobiographies*, p. 302.
85 Pater, *Marius*, II, p. 182. See Lionel Johnson's verse 'to be three years old, / Is to have found the Age of Gold'.
86 Pater, *Marius*, II, pp. 181–2.
87 Ibid., pp. 188–9.
88 James Thomson B.V., *Hymns to Night*, Bodleian Ms. Don. e. 48, 8.
89 O'Sullivan, *The Houses of Sin*, p. 26. For the close relationship between symbolic landscapes and symbolic figures see the juxtaposition of the motif of the dead beloved with that of the dead city in Georges Rodenbach's novel *Bruges-la-Morte* (1892): 'Bruges était sa morte. Et sa morte était Bruges' (p. 19). For an analysis of the motif of the dead city in this novel see Hinterhäuser, esp. 321–5.
90 O'Sullivan, *The Houses of Sin*, p. 62.
91 Poe, *Works*, XIV, *Essays, Miscellanies*, p. 201, 'The Philosophy of Composition'.
92 Ibid., VII, p. 164.
93 Walter Pater, 'Aesthetic Poetry' (1868) in *Appreciations*, 1889 (missing in later editions), quoted from Pater, *Selected Works*, p. 83.
94 Ibid., p. 77. For the case of late romanticism in England this poetological argumentation seems to present a more appropriate perspective than the examples of pathological necrophilia discussed by Praz (p. 122).
95 O'Sullivan, *The Houses of Sin*, pp. 17–18.
96 In 1899 O'Sullivan edited Poe's *The Raven. The Pit and the Pendulum. With some account of the author.*
97 Symons, *Poems*, III, pp. 241–2.
98 Allingham, *Poems*, pp. 189–90.
99 O'Shaughnessy, *Music and Moonlight*, pp. 108–9.
100 Woolner, 'Of my Lady in Death', in *The Germ*, p. 6.
101 *The Works of Francis Thompson*, II, p. 216.
102 Dowson, *Poems*, p. 58. On the question of sources for the title 'Cynara' see Longaker's notes to this edition, pp. 207–8.
103 James Thomson, *Poems*, p. 190, lines 37–40.
104 Ibid., p. 1, lines 49–51.
105 In Rossetti's painting Beatrice appears in a vision lying on her bier.
106 Housman, *The Green Arras*, p. 60, 'The Dead Mistress'.
107 See Swinburne, *PB*, p. 7, 'A Ballad of Death' and L. Johnson, *Complete Poems*, p. 35, 'The Last Music'.

108 See Thomson's most revealing formulation 'as a statue carved in stone', and the stylizing features in Le Gallienne's poems 'Monody' and 'Requiem', written after the death of his first wife, Mildred; Le Gallienne, *New Poems*, 1910, pp. 60 and 63.
109 'My master that was thrall of Love / Is become thrall to Death' (Swinburne, 'A Ballad of Death', p. 9).
110 Yeats, *Collected Poems*, pp. 80–1.
111 Christina Rossetti, *Poetical Works*, pp. 319–20; see also ibid., p. 326, 'Gone Before'.
112 Ibid., p. 292, 'Dream Land' and p. 293, 'Rest'.
113 Wilde, p. 709.
114 Harry Quilter, 'The New Renaissance', pp. 400 and 396.
115 Housman, *The Green Arras*, p. 65.
116 The dead wife appears to her husband prophesying that he shall find the baby that drowned with her; having buried it by her side he, too, dies and all three are happily united in heaven: 'These three of Heaven's honey feed, / And milk of Paradise', Payne, *New Poems*, pp. 108–9.
117 Le Gallienne, *English Poems*, p. 21.
118 See e.g. Bourke Marston's poems 'Sleepland Glorified' and 'Sleepland Forsaken' (*Collected Poems*, p. 89) in which dream embodies the same qualities as the figure of the dead beloved. See also Allingham, *Flower Pieces and Other Poems*, p. 73, 'Unknown Belov'd One'.
119 See *The Works of Francis Thompson*, III, p. 48, 'Paganism Old and New'.
120 The great number of poems in which Dowson uses the motif illustrates the inner relationship between the dead beloved and other stylized forms of the symbolic female figure. It is apparently the same impulses that induce him to turn to the dead beloved and the childbride; see Dowson, *Poems*, pp. 65–6, 'You would have understood me' and p. 47, 'Ad Domnulam Suam'.
121 Ibid., pp. 95–6.
122 Dowson, *Poems*, p. 92, 'Seraphita'; see also the invocation: 'O visionary face; the bright illumination of thy memory; O moon of all my night'.
123 Ibid., p. 68: 'So might she look on me with pitying eyes, / And lay calm hands of healing on my head'; p. 86: 'Grant me one hour of all mine hours, and let me see for a token / Her pure and pityful eyes shine out, and bathe her feet with tears'.
124 *The Works of Francis Thompson*, I, pp. 171, 200; II, pp. 52, 67.
125 Johnson, *Complete Poems*, p. 15; see also 'A Discant upon the Litany of Loretto' (p. 136); 'Cadgwith', III (p. 74); 'Our Lady of the May' (p. 139); 'Our Lady of the Snow' (p. 94).
126 Rossetti, *Poems*, p. 27.
127 Wratislaw, *Orchids*, p. 32; see also pp. 52 and 53.
128   O you, that are too pure to save,
        Immaculate eternally.
        Mother of lilies, pity me!   (Symons, *Poems*, II, p. 66).
129 Symons, *The Symbolist Movement*, p. 95.
130 Swinburne's 'Hymn to Proserpine' presupposes this idea. On this problem see also Francis Thompson's essay 'Paganism Old and New', *Works*, III.
131 Gautier, *Mademoiselle de Maupin*, p. 201.

132 Nerval, *Œuvres*, I, p. 408, *Aurélia*.
133 Ibid., I, p. 403, *Aurélia*.
134 De Quincey, XIII, p. 366, 'Levana and Our Ladies of Sorrow'. It seems symptomatic of the literary parallels that 'Levana Et Nos Notre-Dames Des Tristesses' counts among those pieces Baudelaire adds to his select translation of *The Confessions of an English Opium-Eater*; see Baudelaire, *Les Paradis Artificiels*.
135 De Quincey, XIII, pp. 368–9.
136 James Thomson, *Poems*, p. 65, lines 1–10.
137 Christina Rossetti, *Poetical Works*, p. 320: 'Yet it may be she will yearn / And look back from far before'.
138 James Thomson, *Essays and Phantasies*, p. 9: 'she and many, many others who, like her, could not continue infinite ascension until rejoined by the twinsouls left beneath them on earth, and who also like her were permitted to visit their twinsouls with heavenly consolations until death's consummate beatitude should remove all need and possibility of consolation.' Bourke Marston (*Collected Poems*, p. 133) in 'Divine Counsel' describes the opposite: 'Has not God turned her heart from loving mine?'
139 *The Works of Francis Thompson*, III, p. 44, 'Paganism Old and New'.
140 Ibid., p. 48.
141 Ibid., p. 49. See also Rossetti's painting *Ecce Ancilla Domini*. For an ironical continuation of this tradition see Beardsley's *Hail Mary*.
142 Pater, *Appreciations*, p. 78, 'Aesthetic Poetry'.
143 Gautier, *Emaux et Camées*, p. 211.
144 Ibid., p. 210.
145 O'Shaughnessy, *Epic of Women*, p. 184.
146 Rossetti, *Poems*, p. 4: 'From the fixed place of Heaven she saw / Time like a pulse shake fierce / Through all the worlds'.
147 O'Shaughnessy, *Epic of Women*, p. 178: 'I see you in the Time that's fled, / Long dead; / I see you in the years to be / After me'.
148 Dobson, *Poetical Works*, p. 131: 'That in this place the hours were dead, / And Time was bound'.
149 Rossetti, *Poems*, pp. 3–4.
150 O'Shaughnessy, *Epic of Women*, pp. 46–7, 'A Whisper from the Grave'.
151 Woolner, *My Beautiful Lady*, pp. 39–40.
152 Yeats, *Collected Poems*, p. 80, 'He Wishes His Beloved Were Dead'.
153 O'Shaughnessy, *Epic of Women*, p. 186, 'The Glorious Lady'.
154 Rossetti, *Poems*, p. 305, 'Antwerp and Bruges'.
155 Ibid., p. 5.
156 Woolner, *My Beautiful Lady*, p. 104.
157 Le Gallienne, *New Poems*, p. 40.
158 Nerval, *Œuvres*, I, p. 393, *Aurélia*. A poem like Baudelaire's 'Réversibilité' illustrates that not only religious imagery but even abstract theological concepts are used as metaphors; see Adam's commentary, *Les Fleurs du Mal*, p. 329.
159 Bourke Marston, *Collected Poems*, p. 21.
160 Ibid., p. 20.
161 Baudelaire, *Les Fleurs du Mal*, p. 36, 'De Profundis Clamavi'. The fact that

in 1851 the poem was entitled 'La Béatrix' is further proof of the close relationship between the madonna and her lover's feeling of rejection. See also Payne, *Poetical Works*, II, p. 347, 'De Profundis' and Symons, *Poems*, I, pp. 240–1, 'De Profundis Clamavi'. In addition to such obvious examples there are a great number of poems in which the same situation is described without any direct reference in the title, see e.g. Verlaine's 'A Une Femme'.

162 Apart from the title of Wilde's well-known essay 'De Profundis' compare also his sonnet 'E Tenebris', Wilde, p. 715.

163 Johnson, *Complete Poems*, p. 191, 'De Profundis'; see also Bourke Marston, *Collected Poems*, p. 19, 'Divine Pity'.

164 Even the title of Payne's poem 'Outstretched Hands' seems characteristic:
Is there no sweetness save for ripened fruit?
Lies all men's gladness in fulfilled desire?
. . . Oh! it cannot be.

165 'I, graceless, joyless, lacking absolutely / All gifts that with thy queenship best behove; – / Thou, throned in every heart's elect alcove', Rossetti, *Poems*, p. 221.

166 Bourke Marston, *Collected Poems*, p. 149, 'Fate'; see also the imagery of Dowson's 'Seraphita' sonnet.

167 Bell Scott, *A Poet's Harvest Home*, p. 122, 'Dante and Beatrice'. Bell Scott himself had previously paid tribute to the tradition in two sonnets on Dante.

168 Gautier, *Mademoiselle de Maupin*, p. 314. 'Pre-Raphaelite' tastes are a marked feature in Gautier; they are clearly perceptible in his 'Melancholia' fragment and in such a poem as 'Le Triomphe de Pétrarque'; the protagonist in *Mademoiselle de Maupin* goes so far as to express his disappointment 'de n'être pas né au seizième siècle, où toutes ces belles avaient vécu'.

169 E. R. Curtius, 'Neue Dantestudien', p. 343.

170 Francis Thompson made a most revealing remark on the question of the Beatrice myth: 'There *was* a Beatrice doubtless; but already she is so overlaid with allegory that not a fact about her can be deemed certain – save that she was *not* Beatrice Portanari', *The Works of Francis Thompson*, III, p. 242, 'Dante'.

171 Bodleian Ms. Don. e. 48, introduction.

172 Nerval, *Œuvres*, I, pp. 363–4, *Aurélia*.

173   In that fair pleasaunce, where on Beatrice
The eyes of Dante slaked their lifelong thirst,
My eyes did light upon my lady first.
(Payne, *Poetical Works*, II, p. 96)

174 Symons, *Poems*, II, p. 129.

175 *Les Fleurs du Mal*, p. 135, 'La Béatrice'.

176 Rossetti, 'Hand and Soul', *The Germ*, p. 26.

177 See also *The Works of Francis Thompson*, II, p. 228, 'The Singer Saith of his Song', where the muse appears as a madonna-like bride.

178 'O célestes créatures, belles vierges frêles et diaphanes qui penchez vos yeux de pervenche et joignez vos mains de lis sur les tableaux à fond d'or des vieux maîtres allemands' (p. 103); 'Elle était si diaphane, si svelte, si légère, d'une nature si délicate' (p. 350); 'son corps était si souple et si diaphane' (p. 322).

179 Pater, *Miscellaneous Studies*, p. 247, 'Diaphaneité'.

180 Ibid., p. 248.

181 Ibid., pp. 248 and 250.
182 Ibid., p. 250.
183 Dowson, *Poems*, p. 147.
184 Pater, *Miscellaneous Studies*, p. 253, 'Diaphaneité'.
185 Ibid., p. 253.
186 Le Gallienne, *English Poems*, p. 21, 'Love Platonic'; see also Beardsley's design for *Platonic Affections* and *The Platonic Lament* from the *Salome* cycle.
187 *In the Key of Blue and Other Prose Essays*, pp. 55–86.
188 'La création se moque impitoyablement de la créature et lui décoche à toute minute des sarcasmes sanglants. Tout est indifférent à tout, et chaque chose vit ou végète par sa propre loi' (p. 197).
189 Ibid., p. 53.
190 Ibid., pp. 63 and 57.
191 Ibid., p. 131.
192 Gautier, *Emaux et Camées*, p. 23.
193 Gautier, *Mademoiselle de Maupin*, p. 65.
194 O'Shaughnessy, *Songs of a Worker*, p. 108.
195 Rossetti, *Works*, II, pp. 280ff.
196 Yeats, *Collected Poems*, p. 81.
197 Rossetti, *Poems*, p. 109.
198 See e.g. Dowson, *Poems*, p. 89, 'Sapientia Lunae'.
199 O'Sullivan, 'Serenade' in *A Sextet of Singers*, p. 51. See also 'Come back: with pity in your eyes / . . . Though I become the scorn of all the wise', Douglas, *Collected Poems*, p. 37, 'Plainte Eternelle'.
200 Rossetti, *Poems*, p. 219, 'Heart's Compass'. For the same tendency see also his sonnet 'Heart's Hope'.
201 It is one of the 'three poems printed for private circulation only', added to a few of those copies of the *English Poems* which contain the poem 'Adoration' on p. 108. Quoted from BL Cup. 503, c. 10.
202 Gautier, *Souvenirs Romantiques*, pp. 306–7, Preface to Baudelaire's *Fleurs du Mal*.

6 Late romantic spirituality

1 Arthur Symons, 'The Decadent Movement in Literature'.
2 Ibid., p. 589.
3 Symons, *The Symbolist Movement*, p. 94. His essay on Huysmans constitutes a typical document of the period. *Studies in Two Literatures*, 1897, pp. 299–305, 'M. Huysmans as a Mystic'.
4 Symons, *The Symbolist Movement*, p. vi. After authors like Symons or Léon Blum (*La Revue Blanche* [January 1894], pp. 38–9) commented both favourably and unfavourably on the close relationship between symbolism and mysticism, critics have again and again discussed the problem, see e.g. Cornell, Carter, Bowra, *Heritage of Symbolism*, Rosenblatt, and L. Wolff, *Dante Gabriel Rossetti*.
5 Wilde, p. 887, 'De Profundis'.
6 Ibid., p. 978, 'The Critic as Artist'.
7 Symons, 'The Decadent Movement', p. 865.

8 Pater, *Marius*, I, p. 151.
9 Ibid., I, p. 158.
10 Ibid., I, p. 159.
11 Nerval, *Œuvres*, I, p. 390, *Aurélia*.
12 O'Shaughnessy, *Epic of Women*, p. 165.
13 'The occasion of the poem was a spiritual crisis in the poets' lives, arising out of their grief for the death of their much beloved dog Whym Chow.' The beautifully printed volume is bound in russet suede and, as regards its contents, belongs to the tradition of the *tombeau*.
14 Michael Field, *Whym Chow, Flame of Love*, 1914 (BL C. 99 e. 21), p. 15, 'Trinity'.
15 See also *Poems of Adoration*, 1912 and *Mystic Trees*, 1913.
16 Yeats, *Autobiographies*, p. 320.
17 *The Works of Francis Thompson*, I, p. 118.
18 Ibid., p. 117.
19 Rossetti, *Poems*, p. 120.
20 *Collected Poems* by AE, p. 12.
21 Thomas Gordon Hake, *Maiden Ecstasy*, 1880, p. 43, 'The Visionary'.
22 *The Complete Works of Gilbert and Sullivan*, pp. 188 and 193, *Patience*.
23 Bourke Marston, *Collected Poems*, p. 165.
24 Payne, *New Poems*, pp. 149, 150, 156.
25 Ibid.; see e.g. 'We dwelt within a wood of thought, / I and my days'.
26 Ibid., p. 148.
27 Ibid., p. 155.
28 Wilde, p. 972, 'The Critic as Artist'. Wilde's formulations leave no doubt that the late romantic mysticism constitutes an intensification and specialization of the well-known romantic phenomenon.
29 O'Shaughnessy, *Music and Moonlight*, p. 13.
30 Ibid., pp. 17 and 36.
31 Poe, *Works*, XIV, p. 197, 'The Philosophy of Composition'.
32 O'Shaughnessy, *Music and Moonlight*, p. 35.
33 O'Shaughnessy, *Epic of Women*, p. 27.
34 Rossetti, *Poems*, p. 224, 'Through Death to Love'. See also 'Memorial Threshold', ibid., p. 233; Yeats, *Collected Poems*, p. 73, 'The Valley of the Black Pig'.
35 Yeats, *Autobiographies*, p. 347. See also the formulation like Baudelaire's '. . . introduire artificiellement le surnaturel', *Œuvres*, p. 355, *Les Paradis Artificiels*.
36 Symons, *Poems*, II, p. 106, 'Haschisch'.
37 On the problem see the studies of Senior and Rudd and also of Ralph Tegtmeier, *Okkultismus und Erotik in der Literatur des Fin de Siècle*.
38 Yeats, *Autobiographies*, p. 347.
39 Wilde, p. 951, 'The Critic as Artist'. Nerval's *Aurélia* is an outstanding example of the late romantic interest in these elements and at the same time betrays the eclecticist tendencies of a period that hardly distinguishes between mysticism and occultism; see esp. *Œuvres*, I, pp. 366, 382, 406, 407.
40 See L. Wolff, p. 124; R. Wallerstein, 'Personal Experience in Rossetti's *House of Life*', 500; and Talon, *Rossetti: The House of Life*, p. 38. On the rather special case of Aleister Crowley, see Tegtmeier, p. 74.

41 How widespread the interest in 'mesmerism' and similar phenomena had
   become in the United States of that period, however, can be illustrated by
   a number of examples from the works of Hawthorne: '. . . One of those
   mesmerical seers, who nowadays, so strangely perplex the aspect of human
   affairs, and put everybody's natural vision to the blush, by the marvels they
   see with their eyes shut'; *The Centenary Edition of the Works of Nathaniel
   Hawthorne*, II, *The House of the Seven Gables*, p. 311. For another satirical
   portrait see Doctor Tarrant, the mesmeric healer in Henry James's *The
   Bostonians*. For the widespread fashion in England see Charlotte Yonge's
   novel *Heartsease, or The Brother's Wife*, p. 174: ' "I told mamma of my
   arrangement to go with Georgina Finch to a lecture on mesmerism" she
   said. "Mesmerism!" was the *sotto voce* exclamation of Lord Martindale.'
   Baudelaire's comment in *Les Paradis Artificiels* (*Œuvres*, p. 348) is of
   special interest: 'De même une certaine école spiritualiste, qui a ses représen-
   tants en Angleterre et en Amérique, considère les phénomènes surnaturels,
   tels que les apparitions des fantômes, les revenants etc. comme des
   manifestations de la volonté divine, attentive à réveiller dans l'esprit de
   l'homme le souvenir des réalités invisibles'.
42 Leon, pp. 505–6.
43 *The Works of Francis Thompson*, III, pp. 116–17.
44 Johnson, *Complete Poems*, p. 168, 'Magic', no. I.
45 *The Works of Francis Thompson*, III, p. 119.
46 Johnson, *Complete Poems*, p. 169, 'Magic', no. II.
47 Ibid., p. 170, 'Magic', no. III, 'the King of night is dead'.
48 See the detailed and thorough study by J. A. Cassidy, 'Robert Buchanan
   and the Fleshly Controversy' and the elaborations by the same authors in
   Algernon Charles Swinburne, pp. 128–9.
49 Talon, *Rossetti: The House of Life*, p. 19: 'Il croit atteindre l'âme dans
   l'extase charnelle'.
50 Baum (ed.), *The House of Life*, p. 27.
51 Watts Dunton, quoted from Baum, ibid., p. 27.
52 H. von Hofmannsthal, *Gesammelte Werke, Prosa*, I, p. 199, 'Über die
   moderne englische Malerei' (1894), my translation.
53 Swinburne, 'Simeon Solomon . . .', p. 310. See also his sonnet on
   Gautier's *Mademoiselle de Maupin*: 'This is the golden book of spirit and
   sense'.
54 Ibid., p. 311.
55 Ibid., pp. 313–14.
56 Pater, *Marius*, II, pp. 55–6.
57 Ibid., I, pp. 95–6.
58 Wilde, p. 991, 'The Critic as Artist'.
59 R. Ellmann, *The Identity of Yeats*, p. 75.
60 Rossetti, *Poems*, p. 114, 'Secret Parting'.
61 Ibid., p. 312, 'Heart's Hope'.
62 Ibid., p. 106, 'The Kiss': 'Can rob this body of honour, or denude / This
   soul of wedding-raiment'.
63 Ibid., p. 129, 'Love-Lily'.
64 Swinburne, *PB*, p. 9, 'A Ballad of Death'.
65 Symons, *Poems*, II, p. 135.

66 Ibid., I, p. 204; see also the following verses from Wratislaw, *Orchids*, p. 9, 'The Conquest of Sense':
> You wake to live beneath my kiss,
> And I possess your soul in this
> Sense-stricken body for an hour.

67 Le Gallienne, *English Poems*, p. 106.

68 See also Le Gallienne's remarks in *The Religion of a Literary Man*, 1893, p. 91.

69 Le Gallienne, *English Poems*, p. 100.

70 *The Works of Francis Thompson*, I, p. 102, 'After Her Going':
> For nothing of me or around
> But absent She did leaven,
> Felt in my body as its soul,
> And in my soul its heaven.
> 'Ah me! my very flesh turns soul,
> Essenced', I sighed, 'with bliss!'.

71 Yeats, *Autobiographies*, p. 326.

72 On the question in general see M. Rudwin, *The Devil in Legend and Literature* and M. Milner, *Le Diable dans la Littérature Française de Gazotte à Baudelaire 1772–1861* and H. Jackson, *The Eighteen Nineties*.

73 Johnson, *Complete Poems*, p. 155.

74 On this poem see I. Fletcher, 'Lionel Johnson: The Dark Angel'.

75 *Les Fleurs du Mal*, p. 5, 'Au Lecteur'.

76 Ibid., p. 146: 'O Satan, prends pitié de ma longue misère!'

77 Johnson, *Complete Poems*, p. 67, 'The Dark Angel'.

78 Yeats, *Autobiographies*, p. 310.

79 Pater, *Marius*, I, p. 247.

80 Douglas, *Collected Poems*, pp. 59–60.

81 *A Sextet of Singers*, pp. 43–4:
> She kneels aside
> In the darkened aisle,
> And angels smile
> On the Devil's bride.

82 O'Sullivan, *Poems*, p. 67.

83 O'Sullivan, 'The Houses of Sin', p. 9. See also O'Sullivan's 'The Children of Wrath': 'Last night I wandered in the Devil's close' (*A Sextet of Singers*, p. 33) and Housman's verses: 'Love wrought me at the forge of death, / Love shaped my reins for sin' marked by the same feeling of sinfulness so typical of the period (*An Anthology of 'Nineties' Verse*, p. 81).

84 Rossetti, *Poems*, p. 224, 'Through Death to Love'.

85 Ibid., p. 225, 'Cloud and Wind'.

86 *The Works of Francis Thompson*, I, pp. 107 and 113.

87 Dowson, *Poems*, p. 87.

88 See Praz, *Romantic Agony*, p. 306.

89 On the pessimism of Thomson see the studies of Peyre and R. A. Forsyth, 'Evolutionism and the Pessimism of James Thomson (BV)'.

90 James Thomson, *Poems*, p. 195, 'CDN', canto XIV, lines 39–42 and p. 194, canto XIV, lines 3–6.

91 See e.g. *Les Fleurs du Mal*, p. 195, 'L'Imprévu': 'Dans mon ciboire, / Vous

avez, que je crois, assez communié / A la joyeuse Messe noire?' See also Huysmans's novel *Là-bas* (1891) in which black religiosity takes on such an extreme form that it seems less suited to a comparison with English parallels than Baudelaire's contributions to the movement.

92 Swinburne, *PB*, p. 179.

93 Ibid., pp. 183 and 185. See also: 'Come down and redeem us from virtue, / Our Lady of Pain' (p. 189) or: 'Ah, forgive us our virtues' (p. 193).

94 Ibid., p. 195.

95 Wratislaw, *Caprices*, 'L'Eternel Féminin' (p. 32); in some copies replacing 'At Midnight'.

96 Wilde, p. 718, 'The New Helen'.

97 Swinburne, 'Simeon Solomon . . .', p. 311.

98 Gautier, *Mademoiselle de Maupin*, p. 177.

99 Nerval, *Œuvres*, I, p. 364, *Aurélia*.

100 Wratislaw, *Orchids*, p. 36, 'Modern Friends'.

101 The quality of Baudelaire's verses reveals itself in the striking combination of the image of the seven swords of Mary with that of the juggler ('jongleur') as well as in the tension between seeming playfulness and brutality (*Les Fleurs du Mal*, pp. 63–4).

102 Wratislaw, *Orchids*, p. 10: 'interlace / Their purity with their corrupted grace' and p. 11: 'And with your beauty know the depths of sin'.

103 Symons, *Poems*, I, pp. 203 and 247.

104 Ibid., III, p. 21; see also a poem such as 'To Our Lady of the Seven Sorrows', ibid., II, pp. 59–60.

105 Wilde, p. 868, 'De Profundis'.

106 Ibid., p. 963, 'The Critic as Artist'.

107 'Enfin, sur la cheminée dont la robe fut, elle aussi, découpée dans la somptueuse étoffe d'une dalmatique florentine, entre deux ostensoirs, . . . un merveilleux canon d'église, aux trois compartiments séparés, ouvragés comme une dentelle, contint, . . . trois pièces de Baudelaire: à droite et à gauche, les sonnets portant ces titres "la Mort des Amants" – "L'Ennemi"; – au milieu le poème en prose intitulé: "anywhere out of the world" ' (J.-K. Huysmans, *A Rebours*, p. 45).

108 Wilde, p. 859, 'De Profundis'.

109 Yeats, *Autobiographies*, pp. 333–4.

110 Yeats, *Collected Poems*, p. 79.

111 Verlaine, *Œuvres poétiques*, p. 257.

112 Baudelaire, *Œuvres*, p. 377, *Les Paradis Artificiels*.

113 Pater, *Marius*, II, p. 124.

114 Ibid., II, p. 125.

115 Ibid., II, pp. 28–9.

116 Wilde, p. 991, 'The Critic as Artist'.

117 Ibid., p. 977.

118 Ibid., p. 869, 'De Profundis'.

119 Pater, *Marius*, I, p. 221.

120 Ibid., II, p. 183: 'Given faultless men and women, given a perfect state of society . . . there would be still this evil in the world.'

121 See O'Sullivan, *The Houses of Sin*, p. 63.

122 Ibid., p. 44.

123 O'Sullivan, *Poems*, p. 8.
124 Dowson, *Poems*, p. 42, my italics.
125 Dobson, *Poetical Works*, p. 165.
126 A poem like Christina Rossetti's 'The Convent Threshold' (*Poetical Works*, p. 340) belongs to the broader context of this motif.
127 O'Sullivan, *Poems*, p. 8, 'The Peace of God'.
128 Dowson, *Poems*, p. 83.
129 Ibid., p. 42, 'Nuns of the Perpetual Adoration'.
130 Wratislaw, *Caprices*, pp. 16–17, 'Palm Sunday'.
131 Symons, *Poems*, I, p. 37.
132 Yeats, *Autobiographies*, p. 329.
133 Dowson, *Poems*, p. 54, 'Benedictio Domini'.
134 Johnson, *Complete Poems*, pp. 82–3, 'The Church of a Dream'.
135 *The Complete Plays of Gilbert and Sullivan*, p. 222.
136 Rossetti, *Poems*, p. 106, 'Lovesight'.
137 Bourke Marston, *Collected Poems*, p. 18, 'Brief Rest'.
138 Le Gallienne, *English Poems*, p. 67, 'An Epithalamium'.
139 Rossetti, *Poems*, p. 105, 'Love's Redemption'.
140 Ibid., p. 118, 'Willowwood', IV.
141 Wilde, p. 720, 'The Burden of Itys':
    Those violet-gleaming butterflies
    . . . Are monsignores, and where the rushes shake
    A lazy pike lies basking in the sun.
    His eyes half shut, – he is some mitred old
    Bishop *in partibus* . . .
142 Ibid., p. 775, 'Quia Multum Amavi'.
143 *The Works of Francis Thompson*, II, p. 21, 'Orient Ode'.
144 See Baudelaire, *Les Fleurs du Mal*, p. 43, 'Un Fantôme', no. II, 'Le Parfum':
    Lecteur, as-tu quelquefois respiré
    Avec ivresse et lente gourmandise
    Ce grain d'encens qui remplit une église . . .
145 Yeats, *Collected Poems*, p. 70.
146 Ibid., pp. 78–9.
147 Bourke Marston, *Collected Poems*, p. 131: 'I preach the Gospel of her life'.
148 Ibid., p. 110.
149 Ibid., p. 149.
150 Ibid., p. 152.
151 *Les Fleurs du Mal*, p. 52; Douglas, *Collected Poems*, p. 71, 'Harmonie du Soir' (From the French of Baudelaire).
152 *Les Fleurs du Mal*, p. 32: 'Avec ses vêtements . . .'; see also p. 33, 'Le Serpent Qui Danse': 'On dirait un serpent qui danse / Au bout d'un bâton'.
153 O'Shaughnessy, *An Epic of Women*, pp. 120, 122, 122.
154 Symons, *Poems*, III, p. 27; see also the ballad-like representation of the snake motif in 'The Snake-Soul', ibid., p. 26.
155 See e.g. the use of the snake motif in Swinburne's 'Fragoletta' (*PB*, p. 96: 'Thou hast a serpent in thine hair, / In all the curls that close and cling') and Wratislaw's 'L'Eternel Féminin' (*Caprices*, p. 32: 'So still I reign, for still I weave a snare / With the hot snakes of my lascivious hair').

156 *An Anthology of 'Nineties' Verse*, pp. 69–70, 'A Dying Viper' by Michael Field.
157 Symons, *Poems*, II, p. 231, 'The Andante of Snakes'.
158 Thomas Gordon Hake, *New Symbols*, 1876, p. 83, 'The Snake-Charmer'.
159 According to Marillier (p. 187) even on his deathbed Rossetti had offered to design a sphinx for the frontispiece of the edition of poems and stories he planned to publish together with Theodore Watts. For the connection of the sphinx with the genre of the painting of ideas, see also the use of the sphinx in Carlyle's *Past and Present* (chapter II).
160 *Les Fleurs du Mal*, p. 79; Wratislaw quotes the last three lines where he finds his inspiration:
    Forgotten, old, abandoned to the scorn
    Of desert winds, I would not give one sign
    Of all the torments that my soul has borne,
    And now being tired of all . . .
                    (*Some Verses*, 1892, pp. 17–18, 'The Mad Sphinx')
161 James Thomson, *Poems*, pp. 202, 9.
162 James Thomson, *Essays and Phantasies*, p. 17.
163 Bourke Marston, *Collected Poems*, p. 332.
164 Rossetti, *Poems*, p. 234.
165 Bell Scott, *A Poet's Harvest Home*, p. 65.
166 Ibid., p. 66; see also Wilde, p. 813, 'The Sphinx'.
167 Bell Scott, *Poems* (1875), p. 160.
168 Ibid.: 'priests, with noiseless feet, / Passing around them with a serpent-coil; / And Kings in crowned hoods, / . . . red men and brown-skinned, and swart'.
169 Ibid., p. 161: 'cruellest rites and oaths / Of secrecy'. See also Evelyn Douglas's 'The Memphian Temple' in *An Anthology of 'Nineties' Verse*, p. 47: 'From the shrines come songs of wild priests haunting / All the night / . . . The vast hawk-sphinxes slumber . . .'.
170 Bell Scott, *Poems*, p. 161. The Cleopatra passages calls to mind the special orientalism of a generation which witnessed both the building of the Suez canal and the first performance of Verdi's *Aida*.
171 Ibid., p. 165.
172 'Joy fled thee, and desire / . . . Thou sittest voiceless, without priest or prayer, / As if thou wert self-born', ibid., p. 162.
173 'Crossing the dusky stream / On the chance stepping-stones of time, . . . And when we turn again . . . The interests of the present seem no more / Than fool's play', ibid., p. 164.
174 Wilde, p. 918, 'The Sphinx'.
175 See also the sphinxes in Hofstätter (*Symbolismus*, plates 66–9).
176 J. A. Symonds, *Many Moods*, p. 37.
177 Gautier, *Mademoiselle de Maupin*, pp. 96, 184, 317.
178 Gautier, *Emaux et Camées*, p. 30.
179 Ibid., p. 31: 'Chimère ardente, effort suprême / De l'art et de la volupté, / Monstre charmant, comme je t'aime / Avec ta multiple beauté!' With authors like Symonds and Swinburne the motif of the hermaphrodite also has biographical overtones.
180 Swinburne, 'Simeon Solomon . . .', p. 310. See also Baudelaire's interest in

the Lesbos motif and Swinburne's Sappho poems.

181 Ibid., p. 305.
182 Swinburne, *PB*, p. 91, 'Hermaphroditus'.
183 Ibid., p. 94, 'Fragoletta'.
184 *Les Fleurs du Mal*, p. 72, 'Les Chats'.
185 O'Shaughnessy, *Music and Moonlight*, p. 36.
186 O'Shaughnessy, *Epic of Women*, p. 125, 'The Daughter of Herodias': 'My love shall open thee a paradise'.
187 Ibid., p. 124: 'all their heavens are a cheat', and p. 121.
188 Ibid., p. 119.
189 Ibid., pp. 120 and 119; see Kermode, p. 57, who interprets the late romantic dancer as the 'emblem of the work of art'.
190 Symons, *Poems*, II, p. 229, 'The Armenian Dancer'.
191 *An Anthology of 'Nineties' Verse*, pp. 57ff, 'A Dance of Death'.
192 Ibid., p. 57: 'How strange this ice, so motionless and still, / Yet calling as with music to our feet', and ibid., p. 58: 'sounds that fill / The floor of ice, as the crystalline sphere / Around the heavens is filled with such a song'.
193 Symons, *Poems*, II, p. 36.
194 Ibid., p. 36.
195 Ibid., p. 40.
196 See e.g. the cycle 'Décor du Théâtre' in Symons's *Poems*, I, pp. 187–8.
197 Wratislaw, *Orchids*, pp. 12–13.
198 O'Sullivan, 'Houses of Sin', pp. 27–8.
199 Ibid., p. 28. For the widespread late romantic Wagnerism in England, see the numerous allusions of the young Yeats and the illustrations of Beardsley, as well as several poems by Wratislaw and other poets of the period.
200 Hake, *Maiden Ecstasy*, p. 39.
201 Le Gallienne, *The Lonely Dancer*, p. 17.
202 Ibid., p. 19.
203 Ibid., p. 20.
204 Yeats, *Collected Poems*, p. 245, 'Among School Children'.
205 Wilde, p. 991, 'The Critic as Artist'.
206 Symons, *Poems*, II, p. 40.
207 *An Anthology of 'Nineties' Verse*, p. 55, 'Your Rose is Dead' by Michael Field.
208 On the rose symbol in the works of Yeats see Bowra, *Heritage of Symbolism*, esp. p. 192; N. Jeffares, *W. B. Yeats, Man and Poet*; W. W. Tindall, 'The Symbolism of Yeats', and Ellmann.
209 *PB*, p. 179.
210 Symons, *Poems*, III, p. 205.
211 Johnson, *Complete Poems*, p. 219, 'Flos Florum'.
212 Yeats, *Collected Poems*, p. 79, 'The Travail of Passion'. See also the combination of the rose and lily in 'The White Birds' (p. 47: 'Soon far from the rose and the lily and fret of the flames would we be'), although very different in content, related to 'The Travail of Passion' in its symbolist form and function.
213 Le Gallienne, *The Lonely Dancer*, pp. 25–6, 'Flos Aevorum'.
214 *Selected Poems by John Davidson*, p. 94, 'The Last Rose'. Compare 'Rose of all Roses, Rose of all the World' ('The Rose of Battle') and 'Far-off, most

secret, and inviolable Rose, / Enfold me in my hour of hours' ('The Secret Rose'). The first of these poems was published in Yeats's *The Rose* (1893), the second in *The Wind Among the Reeds* (1899), Yeats, *Collected Poems*, pp. 42 and 77 respectively.

215 Dowson, *Poems*, p. 57.
216 Symons, *Poems*, I, p. 201.
217 Ibid., pp. 185 and 264.
218 Ibid., p. 132.
219 Ibid., p. 214.
220 Swinburne, *PB*, p. 94.
221 The wide range of variations on this motif comes to light in the poetry of Symons. The demanding symbolist title 'Rosa Alba' derives from his special liking for pale women; in the impressionist rendering of 'Oliver Metra's Waltz of Roses' in 'La Mélinite: Moulin Rouge' he achieves effects that come very close to symbolist suggestiveness:

> The perfect rose of lights and sounds,
> The rose returning
> Into the circle of its rounds.
>   . . .
> And, enigmatically smiling,
> In the mysterious night,
> She dances for her own delight.   (I, pp. 190–1)

222 Yeats, *EI*, p. 192.
223 Ibid., p. 189.
224 Ibid., p. 193.

Postscript: a survey of critical works since 1971

1 W. E. Fredeman, *Pre-Raphaelitism, A Bibliocritical Study*. See also G. Metken (ed.), *Präraffaeliten*; exhibition catalogue *Baden-Baden* and *Die Präraffaeliten*; L. C. Dowling, *Aestheticism and Decadence. A Selective Annotated Bibliography*.
2 R. Z. Temple, 'Truth in Labelling: Pre-Raphaelitism, Aestheticism, Decadence, Fin De Siècle'.
3 P. Stansky (*William Morris*, p. 6) cites as an example the fact that both the Tory Prime Minister Stanley Baldwin and the Labour Prime Minister Clement Attlee claimed William Morris as their ideological ancestor.
4 W. V. Harris, 'An Anatomy of Aestheticism', p. 334.
5 *Pre-Raphaelite Writing. An Anthology*, ed. with an introduction by Derek Stanford, p. xvii.
6 See my ' "Point of View" and its Background in Intellectual History'.
7 For a recent assessment of 'Decadence as a Critical Term in England' see R. K. R. Thornton, *The Decadent Dilemma*.
8 U. Horstmann, *Ästhetizismus und Dekadenz*, p. 22.
9 J. Lucas, 'From Naturalism to Symbolism', in *Decadence and the 1890s*, ed. Ian Fletcher.
10 D. Perkins, *A History of Modern Poetry: From the 1890s to the High Modernist Mode*.

11 H. H. Hofstätter, *Symbolismus und die Kunst der Jahrhundertwende.*
12 P. Jullian, *The Symbolists.*
13 A. Mackintosh, *Symbolism and Art Nouveau.*
14 R. Bauer *et al.* (eds.), *Fin de Siècle. Zur Literatur und Kunst der Jahrhundertwende.*
15 H. Hinterhäuser, *Fin de Siècle. Gestalten und Mythen.*
16 David G. Riede, *Swinburne. A Study of Romantic Myth-making*; Francis J. Sypher, 'Swinburne and Wagner'. Since the seventies critics have tended to approach the Pre-Raphaelites and the English aesthetic movement with an increasing awareness of their place in an international context. Robin Spencer (*The Aesthetic Movement: Theory and Practice*, pp. 18, 20, 27, 132, 140) notes several instances; Douglas C. Fricke, 'Swinburne and the Plastic Arts' addresses Swinburne's indebtedness to both 'French Aestheticism and the Pre-Raphaelites', p. 65; Derek Stanford refers to the respective features in Rossetti and Swinburne in the following terms: 'Add Gautier, and you have aestheticism; add Baudelaire, Verlaine and Mallarmé, and the formula for the decadent and symbolic poetry of the nineties is complete', p. xxvi.
17 E. Koppen, *Dekadenter Wagnerismus – Studien zur europäischen Literatur des Fin de Siècle*, p. 113; J. Sänger, *Aspekte dekadenter Sensibilität*, p. 25.
18 J. Goode, 'The Decadent Writer as Producer', *Decadence and the 1890s*, ed. Ian Fletcher, p. 125.
19 M. Lindner, 'Ästhetizismus, Dekadenz, Symbolismus', *Die 'Nineties'. Das englische Fin de siècle zwischen Dekadenz und Sozialkritik*, ed. Manfred Pfister and Bernd Schulte-Middelich, pp. 53–81.
20 G. Monsman, *Walter Pater*, p. 153.
21 L. McKay Johnson, *The Metaphor of Painting*, p. 6.
22 H. L. Sussman, *Fact into Figure*, p. xv.
23 G. P. Landow, *Victorian Types. Victorian Shadows*, p. 109.
24 G. Hönnighausen, 'Emblematic Tendencies in the Works of Christina Rossetti'.
25 Ursula Brumm, *American Thought and Religious Typology.*
26 Cf. the recent studies by W. Lottes, *Wie ein goldener Traum. Die Rezeption des Mittelalters in der Kunst der Präraffaeliten* and L. C. Dowling, 'The Aesthetes and the Eighteenth Century'.
27 Preparing the ground for this, cf. *Literary Uses of Typology from the Late Middle Ages to the Present*, ed. E. Miner.
28 Quoted in George P. Landow, 'The Rainbow: A Problematic Image', *Nature and the Victorian Imagination*, ed. U. C. Knoepflmacher and G. B. Tennyson, pp. 341–69, 345. Landow very interestingly traces the change of the emblematic meaning from Byron and Shelley to Ruskin and beyond.
29 C. T. Christ, *The Finer Optic. The Aesthetic of Particularity in Victorian Poetry.*
30 D. G. Riede, *Dante Gabriel Rossetti and the Limits of Victorian Vision*, p. 66.
31 For a discussion of the relevant features in Swinburne see Robert Peters, 'Swinburne: A Personal Essay and a Polemic', *The Victorian Experience*, ed. R. A. Levine. For Rossetti's problematical relationship to reality, see John P. McGowan, 'The Bitterness of Things Occult: D. G. Rossetti's Search for the Real', *Victorian Poetry. An Issue Devoted to the Works of*

Dante Gabriel Rossetti, ed. William E. Fredeman.

32 G. B. Tennyson, 'The Sacramental Imagination', *Nature and the Victorian Imagination*, ed. Knoepflmacher and Tennyson, pp. 370–90. D. M. R. Bentley, 'The Pre-Raphaelites and the Oxford Movement'.

33 See note 26 and my *Grundprobleme der englischen Literaturtheorie des neunzehnten Jahrhunderts*, pp. 123–8, 'Die Wirklichkeit als Symbol'.

34 K. J. Höltgen, *Aspects of the Emblem*, p. 143.

35 R. L. Stein, *The Ritual of Interpretation. The Fine Arts as Literature in Ruskin, Rossetti, and Pater*, p. 26.

36 See also D. G. Riede, 'The Feud of the Sister Arts', pp. 215–21, and J. R. Prince, 'The Iconic Poem and the Aesthetic Tradition'.

37 See for instance J. D. Hunt, 'A Moment's Monument: Reflections on Pre-Raphaelite Vision in Poetry and Painting', *Pre-Raphaelitism*, ed. J. Sambrook; J. R. Prince, 'D. G. Rossetti and the Pre-Raphaelite Conception of the Special Moment', and J. G. Nelson, 'The Nature of Aesthetic Experience in the Poetry of the Nineties: Ernest Dowson, Lionel Johnson, and John Gray'.

38 Linda Gallasch's dissertation, 'The Use of Compounds and Archaic Diction in the Works of William Morris', contains extensive lists of compounds and archaic diction, but most of the material deriving from Morris's special interest in Old Norse literature is of greater relevance to the linguist than to the student concerned with Rossetti's and Swinburne's means of verbally fusing spirit and senses. Chapter 4, 'Criticism of Morris' Diction by his Contemporaries' contains interesting information for a study of late romantic diction.

39 E. G. Gitter, 'The Power of Women's Hair in the Victorian Imagination'; Pauline Fletcher, *Gardens and Grim Ravines. The Language of Landscape in Victorian Poetry*.

40 'Dreamers of Dreams: Toward a Definition of Literary Pre-Raphaelitism', *The Golden Chain. Essays on William Morris and Pre-Raphaelitism*, ed. Carole G. Silver, pp. 5–51, esp. p. 5.

41 In C. G. Silver (ed.), *The Golden Chain*, pp. 75–95.

42 D. Sadoff, 'The Poetics of Repetition and *The Defence of Guenevere*', *The Golden Chain*, ed. C. G. Silver, pp. 97–113.

43 H. E. Roberts, 'The Dream World of Dante Gabriel Rossetti'; B. Charlesworth Gelpi, 'The Feminization of D. G. Rossetti', *The Victorian Experience: The Poets*, ed. R. A. Levine.

44 F. S. Boos, *The Poetry of D. G. Rossetti. A Critical Reading and Source Study*, pp. 88–91.

45 M. Miyoshi, *The Divided Self: A Perspective on the Literature of the Victorians*.

46 J. Maas, p. 124.

47 Holman Hunt, I, p. 114.

48 D. G. Riede, *Dante Gabriel Rossetti and the Limits of Victorian Vision*, p. 25.

49 A. Staley, *The Pre-Raphaelite Landscape*, pp. 68–9.

50 M. Meisel, ' "Half Sick of Shadow": The Aesthetic Dialogue in Pre-Raphaelite Painting', *Nature and the Victorian Imagination*, ed. Knoepflmacher and Tennyson, pp. 309–40.

51 Quoted in R. R. Howard, *The Dark Glass. Vision and Technique in the Poetry of D. G. Rossetti*, p. 42.
52 D. G. Riede, *Dante Gabriel Rossetti and the Limits of Victorian Vision*, p. 58.
53 Howard, p. 43.
54 J. P. McGowan, ' "The Bitterness of Things Occult": D. G. Rossetti's Search for the Real'.
55 K. Beckson, 'A Mythology of Aestheticism'.
56 C. Snodgrass, 'Swinburne's Circle of Desire: A Decadent Theme', *Decadence and the 1890s*, ed. Ian Fletcher, pp. 61–88; L. Dowling, 'Nero and the Aesthetics of Torture'.
57 R. Taylor, 'Die mystisch-okkulte Renaissance. Rituelle Magie und symbolistische Dichtung', *Die Nineties*, ed. M. Pfister, B. Schulte-Middelich, pp. 100–14; R. Tegtmeier, *Okkultismus und Erotik in der Literatur des Fin de Siècle*.
58 C. S. Nassaar, *Into the Demon Universe. A Literary Exploration of Oscar Wilde*; H. Fritz, 'Die Dämonisierung des Erotischen in der Literatur des Fin de Siècle', *Fin de Siècle*, ed. Bauer *et al.*, pp. 442–64. On Wilde's Salome: N. Kohl, *Oscar Wilde. Das literarische Werk zwischen Provokation und Anpassung*, pp. 306–15.
59 W. Fritzsche, 'Problems and Success in the Mutual Development of D. G. Rossetti's Paintings and Sonnets', 104–7.
60 D. C. Fricke, 'Swinburne and the Plastic Arts in *Poems and Ballads I (1866)*'.
61 Quoted in P. Stansky, *William Morris*, pp. 24–5.
62 Stansky, p. 21.
63 E. Pound, *Selected Poems*, p. 116.

Bibliography

Primary works

Anthologies and miscellanies

Aesthetes and Decadents of the 1890s, Karl Beckson (ed.), N.Y.: Random House, Vintage Books, 1966
American Poems, W. M. Rossetti (ed.), London: E. Moxon, Son and Co., 1872
An Anthology of 'Nineties' Verse, with an introduction, A. J. A. Symons (ed.), London: E. Mathews and Marrot, 1928
A Comprehensive Anthology of American Poetry, Conrad Aiken (ed.), N.Y.: Modern Library, 1944
The Book of the Rhymers' Club, London: E. Mathews, 1892
The Second Book of the Rhymers' Club, London: E. Mathews & J. Lane; N.Y.: Dodd, Mead & Co., 1894
The Faber Book of Modern Verse, new edn, Anne Ridler (ed.), London: Faber & Faber, 1951
Flower-Lore. The Teachings of Flowers, Historical, Legendary, Poetical and Symbolical, Belfast: McCaw, Stevenson and Orr, 1879
The Germ. Thoughts towards Nature in Poetry, Literature, and Art, intro. W. M. Rossetti, London: 1901 (repr. Ams Press, N.Y.: 1965)
Modern American Poetry. Modern British Poetry, L. Untermeyer (ed.), combined mid-century edn, N.Y.: Harcourt, Brace and Co., 1950
The Oxford Book of Modern Verse 1892–1935, W. B. Yeats (ed.), Oxford: Clarendon Press, 1936
The Painter-Poets, Kineton Parkes (ed.), London, N.Y.: W. Scott [1890]
Picture Poesies, Poems chiefly by Living Authors, London: G. Routledge and Sons, 1874
Poets of the 'Nineties'. A Biographical Anthology, D. Stanford (ed.), London: John Baker, 1965
The Pre-Raphaelite Poem, J. D. Merritt (ed.), N.Y.: Dutton, 1966
Pre-Raphaelite Writing. An Anthology, D. Stanford (ed.), London: Dent, 1973
The Pre-Raphaelites in Literature and Art, intro. D. S. R. Welland (ed.), London: Harrap, 1953
Sacred Emblems with Miscellaneous Pieces, Moral, Religious, and Devotional in Verse, London: printed W. H. Birchall, sold by R. Baynes, and E. Palmer, 1828
A Sextet of Singers, or Songs of Six, George Barlowe, J. A. Blaikie, 'Paganus' (L. Cranmer-Byng), Vincent O'Sullivan, Walter Herries Pollock, Sidney R. Thompson, London: Roxburghe Press [1896?]

319

Complete editions and editions of individual works

Allingham, William, *Poems*, London: Chapman & Hall, 1850
   Flower Pieces and Other Poems, London: Reeves & Turner, 1888
   Choice Lyrics and Short Poems; Or Nightingale Valley, London: Bell & Daldy, n.d.
Arnold, Matthew, *The Poetical Works of Matthew Arnold*, C. B. Tinker and H. F. Lowry (eds.), London: Oxford University Press, 1961
Baudelaire. Charles, *Œuvres Complètes*, Y.– G. Le Dantec (ed.), edn revised by C. Pichois, Paris: Gallimard, 1961
   Les Fleurs du Mal, A. Adam (ed.), Paris: Garnier, 1959
   Petits Poèmes en Prose, H. Lemaitre (ed.), Paris: Garnier, 1962
Beardsley, Aubrey, *Illustrations to Edgar Allan Poe*, Indianapolis, 1926
   The Early Work of Aubrey Beardsley and *The Later Work of Aubrey Beardsley*, N.Y.: Dover, 1967
Blake, William, *The Poetical Works of William Blake*, J. Sampson (ed.), London: Oxford University Press, 1913
   The Prophetic Writings of William Blake, D. J. Sloss and J. P. R. Wallis (eds.), 2 vols., Oxford: Clarendon Press, 1926
Burne-Jones, Edward, *Memorials of Edward Burne-Jones*, Georgina Burne-Jones (ed.), 2 vols., London: Macmillan & Co., 1904
   The Flower-Book, London: H. Piazza et Cie., 1905
Butler, Samuel, *Ernest Pontifex, or The Way of All Flesh*, Daniel F. Howard (ed.), London: Methuen, 1965
Carlyle, Thomas, *The Works of Thomas Carlyle*, H. D. Traill (ed.), centenary edn, 30 vols., London: Chapman & Hall, 1896–9
Carroll, Lewis, *The Complete Works of Lewis Carroll*, illustrated by John Tenniel, intro. A. Woollcott, London: Modern Library, 1939
Chapman, Revd. Hugh B., *Sermons in Symbols*, London: Swan, Sonnenschein, Lowrey & Co., 1888
Coleridge, Samuel Taylor, *Biographia Literaria*, J. Shawcross (ed.), London: Oxford University Press, 1907
   The Poems of Samuel Taylor Coleridge, Ernest H. Coleridge (ed.), London: Oxford University Press, 1912
   Coleridge's Miscellaneous Criticism, T. M. Raysor (ed.), Cambridge, Mass.: Harvard University Press, 1936
Crane, Walter, *A Floral Fantasy in an Old English Garden*, N.Y.: Harper & Brothers, 1898
Custance, Olive, *Opals*, London: John Lane, 1897
   Rainbows, London: John Lane, 1902
   The Blue Bird, London: Marlborough Press, 1905
   The Inn of Dreams, London: John Lane, 1911
Davidson, John, *Selected Poems by John Davidson*, London: John Lane, 1904
   A Selection of his Poems, preface by T. S. Eliot, intro. M. Lindsay (ed.), essay by Hugh McDiarmid, London: Hutchinson, 1961
De Quincey, Thomas, *The Collected Writings of Thomas De Quincey*, D. Masson (ed.), 14 vols., Edinburgh: Black, 1889–90
Dobell, Sydney, *The Poetical Works of Sydney Dobell*, 2 vols., London: Smith, Elder & Co., 1875

Dobson, Austin, *The Complete Poetical Works of Austin Dobson*, London: Oxford University Press, 1923

Douglas, Lord Alfred, *The Collected Poems of Lord Alfred Douglas*, London: M. Secker, 1919

Douglas, Evelyn, *Selections from Songs of a Bayadere and Songs of a Troubadour*, Dundee: J. P. Mathew, 1893

Dowson, Ernest, *The Poems of Ernest Dowson*, Mark Longaker (ed.), Philadelphia, Pa.: University of Pennsylvania Press, 1962

Eliot, T. S., *Selected Essays*, London: Faber & Faber, 1932

  Collected Poems 1909–1935, London: Faber & Faber, 1936

  Four Quartets, London: Faber & Faber, 1959

  'From Poe to Valéry' (1948) in Eliot, *To Criticize the Critic*, London: Faber & Faber, 1965

Field, Michael (Katherine Bradley and Edith Cooper), *Sight & Song*, London: E. Mathews, 1892

  Underneath the Bough, London: G. Bell and Sons, 1893

  Wild Honey from Various Thyme, London: F. Fisher Unwin, 1908

  Poems of Adoration, London: Sands, 1912

  Mystic Trees, London: E. Nash, 1913

  Whym Chow, Flame of Love, London: Eragny Press, 1914

Fitzgerald, Edward, *The Letters and Literary Remains of Edward Fitzgerald*, 7 vols., N.Y.: Ams Press, 1966 (repr. from edn of 1902–3)

Gautier, Théophile, *Souvenirs Romantiques*, A. Boschot (ed.), Paris: Garnier, 1929

  Emaux et Camées, A. Boschot (ed.), Paris: Garnier, 1954

  Mademoiselle de Maupin, A. Boschot (ed.), Paris: Garnier, 1955

George, Stefan, *Werke*, Munich: Küpper, 1958

Gilbert, W. S., *The Complete Plays of Gilbert and Sullivan*, N.Y.: Modern Library, 1936

Gilchrist, A., *Life of William Blake 1757–1827*, London: J. M. Dent & Sons, 2nd revised edn, 1880

Glover, Revd. Richard, *The 'Light of the World' or Holman Hunt's Great Allegorical Picture Translated into Words*, London, 1862

Gray, John, *Silverpoints*, London: E. Mathews & John Lane, 1893

Hake, Thomas Gordon, *New Symbols*, London: Chatto & Windus, 1876

  Maiden Ecstasy, London: Chatto & Windus, 1880

Hawthorne, Nathaniel, *The Centenary Edition of the Works of Nathaniel Hawthorne*, W. Charvat and R. H. Pearce (eds.), Columbus, Ohio: Ohio State University Press, 1962–

Hofmannsthal, Hugo von, *Gesammelte Werke*, Frankfurt: Fischer, 1956

Housman, Laurence, *The Green Arras*, London: John Lane, 1896

Hueffer, Ford Madox, *Poems for Pictures and Notes for Music*, London: J. MacQueen, 1900

Hunt, William Holman, *Pre-Raphaelitism and the Pre-Raphaelite Brotherhood*, 2 vols., London: Macmillan, 1905

Huysmans, Joris-Karl, *Là-bas*, Paris: Tresse & Stock, 1891

  A Rebours, Paris: Charpentier, 1961

Johnson, Lionel, *The Complete Poems of Lionel Johnson*, I. Fletcher (ed.), London: Unicorn Press, 1953

Joyce, James, *A Portrait of the Artist as a Young Man*, London: Egoist, 1916

Keble, John, *The Christian Year. Thoughts in Verse for the Sundays and Holydays throughout the Year*, London: Scott, 1887
Keble's Lectures on Poetry 1832–41, trans. Edward Kershaw Francis, 2 vols., Oxford: Clarendon Press, 1912
Le Gallienne, Richard, *English Poems*, London: E. Mathews & John Lane, 1892
Nightingales, London: E. Mathews & John Lane, 1893
The Religion of a Literary Man, E. Mathews & John Lane, 1893
Retrospective Reviews, London: John Lane, 1896
New Poems, London: John Lane, 1910
The Lonely Dancer and Other Poems, London: John Lane, 1914
Lee-Hamilton, Eugene, *Apollo and Marsyas and Other Poems*, London: Stock, 1884
Imaginary Sonnets, London: Stock, 1888
Sonnets of the Wingless Hours, London: Stock, 1894
Marston, Philip Bourke, *A Last Harvest*, London: E. Mathews, 1891
The Collected Poems of Philip Bourke Marston, London: Roberts Brothers, 1892
Morris, William, *The Collected Works of William Morris*, intro. May Morris, 24 vols., London, N.Y.: Longmans, Green, 1910–15
Nerval, Gérard de, *Œuvres*, Albert Béguin and Jean Richer (eds.), 2 vols., Paris: Bibliothèque de la Pléiade, 1956
Novalis, *Novalis' Schriften*, 4 vols., P. Kluckhohn and R. Samuel (eds.), Stuttgart: Kohlhammer, 1960
O'Shaughnessy, Arthur William Edgar, *Epic of Women and Other Poems*, London: John Camden Hotton, 1870
Music and Moonlight, London: Chatto & Windus, 1874
Songs of a Worker, London: Chatto & Windus, 1881
O'Sullivan, Vincent, *Poems*, London: E. Mathews, 1896
The Houses of Sin, London: Smithers, 1897
(ed.), *Edgar Allan Poe, The Raven, The Pit and the Pendulum*, London: Leonard Smithers & Co., 1899
Pater, Walter, *The Works of Walter Pater*, 8 vols., London: Macmillan, 1900–1
Selected Works, R. Aldington (ed.), London: Heinemann, 1948
Paton, Joseph Noel, *Poems by a Painter*, London: Blackwood & Sons, 1861
Payne, John, *New Poems*, London: Newman & Co., 1880
The Poetical Works of John Payne, 2 vols., London: Villon Society, 1902
Plarr, Victor, *In the Dorian Mood*, London: John Lane, 1896
Poe, Edgar Allan, *The Works of Edgar Allan Poe*, James A. Harrison (ed.), textual notes R. A. Stewart, 17 vols., N.Y.: Ams Press, 1965 (reproduced from 1902 N.Y. edn)
Pound, Ezra, *Selected Poems*, T. S. Eliot (ed.), London: Faber & Faber, 1948
Gaudier-Brzeska, a Memoir, London: New Directions Books, 1960
Rimbaud, Arthur, *Œuvres Complètes*, Rolland de Renéville and Jules Mouquet (eds.), Paris: Gallimard, 1954
Rossetti, Christina Georgina, *The Poetical Works of Christina Georgina Rossetti*, W. M. Rossetti (ed.), London: Macmillan, 1904
The Family Letters of Christina Georgina Rossetti, with supplementary letters and appendices, W. M. Rossetti (ed.), London: Brown, Langham & Co., 1908
Complete Poems of Christina Rossetti. A variorum edition with notes and

intro., R. W. Crump (ed.), vol. 1, Baton Rouge, La.: Louisiana State University Press, 1979

Rossetti, Dante Gabriel, *His Family Letters*, intro. W. M. Rossetti, 2 vols., London: Ellis & Elvey, 1895

Letters of Dante Gabriel Rossetti, George Birbeck Hill (ed.), London: T. F. Unwin, 1897

Pictures and Poems by D. G. Rossetti, arranged Fitz Roy Carrington, N.Y.: R. H. Russell, 1899

The Collected Works of Dante Gabriel Rossetti, with preface and notes, W. M. Rossetti (ed.), 2 vols., London: Ellis, 1906

The House of Life. A Sonnet-Sequence by Dante Gabriel Rossetti, Paull Franklin Baum (ed.), Cambridge, Mass.: Harvard University Press, 1928

Rossetti's Poems, intro. and notes, Oswald Doughty (ed.), London: Dent, 1961

Letters of Dante Gabriel Rossetti, Oswald Doughty and John Wahl (eds.), vol. 1, Oxford: Clarendon Press, 1965–7

Rossetti, William Michael, *The PRB Journal: William Michael Rossetti's Diary of the PRB, together with other Pre-Raphaelite Documents*, W. E. Fredeman (ed.), Oxford: Clarendon Press, 1974

Ruskin, John, *The Works of John Ruskin*, E. T. Cook and A. Wedderburn (eds.), library edn, 39 vols., London: Allen, 1903–12

Russell, George William (AE), *Collected Poems*, London: Macmillan, 1913

The Candle of Vision, London: Macmillan, 1918

Scott, William Bell, *Poems by a Painter*, London: Smith, Elder, 1854

Poems by W. Bell Scott, illustrated by 17 etchings by the author and L. Alma Tadema, London: Longmans, Green, 1875

Albrecht Durer, His Life and Works, London: Longmans, Green, 1869

William Blake, Etchings from His Works, London: Chatto & Windus, 1878

A Poet's Harvest Home, London: Stock, 1882

Shrewsbury, H. W., *Brothers in Art*, London: Epworth Press, 1920

Smetham, James, *Letters of James Smetham*, Sarah Smetham and W. Davies (eds.), London: Macmillan, 1892

Solomon, Simeon, *A Vision of Love Revealed in Sleep*, London: privately printed, 1871

Spenser, Edmund, *Faerie Queene*, Thomas J. Wise (ed.), designs by Walter Crane, London: Allen, 1894

The Poetical Works of Edmund Spenser, J. C. Smith and E. de Selincourt (eds.), London: Oxford University Press, 1952

Swinburne, Algernon Charles, *Poems and Ballads*, London: Moxon, 1866

William Blake, A Critical Essay, London: J. C. Hotten, 1868

Essays and Studies, London: Chatto & Windus, 1875

The Poems of A. C. Swinburne, 6 vols., London: Chatto and Windus, 1904

'Simeon Solomon: Notes on His "Vision of Love" and Other Studies', *Bibelot*, 14 (1908), 291–316

Symonds, John Addington, *Many Moods*, London: Smith, Elder & Co., 1878

New and Old, London: Smith, Elder & Co., 1880

In the Key of Blue and Other Prose Essays, London: E. Mathews & John Lane, N.Y.: Macmillan, 1893

Symons, Arthur, 'The Decadent Movement in Literature', *Harper's New Magazine*, 87 (1893), 858–67

The Symbolist Movement in Literature, London: Heinemann, 1899
Studies in Two Literatures, London: L. Smithers, 1897
Dramatis Personae, Indianapolis: Bobbs-Merrill Co., 1923
The Collected Works of Arthur Symons, Poems, vols. I–III, London: Secker, 1924
William Blake, London: Secker, 1924
Tennyson, Lord Alfred, *The Works of Tennyson*, annotated A. Lord Tennyson, H. Lord Tennyson (ed.), London: Macmillan, 1907
Thackeray, William Makepeace, *The Works of Thackeray*, 20 vols., London: Macmillan, 1911
Thompson, Francis, *The Works of Francis Thompson*, 3 vols., London: Burns, Oates & Washbourne, 1925
Thomson, James, B.V., *Essays and Phantasies*, London: Reeves & Turner, 1881
Shelley, a Poem, with Other Writings Relating to Shelley, by the late James Thomson (B.V.): to which is added an essay on 'The Poems of William Blake' by the same author, Bertram Dobell (ed.), 1884 (privately printed) (BM 11825. i. 26)
'Hymns to Night', Bodleian Ms. Don. e 48
Poems and Some Letters of James Thomson, Anne Ridler (ed.), London: Centaur Press, 1963
Todhunter, John, *Selected Poems by John Todhunter*, D. L. Todhunter and A. P. Graves (eds.), London: E. Mathews & Marrot, 1929
Verlaine, Paul, *Œuvres poétiques*, Y.-G. Le Dantec (ed.), Paris: Gallimard, 1957
Whitney, Geoffrey, *A Choice of Emblems*, Leyden, 1586
Wilde, Oscar, *The Works of Oscar Wilde*, intro. G. F. Maine (ed.), London: Collins, 1963
'The English Renaissance of Art', *Essays and Lectures by Oscar Wilde*, Robert Ross (ed.), *Works*, vol. 11, London: Methuen, 1909
Woolner, Thomas, *My Beautiful Lady*, London: Macmillan, 1863
Wordsworth, William, *The Poetical Works of Wordsworth*, Thomas Hutchinson (ed.), new revised edn, E. de Selincourt (ed.), London: Oxford University Press, 1961
Wordsworth, William and S. T. Coleridge, *Lyrical Ballads*, R. L. Brett and A. R. Jones (eds.), London: Methuen, 1963
Wratislaw, Theodore, *Some Verses*, London: G. E. Over, 1892
Love's Memorial, London: G. E. Over, The Rugby Press, 1892
Caprices, London: Gay & Bird, 1893
Orchids, London: Smithers, 1896
(ed.), *Plato, The Republic*, trans. T. Taylor, London: Scott, 1894
Yeats, William Butler, *Autobiographies*, London: Macmillan, 1955
Essays and Introductions, London: Macmillan, 1961
The Collected Poems of William Butler Yeats, London: Macmillan, 1963
Yeats, William Butler and Ellis, Edwin John (eds.), *The Works of William Blake, Poetic, Symbolic and Critical*, 3 vols., London: B. Quaritch, 1983
Yonge, Charlotte M., *Heartsease or The Brother's Wife*, Leipzig: Tauchnitz, 1855

Secondary works

Abrams, M. H., *The Mirror and the Lamp*, Oxford and N.Y.: Oxford University Press, 1953

Actes du Cinquième Congrès International de la Littérature Comparée, 1951, Florence: Valmartina, 1955

Adams, H., *Blake and Yeats. The Contrary Vision*, Ithaca, N.Y.: Cornell University Press, 1955

Alexander, E., *Matthew Arnold, John Ruskin, and the Modern Temper*, Columbus: Ohio State University Press, 1974

Andrews, K., *The Nazarenes*, Oxford: Clarendon Press, 1964

Apostolos-Cappadona, D., 'Oxford and the Pre-Raphaelites from the Perspective of Nature and Symbol', *Pre-Raphaelite Review*, 2, 1 (1981), 78–101

Austin, L. J., *L'Univers Poétique de Baudelaire: Symbolisme et Symbolique*, Paris: Mercure de France, 1956

Babbitt, I., *The New Laokoön*, Boston and N.Y.: Houghton Mifflin Co., 1910

Bahr, H., *Zur Überwindung des Naturalismus, Theoretische Schriften 1887–1904*, G. Wunberg (ed.), Stuttgart: Kohlhammer, 1968

Baker, J. E. (ed.), *The Reinterpretation of Victorian Literature*, N.Y.: Russel & Russel, 1962

Battiscombe, G., *Christina Rossetti*, London: Longmans, 1965

Christina Rossetti: A Divided Life, London: Constable, 1981

Bauer, R. *et al.* (eds.), *Fin de Siècle: Zur Literatur und Kunst der Jahrhundertwende*, Frankfurt: Klostermann, 1977

Bayley, J., *The Romantic Survival. A Study in Poetic Evolution*, London: Constable, 1957

Beckson, K., 'A Mythology of Aestheticism', *English Literature in Transition*, 17 (1974), 233–49

Bell, Q., *Victorian Artists*, London: Routledge & Kegan Paul, 1967

Benson, A., *Dante Gabriel Rossetti*, London: Macmillan, 1906

Bentley, D. M. R., 'The Pre-Raphaelites and the Oxford Movement', *Dalhousie Review*, 57 (1977), 525–39

Bergonzi, B., *The Turn of a Century*, London: Macmillan, 1973

Black, G. A., 'James Thomson. His Translation of Heine', *Modern Language Review*, 31 (1936), 48–54

Bloom, E. A., 'The Allegorical Principle', *English Literary History*, 18 (1951), 163–90

Bøe, A., *From Gothic Revival to Functional Form. A Study in Victorian Theories of Design*, Oslo: Oslo University Press, 1957

Boos, F. S., *The Poetry of D. G. Rossetti. A Critical Reading and Source Study*, The Hague: Mouton, 1976

Bowra, C. M., *The Heritage of Symbolism*, London: Macmillan, 1942

The Romantic Imagination, London: Oxford University Press, 1950

Bradbury, M. and Palmer, D. (eds.), *Victorian Poetry*, London: Arnold, 1972

Brönner, O., *Das Leben Arthur O'Shaughnessys*, Heidelberg: Winter, 1933

Broers, B. C., 'The Pre-Raphaelites. The Germ', *Mysticism in the Neo-Romanticists*, Amsterdam and Paris, 1923

Bronson, B. H., 'Personification Reconsidered', *English Literary History*, 14 (1947), 163–77

Brown, C. S., *Music and Literature*, Athens, Ga.: University of Georgia Press, 1948

Brumm, U., *American Thought and Religious Typology*, New Brunswick, N.J.: Rutgers University Press, 1970

Buckler, W. E., *The Victorian Imagination. Essays in Aesthetic Exploration*, Brighton: Harvester Press, 1980

Buckley, J. H., *The Victorian Temper. A Study in Literary Culture*, London and Cambridge, Mass.: Harvard University Press, 1952

The Triumph of Time. A Study of the Victorian Concepts of Time, History, Progress and Decadence, Cambridge, Mass.: Harvard University Press, 1966

'Pre-Raphaelite Past and Present; The Poetry of the Rossettis', in M. Bradbury and D. Palmer (eds.), *Victorian Poetry*, London: Arnold, 1972, pp. 123–37

Burdett, O., *The Beardsley Period. An Essay in Perspective*, London: John Lane, 1925

Bush, Douglas, *Mythology and the Romantic Tradition in English Poetry*, N.Y.: Pageant Books, 1957

Byron, K. H., *The Pessimism of James Thomson, B.V. in Relation to his Time*, The Hague: Mouton, 1965

Carter, A. E., *The Idea of Decadence in French Literature 1830–1900*, Toronto: University of Toronto Press, 1958

Cassidy, J. A., 'Robert Buchanan and the Fleshly Controversy', *PMLA*, 67 (1952), 65–93

Algernon Charles Swinburne, N.Y.: Twayne, 1964

Cecil, Lord D., 'Fin de Siècle', in Cecil, *Ideas and Beliefs of the Victorians*, London: BBC, 1950

Charlesworth, B., *Dark Passages. The Decadent Consciousness in Victorian Literature*, Milwaukee, Wis.: University of Wisconsin Press, 1965

Charlesworth Gelpi, B., 'The Feminization of D. G. Rossetti', in R. A. Levine (ed.), *The Victorian Experience: The Poets*, Athens, Ohio: Ohio University Press, 1982

Chiari, J., *Symbolism from Poe to Mallarmé. The Growth of a Myth*, London: Rockcliff, 1956

Christ, C. T., *The Finer Optic. The Aesthetic of Peculiarity in Victorian Poetry*, New Haven, Conn. and London: Yale University Press, 1975

Christoffel, U., *Malerei und Poesie. Die symbolistische Kunst des 19. Jahrhunderts*, Wien: Gallus, 1948

Connolly, T. E., *Swinburne's Theory of Poetry*, N.Y.: N.Y. State University Press, 1964

Cornell, K., *The Symbolist Movement*, New Haven, Conn.: Yale University Press, 1951

Crump, R. W., *Christina Rossetti: A Reference Guide*, Boston: G. K. Hall, 1976

Cruse, A., *The Victorians and their Books*, London: G. Allen & Unwin, 1935

Curtius, E. R., 'Neue Dantestudien', *Gesammelte Aufsätze zur Romanischen Philologie*, Bern: Francke, 1960, pp. 305–39

Dale, H., *La Poésie Française en Angleterre: 1850–1900. Sa Fortune et Son Influence*, Paris: Didier, 1954

Dali, S., 'Le Surréalisme Spectral de l'Eternel Féminin Pré-raphaélite', *Minotaure*, 8 (1936), 46–9

Dawson, Carl, *Victorian Noon: English Literature in 1850*, Baltimore and London: Johns Hopkins University Press, 1979

Dingle, H., 'Swinburne's "Internal Centre"', *Queen's Quarterly*, 40 (1933), 212–28

Doughty, O., *A Victorian Romantic: Dante Gabriel Rossetti*, London: Oxford University Press, 1960

'Rossetti's Conception of the "Poetic" in Poetry and Painting', *Transactions of the Royal Society of Literature*, n.s., 26 (1963), 89–102

Dowling, L. C., 'The Aesthetes and the Eighteenth Century', *Victorian Studies*, 20 (1977), 357–77

Aestheticism and Decadence. A Selective Annotated Bibliography, N.Y. and London: Garland, 1977

'Nero and the Aesthetics of Torture', *The Victorian Newsletter*, 66 (1984), 1–6

'Roman Decadence and Victorian Historiography', *Victorian Studies*, 28 (1985), 579–606

Drinkwater, J., *William Morris, A Critical Study*, London: Secker, 1912

Duncan, J. E., *The Revival of Metaphysical Poetry*, Minneapolis, Minn.: University of Minnesota Press, 1959

Egan, R. F., 'The Genesis of the Theory of Art for Art's Sake in Germany and England', *Smith College Studies in Modern Languages*, 21 (1921), 5–61 and 25 (1924), 1–22

Eichbaum, G., 'Die impressionistischen Frühgedichte Oscar Wildes unter besonderer Berücksichtigung des Einflusses von James MacNeill Whistler', *Die neueren Sprachen*, 40 (1932), 398–407

Ellmann, R., *The Identity of Yeats*, London: Oxford University Press, 1954

Emanuel, H., *Diamonds and Precious Stones*, London: J. C. Hotten, 1865

Enzensberger, Ch., *Viktorianische Lyrik, Tennyson und Swinburne in der Geschichte der Entfremdung*, München: Hanser, 1969

Evans, I., *English Poetry in the Later Nineteenth Century*, London: Methuen, 1966

Evans, J., *John Ruskin*, London: Cape/Alden Press, 1954

Fairchild, H. N., *Religious Trends in English Poetry*, vol. IV, 1830–1880, *Romanticism in the Victorian Era*, N.Y.: Columbia University Press 1957; vol. V, 1880–1920, *Gods of a Changing Poetry*, N.Y.: Columbia University Press, 1962

Farmer, A. J., *Le Mouvement Esthétique et Décadent en Angleterre 1873–1900*, Paris: Champion, 1931

Faverty, F. E. (ed.), *The Victorian Poets. A Guide to Research*, Cambridge, Mass.: Harvard University Press, 1968

Fehr, B., 'Walter Pater und Hegel', *Englische Studien*, 50 (1916), 300–8

'Walter Paters Beschreibung der Mona Lisa und Théophile Gautiers romantischer Orientalismus', *Archiv für das Studium der neueren Sprachen und Literaturen*, 135 (1917), 80–102

Studien zu Oscar Wildes Gedichten, Berlin: Mayer & Müller, 1918

Feidelson, C., *Symbolism and American Literature*, Chicago: Chicago University Press, 1953

Fleming, G. H., *Rossetti and the Pre-Raphaelite Brotherhood*, London: Rupert Hart-Davis, 1967

Flemming, H. Th., 'Die stilistische Entwicklung der Malerei von Dante Gabriel Rossetti', unpublished dissertation, Berlin, 1954

Fletcher, A., *Allegory. The Theory of a Symbolic Mode*, Ithaca, N.Y.: Cornell University Press, 1964

Fletcher, I., 'Lionel Johnson: The Dark Angel', in John Wain (ed.), *Interpreta-

tions: *Essays on Twelve English Poems*, London: Routledge & Kegan Paul, 1955

'Some Types and Emblems in Victorian Poetry', *The Listener*, 25 May 1967, 679–81

(ed.), *Decadence and the 1890s*, London: Arnold, 1979

Fletcher, P., *Gardens and Grim Ravines. The Language of Landscape in Victorian Poetry*, Princeton, N.J.: Princeton University Press, 1983

Foakes, R. A., *The Romantic Assertion, A Study in the Language of Nineteenth Century Poetry*, London: Methuen, 1958

Ford, G. H., *Keats and the Victorians. A Study of his Influence and Rise to Fame, 1821–1895*, New Haven, Conn.: Yale University Press, 1962

Forsyth, R. A., 'Evolutionism and the Pessimism of James Thomson (B.V.)', *Essays in Criticism*, 12 (1962), 148–66

Fredeman, W. E., *Pre-Raphaelitism. A Bibliocritical Study*, Cambridge, Mass.: Harvard University Press, 1965

(ed.), *Victorian Poetry*, 13 (1975), no. 3/4, special issue William Morris

(ed.), *Victorian Poetry*, 20 (1982), no. 3/4, special issue D. G. Rossetti

Freeman, R., *English Emblem Books*, London: Chatto & Windus, 1967

Fricke, D. C., 'Swinburne and the Plastic Arts in *Poems and Ballads I (1866)*', *Pre-Raphaelite Review*, 1, 1 (1977), 57–79

Friedrich, H., *Die Struktur der modernen Lyrik. Von Baudelaire bis zur Gegenwart*, Hamburg: Rowohlt, 1956 (extended new edn, 1967)

Fritzsche, M. W., 'Problems and Successes in the Mutual Development of D. G. Rossetti's Paintings and Sonnets', *Journal of Pre-Raphaelite Studies*, 1, 2 (1981), 104–17

Frye, N., *Fearful Symmetry*, Princeton: Princeton University Press, 1947

'Yeats and the Language of Symbolism', *University of Toronto Quarterly*, 17 (1947/48), 1–17

'Lexis and Melos', in N. Frye (ed.), *Sound and Poetry*, N.Y.: Columbia University Press, 1957

Gallasch, L., *The Use of Compounds and Archaic Diction in the Works of William Morris*, Bern: Lang, 1979

Gaunt, W., *The Aesthetic Adventure*, London: Cape, 1945

The Pre-Raphaelite Dream, N.Y.: Schocken Books, 1966 (new edn of *The Pre-Raphaelite Tragedy*, London: 1942)

Gawsworthy, J., 'The Dowson Legend', *Transactions of the Royal Society of Literature of the United Kingdom*, n.s., 17 (1938), 93–123

Gitter, E. G., 'The Power of Women's Hair in the Victorian Imagination', *PMLA*, 99, 5 (1984), 936–54

Goode, J., 'The Decadent Writer as Producer', in I. Fletcher (ed.), *Decadence*, London: Arnold, 1979, pp. 108–29

Gordon, J. B., ' "Decadent Spaces": Notes for a Phenomenology of the *Fin de Siècle*', in I. Fletcher (ed.), *Decadence*, London: Arnold, 1979, pp. 31–58

Green, H., *Shakespeare and the Emblem Writers. An Exposition of their Similarities of Thought and Expression*, 1870, repr. N.Y.: Burt Franklin, 1969

Grigson, G., 'The Pre-Raphaelite Myth', in Grigson, *The Harp of Aeolus*, London: Routledge, 1947, pp. 86–97

Gurd, P., 'The Early Poetry of W. B. Yeats', unpublished dissertation, Zürich, 1916/17

Harper, G. M., 'Blake's Nebuchadnezzar in the City of Dreadful Night', *Studies in Philology*, 50 (1953), 68–80

Harris, W. V., 'Innocent Decadence: The Poetry of the Savoy', *PMLA*, 77 (1962), 629–36

'The Road to and from Eliot's "Place of Pater" ', *Texas Studies in Language and Literature*, 23 (1981), 183–96

'An Anatomy of Aestheticism', in J. R. Kincaid and A. Kuhn (eds.), *Victorian Literature and Society: Essays Presented to Richard D. Altick*, Columbus, Ohio: Ohio State University Press, 1984

Harrison, A. H., 'Swinburne's Craft of Pure Expression', *Victorian Newsletter*, 51 (1977), 10–20

'Swinburne's Losses: The Poetics of Passion', *English Literary History*, 49 (1982), 689–706

Hartley, K., *Oscar Wilde: l'Influence Française dans son Œuvre*, Paris: Librairie du Recueil Sirey, 1935

Hasenclever, G., *Das 18. Jahrhundert in A. Dobsons Dichtung*, Würzburg: Edeltrut, 1939

Hauser, A., *Sozialgeschichte der Kunst und Literatur*, 2 vols., Munich: Beck'sche Verlagsbuchhandlung, 1953

Hayter, A., *Opium and the Romantic Imagination*, Calif.: University of California Press, 1968

Heath-Stubbs, J., *The Darkling Plain. A Study of the Later Fortunes of Romanticism in English Poetry from George Darley to W. B. Yeats*, London: Eyre and Spottiswoode, 1950

Henderson, St E., 'A Study of Visualized Detail in the Poetry of Tennyson, Rossetti, and Morris', unpublished dissertation, University of Wisconsin, 1959

Henkel, A. and Schöne, A. (eds.), *Emblemata. Handbuch zur Sinnbildkunst des XVI. und XVII. Jahrhunderts*, Stuttgart: Metzler, 1967

Henn, T. R., *The Lonely Tower. Studies in the Poetry of W. B. Yeats*, London: Methuen, 1965

Hess, G., *Die Landschaft in Baudelaires 'Fleurs du Mal'*, Heidelberg: Winter, 1953

Hinterhäuser, H., 'Tote Städte in der Literatur des Fin de Siècle', *Archiv für das Studium der neueren Sprachen und Literaturen*, 206 (1970), 321–44

Fin de Siècle: Gestalten und Mythen, Munich: Fink, 1977

Hoffman, H., 'An Angel in the City of Dreadful Night', *Sewanee Review*, 32 (1924), 317–35

Hofstätter, H. H., *Geschichte der europäischen Jugendstilmalerei*, Cologne: Du Mont, 1963

Symbolismus und die Kunst der Jahrhundertwende, Cologne: Du Mont, 1965

Holberg, M. St, 'Image and Symbol in the Poetry and Prose of Dante Gabriel Rossetti', unpublished dissertation, University of Maryland, 1958

Höltgen, K. J., *Aspects of the Emblem*, Kassel: Reichenberger, 1986

Hönnighausen, G., 'Christina Rossetti als viktorianische Dichterin', unpublished dissertation, Bonn, 1969

'Emblematic Tendencies in the Works of Christina Rossetti', *Victorian Poetry*, 10 (1972), 1–15

Hönnighausen, L., 'Dowsons Seraphita-Gedichte', *Archiv für das Studium der neueren Sprachen und Literaturen*, 204 (1967), 192–201

'Austin Dobsons präraphaelitische Gedichte', *Anglia*, 85 (1967), 350–62

'A Stray Letter of Theodore Wratislaw', *Notes and Queries*, n.s., 15 (1968), 428–30

'Algernon Charles Swinburne: *August*', in K. H. Göller (ed.), *Die englische Lyrik von der Renaissance bis zur Gegenwart*, 2 vols., Düsseldorf: Bagel, 1968, vol. II, pp. 203–15

'Aspekte des Blake-Verständnisses in der Ästhetik des 19. Jahrhunderts', *Zeitschrift für Kunstgeschichte*, 33 (1970), 41–53

Präraphaeliten und Fin de Siècle: Symbolistische Tendenzen in der englischen Spätromantik, Munich: Fink, 1971

'Die englische Literatur 1870–1890', *Jahrhundertwende*, pt 1, *Neues Handbuch der Literaturwissenschaft*, vol. 18, H. Kreuzer (ed.), Wiesbaden: Athenaion, 1976, pp. 359–400

Grundprobleme der englischen Literaturtheorie des neunzehnten Jahrhunderts, Darmstadt: Wissenschaftliche Buchges., 1977

' "Point of View" and its Background in Intellectual History', *Comparative Criticism*, 2 (1980), Elinor Shaffer (ed.), Cambridge University Press, 151–66

Horstmann, U., *Ästhetizismus und Dekadenz. Zum Paradigmakonflikt in der englischen Literaturtheorie des späten 19. Jahrhunderts*, Munich: Fink, 1983

Hough, G., *The Last Romantics*, London: Duckworth, 1949

House, H., *All In Due Time*, London: Hart-Davis, 1955

Housman, L., 'Pre-Raphaelitism in Art and Poetry', *Transactions of the Royal Society of Literature*, n.s., 12 (1933), 1–29

Howard, R. R., *The Dark Glass: Vision and Technique in the Poetry of D. G. Rossetti*, Athens, Ohio: Ohio University Press, 1972

Hunt, J. D., *The Pre-Raphaelite Imagination 1848–1900*, London: Routledge & Kegan Paul, 1968

'A Moment's Monument: Reflections on Pre-Raphaelite Vision in Poetry and Painting', in J. Sambrook (ed.), *Pre-Raphaelitism*, Chicago: Chicago University Press, 1974, pp. 243–64

Iser, W., *Walter Pater. Die Autonomie des Ästhetischen*, Tübingen: Niemeyer, 1960. English edition published as *Walter Pater: The Aesthetic Moment*, trans. David Wilson, Cambridge University Press, 1986

Jack, I., *Keats and the Mirror of Art*, Oxford: Clarendon Press, 1967

Jackson, H., *The Eighteen Nineties: A Review of Art and Ideas at the Close of the Nineteenth Century*, London: Grant Richards, 1913

Jeffares, N., *W. B. Yeats: Man and Poet*, London: Routledge & Kegan Paul, 1949

Johnson, H., *The House of Life. Interpretations of the Pictures of the Late G. F. Watts*, London: Dent & Sons, 1911

Johnson, L. M., *The Metaphor of Painting*, N.Y.: Bowker, 1981

Johnston, R. de S., 'Imagery in Rossetti's House of Life', unpublished dissertation, University of Missouri, 1959

Journal of Pre-Raphaelite Studies, 2, 2 (1982): special issue D. G. Rossetti

Jullian, P., *The Symbolists*, London: Phaidon, 1973

Kayser, W., 'Der europäische Symbolismus', in Kayser, *Die Vortragsreise*, Bern: Francke, 1958, pp. 287–304

Kermode, F., *Romantic Image*, London: Routledge & Kegan Paul, 1957

King, C. W., *The Natural History, Ancient and Modern of Precious Stones and Gems*, London: Bell & Daldy, 1865

Knickerbocker, K. L., 'Rossetti's "The Blessed Damozel" ', *Studies in Philology*, 29 (1932), 485–504

Knoepflmacher, U.C. and Tennyson, G. B. (eds.), *Nature and the Victorian Imagination*, Berkeley, Calif.: University of California Press, 1977

Kohl, N., *Oscar Wilde. Das literarische Werk zwischen Anpassung und Provokation*, Heidelberg: Winter, 1980. English edition to be published as *Oscar Wilde: The Works of a Conformist Rebel*, trans. David Wilson, Cambridge University Press, 1988

Koppen, E., *Dekadenter Wagnerismus: Studien zur europäischen Literatur des Fin de Siècle*, Berlin: de Gruyter, 1973

Kusche, L., *Franz Liszt*, Munich: Süddeutscher Verlag, 1961

Küster, E. C., *Mittelalter und Antike bei William Morris*, Berlin: de Gruyter, 1928

Lafourcade, G., *La Jeunesse de Swinburne 1837–1867*, 2 vols., London: Oxford University Press, 1928

Landow, C. P., 'The Rainbow: A Problematic Image', in U. C. Knoepflmacher and G. B. Tennyson (eds.) *Nature and the Victorian Imagination*, Berkeley, Calif.: University of California Press, 1977, pp. 341–69

William Holman Hunt and Typological Symbolism, New Haven, Conn.: Yale University Press, 1979

Victorian Types, Victorian Shadows: Biblical Typology in Victorian Literature, Art, and Thought, Boston: Routledge, 1980

Langbaum, R., *The Poetry of Experience. The Dramatic Monologue in Modern Literary Tradition*, London: Chatto & Windus, 1957

Lauterbach, E. S. and Davis, W. E., *The Transitional Age in British Literature, 1880–1920*, Troy: Whitston, 1973

Lehmann, A. G., *The Symbolist Aesthetic in France: 1885–1895*, London: Blackwell, 1950

Leon, D., *Ruskin. The Great Victorian*, London: Routledge & Kegan Paul, 1949

Levine, R. A. (ed.), *The Victorian Experience: The Poets*, Athens, Ohio: Ohio University Press, 1982

Lhombreau, R., *Arthur Symons. A Critical Biography*, London: Unicorn Press, 1963

Livermore, A., 'J. M. W. Turner's Unknown Verse-Book', *The Connoisseur Year Book*, 1957, pp. 78–86

Lombardo, A., *La Poesia Inglese dall' Estetismo al Simbolismo*, Rome: Edizioni di Storia e Letteratura, 1950

Longaker, M., *Ernest Dowson*, Philadelphia, Pa.: University of Pennsylvania Press, 1945

Lottes, W., *Wie ein goldener Traum – Die Rezeption des Mittelalters in der Kunst der Präraffaeliten*, Munich: Fink, 1984

Lowes, J. L., *Road to Xanadu*, Boston, Mass.: Riverside Press, 1930

Lucas, J., 'From Naturalism to Symbolism', in I. Fletcher (ed.), *Decadence*, London: Arnold, 1979, pp. 131–48

Maas, J., *Victorian Painters*, London: Barrie & Rockcliff, The Crescent Press, 1969

McGann, J. J., 'James Thomson (B.V.): The Woven Hymns of Night and Day', *Studies in English Literature, The Nineteenth Century*, 3 (1963), 493–507

McGowan, J. P., ' "The Bitterness of Things Occult": D. G. Rossetti's Search for the Real', *Victorian Poetry*, 20 (1982), no. 3/4, 45–64

Mackintosh, A., *Symbolism and Art Nouveau*, London: Thames & Hudson, 1975

Mainusch, H., *Romantische Ästhetik. Untersuchungen zur englischen Kunstlehre des späten 18. und frühen 19. Jahrhunderts*, Zurich: Gehlen, 1969

Marillier, H. C., *Dante Gabriel Rossetti. An Illustrated Memorial of his Art and Life*, London: G. Bell & Sons, 1899

Maslenikow, O. A., *The Frenzied Poets. Andrey Biely and the Russian Symbolists*, Berkeley, Calif.: University of California Press, 1952

Mégroz, R. L., *Dante Gabriel Rossetti. Painter Poet of Heaven in Earth*, London: Faber, 1928

Meisel, M., ' "Half Sick of Shadows": The Aesthetic Dialogue in Pre-Raphaelite Painting', in U. C. Knoepflmacher and G. B. Tennyson (eds.), *Nature and the Victorian Imagination*, Berkeley, L.A.: University of California Press, 1977, pp. 309–40

Mercier, A., *Les Sources Esotériques et Occultes de la Poésie Symboliste*, Paris: Nizet, 1974 (vol. I, 1969; vol. II, 1974)

Metken, G. (ed.), *Präraffaeliten*. Exhibition catalogue for Baden-Baden, 23 February 1973–24 February 1974, Baden-Baden 1973

Die Präraffaeliten: Ethischer Realismus und Elfenbeinturm im 19. Jahrhundert, Cologne: Du Mont, 1974

Michaud, G., *Message Poétique du Symbolisme*, 4 vols., Paris: Nizet, 1947

Mills, E., *The Life and Letters of Frederic Shields*, London: Longmans, Green & Co., 1912

Milner, J., *Symbolists and Decadents*, N.Y.: Dutton, 1971

Milner, M., *Le Diable dans la Littérature Française de Gazotte à Baudelaire 1772–1861*, 2 vols., Paris: Corti, 1960

Miner, E. (ed.), *Literary Uses of Typology from the Late Middle Ages to the Present*, Princeton: Princeton University Press, 1977

Miyoshi, M., *The Divided Self: A Perspective on the Literature of the Victorians*, N.Y.: New York State University Press, 1969

Monsman, G., *Walter Pater*, Boston, Mass.: Twayne, 1977

Morse, B. J., 'Dante Gabriel Rossetti and William Blake', *Englische Studien*, 66 (1932), 364–72

Murciaux, C., 'Christina Rossetti, La Vierge Sage des Préraphaélites', *Revue de Paris*, 71 (1964), 74–84

Nassaar, C. S., *Into the Demon Universe: A Literary Exploration of Oscar Wilde*, New Haven and London: Yale University Press, 1974

Nelson, J. G., *The Early Nineties: A View from the Bodley Head*, Cambridge, Mass.: Harvard University Press, 1971

'The Nature of the Aesthetic Experience in the Poetry of the Nineties: Ernest Dowson, Lionel Johnson, and John Gray', *English Literature in Transition*, 17 (1974), 223–32

Notopoulos, J. A., *The Platonism of Shelley*, Durham, N.C.: Duke University Press, 1949

Osborne, C. C., *Philip Bourke Marston*, London: The Times Book Club, 1926

Packer, L. M., *Christina Rossetti*, Berkeley, Calif.: University of California Press, 1963

Parris, L., *The Pre-Raphaelites*, London: Tate Gallery Publications, 1966

Parry, G., 'The Pre-Raphaelite Image: Style and Subject 1848–56', *Proceedings of the Leeds Philosophical and Literary Society, Literary and Historical Section*, 17 (1979), 1–54

Perkins, D., *A History of Modern Poetry: From the 1890s to the High Modernist Mode*, Cambridge, Mass.: Harvard University Press, 1976

Peters, R., 'Swinburne: A Personal Essay and a Polemic', in R. A. Levine (ed.), *The Victorian Experience: The Poets*, Athens, Ohio: Ohio University Press, 1982, pp. 138–57

Peters, R. L., 'The Salome of Arthur Symons and Aubrey Beardsley', *Criticism*, 2 (1960), 150–63

The Crowns of Apollo. Swinburne's Principle of Literature and Art, Detroit: Wayne State University Press, 1965

Peyre, H., 'Les Sources du Pessimisme de Thomson', *Revue Anglo-Américaine*, 2 (1924/25), 152–6

Pfister, M. and Schulte-Middelich, B. (eds.), *Die 'Nineties': Das englische Fin de Siècle zwischen Dekadenz und Sozialkritik*, Munich: Francke, 1983

Pichois, C. and Ruchon, F., *Iconographie de Baudelaire*, Geneva: Cailler, 1960

Pierrot, J., *L'Imaginaire décadent, 1880–1900*, Paris: Presses Universitaires de France, 1977. English translation published by University of Chicago Press, 1981

Powell, K., 'Arthur Symons, Symbolism, and the Aesthetics of Escape', *Renascence*, 29 (1977), 157–67

Praz, M., *The Romantic Agony*, London: Oxford University Press, 1951

Studies in Seventeenth-Century Imagery, Rome: Edizioni di Storia e Letteratura, 1964

Prince, J. R., 'The Iconic Poem and the Aesthetic Tradition', *English Literary History*, 43 (1976), 567–83

'D. G. Rossetti and the Pre-Raphaelite Conception of the Special Moment', *Modern Language Quarterly*, 37 (1976), 349–69

Pütz, H. P., *Kunst und Künstlerexistenz bei Nietzsche und Thomas Mann*, Bonn: Bouvier, 1963

Quilter, H., 'The New Renaissance; or, the Gospel of Intensity', *Macmillan's Magazine*, 42, May–October 1880, 394–400

Preferences in Art, Life and Literature, London: Sonnenschein & Co., 1892

Redgrove, H. St, 'Blake and Swedenborg: A Study in Comparative Mysticism', *Occult Review*, 38 (1923), 288–96

Reid, F., *W. B. Yeats. A Critical Study*, London: Secker, 1915

Renier, G. F., *Oscar Wilde*, London: Albatross Continental Library, 1933

Reul, P. de, *L'Œuvre de Swinburne*, Brussels: R. Sand, 1922

Richardson, J., 'Fullness and Dissolution: The Poetic Style of D. G. Rossetti', *Journal of Pre-Raphaelite Studies*, 1, 1 (1980), 33–68

Riede, D. G., *Swinburne: A Study of Romantic Myth-making*, Charlottesville, Va.: University of Virginia Press, 1978

Dante Gabriel Rossetti and the Limits of Victorian Vision, Ithaca, N.Y.: Cornell University Press, 1983

Roberts, H. E., 'The Dream World of D. G. Rossetti', *Victorian Studies*, 17 (1974), 371–93

Rodenbach, G., 'La Poésie Nouvelle: A Propos des Décadents et Symbolistes', *Revue Bleue*, 47 (1891), 422–30

Roditi, E., *Oscar Wilde*, Norfolk, Conn.: New Directions Books, 1948

Roos, J., 'William Blake' in Roos, *Aspects Littéraires du Mysticisme Philosophique et l'Influence de Boehme et de Swedenborg au Début du Romantisme:*

William Blake, Novalis, Ballanche, Strasbourg: Heitz, 1951, pp. 25–194

Rosenblatt, L., *L'Idée de l'Art pour l'Art dans la Littérature Anglaise pendant la Période Victorienne*, Paris: Champion, 1931

Rothenstein, E., 'The Pre-Raphaelites and Ourselves', *Month*, n.s., 1 (March 1949), 180–98

Rudd, M., *Divided Image. A Study of William Blake and W. B. Yeats*, London: Routledge & Kegan Paul, 1953

Rudwin, M., *The Devil in Legend and Literature*, Chicago: The Open Court Publishing Company, 1931

Sadoff, D., 'The Poetics of Repetition and *The Defense of Guenevere*', in C. G. Silver (ed.), *The Golden Chain*, London: Wm. Morris Society, 1982

Sambrook, J. (ed.), *Pre-Raphaelitism: A Collection of Critical Essays*, Chicago, Ill.: University of Chicago Press, 1974

Sänger, J., *Aspekte dekadenter Sensibilität*, Frankfurt am Main: P. Lang, 1978

Sattler, E., *A. Ch. Swinburne als Naturdichter*, Bonn: S. Foppen, 1910

Savarit, J., *Tendances Mystiques et Ésotériques chez D. G. Rossetti*, Paris: Didier, 1961

Schaefer, W. D., 'James Thomson. A Study in Intellectual Development', unpublished dissertation, University of Wisconsin, 1962

'The Two Cities of Dreadful Night', *PMLA*, 77 (1962), 609–16

James Thomson (B.V.): Beyond 'The City', Berkeley, Calif.: University of California Press, 1965

Schinz, A., 'Literary Symbolism in France', *PMLA*, 18 (1903), 263–307

Schmidt, A.-M., *La Littérature Symboliste 1870–90*, Paris: Presses Universitaires de France, 1955

Schmutzler, R., *Art Nouveau – Jugendstil*, Stuttgart: Hatje, 1962

Schorer, M., 'Swedenborg and Blake', *Modern Philology*, 36 (1938), 157–78

Senior, J., *The Way Down and Out. The Occult in Symbolist Literature*, Ithaca, N.Y.: Cornell University Press, 1959

Sharp, W., *Dante Gabriel Rossetti. A Record and a Study*, London: Macmillan, 1882

Siebold, E. von, 'Synästhesien in der englischen Dichtung des 19. Jahrhunderts', *Englische Studien*, 53 (1919/20), 196–334

Silver, C. G. (ed.), *The Golden Chain: Essays on William Morris and Pre-Raphaelitism*, London: Wm. Morris Society, 1982

'Dreamers of Dreams: Toward a Definition of Literary Pre-Raphaelitism', in C. G. Silver (ed.), *The Golden Chain*, London: Wm. Morris Society, 1982, pp. 5–51

Singer, L., 'The Aesthetics of "Art for Art's Sake" ', *Journal of Aesthetics and Art Criticism*, 12 (1953), 343–59

Sjöden, K. E., 'Balzac et Swedenborg', *Cahiers de l'Association Internationale des Etudes Françaises*, 15 (1963), 295–307

Small, I. C., 'Plato and Pater: *Fin de Siècle* Aesthetics', *British Journal of Aesthetics*, 12 (1972), 369–83

Spencer, R., *The Aesthetic Movement. Theory and Practice*, N.Y.: Dutton, 1972

Staley, A., *The Pre-Raphaelite Landscape*, Oxford: Clarendon Press, 1973

Stanford, D. (ed.), *Pre-Raphaelite Writing*, London: Dent, 1973

Stansky, P., *William Morris*, N.Y.: Oxford University Press, 1983

Starkie, E., *From Gautier to T. S. Eliot: The Influence of France on English*

Literature, 1851–1939, London: Hutchinson, 1960

Stauffer, D. A., 'W. B. Yeats and the Medium of Poetry', *English Literary History*, 15 (1948), 227–46

Stein, R. L., *The Ritual of Interpretation. The Fine Arts as Literature in Ruskin, Rossetti, and Pater*, Cambridge, Mass.: Harvard University Press, 1975

Stevenson, L., *The Pre-Raphaelite Poets*, Chapel Hill: University of North Carolina Press, 1972

Sussman, H., *Fact into Figure: Typology in Carlyle, Ruskin, and the Pre-Raphaelite Brotherhood*, Columbus, Ohio: Ohio State University Press, 1979

Sypher, F. J., 'Swinburne and Wagner', *Victorian Poetry*, 9 (1971), 165–83

Sypher, W., *Rococo to Cubism in Art and Literature*, N.Y.: Random House, 1960

Talon, H., *D. G. Rossetti: The House of Life: Quelques Aspects de l'Art, des Thèmes et du Symbolisme*, Paris: Lettres Modernes, 1966

'Dante Gabriel Rossetti, Peintre-Poète dans la Maison de Vie', *Etudes Anglaises*, 9 (1966), 1–4

Tegtmeier, R., *Okkultismus und Erotik in der Literatur des Fin de Siècle*, Königswinter: Edition Magus, 1983

Temple, R. Z., *The Critic's Alchemy: A Study of the Introduction of French Symbolism into England*, N.Y.: Twayne Publishers, 1953

'Truth in Labelling: Pre-Raphaelitism, Aestheticism, Decadence, *Fin de Siècle*', *English Literature in Transition*, 17 (1974), 201–22

Tennyson, G. B., 'The Sacramental Imagination', in U. C. Knoepflmacher and G. B. Tennyson (eds.), *Nature and the Victorian Imagination*, Berkeley, Calif.: University of California Press, 1977, pp. 370–90

Thomas, D., *Swinburne: The Poet in his World*, N.Y.: Oxford University Press, 1979

Thornton, R. K. R., *The Decadent Dilemma*, London: Arnold, 1983

Tillotson, G., *A View of Victorian Literature*, Oxford: Clarendon Press, 1978

Tillotson, G. and K., *Mid-Victorian Studies*, London: Athlone Press, 1965

Tindall, W. W., 'The Symbolism of W. B. Yeats', *Accent*, 5 (1945), 203–11

The Literary Symbol, N.Y.: Columbia University Press, 1955

Tolles, F. B., 'The Praetorian Cohorts: A Study of the Language of Francis Thompson's Poetry', *English Studies*, 21–2 (1940), 49–64

Uhlig, C., 'Walter Pater und die Poetik der Reminiszenz: Zur literarischen Methode einer Spätzeit', *Poetica*, 6 (1974), 285–327

Ullmann, St von, 'Synästhesien in den dichterischen Werken von Oscar Wilde', *Englische Studien*, 72 (1938), 245–56

'Romanticism and Synaesthesia: A Comparative Study of Sense Transfer in Keats and Byron', *PMLA*, 60 (1945), 811–27

Underwood, V. P., *Verlaine et l'Angleterre*, Paris: Nizet, 1956

Victorian Poetry, 9 (1971): special issue A. C. Swinburne

13 (1975), no. 3/4: special issue William Morris

20 (1982), no. 3/4: special issue D. G. Rossetti

Vordtriede, W., *Novalis und die französischen Symbolisten*, Stuttgart: Kohlhammer, 1963

Walker, I. B., *James Thomson (B. V.). A Critical Study*, Ithaca, N.Y.: Cornell University Press, 1950

Wallerstein, R., 'Personal Experience in Rossetti's *House of Life*', *PMLA*, 42 (1927), 492–504

Weatherby, H. L., 'Problems of Form and Content in the Poetry of Dante Gabriel Rossetti', *Victorian Poetry*, 2 (1964), 11–19

Weintraub, S., 'Three Views of the Nineties', *Review*, 1 (1979), 301–8

Welby, T. E., *A Study of Swinburne*, London: Faber, 1926
The Victorian Romantics, 1850–1870, London: Howe, 1929

Wellek, R., *A History of Modern Criticism 1750–1950, The Age of Transition*, London: Cape, 1966; *The Later Nineteenth Century*, London: Cape, 1966

Whitsitt, J., ' "To See Clearly": Perspective in Pre-Raphaelite Poetry and Painting', *Pre-Raphaelite Review*, 3, 2 (1983), 69–79

Whittington-Evan, R., ' "The Nineties": End or Beginning', *Contemporary Review*, 237 (1980), 255–61

Wilcox, J., 'The Beginnings of l'Art pour l'Art', *Journal of Aesthetics and Criticism*, 11 (1952), 360–77

Wilson, E., *Axël's Castle. A Study in the Imaginative Literature of 1870–1930*, N.Y.: Scribner, 1948

Wolff, E., 'Ruskins Denkform. Ganzheitlich-morphologisches Denken im Werk John Ruskins', unpublished dissertation, Bonn, 1950

Wolff, L., *Dante Gabriel Rossetti*, Paris: Didier, 1934

Wuthenow, R.-R., *Muse, Maske, Meduse. Europäischer Ästhetizismus*, Frankfurt am Main: Suhrkamp, 1978

Index

The terms 'symbolism', 'Pre-Raphaelitism', and *'fin de siècle'* do not occur as individual headings in the index, since they are the overall subject of the book.

337